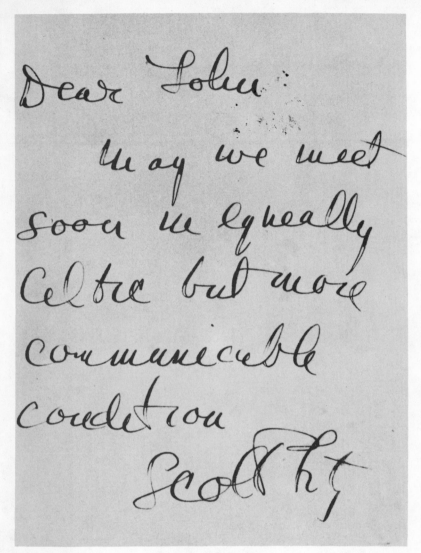

John O'Hara's copy of *Tender Is the Night* (courtesy of Mrs. John O'Hara).

FITZGERALD/HEMINGWAY
ANNUAL
1973

FITZGERALD/HEMINGWAY ANNUAL 1973

Edited by

MATTHEW J. BRUCCOLI

University of South Carolina

and

C. E. FRAZER CLARK, JR.

Microcard Editions Books
An Indian Head Company
A Division of Information Handling Services

EDITORS: MATTHEW J. BRUCCOLI

Department of English
University of South Carolina
Columbia, S. C. 29208

C. E. FRAZER CLARK, JR.

1700 Lone Pine
Bloomfield Hills, Michigan 48013

ASSISTANT EDITOR: Jennifer McCabe Atkinson

EDITORIAL ASSISTANTS: Linda Berry
Margaret Duggan

Address all editorial correspondence to the editors.

Address orders and inquiries to Microcard Editions Books, 901 26th Street, N.W., Washington, D.C. 20037

Library of Congress Catalog Card Number: 75-83781
ISBN: 0-910972-38-9

Printed in the United States of America.

To John C. Guilds

Contents

THE PARIS CONFERENCE

F. SCOTT FITZGERALD

ERNEST HEMINGWAY

FITZGERALD/HEMINGWAY
ANNUAL
1973

THE PARIS CONFERENCE

FITZGERALD AND HEMINGWAY IN PARIS: CONFERENCE PROCEEDINGS

On 23-24 June 1972 the *Fitzgerald/Hemingway Annual* sponsored a conference to explore the significance of Paris for F. Scott Fitzgerald and Ernest Hemingway. It was appropriately held at the Institut d'Études Américaines, Place de l'Odéon. The original plan for the conference was to mark the 30th anniversary of the first meeting of Fitzgerald and Hemingway at the Dingo in the spring of 1925; but we anticipated this anniversary by three years to mark the publication day of Bertram D. Sarason's *Hemingway and the SUN Set* (Washington: Bruccoli Clark/NCR Editions, 1972).

Papers were read by Professor Roger Asselineau and Professor André LeVot, and a panel discussion of "old Paris hands" was presented by Harold Loeb, André Chamson, Florence Gilliam, and Morrill Cody. The proceedings were recorded, and the panelists have corrected the transcriptions published below.

An exhibition of Paris-related material was mounted at the Bibliothèque Benjamin Franklin to help commemorate the conference. The exhibition catalogue, *F. Scott Fitzgerald and Ernest M. Hemingway in Paris* has been published (Bloomfield Hills & Columbia: Bruccoli Clark, 1972).

Special acknowledgment is made for the help of Simon Copans, Director of the Institut d'Études Américaines, Mr. & Mrs. Russell L.

Harris of the American Embassy, Michel Fabre, and Madame André Chamson.

In important ways, Montparnasse was the Paris experience for F. Scott Fitzgerald and Ernest Hemingway, for there the things that seemed to matter could be found: exciting people came; something was always happening; and everthing "seemed to have something to do with art." Montparnasse assaulted the senses of both writers; the sights, sounds, aromas, and tastes were incorporated into their prose. Paris was, as Hemingway wrote, an experience which stays with you for the rest of your life.

The Montparnasse
of Fitzgerald
and Hemingway

The map which follows is keyed to indicate those places in Montparnasse which were significant in the lives of Fitzgerald, Hemingway and their friends.

1   Hôtel Jacob (now Hôtel d'Angleterre), 44 rue Jacob, where, on Sherwood Anderson's recommendation, Ernest and Hadley Hemingway stayed when they first arrived in Paris in December, 1921.

2   Pré aux Clercs, corner of rue Jacob and rue Bonaparte, where Ernest and Hadley's first Christmas dinner in Paris came to twelve francs and a bottle of good Pinard wine cost sixty centimes.

. 3   Michaud's restaurant, corner of rue Jacob and rue des Saints-Pères, where James Joyce ate with his family, and where Lewis Galantière hosted the Hemingways shortly after they arrived in France.

4   74 rue du Cardinal Lemoine, was a fourth-floor, rear, two-room flat the Hemingways moved into on 9 January 1922.

5   The Bal Musette, a workman's dance hall, in an angular building adjacent to 74, rue du Cardinal Lemoine, where the accordian player doubled as a taxi driver and, at four in the morning in August, 1922, took the Hemingways to Le Bourget field for their first flight, to Strasbourg.

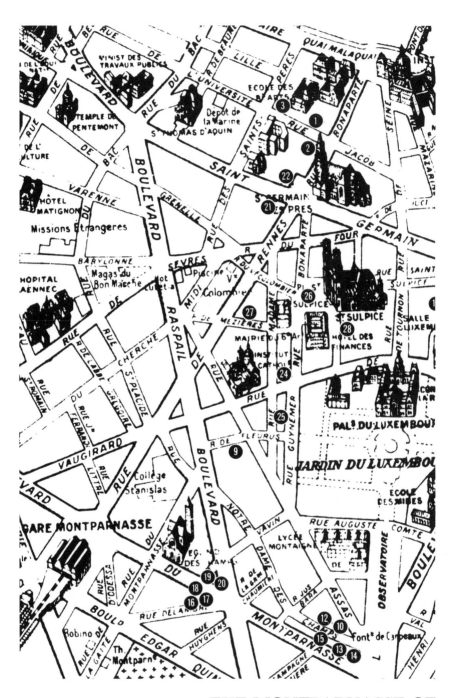

THE MONTPARNASSE OF

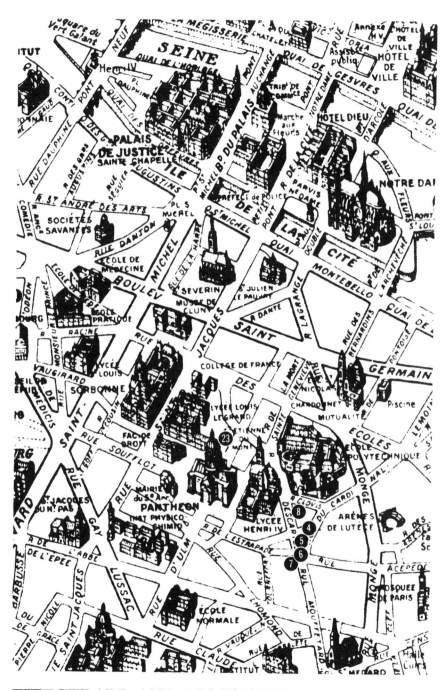

FITZGERALD AND HEMINGWAY

6   Place de la Contrescarpe, a cobblestoned square at the end of rue du Cardinal Lemoine a half a block from the Hemingways' apartment at number 74.

7   The Café des Amateurs, "the cesspool of the rue Mouffetard," where Mouffetard empties into Place Contrescarpe.

8   Hemingway rented a room to work in on the top floor of the old hotel where Paul Verlaine died, at 39 rue Descartes, around the block from 74 rue Cardinal Lemoine.

9   27 rue de Fleurus, the apartment of Gertrude Stein and Alice B. Toklas, first visited by Hemingway in March 1922.

10   The studio of Ezra Pound on the rue Notre Dame des Champs near the Luxembourg Gardens. Hemingway first called on Pound in January or February of 1922 at the suggestion of Sherwood Anderson who had earlier written Pound on Hemingway's behalf.

11   Shakespeare and Company, 12 rue de l'Odéon, the lending library and bookstore operated by Sylvia Beach, Joyce's publisher and staunch friend of Hemingway.

12   113 rue Notre Dame des Champs, the second-floor apartment looking down over a sawmill and lumberyard which the Hemingways rented when they returned to Paris in January of 1924.

13   La Closerie des Lilas, "a good café" on the Place St. Michel where Hemingway often went to write.

14   Hemingway's "old friend," the statue of Marshal Ney, which stands in front of the Closerie des Lilas.

15   The Negre de Toulouse, whose proprietor, Mr. Lavigne, always served Hemingway the good Cahors wine and asked about his work. Harold Loeb and Kitty Cannell invited Ernest and Hadley here for a lobster dinner shortly after they met in the spring of 1924.

16   The Dingo Bar in the rue Delambre (now the Bar Basque), where Fitzgerald and Hemingway met.

17   The Dôme.

18   The Coupole.

19   The Select.

20   The Rotonde.

21   The Brasserie Lipp, where Hemingway would order a *distingué* and *pommes à l'huile.*

22   The Café Aux Deux Magots.

23   André Chamson lived in a small apartment at the top of the Latin Quarter, just behind the Panthéon, 17 rue Thoin, and it was here that Chamson was sought out by F. Scott Fitzgerald.

24   When Scott and Zelda Fitzgerald returned to Paris for the summer of 1928, they stayed for the first time on the left bank, briefly at the Hôtel des Palais, then in a rented apartment, 58 rue de Vaugirard, corner of the rue Bonaparte.

25   14 rue Guynemer, the apartment of Sara and Gerald Murphy.

26   St. Sulpice, where, in 1929, Hemingway attended Mass with his second wife, Pauline Pfeiffer.

27   When the Fitzgeralds returned to Paris in April, 1929, they rented a large apartment near St. Sulpice, presumably on the rue de Mézières not far from where they had lived the year before.

28   Hemingway, back from the States in 1929, lived at 6 rue Férou not far from St. Sulpice and near the Fitzgeralds. Hemingway, hard at work on *Farewell* and anxious to avoid interruption, didn't reveal to Fitzgerald when they again met that they were neighbors.

ROGER ASSELINEAU

HEMINGWAY
IN
PARIS

Roger Asselineau is Europe's leading Hemingway authority – the author of The Literary Reputation of Hemingway in Europe *and editor of the Pléiade edition of Hemingway. His most recent work is* Ernest Hemingway *in the "Ecrivains d'hier et d'aujourd'hui" series. Prof. Asselineau is president of the Association francaise d'études americaines.*

It is generally assumed that Hemingway had no university education. This is wrong. Paris was his university in the same way as a whaling-ship was Melville's Yale and Harvard. Rather than "a moveable feast," it was a capital chapter in "The Education of Nick Adams," for it was there that he graduated from mid-western journalism and teetotalism to creative writing and wine-drinking. At a time when there was no G.I. Bill of Rights to help young veterans to finish their education, he decided, like many other young Americans, to return to Europe to escape the narrow provincialism of his early environment and the depressing effects of prohibition.

One of the reasons why he went to Paris rather than to any other place may have been that he discovered it on his way to the Italian front, for he first arrived in Paris at the beginning of June 1918 with a small group of Red Cross volunteers among whom was his friend

Ted Brumback who had begun work at the *Star* in Kansas City about the same time as Hemingway. They were quartered in a small hotel near the Madeleine. It was the time when Big Bertha was bombarding Paris from the neighborhood of Château-Thierry. High explosive shells were falling in the streets here and there at regular intervals. Hemingway and Brumback found it very exciting. As soon as they heard a shell explode, they took a taxi and rushed to the spot to examine the damage. In the course of this frantic chase from one part of Paris to another, they may have come to the Latin Quarter, for one of the shells fell on Boulevard St. Michel, opposite the Ecole des Mines, the façade of which still bears the scars of the explosion. On returning to their hotel from one of these expeditions, they heard a frightening, hissing sound and a tremendous explosion. A shell had just hit the façade of the Madeleine and chipped some of the columns. They thought for a minute that is was going to land on them.

But Hemingway didn't have time to see much more of Paris. His group was reinforced by another contingent of volunteers coming in from London. Within two or three days they were all shipped off to Italy.

So was it the mere memory of this brief visit under rather tragic circumstances that made Hemingway decide to settle in Paris after the war and his marriage to Hadley? It is unlikely. His love of Paris was not a case of love at first sight. Actually, in 1921 he didn't know what to do and where to turn. Being very ambitious and endowed with a strong competitive spirit, he would have liked to go to a university, and bore his mother a grudge because she had spent money on Grace Cottage on Walloon Lake instead of sending him to Princeton. "But you don't need a university!" Hadley told him. Thus, as he realized that his Italian experience had been crucial in his development, they decided to go to Europe. Hadley, for her part, would have preferred Italy of which he spoke with such enthusiasm, but Sherwood Anderson and his wife Tennessee, whom they happened to meet in Chicago about this time had just returned from France and talked them into going to Paris instead. According to Sherwood Anderson, Italy was all right for tourists, but, if you wanted to make your name, Paris was the place, because people believed in literature there and you could make the acquaintance of such promising or important writers as Gertrude Stein, Ezra Pound, James Joyce, Lewis Galantière and others – and Sylvia Beach ran a bookshop where you could meet everyone worth knowing. These arguments fully convinced Hemingway. He obtained an assignment

Hemingway rented a room on the top floor of the hotel where Paul Verlaine had died; it was here in quiet that he sought the "one true sentence."

from *The Toronto Star* as roving correspondent in Europe; Sherwood Anderson gave him letters of introduction to all the expatriates who counted and the address of a cheap hotel: Hôtel Jacob et d'Angleterre, 44 rue Jacob in the Latin Quarter, close to the church of St. Germain-des-Prés.

Hemingway and his young wife arrived in Paris shortly before Christmas of 1921. He has described his first impressions in a little piece which he contributed to *The Toronto Star Weekly* in 1923 entitled "Christmas in Paris." Apparently it was snowing in Paris that Christmas, if we are to believe the article — and there is no reason for not believing it — and they loved it: "It is wonderful in Paris to stand on a bridge across the Seine looking up through the softly curtaining snow past the grey bulk of the Louvre, up the river spanned by many bridges and bordered by the grey houses of old Paris to where Notre Dame squats in the dusk."[1] They had a special Christmas dinner in "The Veritable Restaurant of the Third Republic," rue Jacob. It was a turkey dinner, but it did not taste like turkey at home. They missed the cranberries. The potatoes were fried with too much grease. In spite of the wine and the beauty of the city outside, they felt terribly lonely and homesick. "I didn't know Paris was like this," said the girl, probably echoing Hadley's own words. "I thought it was gay and full of light and beautiful." The author tries to comfort her by putting his arm around her, "At least that was one thing you could do in a Parisian restaurant", and by telling her: "Never mind, honey. We've been here only three days. Paris will be different. Just you wait" (*By-Line*, p. 131).

And indeed Paris soon was different. They overcame their homesickness, broke their isolation and fell in love with the city. To begin with, they moved to less impersonal quarters as early as January 9, 1922. They rented a small flat, at 74 rue du Cardinal-Lemoine, on Ste. Geneviève hill, behind the Panthéon, not far from that picturesque Place Contrescarpe which he has lovingly described in *A Moveable Feast* (and which still exists—almost unchanged): "The leaves lay sodden in the rain and the wind drove the rain against the big green autobus at the terminal and the Café des Amateurs was crowded and the windows misted over from the heat and the smoke inside."[2] Their apartment on the fourth floor was very small; there was only one cold water tap in the kitchen and no bathroom proper. They had to use squat toilets which they shared with their neighbors. He has described them with wonderful accuracy and some complacency: there was only one toilet "by the side of the stairs on each floor with the two cleated cement shoe-shaped

Hemingway began his writing career in Paris at 74, rue du Cardinal Lemoine, where he and Hadley had rented an apartment. The address, wrote Hemingway, "could not have been a poorer one."

elevations on each side of the aperture so a *locataire* would not slip. . ." (*Feast*, p. 3). People were poor, but very cheerful. There was a *bal musette* two steps from their house and others in the neighborhood. If we are to believe *The Sun Also Rises* there was one in particular: ". . . in the rue de la Montagne Sainte Geneviève. Five nights a week the working people of the Panthéon quarter danced there. One night a week it was the dancing-club. . . .There were long benches, and tables ran across the room, and at the far end a dancing-floor."[3] People danced to the sound of an accordion and paid with tokens at the end of each dance and drank beer or wine. Hemingway and Hadley sometimes went there. He loved the atmosphere of the place, but she was a little frightened by some of the ruffians who occasionally invited her to dance.

Their apartment was so small that Hemingway could not work at home. There were just two rooms and a tiny kitchen. He had to be all by himself, "alone with his ideas and his paper," as he once wrote of Baudelaire (*By-Line*, p. 25). So he rented a room nearby on the top floor (sixth or eighth, he didn't remember exactly by the time he wrote *A Moveable Feast*) in the hotel where Verlaine died in 1896 (39 rue Descartes). The room "looked across all the roofs and the chimneys of the high hill of the quarter. . ." (*Feast*, p. 11). It was very cold there in winter and he had to light a wood fire to warm the place. He bought his wood before going upstairs: "a bundle of small twigs, three wire-wrapped packets of short, half-pencil length pieces of split pine [of a type which can still be found] to catch fire from the twigs, and then the bundle of half-dried lengths of hard wood. . ." to feed the fire (*Feast*, p. 4). It was like camping in the open. When the chimney didn't draw—he looked at the neighboring chimneys to find out before going upstairs — he went to a good café he knew on the Place St. Michel and did his writing there drinking white coffee and rum St. James, as he has told in *A Moveable Feast.*

He was very poor in those days. Though the rate of exchange made living very cheap for Americans, he had to live a Spartan life, but he didn't mind this asceticism. He and Hadley were perfectly happy: "We ate well and cheaply and drank well and cheaply and slept well and warm together and loved each other" (*Feast*, p. 51). "I thought of bathtubs and showers and toilets that flushed as things that inferior people to us had. . ." (*Feast*, p. 50). He didn't care because he was "doing his work and getting satisfaction from it. . . ." (*Feast*, p. 50). Throughout his life he was never so happy as when he was working. He was a true Puritan in this respect: Work is worship; *laborare est orare.* But he described it differently in more secular and

Hemingway's fourth-floor rear apartment at 74, rue du Cardinal Lemoine, was a two-room flat that had no hot water. The stairway up to the flat was narrow and dark with an outside toilet on each landing.

sensual terms. Writing a story, he claimed in *A Moveable Feast* is tantamount to making love: "After writing a story I was always empty and both sad and happy, as though I had made love. . ." (p. 6). When he was not writing, he was filling up his tank for future use, so his trade was his life and his life was his trade, which is the mark of all creative artists.

Thus, at least at the beginning of his stay in Paris, he led a very steady and laborious life with his wife — a petty-bourgeois life in a way — and he didn't mix at all with the American expatriates, the "American Bohemians," as he called them, who crowded the tables of the Café Rotonde. He despised them intensely for their laziness and superficiality and wrote a scathing article on their aimless life of dissipation for *The Toronto Star Weekly:* "The scum of Greenwich Village, New York, has been skimmed off and deposited in large ladlesful on that section of Paris adjacent to the Café Rotonde," the article began (*By-Line,* p. 23). "You can find anything you are looking for at the Rotonde — except serious artists . . . . They are nearly all loafers expending the energy that an artist puts into his creative work in talking about what they are going to do. . ." and never do (*By-Line*, pp. 24-25). And he went on criticizing their costume: "They have all striven so hard for a careless individuality of clothing that they have achieved a sort of uniformity of eccentricity" (*By-Line*, p. 23). (This sounds familiar in 1972.) For his part, in those days, he dressed conservatively and rarely wore anything but business (or lounge) suits — as the photographs taken at that time show. He did not yet feel called upon to wear a disguise and dress like Tartarin de Tarascon on his way to a hunting expedition or, at best, like a cowboy in mufti. It was only after he had left Paris that he indulged in such eccentricities.

Even in those years, however, it was always his method to take some relaxation after the morning's toil at his writing-table. He enjoyed the simple, inexpensive pleasures of moneyless people. He walked along the quays of the Seine, and when the weather was fine spent hours watching anglers in the vicinity of the Île St. Louis: "I would buy a liter of wine and a piece of bread and some sausage and sit in the sun and read one of the books I had bought and watch the fishing" (*Feast*, p. 44). Besides going to a *bal musette* with Hadley in the evening, he often had boxing-bouts in the afternoon in popular clubs like the Ménilmontant, to which he once took Sylvia Beach and Hadley when she was expecting Bumby. On that occasion, the "last fight led to another — in which the spectators participated. Opinion was divided on the referee's decision; everybody got up on the

According to Hemingway, the Closerie des Lilas was the nearest good cafe when he lived over the sawmill at 113, rue Notre Dame des Champs. Driven from the apartment by the whine of the saw, Hemingway would walk to Place St. Michel at the end of the street, take a table at the Lilas, order a *café au lait*, take out his pencil and notebook, and write.

benches and jumped down on each other – a real Western" Sylvia Beach concluded.[4] He dragged some of his literary friends to such places to show them his skill as a boxer and practice with them, notably Ezra Pound who put up a good show and Fitzgerald who didn't particularly like it.

At other times Hemingway and Hadley took the day off and went to the races at Auteuil or Enghien. They sat on his raincoat on the fresh-cropped grass bank, ate sandwiches, drank from a wine bottle, enjoyed the Raoul Dufy scenery: "the old grandstand, the brown wooden betting booths, the green of the track, the darker green of the hurdles, and the brown shine of the water jumps and the whitewashed stone walls and the white posts and rails . . . and the first horses being walked to the paddock" (*Feast*, pp. 51-52). They bet some money, not much, as much as they could afford. And when, by a stroke of luck, their winnings permitted it, they stopped at Prunier's on the way home and had "oysters and *crabe Mexicaine* with glasses of Sancerre" (*Feast*, p. 53).

They loved cycling too, not that they did any cycling themselves, but they attended the famous "Six-Jours" races at the Vélodrome d'Hiver, taking Adrienne Monnier and Sylvia Beach with them, spending hours there, watching the racers tirelessly circling the ring amid the blare of loud-speakers and observing the picturesque crowd of the fans who sometimes camped there for the duration (*Shakespeare & Co.*, p. 89).

Hemingway, however, had also less frivolous pastimes and occupations more fitting to a serious writer. He frequented Sylvia Beach's bookshop regularly. This bookshop, called Shakespeare and Company, was situated in the heart of the Latin Quarter, at 12 rue de l'Odéon. (Sylvia Beach had just moved there from 8 rue Dupuytren shortly before Hemingway arrived in Paris.) In her book of reminiscences she has devoted a whole chapter to him (full of inaccuracies) entitled "My Best Customer." He not only borrowed books and periodicals, but also bought some, for he was much more bookish than one might think, as the long list of his literary forbears which he recited to the interviewer of the *Paris Review* in 1958 proves.[5]

He put painters in this list, because, as he said on that occasion, he learned as much from painters about how to write as from writers. However odd this may sound, it is undoubtedly true. As I showed in passing, his description of the racecourse at Auteuil recalls a painting by Dufy. At the very beginning of *A Moveable Feast*, he specifies himself that the nightmen's "tank wagons were painted brown and

Place Contrescarpe, where "the cold wind would strip the leaves from the trees," was a cobblestoned square at the end of rue du Cardinal Lemoine, only a few doors from the noisy Bal Musette and Hemingway's apartment at number 74. On the other side of the square, at the corner of rue Mouffetard, was the Café des Amateurs.

saffron color and in the moonlight when they worked the rue Cardinal Lemoine their wheeled, horse-drawn cylinders looked like Braque paintings" (p. 4). In *Across the River and Into the Trees* he refers to Degas in the same way in the course of a description of the Grand Canal. To some extent he looked at the world through the eyes of his favorite painters and it might be claimed that, generally speaking, he tried like Cézanne to give an impression of depth and volume without resorting to perspective.

It was in the Art Institute at Chicago that he first saw good pictures and in particular discovered the existence of Cézanne and the French Impressionists, but it was in Paris that he studied their technique thoroughly and used them as models. He went nearly every day to the Musée du Luxembourg which then housed the Cézannes, the Manets, the Monets, and the other Impressionists which were later transferred to the Louvre or the Jeu de Paume. "I was learning something from the painting of Cézanne that made writing simple true sentences far from enough to make the stories have the dimensions that I was trying to put in them" (*Feast*, p. 13).

It was not only in the Musée du Luxembourg that Hemingway would study modern French painting, but also, close by, across the Luxembourg Gardens, in the studio apartment of Gertrude Stein. "It was like one of the best rooms in the finest museum except there was a big fireplace and it was warm and comfortable and they gave you good things to eat and tea and natural distilled liqueurs made from purple plums, yellow plums or wild rasberries. . . ." In other words, "*quetsche, mirabelle* or *framboise*" (*Feast*, pp. 13-14), Gertrude Stein lived at 27 rue de Fleurus. Hemingway and Hadley made their first call on her several months after their arrival in Paris, in March 1922. They had been much impressed by what Sherwood Anderson had told them about her and they had to muster up their courage before they dared to face her. But they were very well received, treated as if they were "very good, well mannered and promising children. . ." (*Feast*, p. 14) — though Hadley was somewhat disconcerted by Alice Toklas' strange way of making one conversation with her, listening to two, and often interrupting the one she was not making between Hemingway and Gertrude Stein. Miss Stein and her companion returned the visit and called rather condescendingly a few days later on Hemingway and Hadley. It was a little as if they were slumming. Later Gertrude Stein did not even remember where Hemingway was living at the time of this visit. In *The Autobiography of Alice B. Toklas* she wrote: "This his first apartment was just off the place du Tertre"[6] — a district where

Hemingway's "old friend," the statue of Marshal Ney, stands in front of the Closerie des Lilas, which suggested to Hemingway "that all generations were lost by something and always had been and always would be."

Hemingway never lived. She probably mistook the Sacré Coeur for the Panthéon. The two ladies must have been pleased with their inspection, for Hemingway was asked to come to the studio any time after five whenever he liked.

He went often. As he said, "The pictures were exciting and the talk was very good" (*Feast*, p. 17). Gertrude Stein did most of the talking. She talked about painting (though more about painters than about painting, Hemingway shrewdly noted) and about literature (though more about her own work than about anybody else's, he added). She was very impressive and Hemingway was duly impressed. Gertrude Stein was Gertrude Stein was Gertrude Stein. He sat at her feet like a little boy, making mental notes of what she said, though not without some reservations. She sat there in the middle of her studio as solid and bulky as a Breton menhir, speaking as if she were God the Mother (as it were). He admired her energy and wealth, but was no dupe, unlike those critics he mentions in *A Moveable Feast* "who . . . took on trust writing of hers that they could not understand because of their enthusiasm for her as a person, and because of their confidence in her judgment" (p. 17). He soon realized that she made two capital errors: she disliked the drudgery of revision and didn't bother to make her writing intelligible. She went on and on like a worn record on a gramophone when the needle keeps to the same groove until you remove it. She was a clever technician and knew all kinds of new tricks, but she had nothing to say, having seen nothing but books and pictures and having had no experience of love and war. Though he often differed with her, he never argued. "That was my own business," he said, "and it was much more interesting to listen" (*Feast*, p. 15). There were things he didn't talk of to her and wrote by himself. Thus, in his own way, he was even more monolithic and solid than she was — though she did not realize it.

During all this period, Hemingway worked very hard both as a roving correspondent for *The Toronto Star* to keep the pot boiling and as a writer. He did not make any money as a writer, but he succeeded (with some difficulty) in getting some of his short prose sketches published in *The Little Review* in 1923, and some of his poems in Harriet Monroe's *Poetry*. 1923 was an important date in his literary career. It was the year when his first book appeared: *Three Stories and Ten Poems* published by Robert McAlmon, editor and owner of the Contact Publishing Company of Paris and Dijon. It was a small beginning, but this slim book already contained great and quite original stories: "Up in Michigan," "Out of Season," and "My

For Clink with love from Popplethwaite.

Paris – August 1923

Eric Edward Dorman-Smith's inscribed copy of *Three Stories and Ten Poems* (courtesy of Mrs. E. E. Dorman-O'Gowan).

To Clink with Hommages Respectueus from his former A D.C. and still, with the occasional permission of His Brittanic Majesty, Companion — Popplethwaite

Paris, October, 1925

Eric Edward Dorman-Smith's inscribed copy of *in our time* — one of the dedication copies (courtesy of Mrs. E. E. Dorman-O'Gowan).

Old Man." They were the first fruits of his Parisian years. Edward O'Brien included "My Old Man" in *The Best Short Stories of 1923* and dedicated the volume to him. Hemingway was delighted and full of hope.

But just then something unexpected happened. Hadley became pregnant. Gertrude Stein has told the story: "He came to the house about ten o'clock in the morning and he stayed, he stayed for lunch, he stayed all afternoon, he stayed for dinner and he stayed until about ten o'clock at night and then all of a sudden he announced that his wife was enceinte [note the old maid's prudery] and then with great bitterness, and I, I am too young to be a father" (*Toklas*, p. 262). This event indeed upset his plans, but he decided to make the best of a bad job. "They would go back to America and he would work hard for a year and with what he would earn and what they had they would settle down and he would give up newspaper work and make himself a [full-time] writer" (*Toklas*, p. 262).

And this is exactly what they did. Hemingway and Hadley sailed for Canada in September 1923 and settled in Toronto. He worked as a reporter for the *Star*, though he hated it — all the more because the chief-editor was a stupid bully. On October 10, the child was born. It was a boy: John Hadley Nicanor Hemingway, thus named in honor of his mother and the matador Villalta, but soon nicknamed "Bumby." Hemingway now felt free to leave as soon as he possibly could. So he resigned from the *Star*, the effective date of his resignation being January 1, 1924. A few months later they were back in Paris.

This time they needed a larger apartment and they found one not very far from Ezra Pound's "pavillon" and Gertrude Stein's studio, 113 rue Notre-Dame-des-Champs. It was thus very conveniently located, and quite close also to the Luxembourg Gardens where Hadley could air the baby and to the Closerie des Lilas, a very nice and quiet café where Hemingway could work whenever he liked. As a matter of fact, he often had to take refuge there, for the windows of his apartment looked out on a small sawmill and the whine of the saw was sometimes unbearable. He said that the Closerie "was one of the best cafés in Paris. . . . Most of the clients were elderly bearded men in well worn clothes. . . . [professors and *savants*] These people made it a comfortable café since they were all interested in each other and in their drinks or coffees, or infusions, and in the papers and periodicals which were fastened to rods, and no one was on exhibition" (*Feast*, pp. 81-82).

It was a different story at the Dôme and the Rotonde in

Montparnasse where he went more often now that he lived closer —
for "In those days many people went to the cafés at the corner of
the Boulevard Montparnasse and the Boulevard Raspail to be seen
publicly. . ." (*Feast*, p. 81) — though even there one met interesting
people like Tristan Tzara, the dadaist poet, Pascin, the painter, Kiki,
the charming model for whose memoirs he was later to write an
introduction, Harold Stearns, the promising author of *America and
the Young Intellectual* (1921), who now could talk of nothing but
horses and had nothing to offer but tips for the races, and many
others.

Hemingway was steadily enlarging the circle of his acquaintances
thanks to Ezra Pound, Sylvia Beach, and Gertrude Stein. He was
great friends, since the war, with Dos Passos and saw him whenever
Dos Passos came to Paris on his way to or from Spain. He has told
himself, in great detail in *A Moveable Feast*, the story of his
friendship with Francis Scott Fitzgerald. He also met Harold Loeb, a
wealthy Princeton alumnus who had recently founded in Italy an
interesting little magazine called *Broom* with the co-operation of
Alfred Kreymborg and Giuseppe Prezzolini. Hemingway used him as
a model for Robert Cohn in *The Sun Also Rises*, but Harold Loeb
has told his own side of the story in a book of reminiscences entitled
The Way it Was (1959).

In those days Hemingway, who sometimes found it very hard to
make both ends meet now that he had no income from the *Star* and
Hadley's patrimony was fast dwindling because of unsound invest-
ments, was particularly eager to make the acquaintance of magazine
editors in the hope of making a name and having his stories and
novels accepted by commercial publishers. That is why he was so
keen to meet Harold Loeb; and why he cultivated the friendship of
Ernest Walsh who eventually founded *This Quarter* in 1925, and
published "Big Two-Hearted River" in the very first issue; and Ford
Madox Ford, the editor of the *transatlantic review*, who on Ezra
Pound's recommendation took Hemingway as sub-editor. This was a
strange association. Hemingway disliked Ford, and believed that
Ford was contemptous of him because he was American and,
consequently, no gentleman. Hemingway was exploited by Ford who
did not pay him for his work, and made him read all the manuscripts
and correct all the proofs. But Hemingway paid himself in kind by
packing the review with his works and those of his friends. Thus the
April number in 1924, contained extracts from *Finnegans Wake* and
a big chunk of Gertrude Stein's *The Making of Americans* and the
earliest reviews of *Three Stories and Ten Poems* and *in our time* and

"Indian Camp." The August number, which Hemingway had to prepare all by himself while Ford was in America trying to raise money for his sinking review, was even more heavily loaded with purely American products since it included a long story by Dos Passos, a short one by Nathan Asch, and another long excerpt from *The Making of Americans.* This was not quite consonant with Ford's ideas of a truly international review. No wonder he accused Hemingway, in the next issue, of having stuffed the *transatlantic* with an "unusually large sample" of work by his American friends.

So one of the things which Hemingway learned in Paris and soon practised with consummate skill was literary strategy. He wanted to come to the front and, in order to achieve his end, he did his very best to ingratiate himself with all the people who counted. He patiently and reverently listened to Gertrude Stein's pretentious and repetitious talk; he bore with Ford's arrogance; he made friends with Ezra Pound, though he originally ridiculed his mannerisms in a satire which he offered to the *Little Review*, but which the editors, luckily for him, refused to print. But, conversely, when he met Katharine Anne Porter, who was a nobody in those days, in Sylvia Beach's shop he cut her dead very rudely. He had little use for other writers except as stepping-stones. After his first collection of short stories, *In Our Time*, was accepted by Liveright on Sherwood Anderson's recommendation, he turned savagely on him in the next book, *The Torrents of Spring.* After Scribners had accepted *The Sun Also Rises* on Fitzgerald's recommendation, he cruelly attacked Fitzgerald by way of thanks in "The Snows of Kilimanjaro." So his was an unscrupulous and ruthless strategy, but it paid. His Parisian apprenticeship was crowned with success.

Unfortunately his success wrecked his marriage. In 1926, as he put it in *A Moveable Feast*, "The rich showed up" in the form of the two Pfeiffer sisters. Pauline, the elder one, was working for the Paris edition of *Vogue.* She was small and delicate, very *chic.* She fell in love with Hemingway − not at first sight, on second thought. She insinuated herself into the company of the couple and soon disrupted it. Hemingway and Hadley set up separate residences towards the end of August 1926. Hadley found a room at the Hôtel Beauvoir near the Closerie des Lilas, and Hemingway took up his quarters in the studio which their rich friends, the Murphys, had put at his disposal at 69 rue de Froidevaux on the sixth floor. Hadley had promised that if Pauline and Ernest would stay apart for a hundred days and were still in love by the end of that time she would give him a divorce. They were divorced on January 27, 1927, and Hemingway married Pauline Pfeiffer in May at a Catholic church in Passy, and moved into a flat at 6 rue Férou (a narrow lane which goes from the Luxembourg Gardens to St. Sulpice). "That was the end of the first part of Paris. Paris was never to be the same again. . ." (*Feast*, p. 211).

The second part was very short, for he did not stay in Paris much longer after that. Less than a year later, in early March 1928, he went back to America and settled in Key West with his second wife. It was the end of his youth, the end of his love affair with Paris. When he came again, at irregular intervals, on his way to Spain or Africa, or even during the mad, intoxicating days of the Liberation, he never stayed very long. He was a rich tourist now and no more a poor expatriate, but he was full of nostalgia: for he never forgot the early days in Paris with Hadley, and this romantic nostalgia permeates *A Moveable Feast* and gives it its penetrating charm. "There is never any ending to Paris . . ." (p. 211). He loved Paris because he loved life and love. He loved Spain for different reasons, because he was fascinated by death.

He resided in Paris from December 22, 1921 to early March 1928, that is to say for five years and a quarter, but actually he was not there all the time. He was always on the go. He had to do a lot of traveling for his newspaper in the early years and spent weeks in Italy, Germany, Turkey, and Switzerland on various assignments. Besides this, there were long stays of three months or more at Schruns in Austria when Hemingway and Hadley fled from the cold winter months in Paris to enjoy the pure air and the sunshine of the mountains, and to ski. There were also the months they spent in Canada. So, if you add up all their absences, you discover that they were away from Paris at least three and a half years and spent in Paris just a little over two years, which is a great deal less than they are generally credited with; and, as they were constantly coming and going, these two years did not give them a chance to strike roots and make friends with French people – except very superficially with the waiters of the Closerie des Lilas and the *femme de ménage* who looked after Bumby. Though some French writers like Paul Valéry, Léon-Paul Fargue, and Valéry Larbaud occasionally visited Sylvia Beach's bookshop and though Adrienne Monnier, her friend who owned a French bookshop at 7 rue de l'Odéon, "La Maison des Livres," almost opposite Shakespeare and Company, tried hard to bring French and English and American writers together, Hemingway had very few contacts with French writers – and those contacts remained epidermic. He met the essayist and novelist Drieu La

Rochelle, who admired his works, only once: "I met Hemingway only once. . . .I liked him very much. . . .He is one of those guys with whom you must go hunting or fishing."[7] Same story with Jean Prévost, though Prévost could speak English and was fond of boxing too: "I boxed with him a few years ago," Jean Prévost wrote in his introduction to the French translation of *The Sun Also Rises.*[8] "I boxed with him," not "I talked with him." In *A Moveable Feast* Hemingway frequently engages in name-dropping. Judging by the way he speaks of Cendrars, you would think he knew him intimately, but a little further he confesses candidly that he *saw* him only once. "Only once" is the burden of all his reminiscences of French writers. And one may wonder why, since he was interested in French literature, in Flaubert, Stendhal, Maupassant. He had even read some of Simenon's novels in French. Why didn't he feel curious to know the French writers he met? One reason may have been that they were useless to him; they were no stepping stones; they had no part to play in his strategy. But another reason was that he was very shy when he had to speak in French with French intellectuals. He was more at ease with waiters than with writers.

At this point one may well ask oneself whether he was not stopped by the language barrier and whether he could speak French fluently. Here testimonies differ. According to Janet Flanner he was "a natural quick linguist who learned a language first through his ears because of his constant necessity for understanding people and for communicating."[9] This was certainly true, and the indignant exclamation quoted by Sylvia Beach: "*Et naturellement le flic est dans la pissottière!*" (*Shakespeare & Co.*, p. 89) though not perfectly idiomatic is a good illustration of what Janet Flanner meant. Hemingway had no doubt picked up a number of picturesque and juicy slang phrases which on occasion enabled him to throw dust in people's eyes, but, unlike Dos Passos who had studied French at Harvard and, before that, as a child in Europe and could write it impeccably, he had never studied French at school (at Oak Park High School they taught only Latin). He had to shift for himself when he arrived in Paris; he acquired a large vocabulary, but his knowledge of grammar was always shaky. He felt embarrassed when he had to converse with French writers. Here I have the testimony of an American professor of French, Roman Guthrie, who taught French at Dartmouth for many years and published several excellent collections of poems, notably *Graffiti* (1959). He first met Hemingway in the twenties and was present, in 1937, when Hemingway was in Paris with Sidney Franklin trying to obtain a visa for Spain for this famous American matador. They were often invited by the leftist poet Robert Desnos to the rue Mazarine. This is what Guthrie wrote to me:

"Desnos, I seem to recall, spoke fair English and at the times when I was there the conversation comes back to me as being in both languages. I don't remember what Hemingway talked about but I am pretty sure it wasn't literature or politics. I remember talking about Stendhal with J. L. Barrault who was present at one of the Desnos dinners, but Hemingway didn't join in. My impression is like yours, i.e., that Hemingway's French was not the kind that one could carry on a philosophical discussion in. (Neither was his English, for that matter.) In short, it is my impression that he was not fluent in French though he could get along in that language without much trouble."[10]

Such is the opinion of a professional. In Ramon Guthrie's eyes, as regards his knowledge of French, Hemingway was only a gifted amateur. Naturally, this relative failure of his as a linguist does not matter in the least. It is worth noticing only in so far as it accounts for his lack of communication with the French intelligentsia. Who cares if he could not carry on a conversation in French about Stendhal? The main thing is that he should have found in Paris the atmosphere he needed to write some of his best short stories and some of his best novels.

He owed to Paris the independence and freedom without which his work would probably have remained stunted; and it was to pay off his debt, as it were, that he wrote *A Moveable Feast* in which he has preserved, in the transparent amber of his tender and cruel prose, the Paris of the twenties: a Paris which has vanished forever, but which he has managed to make immortal.

A few reviewers, especially those of his own generation, have accused Hemingway of unfairness because he has refused to gloss over the failings and failures of some of the expatriate writers and artists who were then living in Paris, even when they were his friends. But why should he have treated them with indulgence? They failed because, unlike Hemingway, they refused to make the necessary sacrifices in order to become great writers. What to him was "a moveable feast" to them was a morass in which they bogged down and lost themselves. They indulged in drink and drugs, like Ralph Cheever Dunning. They let their pens run on-and-on without ever stopping to polish what they wrote, like Gertrude Stein. They allowed their wives to destroy them out of jealousy of their creative powers, like Fitzgerald. They were the true lost generation — "la génération foutue," as it should be called in French — whereas he, the young veteran of the lithe body and the iron will, imposed upon himself and his writings a strict discipline which enabled him to control his despair and create enduring masterpieces.

But Hemingway had to pay a high price for this achievement. Though he never said so in so many words — because unlike Montherlant, he refused to admit it even to himself — he discovered that life is, to a large extent, incompatible with artistic creation. You cannot both live and write. And that charming young wife of his, whom he has painted in such attractive colors in *A Moveable Feast*, was one of the things he had to sacrifice together with Mr. Bumby, his first son — though the first-born is always a miracle — in order to pursue his experiences and devote himself to his career. But the sense of his loss gives pathos to many pages of his book. A creator is doomed to solitude. To create is to suffer.

Yet, in the solitude of his old age, Hemingway had known how to recapture the exhilaration of the young and happy days he spent in Paris, in the crucial years, when he was patiently polishing the tools of his trade all by himself in a cold *mansarde* or a clean well-lighted *café*, in the calm center of the tumultuous city which was revolving round him.

The Sorbonne

[1] *By-Line: Ernest Hemingway*, ed. William White (New York: Scribners, 1967), p. 130.

[2] Hemingway, Ernest. *A Moveable Feast* (New York: Scribners, 1964), p. 3.

[3] Hemingway, Ernest. *The Sun Also Rises* (New York: Scribners, 1926), p. 19.

[4] Beach, Sylvia. *Shakespeare and Company* (London: Faber and Faber, 1960), p. 89.

[5] Plimpton, George. "The Art of Fiction XXI: Ernest Hemingway," *Paris Review*, V (Spring 1958), p. 73-74.

[6] Stein, Gertrude. *The Autobiography of Alice B. Toklas*. New York: Harcourt, Brace, 1933, p. 261.

[7] *L'Adieu aux armes* (Paris: Gallimard, 1932), pp. 9-10. Translated by Maurice-Edgar Coindreau. Preface by Drieu la Rochelle.

[8] *Le soleil se lève aussi* (Paris: Gallimard, 1933), p. x. Translated by Maurice-Edgar Coindreau. Preface by Jean Prévost.

[9] Baker, Carlos. *Ernest Hemingway A Life Story* (New York: Scribners, 1969), p. 138.

[10] Letter to the author, 1 June 1972.

HAROLD LOEB

REMARKS

BY

HAROLD LOEB

Harold Loeb has been many things in American literature: the editor and publisher of Broom, *which has been called the best of the expatriate journals, and the author of three remarkable novels –* Doodab, Tumbling Mustard, *and* The Professors Like Vodka. *He was intricately involved in the life of The Quarter, and he is one of the contributors to* Hemingway and the SUN Set. *Mr. Loeb knows* The Way it Was.

I came to Europe in 1921 soon after Harold Stearns did. He had left America partly because of Prohibition, partly because of the Puritanism which we all supposed enveloped our country – we didn't realize the French were in some respects more puritanical – and partly because of the more serious reception the arts received abroad. After he was over here for about a year, his compilation *Civilization in the United States* came out. I didn't agree with much of it. Nevertheless, we remained good friends.

On landing in June, the Kreymborgs and I went to the Hôtel Jacob, a musty little hotel much frequented by American writers. But I was impatient and soon boarded the train for Italy, not knowing in which country to publish *Broom*. The first person I went to see there was Filippo Marinetti. He exclaimed: "You come from

America: the land of energy! of acceleration! where the new world is being formed!" I was more than a little taken back.

When I returned to France, I met Cocteau, Picabia, Breton, Aragon, Tzara, and many others. I tried to say how wonderful it was to be in France where the arts were respected, where painting was treasured, and literature appreciated. Often someone would remark: "But in America − acceleration, velocity!" This confused me as I was at the time gradually formulating an editorial position. But not very much. I was quite willing to accept the wonders of the United States. Perhaps I did a little more justice to our skyscrapers, jazz, movies, and advertising than I would have done if it had not been for this unexpected foreign reaction. *Vanity Fair* was still under the influence of the American cultured classes who thought of America as provincial. Bunny Wilson maintained in its pages that America had been overshadowed by its skyscrapers and enslaved by its machines. Indignantly I wrote an editorial which said that when I pressed a button, the car ran. I did not understand how I could be enslaved by an apparatus which obviously obeyed me.

I met Scott Fitzgerald before coming over. He went to Princeton three years after I did, but I did not see him there. After his successful novel, *This Side of Paradise*, he arrived one day at the Sunwise Turn Book Shop where I was a partner and asked me to get him an out-of-print book. He came with Zelda. They were quite young then. I remember thinking what a beautiful couple they made, the most striking couple I'd ever encountered. And I was fortunate to find him the book he wanted.

The next time I saw him I was sitting on the terrace of the Select and he came up waving *The Great Gatsby* which he presented to Hemingway, and said, "I hope you'll like it." This must have been early in 1925 because I first met Hemingway at one of Ford Madox Ford's tea parties, and this occurred, I think, after Ford had started to publish the *transatlantic review* in 1924.

Broom had come to an end the year before when the money gave out. We closed the office in Berlin where we had gone in the hope of getting cheaper paper and cheaper printing because of the fall of the mark and returned to Paris. Kitty Cannell had known Ford in London. I was sitting at a table with him when he invited me − he invited everyone he met, partly in the hope of increasing his magazine's circulation, to a Thursday afternoon cocktail party. I ran into Hemingway there, a large man with red cheeks, beautiful teeth, and a lovely smile. We got to talking about shooting quail and fishing for trout in Michigan.

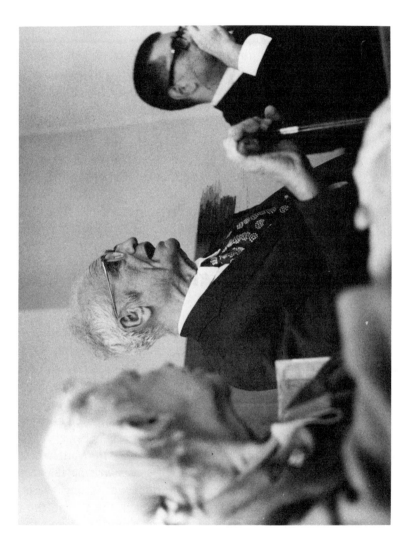

Harold Loeb at the Paris conference: " . . . the story that I planned to shoot Hemingway at Lipps was completely false."

In those days I had the notion that many writing people resembled Oscar Wilde. They mightn't be homosexual, but they were likely to be effeminate; and it was a relief to run into a writer who was enthusiastic about the outdoors and sports.

Hem had written a number of short stories but hadn't had much accepted as yet. He was still sending them out. They usually came back with an editorial comment to the effect that: "This is all very fine writing, Mr. Hemingway, but it's not a story." He was helping Ford on the review. I liked him at once. We started playing tennis on the public courts near the guillotine. Hem was no tennis player. He had a bad eye. I thought it was due to an injury in a street fight. However, Carlos Baker maintains that Hemingway had had it from childhood — that it was a congenital defect. Hem also had a bad leg from shrapnel fragments. He seldom ran up to the net. But he did enjoy the game. So did everyone else when he was on the court. He had such pleasure when he made a good shot and such misery when he missed that the game was never lackadaisical. Paul Fisher was the best of us four. Bill Smith was usually my partner. He and I were about equal to Fisher and Hem. And afterwards Hem and I would box. He could have knocked me out if he had wanted to, but he never did. We boxed pleasantly, and he was a good boxer, but not the great champion that he was supposed to have been. At least I don't think so. I don't know how Hem managed to build up a reputation as a boxer.

We made plans to go skiing in Schruns, Austria, and then to watch the bullfights in Spain. I remember a letter that Donald Ogden Stewart wrote to Hem saying it was alright to go skiing but why choose a town with a name like Schruns. I didn't think it was particularly funny. Instead of going skiing in Austria, I went to the United States. I had a book coming out and had eliminated all the *a's* and *the's* that weren't functionally needed. If it was necessary to say the noun was definite or indefinite I'd put in *a* or *the*, but when it wasn't necessary, I'd leave it out. I thought I was writing telescopic English. Maybe I was. Maybe Horace Liveright was wrong when he wired me: "Will accept your book if you put back the *a's* and *the's.*" I took a steamer all the way to America to put back the *a's* and *the's.*

While I was there I asked about Hemingway's manuscript. I had introduced him to Leon Fleischman, who was then the Paris representative of Liveright. Fleischman had sent the manuscript to New York, and I asked Schneider about it. Schneider told me to see Beatrice Kaufman, George S. Kaufman's wife, who was reading for Liveright. She had it on her desk and she said, "I'm glad you came in;

I was just sending it back." I asked: "Why?"

We had a long discussion, and she promised to read it again. I don't think my intervention was the crucial factor in getting *In Our Time* accepted because Sherwood Anderson, who was then Liveright's best literary seller, also put in a word for it. But Horace finally did publish it. I don't think he sold very many; books of short stories are pretty hard to sell.

After I had put the *a's* and *the's* back — it took me several weeks — I returned to France. Hem and I continued boxing and tennis. But before going off to Pamplona, I went to St. Jean de Luz. It was there that I had a letter from Duff asking me if I'd mind if she joined the party in Pamplona. I thought: if she can take it, I can. So the party came to consist of Duff and Pat, Hemingway and Hadley, Bill Smith, Donald Ogden Stewart, and myself.

Don wouldn't go into the ring in the amateur morning because he had broken three ribs the year before. The bullfighting was alright, except some of us had considerable sympathy for the cat-like quadruped. The horses' injuries didn't bother me much. (That was before the padding, and many of them were gored and dragged their intestines along the ground.) But the bull came out with such splendor, to be gradually weakened and weakened and weakened by picadors and banderilleros until the matador could get near enough to kill him. It seemed pathetic.

In the morning the riff-raff of the town — you had to get up at 6:00 a.m. — used to try their hand at passing small bulls, cows, and steers to right and left. I forced myself to go over the barrier into the arena by an act of will. Hemingway went first. Bill Smith and I followed. We got inside and Bill Smith got knocked down. I took my Fair Isle sweater off. It was blue and red, and had been the gift of a nice young woman. I held it out in front of me, and the bull put his horn through it and ran off. I had to chase him all over the arena to get my sweater back. So the next morning I carefully left the Fair Isle sweater behind and carried a hotel towel. Nobody told me that bulls aren't interested in white. Someone told me that later — I don't know if it's true. In any case, I noticed the bull wasn't looking at the towel which I held in front of me, shaking it slightly and swinging it a little from side to side. He was looking over the towel at my spectacles. People think I made a quick decision. There was no decision to make: it was a scarcity of alternatives. I turned my back and sat on the bull, grabbed the horns and was carried across the arena. The matador, whom Hemingway admired so much, I don't remember his name — he certainly didn't know Duff; we just shook hands with him on the way out — told Hemingway: "One would have thought he had done it on purpose."

So our friendship ended.

REMARKS

BY

MORRILL CODY

In one way Morrill Cody is the most appropriate person for this panel discussion because it was largely through his efforts that the Café Voltaire became the Bibliotheque Benjamin Franklin, which houses the Institut d'Études Américaines. Mr. Cody was a Paris newsman in the twenties and is an old hand in the Foreign Service, having been Information Officer and Public Affairs Officer at American Embassy in Paris. He is presently Paris Bureau manager of Radio Liberty. Mr. Cody is well known to Hemingway buffs for This Must Be the Place, *and also wrote* The Favorite Restaurants of an American in Paris. *Ernest Hemingway once referred to Morrill Cody as his oldest friend in Paris. Although Mr. Cody notes that this compliment is inaccurate, he's pleased that Hemingway said it.*

My friend André Chamson a little while ago said that he didn't know Hemingway very well, but he knew Scott Fitzgerald, and that he was somewhat embarrassed at that time because Scott Fitzgerald paid all the bills in restaurants. I'd like to tell you about the reverse of that. I knew both of these men. But I knew Hemingway particularly well, who never bought any meals in restaurants; and, in fact, I and others lent him money when he was jobless which was never repaid. Not large sums of money – but, you know, five dollars here and five dollars there. So this is the other side of the coin. André Chamson chose the right friend.

As has been mentioned, I wrote a book about Montparnasse which was published under the title *This Must Be the Place*. I did this because I liked Jimmy Charters, the most famous barman of Montparnasse. Jimmy was an uneducated Welsh lad of Irish ancestry with a heart of gold, and I suppose that his best friend was Hemingway. Hemingway adored Jimmy – he just thought Jimmy was *it*. Jimmy helped things along by giving Hemingway occasional free drinks at his bar. They were really great friends. At some point friends said, "Jimmy, you ought to write your memoirs." And Jim would say "Yes." Jimmy wasn't a writer. I finally volunteered to write these memoirs; but I didn't know how to write them, and he didn't know either. Hemingway told me how to write the book, but his ideas weren't very good either. Finally we decided that we'd find a young lady who would take dictation and not be shocked. Jimmy and I spent a year off and on while he dictated his memoirs. And when he got through with his memory test – when we finally exhausted everything that Jimmy had – there were some very thin spots. So I filled in the thin spots about people that Jimmy hadn't known because we wanted to mention everyone that should have been in there. But as I looked over these notes, which were voluminous, I soon saw that at least one third of them were, in those days at least, unpublishable.

Hemingway was in Key West. He wrote me letters about the introduction he would write. I was very happy about that. And then he came to Paris and he said he wanted to see the manuscript. So I showed him the manuscript which he thougth was all right. (I subsequently decided it was not, but that's another story.) I told him there were one third of the notes which couldn't be published. He said, "Where are they?" He was about to go off to Africa, so he said, "Let me take them with me." I said, "Well, I want them back." He said, "I'll send them right back; don't worry about it. I'll send them right back." Well, this is one of the manuscripts which is lost forever; he never sent them back to me; he later claimed that he had destroyed them. Maybe they should have been destroyed – I don't know – but there were a lot of things in there that Jimmy remembered which historically were interesting.

Harold mentioned Hemingway's boxing. Jimmy is still alive, in-cidentally, and lives in London – I saw him a couple of years ago; he does bit parts in the movies over there. He's about 83, but he still does bit parts, character parts. He's quite a person that Jimmy.

Morrill Cody at the Paris Conference: "I knew Scott and Zelda in the old Dingo Bar, but I didn't know Fitzgerald well partly because I didn't have enough money to pay for Scott Fitzgerald. I did have enough money to pay for Hemingway."

Anyway, Jimmy, who had been a professional boxer, boxed once or twice with Hemingway. However, thereafter Jimmy avoided boxing with Hemingway because he said Hemingway knew nothing about boxing. And as he was his client, you see, Jimmy was afraid that he would hit him, and then he would lose a friend.

Well, I don't exactly know what more to say. I didn't know Scott Fitzgerald very well, and partly for the same reason André Chamson mentioned, that I didn't have enough money to keep up with his crowd. I had enough money to pay occasionally for Hemingway, but I didn't have enough money to pay my end with Scott Fitzgerald. I used to see him and Zelda in the old Dingo Bar where we'd have a drink together, but we never became really close friends. Hemingway was different, and he and I became very good friends, and he was very helpful to me in many ways and a very good friend right till almost his last days. I saw him for the last time in Pamplona — that was in the late 50's. He told me than that he was going to get even with those people in Paris in the 20's in a book he was writing. He didn't tell me the name of it, but you all know it — *A Moveable Feast*. He had only written part of it, he said — he'd written it over a long period I believe — different parts. And I think his intention — at least he told me his intention was to have a much longer book in which he'd take more people apart than he did in *A Moveable Feast*. But he did pretty well at that.

FLORENCE GILLIAM

REMARKS

BY

FLORENCE GILLIAM

Florence Gilliam has been described as the typical American literary woman in Paris. She was editor and publisher of Gargoyle, *the first English-language review of arts and letters on the continent between the two wars. She has been Paris correspondent for* Theatre *and drama critic for the* Boulevardier. *She wrote* France *(1945) and* The Joy of Dancing *(1953). Miss Gilliam has been honored by France for her work in war relief, and for years ran the General Secretariat of the American Catholic Women's Organization of Paris.*

I met Ernest Hemingway through George Slocombe, who was a British journalist and who knew Ernest Hemingway because Hemingway was working for the *Toronto Star.* George Slocombe invited Arthur Moss and me to come in and hear some of Hemingway's stories which had not been published, and which George thought were very much worth publishing. So he asked us to come in and give our opinion on them. Hemingway at that time, and as I remembered him for many years, was a very tall, rosy-cheeked, soft-voiced, soft-eyed young man. Entirely different from the Papa with the heavy beard and so forth that we learned to know as his image later on. Anyway he read us some of his stories that night, and we thought they were wonderful. Before very long Bob McAlmon and Bill Bird

43

and other people here with the Contact Editions and the Three Mountains Press had published these in small editions of which we had some very prized copies. And Harold has mentioned the fact that he had something to do in getting these done in America later on in larger editions.

I said when I was asked if I would participate in this panel that I thought I had very little to contribute about my contacts with Hemingway and Fitzgerald, because though I knew Hemingway for years — he was a great friend of ours and we knew both of his first two wives very well — still I didn't have really any very amusing or lively anecdotes about him to contribute. As for Fitzgerald, he was just part of our night life. I mean we saw him at cocktail parties or night clubs, but we didn't have any real close friendship with him. Bricktop — who was, as you know, night-club hostess to the world and to royalty included — told me some very amusing stories about Fitzgerald, because he was a great friend of hers and always in her nightclub. She used to take his money away from him, as he always carried around five or ten thousand francs, which at that time meant something. And she used to take it away because she was afraid that he would lose it or just spend it in some untoward way; then just give it back to him in time for his return. But one night she said the two Fitzgeralds were at the Lido, and Fitzgerald decided that he would jump into the pool. At that time the Lido had a swimming pool and everybody sat around having drinks by the pool. So Scott decided he would jump in just for fun, you know, the way he did everything. Zelda, of course, being a very loving wife jumped in right after him, and they were fished out and put out in the street. Of course the cops seeing them all dripping didn't know what to do with them, so they took them to the station house. And there Zelda finally arranged to get a cab and go home. But Scott would say nothing except that he was a great friend of Bricktop's. So eventually the police got him into a taxicab and took him to Bricktop's apartment — this of course must have been about four or five o'clock in the morning. Bricktop said that it took her until noon the next day to get him out of there. And she was, of course, seeing that he didn't go home alone because of all these thousands of francs, so she just got a cab and took him home herself. This is one of Bricktop's typical stories because she was involved with practically everybody — not only all the artists and all the writers but also all of the socialites that came to Paris. Anyway, I wanted to speak of Bricktop especially in connection with another point that I want to make about the '20s.

What I thought, as long as I said I was just going to talk a little bit

Florence Gilliam at the Paris conference: "Hemingway was a very tall, rosy-cheeked, soft-voiced, soft-eyed young man entirely different from the Papa with the heavy beard. . . . "

about general things, was that the aspect that seemed to me the most
interesting and the most thrilling of *les années vingt,* the '20's — or
les années folles as the French called them — was the international
element that played such a very strong role in all the things that we
did. As Professor Bruccoli said, Arthur Moss and I published the first
of the little magazines on the continent between the two wars which
was called *Gargoyle.* I thought it was interesting — as I looked over
the list of our contributors — that while we had very devoted
American contributors like Malcolm Cowley and Bob Coates and
Lawrence Vail and Mattie Josephson, we also had people from
England like Lett Haines and Bryer and H. D. We were doing
reproductions, of course, of all kinds of paintings and sculpture,
which was one of the main elements in our effort. So we not only
had the French like Cézanne and Matisse and Derain and Braque, but
we had also the other members of *Ecole de Paris* which, as you
know, was completely international. And so we had reproductions of
Picasso and Modigliani, and Foujita the Japanese, and Marcoussis and
Kisling, and Lipschitz and Zadkine — in other words, the people
from central Europe, the Poles and the Italians as well as the French.

An eminently important example of that internationalism was, of
course, the Diaghilev ballets which probably most of you know were
in their heyday during the twenties here. Those of us who had
friends among the artists always had a *carte de circulation* so that we
could go to every performance and see any ballet as many times as
we wished. For Diaghilev, of course, the fundamentals of his ballet
were Russian — there was no question about that. He brought his
painters like Bakst and Benois and Larionov and Gontcharova, and
later on, of course, others such as Tchelitchef. But his ballets were as
much dominated by people like Matisse and Picasso and Braque and
Rouault and Marie Laurençin and also the Italian De Chirico and the
German Max Ernst — so that it was a completely international
picture, you see.

And as for the music, the two outstanding composers naturally
were Stravinsky and Prokofieff. But Diaghilev had ballets from every
one of *Les Six,* which was the French group of the time that was
most in view, largely launched by Cocteau and those people you all
know. There were Poulenc and Auric and Milhaud and various
others, but particularly those were active in the ballet. We also had
Satie — all of them making a completely international picture. The
same thing more or less obtained — well, to a lesser degree — with the
dancers.

Of course, the great choreographers were Russians — like Nijinsky and Nijinska and Massine and Balanchine (who was responsible for the great fame of the New York City Ballet). All of those people were Russian to start with, but Diaghilev also had a great many people that joined the ballet. Among the dancers there were not only the Russians such as Karsavina and Nemchinova and Nikitina and Dubrowska and Idzikowsky and Woidzikowsky; but also people like Sokolowa, an English girl who changed her name to a Russian name; and Markova, one of the most brilliant stars he ever had, who was just Alice Marks from London; and Antonin Doline, who was just an Irish boy by the name of Dolan. It was a very international outfit from the very start.

Swedish ballet was also very international. It was of a lesser degree, I should say, as far as the artistic achievement was concerned. But Swedish Ballet was very international. They had, of course, their own native painters like Nils Dardel for the background. But they also had a great many things by Léger and by Perdrier, with music by all the members of *Les Six*. And among the people who contributed to the scenarios there was Blaise Cendrars, and other people who were of the French or the international picture.

All that had a great influence here in Paris – I mean from the whole artistic point-of-view – this internationalism which obtained everywhere was just, I think, most significant for the enrichment of life of those Americans like myself who were here. It was one of the great elements that made our lives in Paris so important to us at that period.

The theatre, of course, was extremely international. I won't go into all of the details of the repertoire. But starting with Lugné-Poë at the Oeuvre, he took a horrible little stuffy concert hall and made it into a theatre. And there he did all the Scandinavians and also a great many other nationalities including the English. And Jacques Copeau had a completely international repertoire and so did Jouvet and so did Dullin, who were, of course, disciples of Copeau to start with. They not only presented the writers of the day like Giraudoux and Sartre and Cocteau, but they did a really international repertoire beginning way back with Ben Jonson and Shakespeare and coming right down to Bernard Shaw. So that it was a completely international repertoire. Of course, the Pitoeffs not only did all the Russian classics, but everybody you could think of – I mean practically every nationality. Pitoeff was the first man, as you know, to introduce Pirandello to Paris. So that the general aspect of international quality in the life of Paris seemed to me quite an important element.

I would like to say that one of the most important and interesting things to me was the dominance of the American Negro entertainers at that period. I suppose it hasn't completely disappeared, but at that period it absolutely dominated all entertainment life. In the first place, of course, we had the *Revue Nègre* that came to the Champs-Elysses and electrified everyone with Josephine Baker, who became an international star. And then we had the *Blackbirds* with Florence Mills with her lovely, little wistful qualities; and then another version of *Blackbirds* which was run by Lou Leslie and which gave me my first example of how American timing is paced so differently from European timing. And in that company there were a lot of people who later became stars in the nightclubs. Most of the Negro entertainers stayed in Paris. They preferred life in Paris. They found it much more agreeable. They found much less prejudice here. And also they ran their own nightclubs. Some of them had their own nightclubs; some of them appeared with other people. But I think particularly of the ones that stayed here and had experience over long years and made their homes here. I don't want to go on indefinitely, because I could at this point. But I do think that the fact that these people were integrated into French life so thoroughly contributed to this general international aspect that I was talking about.

ANDRÉ LE VOT

FITZGERALD

IN

PARIS

André Le Vot is the most active French scholar of Fitzgerald. He wrote the section on The Great Gatsby *in the "Collection U2" Fitzgerald volume and edited a bilingual edition of Fitzgerald's stories for Aubier-Fammarion. Prof. Le Vot has recently completed a critical book on Fitzgerald.*

During a span of ten years, from his first brief visit to Europe in May 1921 to the moment he left for good in September 1931, Fitzgerald lived for about four and a half years abroad, out of which three years were spent in France — two-thirds of which, roughly twenty-two months, in Paris, the same amount of time he spent in the States during the seven years between 1924 and 1931.

We shall of course go into the details of Fitzgerald's life in Paris, but what is, I think, more important than merely biographical data is the impact another civilization may have had upon his development as a man and a writer, the influence, if any, another culture may have had upon his conception of life and art. At the outset we can assert that, apart from a major exception, his friendship with André Chamson, he had very little communication with the French writers of the period and does not seem to have taken any interest in the literary movements (Dada, Surrealism) of the time. Unlike Hem-

ingway, who shared for a while the life of the poor, his relationships
with the French were those of a rich tourist who spoke the language
badly and dealt mostly with paid employees—taxi-drivers, restaurant
and bar waiters, servants, and nurses and policemen when things were
getting out of hand. It seems he got only what money can buy, and
his awareness, and wistfulness, can be felt in the passage in "Babylon
Revisited" in which Charlie Wales catches sight of a cheap restaurant
and realizes he has never shared the real life of the Parisians, seen
here having their dinner "behind the trim little bourgeois hedge of
Duval's. He had never eaten at a really cheap restaurant in Paris.
Five-course dinner, four francs fifty, eighteen cents, wine included.
For some odd reason he wished that he had." Instead he went to the
expensive places where he met other Americans, living in an insulated
universe where English was the only language and the Americans a
race apart: "We were a sort of royalty, almost infallible, with a sort
of magic around us."

1921

His first reaction to Paris and France, as expressed in a letter to
Edmund Wilson from London in May 1921 is rather blunt and
marked by some of the prejudices he had found in Mencken's essays,
mentioned in the same letter:

> God damn the continent of Europe. It is of merely antiquarian
> interest . . . The negroid streak creeps northward to defile the Nordic
> races . . . France makes me sick. Its silly pose as the thing the world has to
> save. I think it's a shame that England and America didn't let Germany
> conquer Europe. It's the only thing that would have saved the fleet of
> tottering old wrecks. My reactions were all philistine, antisocialistic,
> provincial and racially snobbish. I believe at last in the white man's
> burden. We are as far above the modern Frenchman as he is above the
> Negro. Even in art! . . . When Anatole France dies French literature will be
> a silly rehashing of technical quarrels. They're thru and done.[1]

Three years later, tired of the incessant parties of Long Island,
unable to work satisfactorily on his third novel, he decided to leave
America and look for an entirely new background where he could
work at peace and be somehow reborn: "We were going to the Old
World to find a new rhythm for our lives, with a true conviction that
we had left our old selves behind forever."[2] In a story written the

preceding winter, a winter of hard work almost entirely devoted to pot-boilers, he had to a certain extent crystallized his dream of evasion around the name of Paris: "No Americans have any imagination − Paris is the only place where a civilized woman can breathe."[3]

1924

He landed in May 1924 and stayed briefly in Paris on his way to the south, finding time to have lunch with John Peale Bishop at the Pavillion d'Ermenonville in the Bois de Boulogne. Presumably through Donald Ogden Stewart, he also got acquainted with the Murphys. In her 1934 article, "Show Mr. and Mrs. Fitzgerald to Number −," Zelda Fitzgerald writes that they stayed at the Hôtel des Deux Mondes (avenue de l'Opéra) where they "bathed the daughter in the *bidet* by mistake and she drank the gin fizz thinking it was lemonade and ruined the luncheon table next day."[4] There was Paris, with its unmistakable music: "Outside we could hear the high, clear honk of strange auto horns and we remembered we were in Paris."[5] Six years later the same correlative appears in "Babylon Revisited" when Wales wants to sum up Paris, what he wants to recover, the blue hour spreading over the façade of the Opéra, and imagines "that the cab horns, playing endlessly the first few bars of *Le plus que lent,* were the trumpets of the Second Empire." Again in a story written in 1940, "News of Paris, Fifteen Years Ago," the melody of Paris, like a Gershwin tune, provides the opening note: "Half way across the street, he stopped to a great screech of auto horns playing Debussy."[6]

1925

It was almost a year before he returned to Paris, a year entirely spent writing *The Great Gatsby* in Saint-Raphael and revising it in Italy. They sailed from Naples to Marseilles in April at about the time the novel was issued in New York. They proceeded to drive to Paris, but the six-horse-power Renault, bought the year before on the Riviera, broke down in Lyons and they continued by train. They must have reached Paris by the end of April as Fitzgerald wired Perkins from Lyons about 24 April. In a letter dated 1 May, he mentions that he has rented an apartment for eight months at number 14 rue de Tilsitt, one block from the Arch of Triumph. Meanwhile they lived for about two weeks at the Hôtel Florida, 12 Boulevard Malesherbes, near la Madeleine, until they could move on 12 May into their fifth-floor walkup, a rather gloomy apartment, pompously crowded with copies of eighteenth-century furniture.

The event of that spring was meeting Hemingway who had come to Paris three and a half years before and was now living at 113 rue Notre Dame des Champs, five minutes away from the famous cafés of Montparnasse. The meeting at the Dingo bar, rue Delambre, in the neighborhood, has been recounted in *A Moveable Feast* and it is needless to go through it again. What is more important is that Hemingway had met Gertrude Stein three years before and that he took Fitzgerald to 27 rue de Fleurus even before they went to Lyons to get the Renault and drive it back to Paris. Stein and Fitzgerald seem to have taken immediately to each other. She had been impressed by *This Side of Paradise* that, she wrote, had created the new generation for the public:

> She has never changed her opinion about this. She thinks this equally true of The Great Gatsby. She thinks Fitzgerald will be read when many of his well known contemporaries are forgotten. Fitzgerald always says he thinks Gertrude Stein says these things just to annoy him by making him think she means them, and he adds in his favourite way, and her doing is the cruellest thing I ever heard. They always have a very good time when they meet. And the last time they met they had a good time with themselves and Hemingway.[7]

Her judgments were a source of playful rivalry for the two men. Still, a few years later when she remarked that Fitzgerald's and Hemingway's "flames" had different qualities, Fitzgerald took it that she meant that Hemingway's was brighter. Hemingway had to write an elaborate letter to convince his friend that he was wrong about it, telling him that Gertrude Stein wanted to organize a hare and tortoise race in which Fitzgerald was to be the hare, although, Hemingway reminded him, he modestly preferred to play the tortoise.[8]

Five years later, having completed *Tender is the Night,* Fitzgerald would remember the hare and tortoise metaphor in a letter to Perkins: "After all, Max, I am a plodder. One time I had a talk with Ernest Hemingway and I told him, against all the logic that was then current, that I was the tortoise and he was the hare, and that's the

The Dingo Bar in the rue Delambre (now the Bar Basque) where F. Scott Fitzgerald introduced himself to Ernest Hemingway and told Hemingway how much he admired his work.

truth of the matter, that everything that I have ever attained has been through long and persistent struggle, while it is Ernest who has a touch of genius which enables him to bring off extraordinary things with facility."[9]

However, they saw little of each other at that time. Gertrude Stein left Paris almost immediately for Bellay where she used to spend the warm season; from there she wrote Fitzgerald her famous appreciative letter, dated 22 May on *The Great Gatsby*. In his answer he alludes to the trip to Lyons with Hemingway, adding: "He's a peach of a fellow and absolutely first-rate."[10] Christian Gauss was also in Paris that summer and he met Fitzgerald and Hemingway several times, which later gave him an opportunity to compare their talents in a more perceptive way than Gertrude Stein:

> You two take your places at the opposite ends of the modern spectrum. Without disrespect to him I put Hemingway down at the infrared side and you on the ultra-violet. His rhythm is like the beating of an African tom-tom — primitive, simple, but it gets you in the end.
> You are at the other end. You have a feeling for musical intervals and the tone-color of words which makes your prose the finest instrument for rendering all the varied shades of our complex emotional states.[11]

A fourth significant meeting was with Edith Wharton. On 8 June she had written Fitzgerald a flattering letter about *The Great Gatsby* promising to send in return what she called "the latest product of my manufactory." Is she alluding there to her indifferent novel published that year, *The Mother's Recompense,* or to a book which would have appealed much more to Fitzgerald, *The Writing of Fiction* in which she acknowledged her debt to Henry James? This was followed by an invitation to both the Fitzgeralds to have lunch or tea with her. He went alone. Like Gertrude Stein, Edith Wharton had settled permanently in France where she had been for almost twenty years. She was living in a small chateau on the edge of the forest of Montmorency, at Saint Brice, about ten miles north of Paris. Nothing remains to-day of the Pavillon Colombe which was destroyed to make way for a housing development.

The story of Fitzgerald's nervousness at the prospect of having to meet the grand old lady has been told in different ways by Mizener and Turnbull in their biographies, but the latter, relying on an eyewitness, the composer Teddy Chanler, who claims to have accompanied Fitzgerald to Saint Brice in his car, seems more reliable. However, I have another version which I got from Mrs. Esther Arthur, Gerald Murphy's sister, according to which it was Mrs.

Arthur, also invited by a friend, Mrs. Chanler, who was staying at
Edith Wharton's, who accompanied Fitzgerald in his Renault. He
stopped so often along the way for a quick drink that Mrs. Arthur
had to phone the butler that they would be late for lunch, an
important lunch by all standards as Paul Bourget and Paul Claudel,
together with their wives, were present. Fitzgerald drank a lot during
the meal—only whiskey—and ate very little. Trying to make an
impression, he told the story of a couple of his friends having by
mistake lived in what they took to be a hotel but which was in fact a
brothel or a house of assignation. When Edith Wharton asked him for
a few more details, he was at a loss to provide the missing data and
realized he had made a fool of himself.

About the middle of May he wrote Wilson: "I've gotten to like
France. We've taken a swell apartment until January. I'm filled with
disgust for Americans in general after two weeks' sight of the ones in
Paris ... I suppose we're no worse than anyone, only contact with
other races brings out all our worse qualities ... There's no news
except that Zelda and I think we're pretty good, as usual, only more
so."[12] Three months later, in a letter to Bishop, the note is a little
stronger: "Paris has been a mad-house this spring and, as you can
imagine, we were in the thick of it. I don't know when we're coming
back — maybe never."[13]

In the beginning of August they drove to Antibes where they
settled for a month in the vicinity of the Murphys' Villa America.
Back at the rue de Tilsitt, he tried to set seriously to work, but the
temptations were too great, in Paris and outside Paris. During the fall
they visited the battlefields at Verdun as well as the places where the
Americans had made their great drive in September 1917 around
Verdun and St. Mihiel toward Sedan and Metz. He was at that time
interested in strategy as well as morbidly attracted by picture-books
representing horrible wounds sustained by soldiers. He would pore
for hours at Brentano's over such war books. He also made a visit to
London where he was received by representatives of high society: We
"went on some very high-tone parties with Mountbattens and all that
sort of things. Very impressed, but not very, as I furnished most of
the amusement myself."[14] He continued to see Hemingway and at
the end of the year provided an anecdote for *The Torrents of Spring*
when he sat in the fireplace, so drunk that Hemingway had to take
him back to the Etoile in the middle of the night. Two days later, on
30 November, Fitzgerald sent a characteristic note of excuse: "It is
only fair to say that the deplorable man who entered your apartment
Saturday morning was not me but a man named Johnson who has

often been mistaken for me."[15] He also made friends with other expatriates, Robert McAlmon with whom he quarreled that fall, and Archibald McLeish and Louis Bromfield who were invited for a Christmas party.

Zelda's health was not good and they had to refuse an invitation from Gertrude Stein in the last week of the year. Their lease expiring on 12 January, they left Paris in the second week of the year for the Pyrenees where Zelda was to take a two-month cure. The rest of the year was spent mostly on the Riviera, with the exception of two weeks spent in Paris when Zelda had an appendectomy in the beginning of June at the American Hospital. Sara Mayfield, who was in Paris at that time, tells in *Exiles from Paradise* that Fitzgerald spent much time in the company of Michael Arlen. The Fitzgeralds returned to Juan les Pins in the middle of June and there met Ernest Hemingway back from Spain. Fitzgerald tried to help him with the *The Sun Also Rises.* But on the whole, trying to make themselves conspicuous at all costs, they just managed to be a nuisance, being exiled for a while from the Villa America for having behaved in an unacceptable way. In December they crossed the Italian border and sailed home from Genoa.

1927

They spent sixteen uninterrupted months in America, mostly in Delaware, and on his return to the motherland Fitzgerald was able to take stock of his Parisian experience, comparing it favorably to what he found in New York, exhibiting a new sophistication which made light of all his pranks and all his failures to live up to the models he admired: "I was shocked," he said to a journalist in Hollywood at the beginning of 1927, "I was shocked when I returned to America. I had been, you know, three years in Paris." Here it is interesting to notice that the two years and a half he had spent in Europe from May 1924 to December 1926 are seen in perspective as having taken place in Paris, although he lived there only for seven months, in 1925. Still those months served as a standpoint from which he could judge the rawness and roughness he supposedly found in New York:

> Everything in New York seems mouldy, rotten. We went to the nightclubs. It was like going to a big mining camp in the boom days . . .
> I got a sensation of horror. There were these fat men smoking cigars fat, and big butter and egg men, and half nude women. There was nothing fine

about it all. It was vulgarity without the faintest trace of redeeming wit.

Coming from Paris to New York was like plunging from a moral world to a state of moral anarchy.

It gave me a fear that everyone had gone crazy — that everything was being done for nothing; that human lives were being exploited for nothing.

And it's not the fault of prohibition. Prohibition is just a crazy symptom of a crazy race. I don't know what it is. Perhaps America just came too late — too late to be anything in our own right, but just part of the history and tradition of Europe.

The Country seems like warmed-over hash — warmed over from the day before. America is the place where everybody is always going to have a good time tomorrow."[16]

In an interview for the New York *World* the following April, he makes a further distinction between the Americans he found at home and those he met in Paris: ' "The best of America drifts to Paris. The American in Paris is the best American. It is more fun for an intelligent person to live in an intelligent country. France has only two things toward which we drift as we grow older — intelligence and good manners.' "[17] That is a far cry from the letters he sent to Edmund Wilson on the subject, the 1921 letter about the French and the 1925 one about Americans in Paris!

1928

When they returned to Paris for the Summer of 1928, they stayed for the first time on the Left Bank, first at the Hotel des Palais, then in a rented apartment, 58 rue de Vaugairard, at the corner of the rue Bonaparte, just in front of the Luxembourg Gardens which provided a convenient playground for their daughter. The Murphys had an apartment a hundred yards away, 14 rue Guynemer, in a newly-built house facing the park. This change of location from the bourgeois and touristic Right Bank to the center of the artistic and intellectual life of Paris was paralleled by a change in Fitzgerald's relationship to the life of the city.

Hemingway had left in March 1928, only to return the following year in April, but Gertrude Stein was near at hand, a few minutes' walk from their home. Zelda became a pupil of Egorova, the head of the ballet school for the Diaghilev company with which Murphy had connections. Through Murphy, Fitzgerald met the painter Fernand Leger; and Natalie Barney, a central figure in expatriate and literary circles, came one night for dinner, alone, to their apartment (and was horrified by Fitzgerald's casual treatment of a sick cat). He got to know Sylvia Beach better now that he was living near Shakespeare and Company, 12 rue de l'Odéon. It was through her that he made the acquaintance of two men for whom literature was not only a profession, but a way of life, André Chamson and James Joyce.

André Chamson was then a young novelist of twenty-eight who had written three novels, the second of which, *Les hommes de la route*, published in 1927, had almost won the Prix Goncourt. A friend of André Malraux, he was actively participating in the literary life of the period and was a familiar figure at Sylvia Beach's and Adrienne Monnier's bookshops where he was known as their "Rodrigue," their knight, by the older writers like Valéry, Gide, or Jules Romains. He was working for the Commission of Education and Art at the Chambre des Deputés and lived in a small apartment at the top of the Latin Quarter, just behind the Panthéon, 17 rue Thoin. It was there, on the sixth floor, that Fitzgerald came one morning in May and introduced himself as a friend of Sylvia Beach. Chamson has written moving pages on what he calls their "coup de foudre," friendship at first sight, in spite of their altogether different cultural backgrounds.[18] The Frenchman was a poor scholar of Protestant origins, born (like Edouard Jozan who became later his friend) in Nimes, at the foot of the Çevennes mountains, famous for resistance to the Catholic persecutions under Louis XIV, a man faithful to the memory of his ancestors. Eager to help, Fitzgerald introduced him to King Vidor, the movie director who had made *The Big Parade* in 1925; he also warmly recommended him to Maxwell Perkins who got Van Wyck Brooks to be his translator. Vidor persuaded Chamson to write a script out of *Les hommes de la route* and wanted him to go to Hollywood, but nothing came out of those plans. Still, the following winter King Vidor convinced another of Fitzgerald's friends, Murphy, to help him as an expert on spirituals when he directed *Hallelujah!*, his first sound movie. King Vidor and his wife, Eleanor Boardman, lived in state in their Villa Trianon at Neuilly, but the three men spent hours in the cafés and the cinemas, the two Americans inviting Chamson to expensive restaurants, and he stubbornly returning their hospitality by asking them to have dinners at his home.

Zelda, who was dancing all day long and was too tired at night to go out, rarely joined the men. She was present on a memorable occasion when Sylvia Beach invited the Fitzgeralds and the Chamsons to have dinner with the Joyces at 18 rue de L'Odéon in the apartment she shared with Adrienne Monnier whose own

Michael DeLisio's sculpture of Shakespeare and Company. Left to right: Joyce, Valery, Eliot, Pound, Hemingway, Miss Beach, Fitzgerald, Miss Monnier, Gide. Photo by John D. Schiff.

bookshop, la Maison des Amis des Livres, was as famous a meeting place for the writers of the time as Shakespeare and Company.

Fitzgerald was certainly as nervous as on the day he visited Edith Wharton; Joyce was a god for him, the incarnation of literature. In his very special way, Fitzgerald offered to jump out of the fourth-floor window to illustrate his admiration. Joyce said later that he found him a little mad: "I'm afraid he'll do himself some injury." In a drawing he made on the endpapers of a copy of *Gatsby*, Fitzgerald represented himself kneeling before his deity, with the two "sirens," Sylvia and Adrienne, sitting at both ends of the table. Title for the scene: "Festival of St. James." It is dated July 1928 although the dinner took place on June 29 (the invitation, dated June 23, is for the next Wednesday, the 29th).

In August Fitzgerald visited Bishop who had settled near Paris, in the Château de Tressancourt at Orgeval, with his family. They had long literary conversations, particularly about Flaubert and *Madame Bovary*.

That summer in Paris was otherwise marked by the same excesses as the year 1926. The old rhythms Fitzgerald had tried to escape had caught up with him once more. He landed in jail twice and, when he went back to America, he brought along with him as a valet one Philippe, a taxi-driver from St. Cloud, willfull and dissipated, who was a sort of symbol of what Paris had become for him.

In "Echoes of the Jazz Age," written in 1931 from the perspective of the Depression, he stresses the ominous changes that were perceptible that summer: "And by 1928 Paris and grown suffocating. With each shipment of Americans spewed up by the boom the quality fell off, until toward the end there was something sinister about the crazy boatloads. They were no longer the simple pa and ma and son and daughter, infinitely superior in their qualities of kindness and curiosity to the corresponding class in Europe, but fantastic neanderthals who believed something, something vague, remembered from a very cheap novel."[19]

Despite his disappointment he was back six months later, in the middle of March 1929, landing at Genoa, spending a little time in Nice where he again visited a French jail, and arriving in Paris in April. The Fitzgeralds rented a big apartment near St. Sulpice, presumably rue de Mezieres in the same area where they had lived the year before. Zelda, who was more than ever decided, in spite of her age, twenty-nine, to make a career in ballet, resumed her work with Egorova. Besides the friends he had made in 1928, Fitzgerald saw Hemingway, back from the States, who was also living near St.

Sulpice, 6 rue Ferou, but who managed to conceal his address, remembering the constant interruptions of his work he had suffered in 1925 in the rue Notre Dame des Champs, when Fitzgerald would wake him up at any hour of the night. He was now working hard on the manuscript of *A Farewell to Arms,* which he allowed Fitzgerald to read before publication. Fitzgerald took his critical role as seriously as in 1926 when he had written a long letter about *The Sun Also Rises* after reading the typescript. He also wrote a critical letter about *A Farewell to Arms* but the document he produced has unfortunately not been discovered so far.[20]

Another novelist appeared in Fitzgerald's life at that time, Morley Callaghan, a young Canadian who had worked with Hemingway on the *Toronto Star* and whom he had recommended to Perkins. Callaghan, in his book *That Summer in Paris,* tells a lot, not only about Fitzgerald, but also about his relations with Hemingway and, incidentally, with Joyce. How for instance Fitzgerald's devotion to the author of *Ulysses* was shown by his inviting the Callaghans to dine at Joyce's favorite table at the Trianon restaurant. They went in and Fitzgerald selected the wrong table: Callaghan had dined there a few days before with the Master, but out of charity he said nothing, not to spoil Fitzgerald's excitement. The boxing match between Hemingway and Callaghan, during which Fitzgerald was acting as time-keeper, is too well known to recount here.

What is perhaps more interesting is the way Callaghan became aware of Fitzgerald's ambiguous position toward religion. One day, on their way to Saint Germain-des-Prés, a few minutes away, the conversation turned on the particular quality of the Saint Sulpice quarter, so well expressed later in "Babylon Revisited." This area is notorious for its numerous shops of objects of piety in a rather bad taste. Callaghan reminded Fitzgerald of that:

I made a joke about Scott living in the shadow of bad Catholic art. It amused him. Then he said he liked living near the Cathedral; he liked the neighborhood; he was always aware he was in the shadow of the Cathedral.[21]

When Fitzgerald mentioned that the pillars of the church (St. Sulpice is not a cathedral) were the widest in Paris, the Callaghans urged him to accompany them inside, which he stubbornly refused to do, although his daughter was brought up as a Catholic: "I walked there [the church] for catechism every Saturday morning." But Fitzgerald himself would not go in: ' "I simply won't go into it,' he said. 'Don't ask me about it. It's personal. The Irish-Catholic background and all that. You go ahead.' " In contrast to this attitude, let us remember that Ernest and Pauline Hemingway would go to St. Sulpice, their parish church, every Sunday for mass.

In July the Fitzgeralds drove south in a new Renault, a blue convertible, and rented a house in Cannes for the summer months. He was again uneasy about his health and feared an attack of tuberculosis. Although he had taken life insurance the preceding March with the Sun Life Assurance Co. of Canada and had received a favorable report ("You are to be congratulated on your splendid physical condition"), he went to a doctor in Cannes who diagnosed a veil over the top of the lung and ganglions around the hilum.[22] At this time he was working on the Melarky version of *Tender is the Night,* sending optimistic reports to his agent that the novel would be three-quarters done by September. He went on doggedly when they returned to Paris in October, moving to an apartment situated on the Right Bank near the Bois de Boulogne, south of the Etoile, 10 rue Pergolese. At the end of the same month he again wrote Harold Ober that the novel was almost finished. It was to take almost five more years to see the final version of the book. But he had to interrupt this bout of creativity to write short stories as money was becoming short, in spite of the $32,000 earned that year. Meanwhile Zelda Fitzgerald was going on with her dancing, more and more obsessed by the idea of becoming a professional ballerina.

An interesting point that I have not yet cleared up is raised here. Did France in general, and Paris in particular, provide an incentive, a stimulus for his work? The answer is positive so far as the first year in concerned: *Gatsby* was written on the Riviera immediately after he left America, as if his creative energy had suddenly been released. During the following spring he wrote in Paris one of his finest stories, "The Rich Boy," and during the fall and winter he started the first version of *Tender is the Night,* the Melarky version. But this did not get anywhere. During the summer of 1928 he wrote three Basil stories, looking nostalgically back upon his childhood and adolescence, as if he were trying to recover something he had lost. Until he started the second version of *Tender* in 1929, he managed to produce just one good story, "Majesty." It is to be noted that none of the stories dealing with the Paris scene were written in the city: "The Bridal Party," "One Trip Abroad," and "Babylon Revisited" were all done in Switzerland. The little that was achieved in France after 1925 appears either as a deepening and an enlargement of the American experience, or simply as a way to earn money quickly by writing stories for *The Saturday Evening Post.* Perhaps the fact that Hemingway had completed his second novel, published in September that year, prompted Fitzgerald to come to terms with his own work. Or the singleness of purpose, the mad dedication that drove Zelda to fulfill herself in dancing made him ashamed of his own idleness.

1930 — 1931

The old crowd was still in Paris – the Hemingways who were to leave in January, the Bishops whom they saw from time to time. But the strain was beginning to tell on both Fitzgeralds and, at the beginning of February, they went away on a two-week tour of Algeria.

On their return they again got involved in various parties, with the Bishops, the Murphys, and friends from Minnesota, the Kalmans, who were visiting Paris. In May, the marriage of Powell Fowler took Scott on a series of parties and dinners just as Zelda was going through a nervous breakdown. In April she had suffered a first attack and had had to spend a few days in a clinic at La Malmaison, just outside Paris. One month later, on 20 May, the Fitzgeralds crossed the Swiss border and she was taken first near Montreux for two weeks, then to Prangins, near Rolle on the lake of Geneva, where she was to receive treatment until September 1931.

They left Switzerland on 15 September in their Renault and drove to Paris where the Hotel Majestic was the last place they lived in the city. A visit to the Exposition des Arts Decoratifs, just before they embarked for the States, was a dim echo of the Exposition des Arts Decoratifs of 1925 which had summed up the mood of the Twenties. It was their farewell to Paris, a Paris as remote now as those "lonely rice fields of lonely far off islands" which told, as Zelda Fitzgerald puts it "an immutable story of work and death." And she concludes: "The juxtaposition of so many replicas of so many civilizations was confusing, and depressing."[2][3] This was the last image, and the last impression.

Still during those fourteen Swiss months, Fitzgerald, though living most of the time in Lausanne, was making trips to Paris from time to time to see his daughter who had been left in care of a governess. She was a brilliant little scholar at the cours Dieterlen, rue Marguerite, near the Ternes, where she was a day pupil. In June 1930 she won a first prize in spite of the competition with French children of her age. His visits were bright spots in her life. "It was always very great fun when he came, especially because of the trip to the Nain Bleu.

He always bought me a new Becassine doll or a new outfit from La Semaine de Suzette, a *marvellous . . .* magazine."[24]

Scottie's recollections perfectly fit with some of the details of "Babylon Revisited." The Nain Bleu, which still exists, is situated at the corner of the rue St Honoré and the rue Richepanse, one block from the Place de la Concorde and just in front of the Restaurant Le Grand Vatel where Honoria and her father have lunch. At the end of the meal, Charlie Wales maps out what they are going to do:" First, we're going to that toy store in the rue St Honoré and buy anything you like. And then we're going to the vaudeville at the Empire."

This brings us to the question of the extent to which the streets and the monuments, the mood and the atmosphere of Paris play a part in Fitzgerald's work. That he was familiar with the city is obvious, with the Right Bank and the Left Bank alike. First the Murphys, then many others served as knowledgable guides to the places of interest. He became a famous figure at the Ritz, place Vendôme, and the near-by Crillon, place de la Concorde. The head barman of the Ritz, Frank, who died in 1957 and was replaced by George, a bell-boy in the twenties, seems to have remembered him well, whatever Hemingway may say about being the *one* who was never forgotten. He was also on familiar terms with Julien at Ciro's, on the Champs-Elyseés. Not long ago Maurice, Julien's brother, could show the small back room which was his favorite dining place. Another restaurant, Voisin, near the Smith bookstore, was also a favorite and appears in *Tender.* In Montmartre he would haunt Zelli's, rue Fontaine, which was the meeting place of the American journalists, or Bricktop's with its black performers, or le Perroquet, on the first floor next to the Casino de Paris. Those were the show places but he also knew the small bistros of the Left Bank where he would spend hours with Chamson, or the famous cafés of Montparnasse, le Dôme, la Coupole, le Select.

Still very little of this inside knowledge appears in his fiction. Some fifty pages in *Tender in the Night* and a handful of stories, among which only three, "The Bridal Party," written in May 1929, "Babylon," written in December 1930, and "News of Paris, Fifteen Years Ago," written in 1940, have Paris exclusively as a background. To these we may add the beginning of "The Swimmers" (written in July 1929), the end of "One Trip Abroad" (August 1930), a few scenes in "A New Leaf" (April 1931), "The Initimate Strangers" (June 1935), "A Penny Spent" (July 1925), "Not in the Guide Book" (February 1925).

In the stories specifically devoted to Paris, the atmosphere is wonderfully evocative, the various moments of the day, the quality of the light, the charm of twilight on the old monuments, all that recaptures with felicity the immediacy of the there and the now. One sentence out of "A Penny Spent" will illustrate that intense poetical feeling for the city: "One thing is certain — that before you melt out into the green-and-cream Paris twilight you will have the feel of standing for a moment at one of the predestined centers of the world."

His topography is practically fautless and I have been able to find only one little mistake. In the story "The Swimmers," and in *Tender* at the beginning of the description of the party in which Dick and Rosemary encounter the lesbians, the places are described in about the same terms, which cannot apply to the street where they are set, rue Monsieur. In the first instance: "Home was fine high-ceiling apartment hewn from the palace of a Renaissance cardinal in the Rue Monsieur"; in the second case: "It was a house hewn from the frame of Cardinal de Retz's palace in the Rue Monsieur..." Now rue Monsieur is part of the Faubourg St Germain which was built in the eighteenth century; at the time of the Renaissance there were only fields belonging to the Abbaye and the University. And of course the Cardinal de Retz lived in the seventeenth century. Fitzgerald who certainly was familiar with the area (Michael Arlen's apartment was a hundred yards from the rue Monsieur, 11 rue Masseran, on the other side of the Boulevard des Invalides) may have thought of the Hôtel de St. Simon, n°3, or the small "folie" at n°7 where Paul Bourget, whom he knew, lived for a long time. But both are definitely eighteenth century buildings.

Mentioning topography, I should like to discuss here a little problem which has puzzled American critics who, map in hand, were at a loss to understand the route followed by Charlie Wales in the first chapter of "Babylon Revisited." They were right only in assuming that Fitzgerald was not wrong. Wales, leaving the Ritz, is shown directing his taxi toward the place de la Concorde, enjoying the pink twilight on the classical facades of Gabriel, then crossing the Seine and coming back on the Right Bank to admire the blue hour spreading over the Opéra, then back again to the Left Bank and St Sulpice.

The habit of using sentences or paragraphs lifted out of his stories in his novels has done a bad turn to Fitzgerald here: he had originally used the passage about the place de la Concorde in "Babylon" as it was published in the *Post*, then transfered it with a few changes to *Tender is the Night*. But when he included "Babylon" in *Taps at*

Reveille, one year later he realized that this paragraph had to be changed in order to avoid duplication of the same lines in the novel and the collection of stories. Accordingly he replaced the passage about the place de la Concorde by the passage about the Opéra: instead of going west in his taxi, Wales goes east, a shorter route in fact, then down the Avenue de l'Opéra and the Caroussel bridge to the Left Bank:

Post version with the words used in *Tender* in italics:

> Outside, *the fire-red, gas-blue, ghost-green signs shone smokily through the tranquil rain.* It was late afternoon and *the streets were in movement; the bistros gleamed.* At the corner of the Boulevard des Capucines he took a taxi. *The Place de la Concorde moved by in pink majesty;* they crossed the logical Seine, and Charlie felt the sudden provincial quality of the left bank.

In the *Taps* version only the following passage, starting with "Charlie directed his taxi to the Avenue de l'Opéra" and ending with the same remark about the "sudden provincialism" of the Left Bank should stand. Both were printed because the proof-reader misunderstood his correction and did not cancel the first one, to Fitzgerald's dismay when he happened upon the passage in *Taps at Reveille*[2][5].

The picture Fitzgerald has given of Paris is a true and precise one, although limited in scope, and dealing chiefly with the international set. Nothing in it is evocative of the French problems or the French way of life. If it uses a true fact from the chronicle of the Twenties, such as the murder in the Gare St. Lazare which appears in *Tender,* it is sure to be a *fait divers* dealing with the only types of people he was bound to meet and to know: in that case the actual shooting of an Englishman, Raymond de Trafford, by his American mistress, the Countess de Janze. The deceptively French-sounding names are in a way here symbolic of the thin disguise under which Anglo-Saxon attitudes asserted themselves in a city which was nothing but a dream setting for compulsions and passions born elsewhere.

This city might just as well have been London or Rome, a mere backdrop for Fitzgerald's imagination, a stimulus for his sensibility, playing the role New York had played from 1922 to 1924 before he came to France. With the difference perhaps that, just as was the case for some other exiles, it possessed some quality of freedom and excitement which had been blunted in the native country. He went to Paris when New York had lost its "iridescence of the beginning of the world," its capacity to arouse wonder, when, as he writes in "My

Lost City," "Whole sections of the city had grown poisonous."[26] We may apply to him in a certain way the diagnosis Henry Adams imagined to justify his attachment to the city when America was no longer the nourishing, vital country it used to be in his youth: "At length, like other dead Americans, he went to Paris because he could go nowhere else." Was Fitzgerald reborn in Paris? Let us not be sentimental about it. He could not escape his older self and his old rhythms. The same process of deterioration, the deterioration of a city reflecting the deterioration of the spirit, took place there. Paris was bound to get as poisonous as New York had been. Such is the lesson of "Babylon Revisited" when, after having felt that "provincialism" of the Left Bank, Charlie Wales suddenly realized what is wrong with him — and this will serve as a conclusion: "I spoiled this city for myself. I didn't realize it, but the days came along one after another, and then two years were gone, and everything was gone, and I was gone."

Sorbonne Nouvelle

---

[1]*The Letters of F. Scott Fitzgerald*, ed. Andrew Turnbull (New York: Scribners, 1963), p. 326.

[2]"How to Live on Practically Nothing a Year," *The Saturday Evening Post*, CXCVII (20 September 1924).

[3]"Rags Martin-Jones and the Pr-nce of W-les," *McCall's*, LI (July 1924).

[4]*Esquire*, I-II (May-June 1934).

[5]"How to Live on Practically Nothing a Year."

[6]*Furioso*, III (Winter 1947).

[7]*The Autobiography of Alice B. Toklas* (New York: Harcourt, Brace, 1933), pp. 268-269.

[8]Fitzgerald Papers, Princeton University Library.

[9]*Letters*, p. 247.

[10]*Letters*, p. 484.

[11]*The Papers of Christian Gauss*, ed. K.G. Jackson and Hiram Haydn (New York: Random House, 1957), p. 218.

[12]*Letters*, p. 342.

[13]*Letters*, p. 358.

[14]*Letters*, pp. 194-195.

[15]Carlos Baker, *Ernest Hemingway* (New York: Scribners, 1969), p. 159.

[16]Unlocated clipping. Reprinted in *F. Scott Fitzgerald in his Own Time*, ed. Matthew J. Bruccoli and Jackson Bryer (Kent: Kent State University Press, 1971), pp. 271-273.

[17]3 April 1927. Reprinted in *F. Scott Fitzgerald in his Own Time*, pp. 274-277.

[18]André Chamson, *La petite odyssée* (Paris: Gallimard, 1965), pp. 45-52.

[19]"Echoes of the Jazz Age," *Scribner's Magazine*, XC (November 1931).

[20]*Letters*, pp. 309-310. In a 16 December 1935 letter in the Fitzgerald

Papers at Princeton, Hemingway alludes to a fifteen-page letter from Fitzgerald about *A Farewell to Arms.*

[21] *That Summer in Paris* (New York: Coward-McCann, 1963), p. 206.

[22] Fitzgerald Papers, Princeton University Library.

[23] "Show Mr. & Mrs. F. to Number—," *The Crack-up* (New York: New Directions, 1945), p. 54.

[24] Unpublished letter, 1972.

[25] *Letters,* p. 262: "Just found another whole paragraph in *Taps,* top of page 384, which appears in *Tender is the Night.* I'd carefully elided it and written the paragraph beneath to replace it, but the proofreaders slipped and put them both in."

[26] *The Crack-Up,* p. 30.

ANDRÉ CHAMSON

REMARKS

BY

ANDRÉ CHAMSON

André Chamson is a member of the Académie française, a distinguished man of letters and civil servant, and a decorated soldier. Beginning with Attitudes, *his first book in 1923, he has published more than 16 books — including* Les hommes de la route *and* La Superbe. *M. Chamson was F. Scott Fitzgerald's closest friend in the French literary world.*

If we were in the Midi instead of in Paris, I would say that your meeting was taking place under multiple auspices. We are here, rue de l'Odéon, very close to what were Sylvia Beach and Adrienne Monnier's bookshops, almost across from Adrienne and Sylvia's apartment, framed by la place Saint Sulpice at the back of which was the apartment, at number 28 [rue de Vaugirard], where Scott Fitzgerald lived at that time, and, for that matter, very close to the house in which I was living then on la montagne Sainte Geneviève.

Fishing for memories, especially when one has lived during a century as confused as ours, is sometimes very difficult. To accompany me in this harvest, there is my wife who has a good memory, not quite the same as mine . . . I, too, have a good memory . . . and two good memories don't necessarily make a complete memory when we are dealing with human events. My wife remembers that we met Scott Fitzgerald at Shakespeare & Co. She talks about this in a book she has just had published.[1] At first we didn't pay much attention because, at that time, in the years 1925, '26, '27, and '28, relations between foreign writers, particularly Americans, and French writers were frequent and very intimate. We used to run into Bromfield there, and we'd see Hemingway.

I would like only briefly to cover Hemingway. Bad luck presided over my meetings with Hemingway. I didn't know him at the same time that I knew Scott Fitzgerald, which could have been possible, but I had heard much about him from Jean Prévost, my friend who was killed when he was in the maquis du Vercors.[2] When Jean Prévost, met him, they immediately told each other that they were both boxers. They put on their boxing gloves and they learned to respect each other because, as Prévost told me, neither could beat the other; Prévost being as strong as Hemingway, and Hemingway being as strong as Prévost. Later on, I went, during the Spanish Civil War, to Madrid; and I believe, in fact, I inherited the room which Hemingway had lived in. Hemingway had left, leaving behind him numerous legends, but I didn't meet him. And, at the time of the liberation, when he had returned to Paris and, naturally, to Shakespeare and Co., he had just left when I, dressed as a major of the First French Army, entered Sylvia's place. She said to me, "Hemingway has just left." This is how one fails to meet people one could have known.

For Scott Fitzgerald things were very different. We first met him at Sylvia's; then he came to the little apartment where we lived on the sixth floor at the top of la montagne Sainte Geneviève, with — even though the apartment wasn't sumptuous — one of the most beautiful views of Paris from our balcony. Scott Fitzgerald came to ask me if I would like to meet King Vidor who wanted to see me. Some days later, King Vidor and Scott Fitzgerald came to see us in our little apartment. I can still see it. I open the door myself. I see two boys. I will not try to present a detailed portrait: one was actually rather stocky, this was King Vidor. The other, by contrast, was tall and lanky, more aristocratic, more elegant. And he said to me, "We asked Sylvia Beach with which young French writer — how shall I say it — we would have the best chance of collaborating." All this was accompanied by extremely kind considerations. "And so we've come to see you. If you would like, we could try to make a film together." I don't mind telling you that we were very poor. Scott Fitzgerald and King Vidor weren't poor — neither of them. We had several months of friendship during which my comportment — I

The Bibliothèque Benjamin Franklin. Left to right: André LeVot, Barbara Loeb, Andre Chamson.

won't say of a French bourgeois – but of a Frenchman who came from the peasant class, played bad tricks on me. I couldn't accept the fact that my American friends were always paying the tabs. But at that time, to pay back one meal in ten was a financial catastrophe for the Chamson household. This financial catastrophe lasted for several months, during which I was under a terrific strain due to the recent publication of my novel *Les hommes de la route,* which is still being read since it is in the *livres de poche* collection. I see the young people of today reading it as though it were a book which has just come out. King Vidor said to me, "We will start with the general theme of this book, then you can make something more and more narrow until you arrive at a concept. When we arrive at a significant statement, it will be over; we will have won." Then we got down to work. Much of the hard work was due to the fact that I knew very little English. Scott Fitzgerald often made fun of me when I tried to speak English. He would look at me and say, "Here's André speaking English: 'This is one finger, this is two fingers, this is three fingers . . .' " I learned from M. LeVot that this was not Scott's improvisation, but a borrowing from Shakespeare.[3] That was very nice, but at any rate my English was limited more or less to that. Nonetheless, we were working: we worked a lot, and we arrived, I remember, more or less, at this formula: a mountain community, cut off from the world, puts itself to a huge collective task in order to be able to continue to live. And then all of a sudden King Vidor said to me, "André, I must go back to Hollywood. It seems that they have discovered how to make talking movies. I want to go film something over there. So we will make a gentleman's agreement." I did not know what a "gentleman's agreement" was. He said to me, "We will make a gentleman's agreement formally and legally." I knew enough English so that this last formula appeared to me completely satisfactory. I said to him, "Good, all right – you work only with me, I only with you." He left, and several years later a film came out. I remember that Adrienne Monnier and Sylvia Beach were very angry with King Vidor because they said to me – I believe this film was *Le pain quotidien [Our Daily Bread]* – "The formula that you found as a final formula for *Les hommes de la route* is the exact formula used in *Le pain quotidien.* You should file a lawsuit." I told her that for a grandson of a French peasant to bring a lawsuit against – what is the name of that big company – Goldwyn Mayer is an absurd idea. The crockery pot which throws itself against the iron pot is completely unreasonable.[4] So we didn't bring a lawsuit; we let it drop. In fact, King Vidor was very nice. Several years later there was a special

article on him in *La revue du cinema,* which was published by
Gallimard, and when he was asked, "Who would you like to do a
personal article on you?" he answered, "My friend André Chamson."
We, therefore, remained friends; but nevertheless, this is not what
kept us from not making a film together, which could perhaps have
changed my life. Note that he did ask me to go to Hollywood, but I
think I was wise in saying to him, "I am not a lemon that wants to be
squeezed to death. I am a French peasant; I'll stay in France . . . for
"money unlimited" . . . well and good . . ."

On the other hand, my friendship with Scott Fitzgerald was
infintely more fruitful. First of all I'll speak about the material side,
because there was a material side. When he had read my first three
books — at that time I had only written three books — Scott became
entranced. Then there were telegram exchanges between him and
Scribners. These telegrams were absolutely imperative and stated that
they had to translate my works immediately and without delay. I
was translated. I had four books translated at Scribners by Van Wyck
Brooks whom I had the chance to meet later on; in fact with rather
great astonishment, because he didn't speak French very well. He was
a very good translator, but his wife was the one who spoke French
well. When I heard how he spoke French I said to myself, "But how
could he have made these excellent translations of my work?" This
proves that even without oral use of the language there can be very
good translators. So, at that time Scott rendered me a great material
service.

It wasn't his fault that my popularity in America was what the
director of Scribners told me several years later. He said to me, "You
had a very good press for each of your books; unfortunately, you
didn't sell very well." *Unfortunately,* I can still hear that. "You are a
writer's writer." I thought a great deal about this. I wondered if this
"writer's writer" was a writer who received a good press and whose
books didn't sell. It was perhaps for this reason that he was restricted
to America, this writer's writer. Well, what the devil, it's done, and I
owe this to Scott Fitzgerald. But then that's the material side of this
affectionate friendship — and I'll say protective friendship — that
Scott Fitzgerald had for me.

Then there is the anecdotal side of this friendship. M. LeVot this
morning related some of my adventures with Scott Fitzgerald. Scott,
for example, arrived one day and I was with him, with an enormous
bucket of ice with bottles of champagne. We were going up to my
sixth-floor apartment, which had no elevator, and, all of a sudden, at
the first or second floor, Scott put down the bucket of ice and said

to me, "Dear André, can you swim?" I said, "Yes, I know how to swim." "Can you swim here?" pointing at the ice bucket. I said to him, "It's absolutely impossible!" He began to undress. He took off his jacket; he took off his shirt; and he was ready to drop his trousers, on a stairway where many people went by. I begged him to come swimming in the apartment because that would be much more . . .

Whether it was that day or another . . . I can still picture Scott, unfortunately a bit too drunk, climbing on the railing of my balcony on the sixth floor, rather giddy, and standing on one foot, and holding on with the tip of his finger on the other side, balancing, and me not daring to make a move towards him, saying to myself, "If you do anything, he's going to try to move and he will go crashing down from the sixth floor on his face." He was declaring he was Voltaire, that he was Rousseau, while pointing out the Panthéon where, theoretically, these two gentlemen were sleeping. "I am Voltaire, I am Rousseau, etc. . . ."

I must add that I remember, for example, the *foire à Neuneu.* [5] We were going to the *foire à Neuneu,* and Scott, quite drunk, all of a sudden stopped in front of two policemen on bicycles – the ones we call *des hirondelles* [6] – we see fewer of them now than we saw at that time. And he said to the policeman, "How much is the bicycle?" The policeman said to him, "What's that?" Scott said, "How much bicycle? If I wanted to buy you, it would be cheap. So bicycle how much?" Well, then the policeman began to understand: insulting officers in the exercise of their duties, that could be serious. I interfered. I explained to the policeman that he was dealing with a great American writer and that he musn't bother him, etc. I finally convinced him, but it was a close call that day at the *foire à Neuneu.*

Our relationship was based on a sort of frankness which led up, for example, to this. When he was around Senlis, he would send me cards. And he generally picked out anti-alcoholism cards – where there is on one side the liver of a healthy man, and on the other side the liver of an alcoholic. On the liver of the healthy man he wrote "yours," and on the liver of the alcoholic he wrote "mine." It was true, and I tried – how shall I say it – to rid him of this vice that I clearly saw was ruining him. It was all too evident. But I don't want to play Protestant pastor, or health advisor, which is too strong.

But, at any rate, I remember certain days – for example, one day when he was completely drunk, it was three o'clock in the morning. I sent for a taxi since I was too tired to accompany him home. So I explained to the taxi driver who he was, etc. . . . I must say that the taxi driver didn't roll him, which could have happened. There was some sort of protection for a fellow like him.

There are also other anecdotes which come back to me. Zelda used to buy him neckties and handkerchiefs and he would give them to me. Zelda would become furious: "You don't like these handkerchiefs and ties I gave you?" He would answer, "But if I didn't like them, I wouldn't give them to André," which was an extremely convincing argument, but one which didn't convince Zelda.

I remember his little girl who came when we had problems in the apartment over there next to the *Commissariat de Police de la place Saint Sulpice.*

Well, all this creates a series of very touching memories, and I ask you to believe that today in this meeting my wife and I are submerged in this return to the past. What touched me most about Scott is when I read his *Letters* which Gallimard published a few years ago — allusions he makes to me, such as the time I was fleeing from Pissenbourg to Rocamadour with the French Army. He wrote such affectionate things about me. He even mentioned certain successes. It was actually at a time when I couldn't think about success. I was caught up in the defeat of a country and all this was so tender, so friendly, so affectionate that it moved me very deeply.

I would like to end by telling you the following thing: in this friendship, this friendship which united us, my wife and I to Scott and Zelda — and we are perhaps the last surviving French witnesses to these events — what seemed to us the most astonishing is the following thing. It is that two men as different as Scott and I, for we are profoundly different — and what we have written is perhaps as diametrically opposed as anything two writers could write — is how our friendship could have been so easy, so immediate, so deep. I see it from Scott's point of view, who was more lucid than I, and who must have more clearly seen what went on. For me, he was the emissary from across the Atlantic who arrived with fabulous stories, King Vidor beside him — the movies, etc. Then there was this personal gentleness, interrupted only by the excesses of alcoholism. Since I am not trying to be a defender of alcohol here, I wonder to what degree at the fringe of his alcoholism there could have been a triggering of something — I won't say cruel — but cutting and sharp. There was ... there was ... I don't know, it seems .... And certainly at the base of all this there was a sort of revenge in this man carried along by anti-puritanism, if you will, Now, my household, our way of living, the books I wrote, all this registered itself at polar opposites to what Scott was able to write. If he had been French or if I had been American, I'm not at all sure that we wouldn't have been hurled against each other in heated debates. But the fact that he was American and that I was French brought about, in spite of the differences, our finding the way of our brotherhood. We found the path of brotherhood; and when you think about it, when you try to see beyond the formal differences, what can unite two human beings, is perhaps – and this is most important at the present time – that which, beyond even their will and their creative involvement, can unite them, augment them, and ends up being one way of seeing the world, of understanding life. Beyond our personalities, our work as well, there is a brotherhood of spirit – and even more than a brotherhood of spirit – a brotherhood of the heart which can establish itself between beings. It is this fraternity of both the spirit and the heart that I had with Scott. It's because of this that I continue to hold a memory of a very profound friendship and that I am happy you gave me the chance today to again find myself in that atmosphere, so close to the apartment where one day we were dining together; James Joyce, Sylvia Beach, Adrienne Monnier, my wife and I, Zelda and Scott Fitzgerald, who that day took a pencil and made a drawing which I believe is reproduced in quite a few books today.[7] I don't know why he drew a police cap on my head. I understand why he drew sun-rays around James Joyce's head. But, after all, all that was the sign of a time which predestined all the misfortunes and all the cruelties which he suffered later on. And it was at that time that we called it *l'époque des années folles.* We also called it *l'époque des années sages* . . . wise or foolish, they were the years when one human being could approach other human beings.

Translated by Surget Lane and
Regis Robe, *University of South Carolina*

---

[1] Lucie Mazauric (avec André Chamson), *A Dieu! que la paix est jolie* (Paris: Plon, 1972).

[2] The Resistance.

[3] See *Henry V,* III.iii.

[4] This is a French proverb.

[5] The Neuilly Fair, an amusement park which extended from the Porte Maillot to the Neuilly Bridge.

[6] The swallows – so nicknamed because their black capes resemble sparrows' wings when they are riding their bicycles.

[7] Fitzgerald's "Festival of St. James" drawing is reproduced in Sylvia Beach's *Shakespeare and Company* (New York: Harcourt, Brace, 1959).

*Following the panel, the conference was opened to discussion
from the floor, part of which is published here. It was a particular
pleasure to have James Jones, who lives in Paris, participate.*

JAMES JONES:

Mr. Cody, I wanted to ask you if Jimmy-the-barman had his own
bar?

MORRILL CODY:

No. Jimmy started out in the Dingo, which is now the Bar Basque in
the rue Delambre. Incidentally, the inside of this bar is exactly the
way it was in the days of the Dingo. It hasn't changed one iota. It
was at the Dingo that Jimmy got his reputation and collected his
friends. Jimmy was a difficult person because he himself went for a
little alcohol once in a while and wouldn't show up the next day, so
he was finally fired. Then he moved around to a number of other
bars, the Maurice, the Falstaff, which exists today in the rue
Montparnasse and where you can see a picture of Jimmy. But the
Dingo was the center for most of the writers of that period, with a
few exceptions, like James Joyce who never went there, but that was

for other reasons. If you could reconstruct today the list of characters, twenty or thirty of them, who might be found in the Dingo at one time you would have American, British, and French literature in front of you.

MATTHEW BRUCCOLI:

Mr. Cody, what made the Dingo such a popular place?

CODY:

The Dingo was run by an American named Wilson and his wife who was Dutch, called Yopi, and Wilson and Yopi were personally very attractive people and they knew how to deal with this amorphous group of artists and writers of various nationalities in a way which was very sympatique.

JONES:

Was it at the Dingo where Jake Barnes, Duff Twysden, and Mike met to make the arrangements to go to Pamplona?*

CODY:

No, Hemingway wrote about that bar which was called the Trois et As which was in the rue de Trianon; it's no longer there. But Jimmy also served in the Trois et As bar. But of course it had some of the clientel and was run by Madame Camis, again a woman who had a great personality for drawing people to her.

JONES:

I think that Mr. Loeb's book in which he deals with the trip to Pamplona — in the last chapter mentions the fact that the meeting between Hemingway, Duff, and Pat did not in fact take place.

HAROLD LOEB:

They met in Paris. I was in St. Jean de Luz, but Hem and I had planned the trip months before. Then I got a letter from Duff saying could she come.

JONES:

But you invited her?

---

*Note: Mr. Jones was correct. See the opening of Chapter 9 of *Sun.*

Part of the audience at the Paris conference, including (L to R) two representatives of Radio France; Roger Asselineau, President, European American Studies Association; and James Jones, author of *From Here to Eternity*.

LOEB:

I didn't invite her, but I maybe let her in. I think Kiley — is that his name? — wrote the book that is all false . . .

CODY:

Kiley, oh Kiley's book has no word of truth in it.

JONES:

It was all very suspect to me.

FRAZER CLARK:

Hemingway's letter to Jed Kiley protesting the whole book is downstairs in the exhibit today. Hemingway tells him that his book is all false.

LOEB:

It's absolutely false. There's not a word of truth in it.

FLORENCE GILLIAM:

And the final line is wonderful, it says, "You were never a friend of mine in Paris or anywhere else."

CLARK:

There was speculation this morning about Hemingway's ability in French.

CODY:

Hemingway, he spoke French moderately well. He spoke it as well as most American newspapermen do in Paris. Enough French to get around. He wasn't any linguist or anything, but sufficient. He could understand everything sort of like the rest of us. I saw him mostly from the journalistic side because we both belonged to the Anglo-American Press Association which was then a small institution. He was an active member of it, and we had lunch anyway once a week and often more frequently.

BRUCCOLI:

Mr. Cody, where was the Hole-in-the-Wall Bar?

CODY:

That was a tourist trap. It never had any significance unless you were terribly dry — it had no other significance. Really it was just a tourist trap.

BERTRAM SARASON:

I believe that was the place where he was supposed to have met Harold Loeb after having heard that Harold Loeb was going to assassinate him.

LOEB:

That was Lipps, wasn't it?

SARASON:

Well, Lipps and also the Hole-in-the Wall Bar.

LOEB:

Hemingway and I ate oysters down at the Versailles or the Trianon, where Joyce ate.

JONES:

Was this after the publication of *The Sun Also Rises?*

LOEB:

No, I saw him only once again. The Hotchner story about me chasing Hemingway around with a gun isn't true. It has no basis whatsoever.

DONALD OGDEN STEWART

A N

INTERVIEW

Donald Ogden Stewart, one of the favorite humorists of the twenties, became part of Hemingway's Bill Gorton. His books include The Parody Outline of History, Mr. and Mrs. Haddock Abroad, *and* Perfect Behavior. *Mr. Stewart was prevented from participating in the Paris conference by illness, but he generously provided a follow-up interview on 4 July 1972 at his London home.*

STEWART:

We could really start with your question about what Hemingway had when I first met him.

BRUCCOLI:

Yes, people reacted to him with an almost sexual intensity.

STEWART:

It probably was. You liked the guy, and he was so full of life and so full of beans. He loved to eat and drink.

BRUCCOLI:

Did you have the impression that he was turning it on and off like a faucet?

STEWART:

No.

BRUCCOLI:

Was he making an attempt to charm you or did it seem completely natural?

STEWART:

No – it seemed awfully natural to me and very real, and it worked until the episode in MacLeish's flat in Paris in the fall of '26.* But it was a magnetic personality, and as far as I was concerned a marvelous personality. You wanted to – this is in a way a comment on myself – but I didn't want to let Ernie down, about bullfighting for instance. Really at my age now I wouldn't say that I loved bullfighting. But I was so damn anxious to please Ernest; I was so damn anxious for him to like me that I wouldn't have dared to criticize bullfighting. And when he explained to me why they had to use the horses so that the bull would get his head down, that seemed perfectly alright: that's fine, Ernest. And when I got my ribs broken, that was his fault. I wouldn't have gone into the goddamn ring, but there was Ernest in there going around chasing bulls, and, as I have told you before, I was sort of hanging around the outside of the crowd not wanting to – because I'm scared to death of animals. Especially bulls. Even though they're young bulls with their horns wrapped and everything. I was just trying to show Ernie that I was there – "old Don" – I didn't really want to face it. And, also as I think I've told you, these two Spaniards came up to me with a red cape or rag or something like that and took me by the arm, and – who am I to break up a friendship with Spain! So I went with them and used the wrong maneuvers. I held the cape right up in front of me, and the bull hit me and knocked me up in the air. The marvelous thing about it was that the minute he'd hit me I wasn't afraid anymore. I grabbed the cape like an idiot and started chasing the bull, and, of course, got hit again and cracked a couple of ribs. But I

---

*Hemingway read a scurrilous poem about Dorothy Parker, and Stewart rebuked him.

had really done that for Ernest Hemingway. I mean I wanted to show him that "old Don" could take it, you see. I think my feeling about him was something like that. I wanted Ernest Hemingway to have respect for me and like me. And both of those Pamplona episodes were examples of "old Don" trying to make good with the master. I've said, the first one was a college reunion; but then into the 1925 fiesta came sex and Harold Loeb and Duff Twysden. It sort of changed – it wasn't the same thing. And I certainly didn't any longer go out after any bulls. But the charm – charm isn't exactly the word – but I think that I sort of fell in love with Ernest Hemingway and Hadley – both of them. They were such marvelous people to be with. There was always fun going on or excitement going on. I think in those days – at least between '23 and '26 – before *The Sun Also Rises* came out – he too was doing a bit of charming. I wouldn't put it past him that he also was selecting the people he wanted to be with. But I never had the slightest suspicion of that, and I really wouldn't want to defend that thesis now. Here's an example. He fell in love with motor bike pacing: a man on a bicycle is behind a motorcycle racing around a track inside at night, and he's in the – I don't know whether it's the suction or something – of the motorcycle so that he's really riding in a vacuum so he can go as fast as hell. On account of Ernest I got to like that. Now the more I think about motor bike pacing – I'd run 8,000 miles rather than go to see one of those damn things; but I used to go with Ernie in Paris and also to prize fights. Well, I rather liked boxing. This is not a terrible criticism of me – but I wanted Ernie to like me – I wanted to live up to his ideal of manhood, you see. It was as simple as that, and all I got were two broken ribs and a lot of hangovers. But I made good. He and I were great friends from '23 until '26, and then the thing happened that I think eventually happened to most of Ernest's friends: the minute he began to love you, or the minute he began to have some sort of an obligation to you of love or friendship or something, then is when he had to kill you. Then you were too close to something that he was protecting. He, one-by-one, knocked off the best friendships he ever had. He did it with Scott; he did it with Dos Passos – with everybody. I think that it was a psychological fear he had that you might ask something from him. He didn't want to be overdrawn at your bank.

BRUCCOLI:

What about Duff? Do you think there was anything between Duff and Hemingway?

STEWART:

Toots, I wouldn't know how there couldn't have been. He was by far the most attractive man that was down there at Pamplona. He was certainly more attractive than Pat Guthrie or Harold Loeb or me; and that they hadn't had a bash at it would have been very surprising. I wasn't watching Hadley, but I would've thought that she would've known about it because she was a terribly attractive girl. She was really the right wife for Ernest — for anybody. She was attractive — she wasn't a *Follies* beauty or anything like that, but she had such a good personality — a marvelous woman to have around. And to be married to Ernie must not have been one of the most dream-like marriages that you could imagine. But she handled him and gave him Bumby. I've never been able to understand — unless it was that Hadley was getting too close to Ernest, and he was becoming indebted to her, and he had to get out into what he thought were the free pastures — because there was no other reason for him to leave her. I mean if I'd had a son that married Hadley, I'd be the happiest father in the world.

BRUCCOLI:

There's only one photograph known of Duff and it's a very bad photo. It may even be a passport photo. What did she look like?

STEWART:

Christ — God — yes. The first time I saw her she was sitting at this table in a bar in Pamplona. She had bought, with her marvelous instinct, one of those bullfighter hats with a flat round top; and she sat there in that, and God, she really was terribly attractive. She was fun to be with. Well, this first time I met her she had a hangover which endeared me to her immediately because I had a bit of a one myself. But she was, I would say, one of the most attractive women that I have ever met, and down-to-earth — there was no falseness about her. I felt that this is really a wonderful woman, and I think she was. I can understand anybody going crazy about Duff.

CLARK:

Was that the first time you met Harold Loeb?

STEWART:

Yeah, that was the first time. We all got together around the remains of poor, dear St. Fermin. And it exploded. But, as I said, it didn't explode into a college reunion — it exploded into sex, which at a bullfight there's no room for that. I mean there shouldn't be any sex at a bullfight. It's a male festival.

BRUCCOLI:

Did you see Duff subsequently?

STEWART:

No — I never saw her again. The unfortunate thing that happened — we had these marvelous five or six days shooting wine into our mouths from goatskin bags and dancing, and it really is a beautiful fiesta. We, in a way, got to love everybody. But then came the end of the fiesta, and the hotel bills were presented. Suddenly Ernie found out that Duff and Pat didn't have a cent, you see. He had recommended them to the proprietor of the Montoya, and suddenly everything went awful in terms of what a good time we had and everything. Harold Loeb had already left; but here were two or three hotel bills that couldn't be paid. Ernie didn't have the money, and fortunately I did. It was just a thing you did. You asked me if I ever saw her again. Yes — after the bills had all been paid then I went up to — I forget where it is on the coast of France . . . I was going back to Gerald and Sara Murphy's, and there she and Pat were and Dos, I think. We had a marvelous drink or two at the bar there, and I left that night. But Duff was worth everything, I think. I still remember her as one of the best women. In an entirely different scale of values she and Hadley were both wonderful women, and I wish to God I could see both of them again.

CLARK:

How did you know that Ernest Hemingway was at Madame Lecomte's in Paris when you went there?

STEWART:

I didn't know he was there, but Bunny Wilson had written me to get in touch with Hemingway, and he may have given me the address or something like that — I don't know. Before I went to Paris for the first time — this was in 1922, I think or '21 — and Dos's *Three Soldiers* I thought was a great book, and I went to see him. He sort of briefed me on Paris. He gave me the name of Madame Lecomte's restaurant, and he gave me the name of a wine called Burgundy which I later developed. But that was — I'm not sure whether we made a rendezvous at Madame Lecomte's or whether Ernest just happened to be there.

CLARK:

Then you went and stayed with him for . . .

STEWART:

Well, he left that night for Switzerland, but I slept in his bed there and I forget — it was the place where they lived before the sawmill. I'm pretty sure it was. Actually, we didn't talk literature, and we didn't want to see where we worked. It was fun . . . . Well, I don't know how it is now, but, for instance, my best friends in literature were Bob Benchley and Dorothy Parker and Ernie and so forth. We never talked technique or about our writings, and I can't remember now ever discussing literature with Ernest. I really was terribly ignorant as to how good he was. I liked him as a person. If he was a writer — well, that was alright with me too, but I never knew how good he was. And even, as I've said, when *The Sun Also Rises* came out in '26 I didn't have any idea it was any good. It was just what had happened. To me it seemed journalism, and he hadn't really written it at all. He just told the way it was. I think I was a little wrong about that.

BRUCCOLI:

You had a lot of company at the time. Were you ever with Fitzgerald and Hemingway at the same time?

STEWART:

Yeah — but I couldn't now ever remember it. I may have brought them together. I was the first one I think that knew the Murphys — Gerald and Sara. I think I introduced Scott and Ernest to Gerald, but I'm not sure. I do know that in '24 when I was writing what I think is my best book of humor . . .

BRUCCOLI:

Mr. and Mrs. Haddock.

STEWART:

Abroad, yes. That's fine. I shouldn't put in that plug for it — I don't think you can buy it today. But I went over to Paris in the spring of '24 and I had just published — just published and had panned by the critics — a book of satire called *Aunt Polly's Story of Mankind.* That was in '23. And sort of as a reaction against the panning of the satire I just sat down at my little room at cent-cinquante-neuf Boulevard Montparnasse, that's where I always lived in Paris. I had gone there because Edna St. Vincent Millay had gone the year before, and it was marvelous. Well, anyway, I started to write *Mr. and Mrs. Haddock Abroad.* And the luck was that every night I would go over to Gerald and Sara Murphy's and there would be either Ernest or Scott of Dos or somebody like that, and I'd read what I'd written that day. It was simply marvelous because it worked — they laughed. The Murphys were the most wonderful people to be in the room of. They both had the great ability to make you feel that they loved you and wanted you there, and right beside you by a curious coincidence would be just the drink that you wanted. Their effect on our group was that of mother and father sort of nursing these fledglings. They were living then at the — oh, I'm sorry I can't remember it now, but it was just off of the Place St. Michel. It was the third or fourth floor of a building there, and they had this — I wish I could remember the name of that but I can't. But as I say that was the most blessed spring to write *Mr. and Mrs. Haddock,* and then every night to have this wonderful audience. And then when July came around to go down to Pamploma with Ernest and his gang, it was . . .

CLARK:

Do you remember the Dingo bar?

STEWART:

The Dingo and all of those bars, the Rotonde and so forth and so on — I just remember them as names. The only place I'm sure of is cent-cinquante-neuf Boulevard Montparnasse because I had to tell taxi drivers to please get me there.

F. Scott Fitzgerald

FRANCES RING AND R. L. SAMSELL

Sisyphus in Hollywood: Refocusing F. Scott Fitzgerald

F. Scott Fitzgerald has become a myth, and intriguing as myths may be, they give us a picture that is imaginary – with only a partial basis in fact. Some of the writings that have created the legendary Fitzgerald are sensitively rendered by earnest biographers, but most have perpetuated an image of alcoholism and despair, which image has been overblown in their blurry focuses on his last Hollywood years. As his secretary, I worked with him daily for almost two years, and what I've read about him seldom resembles the man I knew so well. Just recently, an editor in a national publication stated: "... the whole Hollywood experience was only an extension of the nightmare that was his later life ... he was a zombie – out of fashion, no family, no self-confidence, a sporadic but psychopathic drunk who alienated people as if it were his vocation." This writer spoke with conviction, with authority – but wasn't he only echoing others?

Nowadays, everybody is an authority on F. Scott Fitzgerald. After all, doesn't knowing the many details of the author's Hollywood romance with Sheilah Graham pretty much cover anything that was truly important in the man's life in the film city? Indeed, *Beloved Infidel* was such an entertaining book that subsequent scribes thrive on re-telling the more flamboyant episodes virtually verbatim. Even eminent scholars have given short shrift to Fitzgerald's Hollywood days, perhaps feeling that *Beloved Infidel* said it all. Prior to Miss Graham's *Beloved Infidel,* Arthur Mizener barely touched upon Fitzgerald's life in Hollywood. His revised edition, however, faithfully adhered to *Infidel,* paralleling Andrew Turnbull's Hollywood report, which just as faithfully followed *Infidel's* lead. And so it goes. Other scholars' shorter Hollywood renditions capsule those same erratic episodes in the Fitzgerald-Graham relationship which *Beloved Infidel* had dramatized in a fuller, more understandable narrative. This brings us to an important point: the shorter the coverage the greater the emphasis on the sensational conduct of the anti-hero, Fitzgerald. And, for each biography there may be numberless reviews, each one of which fires the would-be reader's imagination by pinpointing the biography's more dramatic episodes. The 'zombie' quote above, for example, typifies how a reviewer draws convenient inferences from what a biographer learned from what somebody else saw, heard, perhaps vaguely remembered. Whatever the mythic process, the result has been the creation of an image of F. Scott Fitzgerald in Hollywood as a physically faded, anti-social alcoholic, irresponsible, an all but defeated man. I do not agree.

When I think of Scott Fitzgerald, I think of work, discipline, responsibility, humor, generosity (of time, energy, emotion and money), lively and instructive discussions. But has my fondness and loyalty for my employer affected my memory and judgment? Then why not go to others who knew him in Hollywood before I did, find out how they remember Scott? I say those who *knew* him – percipient witnesses.

In July, 1937, arriving at MGM, Scott visited with Edwin Knopf, the story editor responsible for bringing him to Hollywood. Knopf tells us, "Scott was determined to succeed. No one worked harder or more sincerely. He was completely responsible." What were his mannerisms? How did he behave socially? "Scott was like a fire in a grate – you went to him. He never sought you. He received; and, when he received, no one was ever rebuffed. He could do more with the lift of a shoulder than somebody else could do with a shout. A little faint smile meant more than somebody else's snarl." Did he drink? "I never saw Scott drink in Hollywood. He always had a glass in his hand, yes – but it was a Coke. I saw him often, very often, at my place; at other parties, too."

During Fitzgerald's first week at MGM, the British writer, Anthony Powell, tells us they lunched together at the commissary, recalling: ". . . one was immediately aware of an unassuming dignity. His air could be thought a trifle sad, but not in the least broken

Fitzgerald's last residence, 1403 North Laurel Avenue, Hollywood – third floor right.

down, as has sometimes been described during this period. In a
railway carriage or bar, one would have wondered who this man
could be." And, more: "Fitzgerald, who was off alcohol, drank milk,
ate cold cuts; the rest of us had beer . . ."

H. N. Swanson was Scott's agent for most of the Hollywood
assignments. Interviewed in his Sunset Strip office, "Swanie" said,
"With me, it was hero worship. The man was a poet. He had more
talent in his little finger than most of those other fellows." Asked
how he most clearly recalled Fitzgerald, Swanson told us – "What a
lot of people don't know is that he had a great fun side to him. If
you sat in a room with Scott, he'd give you the feeling that somewhere around the corner something wonderful and exciting was
going to happen." How was he thought of at the studio? "They
looked up to him with awe. They were overly kind, leaning over
backwards, hoping he would turn out to be a fine screenwriter."

In February, 1938, Scott wrote his daughter, "I am half sick with
work, overwhelmed with it and yet vaguely happier than I've been in
months." By the year's close, however, the novelist, who admittedly
did his best work alone, apparently could not become part of the
team. He bickered with colleagues, finally differing with studio
executives over scripts. For whatever reasons, MGM did not renew
Scott's contract as of 1 January 1939. But, during his eighteen-
month stint at the Culver City studio, Fitzgerald filed more than
twenty-four hundred pages of completed scripts, worked on six film
assignments *(A Yank at Oxford, Three Comrades, Infidelity, The
Women, Marie Antoinette, Madame Curie)*, earning in excess of
$85,000.00.

Free of what he described as big heartbreaking doses of work, and
with savings, Scott's free-lancing career began with two weeks' work
on Selznick's *Gone with the Wind*, followed by an equally lucrative
assignment on Walter Wanger's *Winter Carnival*. He had been taking
notes throughout 1938 for a new novel, finding time to read, browse
at favorite book stores, simply getting out to see what he liked and
disliked about Los Angeles: dining out often – he preferred Musso-
Frank's in Hollywood to his other favorites, the Hollywood Brown
Derby and Victor Hugo's on Sunset Boulevard (now the Saratoga) –
taking in previews with Sheilah Graham, dropping in at the Beverly
Hills Tennis Club, or going to Gilmore Stadium's midget automobile
races at Beverly & Fairfax. He occasionally dined with Ogden Nash,
partied at Gladys Swarthout's, with Frances and Albert Hackett, at
the Knopfs' where he and Thomas Mann once enjoyed each other.
But Scott stayed away from large gatherings. When trapped, how-

Fitzgerald's house at Edward Everett Horton's "Belly Acres" estate, Encino, California.

ever, he could bear up under the task, and, as screenwriter-producer
Nunnally Johnson tells us — "Scott and I probably saved each other
a lot of strain and boredom at some of those parties." Scott had
moved in the spring of 1938 from his four-hundred-dollar-a-month
suite at the Garden of Allah to a comfortable beach house at Malibu.
Ironically, while the town was on its golden spree, Fitzgerald, with
plans for his novel, began to withdraw, finally isolating himself in the
fall of 1938 in a rambling cottage at Edward Everett Horton's Belly
Acres estate in Encino.

Scott was living at Belly Acres when MGM let him go. For a time,
financial pressures were only in the wing. When he worked, he
commanded $1,500.00 a week, but his expenses kept mounting.
There was the relentless drain of medical bills (Scott insisted on the
best possible care for Zelda); and he would have only a Vassar education for Scottie. These responsibilities came first with Scott. I
think it's fair to state here that such obligations haunted him, daily.
But resolved to work on his novel, he also had to maintain his own
household, which now included a cook and secretary. Then, after an
Easter visit with Zelda, he came back depressed and anxious. This
was his period of drinking. Simultaneously, he was quarreling with
editor Kenneth Littauer and agent Harold Ober, seeking out local
agents for movie work. But he was almost five months between
assignments. The drinking during this time required the services of a
nurse for several months, also frequent visits by a doctor. And the
money was going. Despite the twenty-one thousand dollars Scott
earned over the course of 1939, there were those long months when
he could not be certain the year would prove that successful. It was
an anxious, desperate year. Worried over the unpredictability of
movie work, Scott turned once again to the magazines. One of his
first efforts, "Design in Plaster," in the November 1939 *Esquire,* won
a place in O'Brien's *Best Short Stories 1940.* It was a year of work,
worry, work — but relieved, of a moment, by his natural zest for
enjoying people and himself. Scott's work alternated between *The
Last Tycoon,* short stories, brief movie assignments, and, in late
1939, his studio hack writer, Pat Hobby, was created for *Esquire.*

Of his four Los Angeles residences, Scott's stay at Belly Acres was
his longest (eighteen months), and in many respects his pleasantest.
He loved the rural environment of Encino. It was like a country
village — a small grocery, drug store, and post office just down the
road. His cottage at Belly Acres was ideal for writing. It was here that
my recollections of him begin. Working, hours meant nothing to
Scott. I would sometimes receive telephone calls at one or two in the

The courtyard at 1443 North Hayworth. The apartment where Fitzgerald died is at the right.

morning, or occasional telegrams specifying what time I was expected. If he had been writing through the night, or rearranging notes, or making one of his characteristic lists, he would simply leave a message – *am sleeping* – indicating what he wanted me to do. By the time I was under way, he would appear in a somewhat tattered terrycloth robe and slippers, wanting some breakfast, worried that his instructions were not clear enough, and wanting to talk – about almost anything, books, politics, the impending war.

What I remember most is his warm interest in people: there was Bob Bennett, for example, the young man who helped Scott at the Holmes Book Co. on Sixth St. in Los Angeles, where Scott went looking for good second-hand copies of *Crime and Punishment,* Kipling, Shaw's *The Intelligent Woman's Guide to Capitalism and Socialism,* or a special edition of *Alice in Wonderland* with Tenniel illustrations, or Chapman's *Homer,* etc. His novelist's curiosity generally encouraged people to talk about themselves and when Bob mentioned that he wrote poetry, Scott asked if he could see some of his work. When next they met, they went to Mackie's for coffee, where, as Bob Bennett tells us – "He only pointed out the lines he liked. He was very very helpful." Bob remembers that Scott was quiet, calm, apparently in good health, arriving at the book store on one occasion in white tennis cap and sneakers. Scott's interest in others, the willingness to help, extended itself over the years. It was pleasant for me to hear Nunnally Johnson recall how Scott, even before the men knew each other, suggested to Max Perkins that Scribners publish a collection of Johnson's short stories – "Such a kind, thoughtful thing for a man to do." Of the countless kindnesses to others, I like to recall his escorting the Smiths – Erleen, his cook, and her handsome husband – to the Coliseum to see UCLA's great halfback, Kenny Washington. The Smiths were a charming couple. Scott responded to their beauty and intelligence, and the football game was just one way he thought of pleasing them.

There was often much humor to his generosity. When Scott's lawyer asked him to inscribe his four novels, he obliged, but also sent along an orange crate jammed with other authors. Or, when a member of the Horton family asked if he had a tennis ball, he retorted: "You want some tennis balls?" and promptly scurried around the house, bringing every tennis ball he could find. Or, knowing I wanted a toaster, he was careful to save his Raleigh coupons for me, and since he was a chain smoker, the coupons accumulated rapidly. His humor could be unpredictable, devilish: once, driving through Beverly Hills, he burst into zany song – "On

The mantlepiece near which F. Scott Fitzgerald died at 1443 North Hayward, Hollywood.

La Cienega, there's no Five & Tenega . . ." And a prized example of his wit is his inscription to me in a copy of *Taps at Reveille:*

> Frances Kroll
> She has a soul
> (She claims to know it)
> But when young Frances
> Does her dances
> She don't show it.
>
> From the bald-headed
> man in the front row
>
> Scott Fitzgerald
> "The Gayieties"
> 1939

While Scott's public manner may have seemed reserved, even somewhat shy, he was completely at ease and spontaneous with those he knew well. While he was adapting his short story "Babylon Revisited" for motion pictures, he paced back and forth dictating, playing all the parts. His portrayals of some of the scenes were so compelling that it was difficult not to get caught up in his outpouring and forget about the dictation. During this period he had moved to an apartment on Laurel Avenue in Hollywood — this to cut expenses and save the long ride from the valley on those evenings when he met Sheilah Graham. Though he had sold a series of Pat Hobby stories to *Esquire,* he complained to editor Arnold Gingrich, "I wish to God you could pay more money. These have all been stories, not sketches or articles." Scott wasn't broke, but the financial drain was unrelenting. His hopes were up, however. He felt *The Last Tycoon* was going well. He worked on the novel every day — writing, re-writing, changing his notes which were outlined chapter by chapter. Even in its unfinished state, critics have generally acclaimed the novel. Nunnally Johnson, who certainly knows literature and Hollywood, has this to say about Fitzgerald's last effort: "He saw this town with a clear eye. No other novelist did — before, or since. Scott began to appraise Hollywood — as though an intelligent, cultivated man were appraising his characters — not funny paper characters, not stereotypes. I think *The Last Tycoon* would have been the greatest book on Hollywood."

"Work is dignity," Scott Fitzgerald tells us, and he lived his own maxim. During those forty-one months of his last Hollywood stay, Scott's work-product resulted in the publication of thirty-one stories

Frances Kroll Ring at the Musso & Frank Restaurant, 1972.

and articles, the beginning of a major novel – all this while working on fifteen movie assignments. He earned over $125,000.00, paying off debts, meeting his responsibilities, dying solvent and with a life insurance policy approximating $30,000.00 intact. The continuing drain on his resources – physical and financial – must have taken its toll. The pressure was always there. There were, of course, those times of emotional lows when Scott did drink. But the drinking did not dominate or control his life and actions. He was a man, who, between battles of hard work, had his few bouts with hard drinking – but let's put the focus where it should be: on the work. Scott was a writer. Those who knew him remember and think of him as a writer. Moreover, they remember him with great affection. Finally, he was always looking ahead, working up new dreams, firing up new hopes, planning one project after another. His perspective was positive. Scott's own words say it best: "the test of a first-rate intelligence is the ability to hold two opposed ideas in the mind at the same time, and still retain the ability to function. One should, for example, be able to see that things are hopeless and yet be determined to make them otherwise."

Los Angeles, California

"NO,
I AM NOT PRINCE CHARMING":
FAIRY TALES IN
Tender is the Night

In his pre-publication instructions to Maxwell Perkins, Scott Fitzgerald was careful to emphasize the seriousness of *Tender is the Night*. Don't mention the Riviera or "gay resorts" in advertisements, he warned Perkins: that territory had been too thoroughly exploited by E. Phillips Oppenheim and others. Furthermore, he twice proposed to his editor, "If it could be done, a suggestion that, after a romantic start, a serious story unfolds would not be amiss...."[1] Clearly, Fitzgerald hoped that the advertisement and jacket copy would guard against the widespread notion, a hangover from his image as laureate of the jazz age, that he was a mere chronicler of the foolish and the frivolous.

The novel itself is of course no paean to the glamour of the "gay resorts." Instead, it condemns the corruption, decadence, and insensitivity of the rich expatriates who appropriate Dick Diver to their purposes and as casually discard him, like any other passing bicyclist, when his usefulness and charm has been exhausted. And in the course of *Tender is the Night,* Fitzgerald took careful steps to separate his book from the sentimental, romantic fairy tale which, it is strongly implied, has been responsible for much of the moral irresponsibility he deplores.

The brief summary of Dick Diver's student days at New Haven, Oxford, and Vienna characterizes him as "Lucky Dick," a young man afflicted with "the illusions of eternal strength and health, and of the essential goodness of people," the illusions of a nation whose frontier mothers had always denied the existence of the wolf at the door. That Dick's illusions will come tumbling down is specifically hinted at in the curious intrusive reference to Thackeray's humorous fairy tale, *The Rose and the Ring,* wherein the Fairy Blackstick, who among other things has the power to turn people into door-knockers, remarks that "The best I can wish you, my child . . . is a little misfortune."[2] The reasoning behind the Fairy Blackstick's observation is that those she has blessed with good fortune — like the two god-daughters she rendered eternally charming in the eyes of their husbands — become "capricious, lazy, ill-natured, absurdly vain," but that those who suffer, like Prince Giglio (whose throne is unsurped by his uncle) and Princess Rosalba (who is cast out into the wilderness to be nurtured by lions), develop such admirable traits as humility, honesty, and courage. Hence, the Fairy Blackstick wonders "What good am I doing by sending this Princess to sleep for a hundred years? by fixing a black pudding on to that booby's nose? by causing diamonds and pearls to drip from one little girl's mouth, and vipers and toads from another's?" and concludes that she "might as well shut my incantations up, and allow things to take their natural course."[3] Thackeray's entertainment for children, in short, is by way of an anti-fairy tale, in which virtue triumphs over misfortune more or less naturally, without much assistance from benevolent fairies, and is particularly appropriate to the case of Dick Diver, whose attempts to render himself forever Prince Charming lead to his downfall.

The course of Diver's deterioration is traced by way of two other literary references. Having lost control of his emotions, he parades round the block waiting for Rosemary to emerge from the studio in Passy as fatuous as "one of Tarkington's adolescents" — as smitten and ridiculous as Willie Baxter himself, in love at seventeen.[4] Later, when he has determined to abandon his *magnum opus* ("He had about decided to brief the work in its present condition and publish it in an undocumented volume of a hundred thousand words as an introduction to more scholarly volumes to follow"), Dick encounters the society pilot fish Bartholomew Tailor in Cannes. "It was a beautiful sight," [he tells Nicole,] "he and I shaking hands there on the boulevard. The meeting of Sigmund Freud and Ward McAllister."[5] Ward McAllister, a kind of self-appointed gatekeeper to American society, is best known as the author of *Society as I Have Found It* (1890), an account of his triumphs at initiating "little dances," forming clubs of the best people, organizing the first private balls at Delmonico's, attending famous Newport gatherings, seating people properly at dinners, and knowing how to issue formal invitations to receptions on a yacht. Freud was interested in the hidden, the interior wellsprings of human behavior; McAllister in the surfaces, the glossy veneer of civilized behavior. Diver, in abandoning his scientific quest for the truth within, has moved toward McAllister's world of social snobbery, but he does not qualify, by birth or inclination, for full membership among the blue bloods. His strength drained by the transference to Nicole, he is without occupation, desperately at liberty.

If *The Rose and the Ring* aptly predicts Dick Diver's collapse, other kinds of fairy tales — some written for children, some for adults — perform a double function in *Tender is the Night*. They are associated with specific characters to indicate how they fail in perception or how they have become corrupt, and they are so vigorously repudiated as to emphasize the distance between the conventional romanticized tale and Fitzgerald's novel. Rosemary for example comes to her worship of Dick, in his jockey cap and red-striped suit the Pope of the beach, "as dewy with belief as a child from one of Mrs. Burnett's vicious tracts. . . ." But in what sense can Frances Hodgson Burnett's *Little Lord Fauntleroy* (1886) or *The Secret Garden* (1911) or her other books, still read by children, be considered *vicious tracts?* They are vicious because they inculcate an almost religious faith in the existence of an oversentimental dream world: in this specific instance, because they lead Rosemary to so idealize Dick Diver that he cannot possibly, "for even a moment," relax into imperfection without undermining her dewy belief.[6]

Being brought up on fairy tales can have still uglier and more damaging effects, Dick proposes in a speech delivered when he, Abe, and Rosemary visit the battlefield near Amiens. That World War I battle, Dick tells Rosemary, had cost "twenty lives a foot" and "No European will ever do that again in this generation." What is more, the slaughter had been precipitated by the "whole-souled sentimental equipment" characteristic of the English, French, and Germans, but not the Russians and Italians. "You had to remember Christmas, and postcards of the Crown Prince and his fiancée, and little cafés in Valence and beer gardens in Unter den Linden and weddings at the mairie, and going to the Derby, and your grandfather's whiskers." Abe attempts to bring Dick down to earth by commenting that General Grant had invented that kind of battle at Petersburg, but Dick insists that Grant only invented the mass butchery.

"This kind of battle was invented by Lewis Carroll and Jules Verne and whoever wrote *Undine,* and country deacons bowling and marraines in Marseilles and girls seduced in the back lanes of Württemberg and Westphalia. Why, this was a love battle — there was a century of middle-class love spent here. This was the last love battle."

Again Abe pokes fun at this rhetoric, observing that Dick wants "to hand over this battle to D. H. Lawrence," but Diver will have none of his levity, nor respond to Abe's mocking volley of pebbles.

"All my beautiful lovely safe world blew itself up here with a great gust of high explosive love," Dick mourned persistently. "Isn't that true, Rosemary?"

"I don't know," she answered with a grave face. "You know everything."

This is a complicated scene to interpret. One is tempted to adopt Abe's jocular attitude toward Dick's high-sounding language, in the conviction that the doctor is here, as elsewhere, showing off for Rosemary. Yet Dr. Diver's point strikes home: that behind the carnage lay generations of unquestioned fidelity to "beautiful lovely safe" traditions and uncritical acceptance of "whole-souled sentimental" fairy tales having no more relation to the truth than the adventures of Alice or Captain Nemo or the knight and the magical water sprite in Motte-Fouqué's *Undine.* For Dick himself, as his inflated rhetoric demonstrates, remains the partial victim of the false values he rails against; he cannot totally escape them; he is moved by them as by the "gold star muzzers," and so cannot joke with Abe: "I couldn't kid here . . . . The silver cord is cut and the golden bowl is broken and all that, but an old romantic like me can't do anything about it."[7]

Fairy tales cloud perception. Rosemary can perceive the truth only dimly through the haze provided by Mrs. Burnett's stories — and even Dick Diver, who knows better, cannot entirely repudiate the enchantments of his childhood. Still more damning, however, is Fitzgerald's association of the most conventional sentimental reading matter with the moral decadence of postwar Europe. "You're not going to like these people," Dick warns Rosemary when they stop at the party in the Rue Monsieur, and indeed she does not, for it "was an electric-like shock, a definite nervous experience, perverted as a breakfast of oatmeal and hashish, to cross that threshold," and be confronted by the "neat, slick girl with a lovely boy's face," who attempts to secure an assignation with Rosemary and by the tall and slender girls, their small heads waving gracefully "rather like long-stemmed flowers and rather like cobras' hoods," who gossip mercilessly about the Divers and their circle. Surely there is no more decadent scene in Fitzgerald (the Wanda Breasted episode having been cut from *Tender is the Night*) than this Frankenstein of a party which takes down Dick and Rosemary at a gulp. And who is in attendance? "There were about thirty people, mostly women, and all fashioned by Louisa M. Alcott or Madame de Ségur . . . ."[8]

Alcott had begun by composing unsuccessful melodramas, but ended, as everyone knows, as the bestselling creator of a sugar-coated world in which Jo, Meg, Amy, and the sentimentally stricken Beth of *Little Women* masquerade as real girls. Sophie (Rostopchine), Comtesse de Ségur, corresponds to Louisa May Alcott, for she too wrote popular, genteel confections for children in whose romantic plots abandoned orphan girls are miraculously rescued. In depicting a Lesbian demimonde whose inhabitants have been "fashioned" by Alcott and de Ségur, Fitzgerald issues a warning that such culturally approved fiction for schoolgirls was anything but safe for them to read, since the most depraved corruption might stem from the propagation, as real, of entirely false views of the world. For example, the tone of Nicole's schizophrenic letters to Captain Diver – and, perhaps, her traumatic incest as well – was derived "from *Daddy-Long-Legs* and *Molly Make-Believe*, sprightly and sentimental epistolary collections enjoying a vogue in the States." One wonders what Scottie had been reading.[9]

The character of Baby Warren nicely combines the qualities of lack of perception and moral callousness, and once again the point is underscored by reference to well-known writers. Baby is very much taken with Englishmen, who figure prominently among her lovers, and regards the English as "the best-balanced race in the world," an assertion Dick Diver categorically denies. It would be good for Nicole and him, she suggests, to take a London house and live "with sane, well-balanced English people."

> She would have gone on to tell him all the old propaganda stories of 1914 if he had not laughed and said:
>
> "I've been reading a book by Michael Arlen and if that's –"
>
> She ruined Michael Arlen with a wave of her salad spoon.
>
> "He only writes about degenerates. I mean the worth-while English."

But in "ruining" Micahel Arlen, Baby has also "dismissed her friends" in the Mayfair set which Arlen dissected in *The Green Hat* (1924).[10]

Though Fitzgerald by 1930 had come to regard Arlen as a writer who had tried and failed to fool the public with second-rate work, he had earlier, in a 1925 letter to Perkins, extended a "profound bow to my successor, Arlen," for having written *The Green Hat.* Now superficial and badly dated, Arlen's novel had created a sensation with its behind-the-scenes exploration of morally bankrupt high society in England. As best he could, the Armenian author had tried to penetrate the imposing facades erected by the upper class English, and for this Fitzgerald respected him. Baby, however, will not recognize the truth when she sees it. "If she had ever suspected the rotted old truth, the real reason for Nicole's illness, she had certainly determined to deny it to herself, shoving it back in a dusty closet like one of the paintings she bought by mistake."[11]

Having gone south for the winter, Baby Warren lies reading late at night, in Rome, "one of Marion Crawford's curiously inanimate Roman stories" before falling off to sleep. Three hours later, she is awakened and sets about to extricate Doctor Diver from the Italian jail where he languishes following what could hardly have been a more animated series of Roman quarrels, flirtations, and fights. In the course of securing Dick's release, Baby exhibits certain qualities — a habit of command, an appeal to connections, a readiness to loose her tear ducts — that have enabled her, always, to have her way. And at the end of the affair, she exhibits her cool callousness in reflecting that it "had been a hard night but she had the satisfaction of feeling that, whatever Dick's previous record was, they now possessed a moral superiority over him for as long as he proved of any use."[12]

It is appropriate that Baby Warren should be reading one of the many Francis Marion Crawford novels laid in Italy, for though American by birth, Crawford (1854-1909) was like her (Baby is "very English," Nicole observes) an expatriate, "a deracinated European, a multilingual cosmopolitan." Primarily a romanticist and a romancer, Crawford wrote prolifically, turning out two novels a year abounding in plot complications, marked by charm and picturesqueness, but as to their underlying philosophy "often . . . very shallow." Crawford, in short, wrote picturesque romantic fairy tales for adults, and Baby Warren is attracted by the glittering surfaces of his novels, which inspire her to contemplate an affair with an Italian officer and to put out of her mind the foul dust that she's swept back into the family closet.[13]

Certainly Fitzgerald's references to various fairy tales in *Tender is the Night* provide a gloss on his characters: Dick and Thackeray's

Fairy Blackstick, Rosemary and Frances Hodgson Burnett, Baby Warren and Marion Crawford. Just as certainly, the references suggest the drastic consequences in failure of perception and in moral corruption of swallowing whole the sentimentalized view of the world implicit in this kind of fiction. But the frequent derogatory references – to Mrs. Burnett, to Lewis Carroll, Jules Verne, and Friedrich Heinrich Karl de la Motte-Fouqué, to Louisa May Alcott and Madame de Ségur, and to Francis Marion Crawford – also function to distance these sentimental writers from Fitzgerald himself. All right, he seems to be saying, perhaps I have been frivolous, perhaps I have romanticized flappers and sheiks, but this novel about Dick Diver's "little misfortune," this *Tender is the Night* is different. This is serious.

College of William and Mary

---

[1] Fitzgerald to Maxwell Perkins, 5 February 1934, *The Letters of F. Scott Fitzgerald*, ed. Andrew Turnbull (New York: Scribners, 1963), pp. 241-242; Fitzgerald to Perkins, 13 January 1934, *Letters, p.* 239: "Don't forget my suggestion that the jacket flap should carry an implication that though the book starts in a lyrical way, heavy drama will presently develop."

[2] F. Scott Fitzgerald, *Tender is the Night* (revised edition), introd. Malcolm Cowley (New York: Scribners, 1951), pp. 3-6. References throughout are to this edition, which, beginning with Dick Diver's return to the Zurich sanitarium after the war, brings the doctor on stage immediately, introduces the Fairy Blackstick's warning on p. 5, and thus foretells "heavy drama" at the beginning.

[3] W. M. Thackeray, *The Rose and the Ring* (New York: Stokes, 1909), pp. 12-15. Fitzgerald slightly misquotes the Fairy Blackstick, whose blessing on the new-born Prince Giglio is "My poor child, the best thing I can send you is a little misfortune."

[4] Fitzgerald, *Tender,* p. 153. The reference is undoubtedly to Booth Tarkington's *Seventeen* (1916).

[5] Fitzgerald, *Tender,* pp. 178, 182. Ward McAllister, *Society as I Have Found It* (New York: Cassell, 1890).

[6] Fitzgerald, *Tender,* pp. 91, 147. "Burnett, Frances [Eliza] Hodgson," *The Reader's Encyclopedia of American Literature,* ed. Max J. Herzberg (New York: Crowell, 1962), p. 125. Fitzgerald may have nurtured a resentment against Mrs. Burnett for having been dressed in his boyhood, like thousands of others, in the curls and velvet suit with lace collar which Little Lord Fauntleroy wore.

[7] Fitzgerald, *Tender,* pp. 117-118.

[8] Fitzgerald, *Tender,* pp. 132-134.

[9] Madame de Ségur's stories, I have been informed by Prof. Luke Martel of the College of William and Mary, were standard reading material in French schools at least through the 1920s, and Fitzgerald's daughter – and her parents – might well have been exposed to them, as well as to Alcott and the fairy tales, during the years when Fitzgerald was working on *Tender is the Night.* Fitzgerald, *Tender,* p. 10.

[10] Fitzgerald, *Tender*, p. 233.

[11] "Arlen, Michael," *Twentieth Century Authors*, ed. Stanley J. Kunitz and Howard Haycraft (New York: Wilson, 1942), p. 39. Fitzgerald to Perkins, ca. 1 May 1930, *Letters*, p. 221; Fitzgerald to Harold Ober, received 13 May 1930, *Letters*, p. 395; Fitzgerald to Perkins, 1 May 1925, *Letters*, p. 182; *Tender*, p. 233.

[12] Fitzgerald, *Tender*, pp. 245-253.

[13] "Crawford, Francis Marion," *American Authors 1600-1900*, ed. Stanley J. Kunitz and Howard Haycraft (New York: Wilson, 1938), pp. 190-191.

HERBERT GORMAN

GLIMPSES

OF

F. SCOTT FITZGERALD

In the literary and artistic worlds of the 1920's there were various groups, commonly called cliques by those who didn't know the exact meaning of the word, quite independent; but which, often enough, cut into one another to greater or lesser extents much like circles that overlap. Many of these groups were quite sympathetic in aims and general purposes but others were violently antagonistic in everything, including personalities. For example, Matthew Josephson distinctly did not belong to the same group as the late Ernest Boyd. Thus it was possible to be in the midst of the yeasty ferment and know much about others whom one physically encountered but seldom, only, so to speak, when the circles overlapped. It was because of this somewhat arbitrary group arrangement, I imagine, that I saw so little of F. Scott Fitzgerald; and yet because our diverse groups *did* impinge occasionally I happened upon him often enough to conceive some idea of his place in the great whirl of things. For a time my group circled about the poet, Elinor Wylie, and, as it included Edmund Wilson and John Peale Bishop, both former Princeton undergraduates with our subject, it did, in a remote way, involve Fitzgerald, certainly by copious rumor if not by actual

---

*Published from the typescript in the possession of Mrs. Herbert Gorman. All rights to this article remain the property of Mrs. Gorman.

presence. Of the times I met him, most of them casual encounters in crowded places, there are three that I would like to recall, for they seem now — at this late date — to illuminate a sort of Pilgrim's Progress of his career.

During most of the summer and autumn of 1926 my wife and I were living in the Hotel Royal at Cannes, France, one of the smaller hostelries on the Croisette facing the long narrow beach and the Mediterranean Sea. While it was Cannes out of season, it was Cannes very crowded, for it had lately become a sort of snobbish fashion for footloose foreigners to establish a season of their own in the Riviera watering-places. True enough, there was no casino open (one would open later in the decade for midsummer gamblers) but Juan-les-Pins was near enough — a short bus-or-car-ride away — and there was a neat little casino there where one could play *boule* all evening without losing one's inheritance. The days were long and pleasant; the sun shone nearly all the time; the food was excellent; and prices had not started to climb to the heights they were to reach before the dreadful 30's ruined us all, and a lot of the Generation sought refuge on Marxian band-wagons! One morning near noon from my second-floor window I heard the shrill honking of a motor-horn and a few minutes later a porter knocked to inform me that friends of mine waited below. I went down to the side-entrance of the hotel and there was Scott Fitzgerald in a small open French car (a Citroen, I believe) with Mrs. Dorothy Parker seated beside him. He jumped over the side of his *voiture* and greeted me with enthusiasm.

At this time Scott was about thirty years old but he seemed much younger, in actions as well as appearance. He was dressed in wrinkled white trousers, a white sports-shirt open at the neck and a pair of soiled white sneakers; his face, neck and arms were rather ruddy than tanned and his hair appeared bleached by the bright sun of the Esterel. There was a Golden Boy aspect about him. He was extremely active, jumping about constantly and making elaborate gestures. When my wife joined us we all rode in the little car down the Croisette to the Old Town where we sat at a table facing the tiny port harboring the small motor-boats that made regular trips to the islands of Sainte-Margueritte and Saint-Honorat. It was pleasant under the leafy trees and a comfortable breeze was blowing. Little remains to me of what was said during the two hours or more that we sat there and drank *apéritifs*, but I do remember that for a long time Scott insisted in conversing in doggerel rhyme and that at several instances he repeated almost lovingly that last sentence from his recent novel, *The Great Gatsby*, the one about the orgastic future which "year by year recedes before us."[1] Of the doggerel I recall only:

> All the girls and mans
> Love to come to Cans
> To meet that dear old Morman
> Herbet Sherbet Gorman.

He spoke, too, of his new novel (which I gathered was well under way), inquired about James Joyce and Ford Madox Ford and invited me to a swimming party on the Cap d'Antibes. He gave neither date nor place and so I never went. As for Mrs. Parker, renowned for her wit and generally the bright soul of every occasion she adorned, I do not remember one word she said.

This was due, perhaps, to my concentration on Scott, for I was quite aware of his immediate attainment. With the unequivocal success of *The Great Gatsby* buoying him up and plans for a new novel already seething in his mind, he was riding the crest of a wave of good fortune and self-realization that I know now he was never to experience again. But I saw no shadows before him then. All things excellent appeared to be coming his way and he was revelling in his own luck. To me it was significant that he repeated several times his own sentence about the orgastic future. Why orgastic? His delight in spontaneous doggerel, his constant laughter, his bouncing manner, all spelled out a personality that was intoxicated with itself: but in a happy non-Narcissistic way. He had demonstrably accomplished; he had absolved himself of past doubts and dubious successes; he was on the road to riches and justified fame (actual achievement) combined. My total impression of him that bright day in Cannes was one of exquisite and luminous self-confidence in what he had just done and what the future, orgastic or not, would make it possible for him to do.

The second encounter I desire to recall has been fragmentarily adumbrated (at second-hand through Edmund Wilson) in Arthur Mizener's *The Far Side of Paradise*. I believe this meeting took place in 1928, although it may have been almost a year later. Memory sometimes shuffles the years when the birth-sign-posts exceed sixty. Anyway, the meeting place was Adrienne Monnier's apartment on the rue de l'Odéon on the Left Bank in Paris and the occasion was a dinner in honor of Miss Sylvia Beach, the original publisher of James Joyce's *Ulysses*. Joyce and I had walked some distance from the *bistro* where we indulged often in our two Pernods before dining and we were somewhat tardy when we arrived at Mademoiselle Monnier's apartment. Over the charming period furniture, paintings, marvellous silkwork and bibelots a blur of voices greeted us and the first persons we saw were Zelda and Scott Fitzgerald. Joyce stiffened slightly as though he were about to run the gauntlet. We were greeted by Adrienne and Sylvia, waved to by Nora Joyce who had arrived (as she generally did) with my wife before us and immediately approached by Scott. He rushed forward, sank upon one knee and kissed Joyce's hand. To me he gave a bright and happy greeting as though we had parted but yesterday. During the dinner (a very fine one, by the way) he called several times across the table to Joyce such remarks as "How does it feel to be a great genius, Sir?" and "I am so excited at seeing you, Sir, that I could weep." In contrast to his ebullience was Zelda Fitzgerald's silence and aloof poise, her face, so Indian-like at times, cold and noninterested. Joyce, who, while certainly dignified and master of himself at all times, was never quite comfortable in an heterogeneous gathering of any respectable size (he always preferred a small party of four to six except upon his birthday), mumbled short responses to Scott and appeared to secrete himself behind the thick lenses of his glasses. His desire was to get away as soon as possible and this disappearance we achieved as soon as it was reasonably tactful after the dinner was terminated.

As Nora, my wife, Joyce and I drove away in a squeaking taxi he explained what had made him stiffen slightly at the unexpected sight of Scott. It was not dislike. It was something else altogether. It was fear. It appeared that sometime before Scott had called upon Joyce while he was living on the sixth floor of the apartment-house at 2, Square Robiac, just off the long winding rue de Grenelle. Scott may have been drinking but I think his deportment, as Joyce described it, was not particularly due to any artificial exhilaration. They were a sincere part of the man himself and betrayed his indubitable worship of actual greatness in letters. He had kissed Joyce's hand then, enlarged upon Nora Joyce's beauty, and, finally, darted through an open window to the stone balcony outside, jumped up on the eighteen-inch-wide parapet and threatened to fling himself to the cobbled thoroughfare below unless Nora declared that she loved him, too. Nora declared hastily that she did and Joyce, always a fearful man where heights were concerned, recovered from a near-fainting lapse. "I think he must be mad," added Joyce to me after relating the tale. "He'll do himself some injury some day." Nora closed the story by remarking airily: "Ah, he's a good lad, Herbert. I think I'll do a bunk with him some day." This made Joyce smile (Nora was always threatening to do bunks with all sorts of people) and the subject was dismissed.[2]

There seemed to me to be a decided difference between the Scott Fitzgerald of this meeting and the one in Cannes a couple of years before. The happy and auspicious excitement in himself, the naive and almost childlike triumph in accomplishment, had somehow diminished and in its place was an over-anxious adulation of another man who had achieved literary greatness by the arduous discipline of his own defiant mind. I think, too, it didn't *have* to be Joyce; it could have been any illustrious creative artist who dominated his wavering will and forced it into accomplishment. Indeed, at this time Scott seemed somewhat coarsened in appearnace although there was what might be called a *generous* envy in his attitude. The constant use of the appellation "Sir," the references to "great genius," the incident related by Joyce which revealed a kind of hysteria in the man, and the loss of that luminous quality of enthusiastic youth may all have their matter-of-fact explanations, but to me it seemed that Scott had lost something that he would never be able to regain. The Golden Boy was gone. The orgastic future had monstrously receded. This may seem like arriving at a summation after the evidence is all in (and to a degree it may be so: — no matter how impartially we endeavor to recover the past the intervening period and its inexorable events and post-proofs color our best trials); but I am convinced that what I saw and heard that evening was significant and true and that I knew it at the time. Scott no longer existed in the juvenescence of his years and he had reached — it is even possible, unconsciously — the level plain of his own limitations and was quite frightened to fully face them.

This appeared to me to be confirmed by the third meeting with him that I prefer to remember. It occurred at an after-dinner party at the home of Lawrence Langner in New York City. This must have been early in the spring of 1929. A number of celebrated actors and actresses were present (for Lawrence who was a director of the Theatre Guild was a sort of generous and urbane godfather to them all) but Scott I soon discovered seated in a window embrasure conversing with Mrs. Blanche Hays. He rose and seemed quite glad to see me, shaking hands almost fiercely and then walking across the room with his arm thrust about mine. He seemed paler than I had ever seen him before, the ruddy hue quite gone; but this may have been emphasized by his black tuxedo. He was holding a highball in his hand but he did not appear exhilarated at all. Indeed, he seemed rather morbid. He inquired about Joyce and how he was getting on with *Work in Progress* (the name by which *Finnegans Wake* was known until its publication) and I asked how he, Scott, was getting on with his novel. He replied somewhat gloomily that it was coming along all right and then asked me suddenly if I had seen Edmund Wilson lately. I replied that I hadn't and he requested me to send his "obeisances" to Joyce. There was some small talk about Paris and the Riviera and then he was diverted by some blond young creature and that was the last I saw of him during the evening.

As I look back at the encounter now it seems to me that there was a lassitude there that I had never expected to recognize in Scott Fitzgerald. He had visibly grown older and the fine bounce of the Cannes days was completely gone. Or perhaps it was for me that evening. Time was drawing in for all of us; the crazy happy era was ending; rumbles of the approaching economic storm were in the air although we did not quite recognize them for what they were. It was the fag-end of a period and the Marxian bandwagons were waiting just around the corner. In a few months the Stock Market would crash with a sound heard round the world. Nearly five years were to pass before the novel which Scott mentioned as being "in the works" in 1926 was to be published (1934) and, as I was not in touch with him, I am quite unaware of what trials and tribulations he endured to complete it. However, it seems to me that the period from, say, 1925 to 1929, included the actual years of the swift rise and unhappy descent of Scott Fitzgerald. I cannot agree with those critics who assert that *Tender is the Night* (the novel published in 1934) ranks as a fit successor to *The Great Gatsby.* Scott was of his era and he hardly lived in creative letters beyond it. These three meetings that I have described, in my judgment, epitomize it. It was a Pilgrim's Progress with no Celestial City waiting in the clouds.

Hughsonville, New York

---

[1]*Editor's Note:* Herbert Gorman's typescript uses *orgiastic* throughout. It has been emended to *orgastic* because that was the word Fitzgerald intended and which was printed in the first edition. The word *orgiastic* did not enter *The Great Gatsby* until it was published with *The Last Tycoon* in 1941. A good guess is that Herbert Gorman used one of the *orgiastic* texts to check the quotation when he wrote this article.

[2]*Editor's Note:* Until publication of this article it has been assumed that Fitzgerald's threat to jump out of the window occurred at Sylvia Beach's "Festival of St. James" in 1928 — see André Chamson's recollections of Fitzgerald in this number of the *Annual.* Although Sylvia Beach describes the dinner in *Shakespeare and Company*, she does not mention Fitzgerald's threat. Since Herbert Gorman's account of Adrienne Monnier's dinner party does not mention the Chamsons, it seems clear that Fitzgerald dined with Joyce at least twice at the rue de l'Odeon (once with the Gormans and once with the Chamsons) — in addition to calling on Joyce at the Square Robiac, where the threatened act of defenestration actually occurred.

ROBERT E. MORSBERGER

THE ROMANTIC ANCESTRY
OF
The Great Gatsby

Published in 1925, halfway through the decade, *The Great Gatsby* is often considered the quintessential novel on the 1920's, the fictional distillation of the Jazz Age that Fitzgerald called "the greatest, gaudiest spree in history . . . . The whole golden boom . . . — its splendid generosities, its outrageous corruptions and the tortuous death struggle of the old America in prohibition."[1] At the same time, Gatsby's romantic and frustrated desire for Daisy is recognized as an expression of the author's youthful obsession first for Ginevra King and later for Zelda Sayre. With his obscure and penniless background, Gatsby represents the young Fitzgerald, "one of the poorest boys in a rich boys' school,"[2] having his winter dreams of wealth and beauty while haunted by insecurity. Like Gatsby, Fitzgerald met a desired and desirable belle and had entrée to her society while he was an Army officer and thus temporarily a "gentleman" by official decree. Back in civilian life, each had to regain that entrée by finding the wealth that was its open sesame. As Scott recalled, " — I was in love with a whirlwind and I must spin a net big enough to catch it out of my head, a head full of trickling nickels and sliding dimes, the incessant music box of the poor. It couldn't be done like that, so when the girl threw me over I went home and finished my novel."[3] Gatsby becomes rich too late and by questionable, even sinister means.

Both of these readings are valid, yet the novel is more than social criticism and fictionalized autobiography. The plot may also embody and criticize the American dream, yet the basic fable is much older and more fundamental. Daisy may be only a spoiled socialite of the 1920's, a member of the idle rich; but Gatsby transcends the era. A man of mystery, he conveys a quality of timeless myth and romance. John Henry Raleigh finds Gatsby to be the legendary Dutchman.[4] Perhaps, but there are other and stronger sources, both in legend and in literature.

It is a critical commonplace that Fitzgerald was an intense romantic; *The Romantic Egotist,* his first title for *This Side of Paradise*, fits him precisely, though he could sometimes subject the romantic vision to ironic appraisal. It is instructive to compare *Gatsby* to another book appearing in the same year, Dreiser's *An American Tragedy.* Like Dreiser's Clyde Griffiths, Gatsby has the American dream, is intoxicated with the romance of money and of beauty; but Dreiser's novel is largely documentary, while Fitzgerald's is poetic. A sometime naturalist, Dreiser made his novel a study in environmental conditioning; Clyde is an inversion of the Horatio Alger hero. But Gatsby has a nobility lacking in Clyde; he wants wealth only as the necessary prelude to an ideal of beauty. He says of Daisy: " 'Her voice is full of money.' That was it. [thinks Nick] I'd never understood it before. It was full of money — that was the inexhaustible charm that rose and fell in it, the jingle of it, the cymbals' song of it. . . . High in a white palace the king's daughter, the golden girl. . . ."[5]

It is not just money; rather it is the cymbals' song, the white palace, and the golden girl. Certainly Gatsby is the antithesis of the fortune hunter. Rather than intriguing for Daisy's wealth, he drives himself to make his own fortune so that he can offer it to her. He is wealthy when the book begins, and his money is meaningless without Daisy. Unlike Henry James' Morris Townsend, who jilts Catherine Sloper when he fears she will be disinherited, Gatsby would never give Daisy up. His is a dream of beauty beyond mere wealth, and we are told that he was dedicated to Daisy like a knight in quest of the Holy Grail. Self-absorbed, he has a "Platonic conception of himself" that must be fulfilled and can be fulfilled only through Daisy.

But Gatsby's romantic vision of wealth and beauty consummated in love is born of and ends in frustration. For he is not to the manor born; his ideal is baffled by poverty and caste. He is like a stableboy looking into the king's palace, which he is forbidden to enter. Like Aladdin, he can win the princess only by offering enough gold to charm the emperor, and even then he remains an upstart. He is Gareth the scullery boy, who must prove himself a knight; he is all the lowborn lovers smarting with frustration under the insolence of hereditary aristocrats who have free access to the lady the Gatsbys are not to contaminate with a look or a word.

Where did Fitzgerald get his romantic values and attitude? Ultimately they may be a matter of temperament, but there are numerous works of romantic fiction that parallel to a degree the basic situation in *Gatsby*. We do not know that Fitzgerald read all of these, but he was sufficiently impressed by a number of them so that in the final years of his life he urged them upon Sheilah Graham as part of her essential reading program. Among the novels that follow, Fitzgerald specifically recommended to Miss Graham *Kenilworth, A Tale of Two Cities, Great Expectations, Wuthering Heights*, and *The White Company*.[6] In addition, it is reasonable to assume that he encountered a fair amount of the romantic fiction popular during his youth. "The Diamond as Big as the Ritz" is among other things a deadpan satire of the sort of extravagant, exotic romance that makes the substance of Walter Mitty's fantasies. (And Thurber, just two years older than Fitzgerald, also came from a Midwestern middle-class background.) It may therefore be profitable to consider some literary analogs that precede and may have influenced *The Great Gatsby*. These may not be immediate or conscious models, but they helped create the romantic outlook still prevalent during Fitzgerald's formative years, despite the rise of realism and naturalism.

As the current nostalgia for old movies and comic strips of the 1930's reveals, some of the most potent and enduring influences may not be great art but childhood and adolescent enthusiasms. Norman Mailer has several times stated that the two writers who most influenced him were Raphael Sabatini and Jeffrey Farnol and that the novels that most moved him as a boy were *Captain Blood* and *The Amateur Gentleman*. Interviewing the astronauts at Houston, science fiction writer Ray Bradbury found that they had grown up, like himself, on a diet of adventure and science fiction and films — the exploits of Edgar Rice Burroughs' John Carter, Warlord of Mars; Buck Rogers vs. Killer Kane; *King Kong* (which Bradbury saw at least twelve times and calls "one of the greatest adventure movies ever made"). The sophisticated scientists in the space program were "the boys who used to read *Astounding Stories* beneath winter bedsheets in olden nights or hid Jules Verne behind algebra texts and then grew up to cog fiction into science." And he discovered that their adventurous spirit was the inheritance of Gary Cooper, Tom Mix,

Buck Jones, and other Western movie heroes whose images fill "our personal data memory system"; that "In going back to Houston I not only went back to a country learned from science-fiction stories and comic strips as a boy, but to movies seen and loved when I was 10, 11, and 12."[7]

A similar process seems to have been at work on Fitzgerald. His interest in movies is well-known, but he was already grown-up when movies came into their own. In his case, the influence would have been mainly literary. English literature is of course full of ballads and songs about squires of low degree who long for the love of a great lady. As Sir Walter Scott appropriated such material for the romantic novel, we find in *Quentin Durward* a poor expatriate Scott who falls in love with the unattainable Countess Isabel at the French court of Louis XI. As her escort on a journey beset with dangers, he gains her love; but to win her over nobel competitors, he must perform the sort of ordeal frequently set for aspiring lovers of fairy tale and legend (just as Gatsby must acquire a king's ransom before he can compete for Daisy) – in this case to be the man who in the final battle brings King Louis the head of the outlaw Wild Boar of Ardennes. Nineteenth-century fiction has many poor soldiers of fortune who similarly aspire to the hand of high-born ladies. Notable among the imitations of Scott are Sir Arthur Conan Doyle's *The White Company* (1891) and *Sir Nigel* (1906) in each of which a penniless squire of the lesser nobility must perform feats of valor in order to be worthy of marriage to a lady above him. In Charles Major's *When Knighthood Was In Flower* (1898), Charles Brandon, a poor guardsman newly arrived at the court of Henry VIII loves the king's sister, but she is married off to Louis XII of France. Brandon must wait anxiously while she outlives Louis and avoids seduction by François I; then he has to rescue her from the evil and arrogant Duke of Buckingham before he finally marries her and is thus raised to the nobility.

In these examples, frustrated romance has a happy consummation, but several other novels anticipate *Gatsby* in their presentation of thwarted love. Thus in Scott's *Kenilworth* the protagonist Sir Edmund Tressilian, an impoverished knight, loses his long-loved Amy Robsart to Queen Elizabeth's favorite, the Earl of Leicester, just as Gatsby loses Daisy to Tom Buchanan. A rather ineffective hero, Tressilian resembles Gatsby only in the frustration of his continued love for another man's wife; but the arrogant and ruthless Leicester is a close counterpart of the millionaire Buchanan. Likewise, Dumas père's Vicomte de Bragelonne (in the novel of that title) loses his boyhood sweetheart Louise de la Vallière to the haughty sun-king Louis XIV. In both books, the protagonist suffers the prolonged torment of watching impotently while his lady-love is swept off her feet by the swaggering lord who enjoys her briefly, and then mistreats her in favor of another, just as Buchanan, while possessing Daisy, has a sordid adulterous affair. We know that Fitzgerald was familiar with Dumas; he read *The Three Musketeers* as a boy and was so enthusiastic that he taught the Scandal Detectives to fence.[8] (The Scandal Detectives was a club that he organized among his classmates at St. Paul Academy, to play at "adventures.") And as late as 1935, he wrote to his daughter about an unspecified Dumas series: "I always thought the first book of that series was one of the most exciting books I ever read."[9] In Charles Kingsley's popular *Westward Ho!* not one man but all young swains of Devon are bereft when the fair Rose Salterne is lured away by the seductive blandishments of a haughty Spanish hidalgo. Led by the brothers Amyas and Frank Leigh, a pair of rustic squires, the luckless lovers band together into the Fellowship of the Rose, determined to win her back; but they sail to La Guayra only to find that her husband Don Guzman has allowed the Inquisition to put her to death for heresy.

In Anthony Hope's perennially popular *The Prisoner of Zenda* (1894) (made into one of several successful film versions in 1922 — with Lewis Stone, Ramon Novarro, and Alice Terry — three years before the publication of *Gatsby*), the dashing hero, Rudolph Rassendyl, is an English commoner, descended via the bar sinister from the ruling house of Ruritania. When Ruritania's weak Rudolph V is drugged and kidnapped on the eve of his coronation, Rassendyl (his identical likeness) has to impersonate him to prevent Rudolph's bastard brother Black Michael from seizing the throne and fair Princess Flavia. So far, this has little relation to *Gatsby*. But pretending to be king, Rassendyl falls in love with Flavia while wooing her for the missing monarch. When he finally rescues the king from the dungeons of Zenda castle, noblesse oblige requires him to yield the princess, though she loves the imposter. Colonel Sapt's final words to Rassendyl, "Heaven doesn't always make the right men kings," anticipates vaguely Nick's epitaph for Gatsby, " 'You're worth the whole damn bunch put together.' "[10] Rassendyl's impersonation of royalty and the loss of the woman he loves to an inferior man has some similarity to Gatsby, and his romantic dedication has even more.

Furthermore, in the sequel, *Rupert of Hentzau* (1898), Rassendyl (again like Gatsby) has a chance to win back the woman whom the obligations of rank and duty have denied him. For King Rudolph has not kept his promises of reform. In self-indulgent debauchery, he is as poor a husband to Flavia (who all the while retains her love for Rassendyl) as Tom Buchanan is to Daisy. Eventually Rassendyl has to return to save Flavia from the dastardly plotting of Rupert of Hentzau, the swashbuckling villain who uses the king's weakness for his own ends. In the climax, both Rupert and King Rudolph are killed. Rudolph's body is identified as Rassendyl's, and Rassendyl is believed to be the king. Here is his chance to hold the throne and marry Flavia in secret. As he walks alone in the palace garden, wrestling with his conscience over whether to take the queen and the kingdom, he is shot to death by one of Hentzau's vengeful henchmen. The scene anticipates Gatsby's murder at the poolside by Wilson, the jealous husband cuckolded by Buchanan.

The disreputable vagabond who becomes a nobleman and wins the lady is best seen in Justin Huntly M'Carthy's melodramatic but popular *If I Were King* (1901), which was a hit on stage; in three movies respectively starring Dustin Farnum (1920), John Barrymore (1926), and Ronald Colman (1938) (whom Fitzgerald singled out for praise in both *Tender Is The Night* and *The Last Tycoon* and who also starred in the 1937 *Prisoner of Zenda*); and still survives in the Rudolph Friml operetta *The Vagabond King.* Here François Villon, the poor rogue and poet from the slums of Paris is metamorphosed into a suave and dashing hero. For love of the lady Katharine de Vaucelles, he accepts King Louis XI's offer that he impersonate the Lord Constable of France for a week, during which he performs heroic exploits that save France from the Burgundians and win him the lady's hand. Such fustian as the verses of the title poem (actually written by M'Carthy, which ironically has become the best-known "work" by Villon!) in which the low-born lover rhapsodizes over the tributary nations and priceless treasures he would bring before his beloved if he were king is certainly in the spirit, though not the style of Gatsby.

Another more literary version of "god's own mad lover" is Jack London's *Martin Eden* (1908), in which again a young tough aspires to refinement, fortune, and beauty in order to win a lady of higher station. A basic difference, though, is that Gatsby, despite acquiring enough polish that he is described once as "an *elegant* young roughneck" [italics mine], does not have Eden's artistic and intellectual development. Still, Eden "had discovered that he loved beauty more than fame, and that what desire he had for fame was largely for Ruth's sake. It was for this reason that his desire for fame was strong. He wanted to be great in the world's eyes; 'to make good,' as he expressed it, in order that the woman he loved should be proud of him and deem him worthy."[11] This is the essential spirit of Gatsby. Eden eventually becomes disillusioned with Ruth's anemic gentility and hollow standards. London rejects the romantic illusion, which he manages to see in ironic perspective, whereas Fitzgerald was, in James Thurber's words, lost "because he was caught in the romantic tradition."[12] To be sure, Fitzgerald criticized Daisy, the unworthy object of Gatsby's dedication, but not the dedication itself.

In Jeffrey Farnol's *The Amateur Gentleman*, a best-seller of 1913, we again find a situation somewhat analagous to *Gatsby*. The hero, Barnabas Barty, is a commoner — the son of a prize fighter. Inheriting a fortune from a relative in Australia, he assumes his mother's more genteel name and endeavors to enter the glittering high society of Regency England. Naturally a noble lady becomes his inspiration; but though he outdoes everyone in aristocratic accomplishments, his origins prevent his being more than an "amateur gentleman."

Yet another analogy, written only three years before *Gatsby*, is Rafael Sabatini's *Captain Blood* (1922), in which a political prisoner sold as a plantation slave in Barbados falls in love with the Lady Arabella Bishop. At first she spurns him because of his servitude; later, when he escapes and becomes a rich and powerful buccaneer, she rejects him because he is "thief and pirate" (though he has done it for her; he even names his flagship the *Arabella*), just as Daisy first rejects Gatsby as ineligible and finally fails him because of his sordid business activities. (Unlike Gatsby, Barnabas Barty and Peter Blood do get the girl at the end.)

No doubt there are more novels with comparable situations; the fact that there are so many attests to the potency of the concept. As *Martin Eden* perhaps reveals, the line between serious and popular fiction was not so sharply drawn in Fitzgerald's youth. Serious writers (Conrad, Kipling, Norris, Stevenson, even Henry James) used some of the same ingredients as potboilers — the difference being mainly in tone, style, depth of insight, and characterization. When Gene Stratton Porter, Mary Johnston, Winston Churchill, John Fox, Jr., F. Marion Crawford, and Maurice Thompson were considered major American writers, when even Harold Bell Wright was taken seriously by much of the public, it should not be surprising if works of marginal literary merit helped form the attitudes of serious artists. The mature Ftizgerald scoffed at *Gone with the Wind*, but he retained his nostalgic admiration for Dumas.

But there are two major nineteenth-century novels that particularly resemble *The Great Gatsby* in plot and even more in emotional tone. In *Great Expectations*, young Pip the blacksmith's apprentice falls desperately in love with Estella, the ward of rich Miss Havisham. A mysterious legacy enables him to become an "amateur gentleman" and to hope that his great expectations include marriage to Estella. To his dismay, he learns that his secret benefactor is an ex-convict and that his fortune is precarious. Estella meanwhile spurns him and marries the rich blackguard Bentley Drummle, Dickens' equivalent of Tom Buchanan. Malcolm Cowley observes that *Gatsby* is like *Great Expectations* in its account of how a young man will rise in a society with false standards, but the resemblance is even closer in the fact that an unattainable girl is in each case the object of devotion and the symbol of success and that the money of both Gatsby and Pip is tainted.[13] Fitzgerald told Sheilah Graham that he "saturated himself in Dickens and Dostoevsky before starting a new novel," and *Great Expectations* is one he specifically had her study.[14]

The major work that anticipates Gatsby in both plot and passion is *Wuthering Heights.* Both Gatsby and Heathcliff come from obscure and base origins; Heathcliff an orphan gypsy, Gatsby (really James Gatz) the son of "shiftless and unsuccessful farm people." But Ellen Dean tells Heathcliff, "Who knows, but your father was Emperor of China, and your mother an Indian queen. . . . And you were kidnapped by wicked sailors, and brought to England. Were I in your place, I would frame high notions of my birth; and the thoughts of what I was should give me courage and dignity to support the oppressions of a little farmer!"[15] Goaded by similar compulsions, James Gatz transforms himself into Gatsby, "educated at Oxford"; " 'After that I lived like a young rajah in all the capitals of Europe — Paris, Venice, Rome — collecting jewels, chiefly rubies, hunting big game, painting a little, things for myself only, and trying to forget something very sad that had happened to me long ago' " or such is the fiction he tells Nick.[16]

Each intense lover, when rejected for a wealthy and socially prominent rival, disappears for some years only to reappear with mysterious wealth from undisclosed sources, which he uses to gain access to the lady he wishes to reclaim. Gatsby's single-minded obsession is more than matched by the brooding intensity of Heathcliff. Each purchases the neighboring manor; Heathcliff becomes the master of Wuthering Heights across the moors from

Cathy's present residence at Thrushcross Grange; and Gatsby buys an opulent estate at West Egg, across the bay from the Buchanans' more fashionable East Egg, his only pleasure being to look at the green light on the end of the Buchanans' pier — the beacon that lures him to Daisy.

There are, of course, some deviations, one of which is that Edgar Linton, whom Cathy marries, is a gentleman of refined sensibility; Cathy's coarse and brutal brother Hindley is a closer equivalent to Tom Buchanan. Another difference is that Cathy responds to Heathcliff's intensity far more than Daisy does to Gatsby; "Nelly, I *am* Heathcliff," she exclaims at the moment of his flight.[17] Furthermore, on his return Heathcliff tries to revenge himself on Cathy rather than win her from her husband; his savage ferocity and violence are never tamed to Gatsby's pseudo-sophisticated "Hello, old sport." And of course the isolated Yorkshire of *Wuthering Heights* is a far cry from Gatsby's Jazz Age society. Nevertheless, on a profound level, Gatsby is Heathcliff.

The plot similarities are striking enough, though perhaps they have been somewhat obscured in *Gatsby* by the secondary characters and subordinate events of Nick Carraway and Jordan Baker and of the Wilsons. And in *Wuthering Heights* after Cathy's death, the account of the second generation also diverts attention. Perhaps the 1939 film, which cut the second half entirely, captured more of the tortured intensity of the hopeless passion between Heathcliff and Cathy. It is this thwarted intensity (coupled with the insurmountable social barriers) even more than the plot that makes *Gatsby* the spiritual heir to *Wuthering Heights.* Fitzgerald recalled after his marriage to Zelda that:

> The man with the jingle of money in his pocket who married the girl a year later would always cherish an abiding distrust, an animosity, toward the leisure class — not the conviction of a revolutionist but the smouldering hatred of a peasant. In the years since then I have never been able to stop wondering where my friends' money came from, nor to stop thinking that at one time a sort of *droit de seigneur* might have been exercised to give one of them my girl.[18]

It is precisely this "smouldering hatred of a peasant" that Heathcliff, the manure-daubed stable boy, feels towards Hindley and Linton.

Whereas most of the romantic fiction previously cited ends either in wish fulfillment or on a noble gesture of renunciation, Fitzgerald himself was closer in spirit to Heathcliff; recalling his "two-cylinder inferiority complex," he concluded, "So if I were elected King of Scotland tomorrow after graduating from Eton, Magdalene to Guards, with an embryonic history which tied me to the Plantagenets, I would still be a parvenu. I spent my youth in alternately crawling in front of the kitchen maids and insulting the great."[19]

Wuthering Heights and *Great Expectations* are great novels; the others previously discussed vary from second-rate to pot-boilers. Yet the recurrence of the myth attests to its vitality. Since Gatsby there have been more in the genre, mostly undistinguished works like Edison Marshall's *Benjamin Blake* (better known as the Tyrone Power film *Son of Fury*), in which the true heir to the 18th-century English estate is robbed of his inheritance, bonded as a stable hand, falls in love with the lady of the manor, and returns after several years' disappearance to the South Seas with a fortune in pearls only to find that the lady betrays him.

What makes *Gatsby* superior to such melodrama is its superb style, the perspective provided by Nick Carraway's commentary, and the fact that it is not only a romance but a potent criticism of the American dream, localized in the glittering vulgarity of the Jazz Age. In the Coolidge era, Gatsby's Keatsian "capacity for wonder" is singularly out of place. As Richard Chase observes, "The special charm of *Gatsby* rests in its odd combination of romance with a realistic picture of raw power — the raw power of the money that has a plutocracy and the raw power the self-protective conventions of this plutocracy assume when they close in a united front against an intruder."[20]

Gatsby reflects Thorstein Veblen as well as tales of romantic aspiration. The Buchanans perfectly exemplify the conspicuous consumption of the leisure class: their eyes are impersonal "in the absence of all desire."[21] Even the moon can be provided by a caterer. Gatsby's attempts to impress Daisy by emulating her opulence are pathetic; lacking inbred taste, he throws gaudy parties, drives a "gorgeous" yellow car, and has an extravagant wardrobe complete with stacks a dozen high of shirts in coral, apple-green, orange, and lavender stripes and scrolls. What finally ruins Gatsby with Daisy is not her fear or love of Tom but her dismay at the vulgarity of Gatsby's defending the way he made his wealth. Here is Gatsby's fatal defect. He ruins himself with her simply by being what he is; he himself realizes that his dream is shattered, though a desperate hope lingers. Daisy has left him even before the final violence.

But the violence is symbolic; it is the combination of Gatsby and

Daisy that is destructive. His frustration and the dream are essentially immature, but they possess an intensity and an idealism that ennobles them above Clyde Griffiths' mere longing for sex and possessions. Daisy, however, can never transcend the limitations of her time and class. Though Hemingway ridiculed Fitzgerald's statement in "The Rich Boy" that the very rich "are different from you and me" by replying, "Yes, they have more money," it is nevertheless true; and in the very story in which he makes that sarcasm ("The Snows of Kilimanjaro") Hemingway concedes the truth of Fitzgerald's observation: "about the very rich; that you were really not of them but a spy in their country. . . ."[2 2] The penalty for spying is death. Driving Gatsby's large, gaudy car instead of her own conservative blue coupé, Daisy accidentally kills her husband's mistress; and Tom, doubly guilty, directs Wilson to Gatsby, who pays for the sins of both Buchanans.

In them is Fitzgerald's deadliest indictment of the wealthy. "They were careless people, Tom and Daisy — they smashed up things and creatures and then retreated back into their money or their vast carelessness, or whatever it was that kept them together, and let other people clean up the mess they had made. . . ."[2 3] In his last words to Gatsby, Nick says, " 'They're a rotten crowd. . . . You're worth the whole damn bunch put together'. . . . The lawn and drive had been crowded with the faces of those who guessed at his corruption — and he had stood on those steps, concealing his incorruptible dream, as he waved them good-by."[2 4]

Here we have at its most effective the double vision of Fitzgerald himself; as he shared Gatsby's dream, winning fortune, Zelda, and fame, so he shared Nick's disillusion and criticism of that life and perhaps wished that he could, like Nick, go back to the more secure moral virtures of his youth in the Middle West.

California State Polytechnic College

[1]F. Scott Fitzgerald, "Early Success," *The Crack-Up*, ed. Edmund Wilson (New York: New Directions, 1945), p. 87.

[2]Interview of Martin Amorous by Peggy Mitchell, *The Atlanta Journal*, 1924, quoted in Arthur Mizener, *The Far Side of Paradise* (Boston: Houghton Mifflin Sentry Edition, 1965), p. 24.

[3]Fitzgerald, "Early Success," *The Crack-Up*, p. 86.

[4]John Henry Raleigh, "Fitzgerald's *The Great Gatsby:* Legendary Bases and Allegorical Significances," *University of Kansas City Review*, XXIII (Summer, 1957), 283-291.

[5]*The Great Gatsby* (New York: Scribners, 1925), p. 144.

[6]Sheilah Graham, *College of One* (New York: Viking, 1967), pp. 77, 116, 208, 214.

[7]Ray Bradbury, "An Impatient Gulliver Above Our Roofs," *Life*, LXIV (November 24, 1967), 32, 36.

[8]Mizener, p. 17.

[9]*Letters of F. Scott Ftizgerald*, ed. Andrew Turnbull (New York: Scribners, 1963), p. 8.

[10]*The Great Gatsby*, p. 185.

[11]Jack London, *Martin Eden* (New York: Holt, Rinehart and Winston, 1963), p. 175.

[12]James Thurber, quoted in Harvey Breit, *The Writer Observed* (Cleveland and New York: World, 1956), p. 257.

[13]Malcolm Cowley, "Introduction," *The Stories of F. Scott Fitzgerald* (New York: Scribners, 1951), p. xvii. Cf. also Norman Friedman, "Versions of Form in Fiction — 'Great Expectations' and 'The Great Gatsby,'" *Accent*, XIV (Autumn, 1954), 246-64.

[14]Graham, p. 77.

[15]Emily Brontë, *Wuthering Heights* (New York: Holt, Rinehart and Winston, 1963), p. 59.

[16]*The Great Gatsby*, p. 79.

[17]*Wuthering Heights*, p. 86.

[18]F. Scott Fitzgerald, "Handle with Care," *The Crack-Up*, p. 77.

[19]To John O'Hara, 18 July 1933, *Letters of F. Scott Fitzgerald*, p. 503.

[20]Richard Chase, *The American Novel and Its Tradition* (Garden City: Doubleday Anchor Books, 1957), p. 162.

[21]*The Great Gatsby*, pp. 6, 12, 14, 15.

[22]Ernest Hemingway, *The Fifth Column and the First Forty-nine Stories* (New York: Scribners, 1938), p. 157.

[23]*The Great Gatsby*, p. 216.

[24]*Ibid.*, p. 185.

THOMAS E. DANIELS

PAT HOBBY:
ANTI-HERO

Fitzgerald's Pat Hobby Stories represent a collection of his writing and thought during the last couple of years of his life which probably have not received the attention due them.[1] They well indicate the direction his fiction was to take during the last phase of his career and interestingly they forecast that which a good deal of modern American literature would follow in the next two decades. There are definitely in Pat Hobby character traits which would appear in *The Last Tycoon*. Particularly noticeable is the similarity between Pat Hobby and Wylie White, the writer in *The Last Tycoon*. In fact, most of Fitzgerald's characterizations of writers in his later life are rather bitter portraits of men who though extremely sensitive and extremely articulate cannot "cope" with the system simply because they are better than most men who surround them. Pat Hobby is not the sensitive, articulate failure that many of the other writers are but he is similar in other respects, and the writers in the Hobby series who are enjoying varying degrees of success are never successful in ultimate terms (which to Fitzgerald's mind at this point in his career would certainly include economic success) and are often similar to Pat in their degree of alcoholic dissipation, if not in his economic straits.

The Hobby series was written during 1939 and 1940. All the stories were submitted to Arnold Gingrich of *Esquire*. There is no

131

doubt but that their specific purpose was to make money to help pay the bills, but, as Gingrich argues, certainly all of Fitzgerald's work was written for the same purpose. Though he attempted to distinguish between his good work and his "hack" material, I feel that he had a difficult time doing so, and indeed some of the so-called "hack work" is superior in quality to the novels, which were supposedly the "serious" material.

There is in the Hobby stories good evidence of the evolution of Fitzgerald's thought from the stance of the young man to the middle-aged man. In fact, I think we see a significant shift from his authorial stance in *This Side of Paradise*, or perhaps better in *The Great Gatsby*, to Pat Hobby or Monroe Stahr. Nick Carraway is not portrayed as the "new rich" or the "old rich," more as the representative of certain values which emerged from his particular type of background, perhaps the old lower upper-class. We see in Nick the positive values, as opposed to the negative and destructive values held by the characters with money.

Between the writing of *The Great Gatsby* and *The Last Tycoon*, then, we see a definite shift on Fitzgerald's part. Monroe Stahr, the man who went from "rags to riches" is the hero of the work, from the beginning through Fitzgerald's notes for the completion of the book. He was to have been finally corrupted by the Brady world with which he had to deal, but it was to have been an "aware" destruction unlike the totally naive and ignorant demise of Jay Gatsby.

Similarly, the entire series of the Pat Hobby stories exhalt the "Tycoons" in the industry, who generally are the men who "know," even opposed to Pat Hobby who like many other writers is sympathetically portrayed but is generally the incompetent fool who lives for alcohol, dreams of his past in silent pictures when he "almost" made it, and an eternal "gate pass" which will bring him into contact with the men in command who dole out the weeks at $250 on which he survives. All of the "Tycoons" of the industry are intelligent, perceptive men who though they are fully aware of Pat's incompetence and complete degeneracy nevertheless keep him around and even pay him. All of the stories indicate Ftizgerald's shift in attitude in this regard, but perhaps two, "No Harm Trying" and "Pat Hobby's Christmas Wish" best exemplify it.

"No Harm Trying" begins with the usual portrait of Pat doing nothing though — "If I could get out to Santa Anita, . . . I could maybe get an idea about nags."[2] Mr. LeVigne, who is one of the moguls at the studio, calls him. The "job" LeVigne offers him is no job at all. The purpose of the paycheck of $250 a week is to provide one of Pat's ex-wives with hospital care — she attempted suicide, but failed. She was at one time a script girl for the studio. LeVigne is then portrayed as a very humane and generous person while Pat grumbles because he has to give up $150 a week for the care of his ex-wife, though he is not required to do anything for the money. In the best tradition of the anti-hero, he was upset by the arrangement: "He did not mind not *earning* his salary, but not getting it was another matter."[3]

With his righteous indignation providing the spur, Pat decides to collect all the people he knows who are on the lot and who are on salary but not working and put together a film. He discovers a call boy, Eric, who wants to be a writer, and who is quite good with ideas; he cons his ex-wife, Estelle, into helping Eric with the script; he convinces Harmon Shaver, an eastern representative for money interests in the studio to back the project; he finds Lizzette Starheim to star in it, Dutch Waggoner will direct it, and Jeff Manfred will supervise it.

When the project is defiantly presented to LeVigne he informs the company gathered that Miss Starheim has not been able to learn enough English to even be considered for a role in a picture; Dutch Waggoner is on drugs; Jeff Manfred is absolutely talentless and is only on the payroll because his wife's cousin had enough influence to place him there; and Pat Hobby is a drunk and a liar. LeVigne, by visiting Estelle, discovered the script was written by Estelle and Eric and not by Pat, and he finally convinces Pat that the studio is right and Pat's plan for the movie is foolish. LeVigne also gives Pat another month at two-fifty, simply because he likes to have him around.

The important element here is that LeVigne comes through as the intelligent, perceptive, humane person. It's Pat and his cronies who are the fools, both to themselves and to the world. They are all cripples in one way or another, and are masquerading as competent people. The studio, represented by LeVigne, is willing to put up with them, even pay them, primarily because of humanitarian inclinations on the part of its executives — certainly a shift from the Warrens or the Buchanans of Fitzgerald's earlier work.

In "Pat Hobby's Christmas Wish" similar character traits emerge, though Pat is the only character who is the same. The story is very simply a blackmail attempt on the part of Pat and Helen Kagle. He has been doing his usual hack script work, and rather than giving his secretary a present he fires her the day before Christmas. She is replaced by Helen Kagle who was the former secretary, and girlfriend, of Mr. Harry Gooddorf, one of the studio executives. Miss Kagle has just been sent "back to the department" because she reminds Harry that "he was getting on." She indicates to Pat that she, though still in love with Gooddorf, has some "information" that could ruin him. Given Pat's predatory nature, and his belief that "deals" always make the man, Pat decides to find out the information and use it for his and Helen's benefit — he even suggests the possibility of their marriage.

The point at which Pat decides to confront Gooddorf is one of the most effective ironies of the series. On his way to the executive's office he remembers that "back in the brief period when he had headed a scenario department Pat had conceived a plan to put a dictaphone in every writer's office. Thus their loyalty to the studio executives could be checked several times a day.

"The idea had been laughed at. But later, when he had been 'reduced back to a writer,' he often wondered if his plan was secretly followed."[4] With this fear in mind, then, he decides not to mention any details while in Harry's office, but in a bar in which Helen is waiting.

The "information" which Helen had was a note that Harry Gooddorf had written years before when she was his secretary, which she had stolen; it read:

To Will Bronson
First National Studios
    Personal

Dear Bill:

We killed Taylor. We should have cracked down on him sooner.
So why not shut up.

Yours, Harry (p. 7)

The note indicates that Gooddorf had murdered William Desmond Taylor, and indeed Taylor had been murdered and no one had been convicted of the crime; since Gooddorf had thrown Helen over she decides to get even.

Harry plays the game with them for awhile thinking that perhaps the 1 February 1921 date that Pat mentioned while in Harry's office was a reference to the night Harry and Helen first fell in love — and waits while Pat demands to be made a producer, and other things while drinking "three large whiskeys." Then Harry informs the group that he and his friends in the industry had decided to quiet things down a bit and Taylor wouldn't so they let him "hang" himself. The note is an admission on Gooddorf's part that "they" — the other tycoons of the industry and himself — were guilty of Taylor's financial demise by "giving him 'too much rope;'" however, they had nothing to do with his physical murder. "Some rat shot him" is the only explanation Fitzgerald gives for the real murder. The money group in 1921 again is portrayed as a collection of perceptive men who tried to keep Taylor from self-destruction, and Pat and Helen had completely misconstrued the letter. Gooddorf gives Pat a Christmas wish, however, that he will say nothing and forget the incident.

As in "No Harm Trying" Fitzgerald again characterizes the tycoon as the good guy while Hobby and his friends, though likeable as blundering rogues, are not to be taken seriously. They are ill-informed misfits who try every scheme possible to make the big time, but they are generally talentless and ambitionless and therefore fail — though they are always saved from total self-destruction by the "big" men in the industry.

Not only is there the interesting shift in Fitzgerald's thought related to the Tycoon of Hollywood as opposed to his earlier more hyper-critical stand towards such people, but we also see Fitzgerald moving in the direction of the so-called anti-hero. Pat Hobby is the sort of "likeable rogue" that has been in literature for a long time, and who has become quite prevalent in modern fiction — especially the rogue with the generally ironic stance towards himself and society. Fitzgerald's portrait of Pat Hobby is strikingly objective compared to many of his earlier characters, and a good deal of his success in the portrayal is his ability to present Hobby in such a way that he is neither authorially condemned nor approved.

In one of the most effective stories in the group, "A Patriotic Short," Fitzgerald weaves together all the major characteristics of Hobby which are developed throughout the series. Pat is again employed by the studio for " — one week at two-fifty —" to do a touch-up job on a script. The script has to do with a post-civil war scene in which President McKinley is awarding a commission to Fitzhugh Lee, a nephew of Robert E. Lee, and Pat is constantly reminded of the days a decade earlier when he was invited to lunch at the studio with a party of executives and the President of the United States, who was visiting Hollywood at the time. He dredges up memories of his swimming pool and his past successes, which

Fitzgerald very effectively contrasts with Pat's present plight. In fact, this story is one of the most effective in the entire series for a number of reasons. The weaving of Hobby's past with his present situation is better done here than in any of the other stories, though the contrast is through them all, and there is perhaps a significant bit of perception on Pat's part when he changes the script right at the point when McKinley is giving the commission to Lee, and Pat has Lee tell him, *"Mr. President, you can take your commission and go straight to hell"* (120).

Pat's realization that the "promise" of America has not been fulfilled for him, and perhaps even his realization that the promise the United States made to the South was not fulfilled is stated quite effectively here. The ending of the story also helps a great deal in eliciting the sympathy necessary for an anti-hero. The symbols in the story, the swimming pool he once had (though it leaked a bit, it was nevertheless a swimming pool), the luncheon with the President back when, and the contrasting symbol of his being generally ignored by a group of important personages who are escorting a new female star down the hallway, are all very nicely woven into the general fabric of the story in much the same way Fitzgerald was capable of injecting symbolic import into prosaic action in his better-known material.

"A Patriotic Short" is one of the few stories of this particular series in which Fitzgerald allows Hobby any self-perception, or gives him any action which indicates Hobby realizes his plight. It is, therefore, quite important to the series since we see for once a Pat Hobby who, though worthless and degenerate in all ways, perhaps begins to understand that so also is the organization and the civilization which has victimized him. There is a very similar construct that Fitzgerald worked on in *The Last Tycoon* when Monroe Stahr is also to conclude that his fall was not due to the plotting of Brady, but to the entire fragmentation of the American Corporation, and therefore the sort of individual which he himself was has no place left in the system. Pat, though a much different type of character in many ways, comes to a similar realization in this particular story, which enhances the story and the entire series.

One of the tightest and most effective stories of the group is "Two Old-Timers." Pat is portrayed very sympathetically in this story. He and another "has-been" of Hollywood, Phil Macedon, "collided" in their automobiles early one morning. Macedon, a former star, had saved enough money to retire on his "hacienda" in the San Fernando Valley, "with the same purposes in life as Man o'War"; Pat had not been as fortunate, or provident, and Fitzgerald very effectively and concisely sets Pat's economic plight by stating simply that "the accident found him driving a 1933 car which had lately become the property of the North Hollywood Finance and Loan Co." Sergeant Gaspar, of the local police department, finds both "drunks" in a belligerent frame of mind primarily because Macedon refuses to acknowledge that he and Pat are old acquaintances.

Pat, as expected, is the more truculent of the two and is put in a cell to wait for the Captain's return. Most of the story takes place with Pat in the cell while Sergeant Gaspar tells Macedon what an excellent actor he was and how well Macedon had "explained" World War I to the people who had not been through it by his role in a picture titled *The Final Push*. Pat, who is within hearing distance of this conversation, tries to jolt Macedon's memory concerning their former relationship by interjecting into this discussion the details of what had really happened when the great "shell hole" scene of the movie was shot. Pat explains that the director, Bill Corker, knew that Macedon was "the toughest ham in Hollywood to get anything natural out of" – so he devised a scheme to do so. Macedon, primarily concerned about the fit of his uniform, was unexpectedly pushed into a hole, then while he tried to claw his way out Corker had cameras on him. Finally, Macedon gave up and cried. Of course Macedon is not happy about Pat's revealing to the Sergeant the reality of the making of the movie and refuses still to acknowledge he knew Pat. When the Captain arrives at the police station both Pat and Macedon are taken to the hospital for the drunk test. Macedon is held for bail while Pat is let go – though he has no place to go since he has been evicted from his room.

Sympathy is elicited for Pat when Sergeant Gaspar offers to lend him a couple of bucks for a room, and then finally believes Pat's story about his earlier relationship with Macedon. All the feeling built for Pat is built by the action of the story; none is attempted through authorial intervention. Sergeant Gaspar's final realization that Pat is telling the truth is most significant in that the reader is given to understand that, though Pat is a "has-been," at least he is honest about the past. He does not, like Macedon, attempt to live a past that never existed, and at least in this story he is perfectly candid about his current situation – which is something less than admirable. He also understands that movies are movies and that Macedon's acting is only Hollywood type of acting. Pat is aware of, and more importantly admits to, the phoniness of making movies, which makes him more admirable than Macedon. He is also far more sympathetic because he has not benefitted from Hollywood even in crass economic terms, which enhances his stance as the likeable rogue.

The Pat Hobby stories are better as individual units than as a series. When presented as a series there is too much repetition of character, setting, and devices Fitzgerald found necessary to tie the stories together. Arnold Gingrich, in his introduction to the volume, argues that " . . . while it would be unfair to try to judge this book as a novel, it would be less than fair to consider it as anything but a full-length portrait." It is not a "full-length portrait" in the sense that it totally develops the character, and it appears that Fitzgerald intended each individual story as an entity in itself by his obvious attempt to include in each story all the background material necessary for an understanding of each story — therefore the repetition.

Further, most of the stories rely very heavily on what may be called a "trick" ending. Or, perhaps better, an element exterior to the general development of the story which is brought in to solve whatever the problem is. In "Pat Hobby's Secret" Pat is hired by an executive to discover how "the artillery shell [got] in the trunk of Claudette Colbert or Betty Field." A playwright, R. Parke Woll, had written most of the script, but refused to supply the ending until given a contract. Pat, then, was hired to find Woll and discover from him what the final solution to the problem was. He did find Woll, in a bar, and he did discover the conclusion of the story, but when Woll's intuition told him Pat was sent by Benizon, the studio executive, for that very purpose, he chased Pat out of the bar. Woll was hit and killed by the bouncer, and Pat was offered $1,000 for the secret; however, just when he was to deliver the secret everything went white — he, Pat forgot it.

"Pat Hobby's College Days," "Pat Hobby, Putative Father" and other stories of the series rely heavily on the same sort of devices for their conclusion, the only possible motivation for which being that Pat is such a degenerate and so incompetent that indeed such happenings are believable incidents in his life. I doubt that sort of justification is sufficient to save many of the stories from melodrama.

Many of the stories do survive very well, though it is quite apparent in most cases they were hurried in composition. Gingrich does point out that Fitzgerald was concerned enough with them beyond their monetary value, however, that he revised most of them after submitting them to *Esquire*.

Perhaps the major significance of the collected stories is Fitzgerald's ability here to create a character quite different from what he had done in the past, and then to present Hobby in a very objective way. His portrait of a rogue who is likeable and worthless is most effective, and indeed is exactly what Fitzgerald had in mind in the series. Also, there is the portrayal of Hollywood and the movie industry which interested him very much, and which he was to develop in greater detail in *The Last Tycoon.* The stories may be seen as apprentice work for the novel, but in many instances I feel they are much more important than mere warm-up exercises. They deserve more serious consideration than they have received in the past in any attempted understanding of the last phase of Fitzgerald's work.

University of Wisconsin, Green Bay

---

[1] Of the few commentators on the Hobby stories, probably the best is Sergio Perosa, in *The Art of F. Scott Fitzgerald* (Ann Arbor: The University of Michigan Press, 1965). His major concern is with the style Fitzgerald used here, though he points out very effectively Fitzgerald's objectivity: "Like the artist envisaged by Joyce in the *Portrait,* Fitzgerald succeeded in assuming the passive indifference of the author who watches from above the movements of his characters and no longer intervenes to correct or determine them" (pp. 150-151).

Robert Sklar, in *F. Scott Fitzgerald, The Last Laocoön* (New York: Oxford University Press, 1967) evaluates the stories primarily as satire, which seems to me rather absurd. He also suggests " . . . the Pat Hobby stories served him best — besides their primary purpose as a source of income — as a purgation, a clearing away of the debris of his aborted Hollywood career, a cleansing of whatever bitterness or self-reproach he felt for having tried and failed as a screenwriter" (pp. 327-328). Sklar feels this "purgation" necessary in order for Fitzgerald to gain the objectivity necessary for writing *The Last Tycoon.*

Kenneth Eble, in *F. Scott Fitzgerald* (New York: Twayne Publishers, 1963) argues the objectivity of the stories is a significant achievement, but that they should be "read singly [in which case they] leave the impression of minor but distinctive achievements" (p. 143). Arnold Gingrich's introduction to the volume of the stories is a good account of the problems Fitzgerald had with publication, and the revisions of the stories, though there is very little useful critical commentary on them. He also wrote a note about the publication of the volume when it appeared in *Esquire,* but it was incorporated almost entirely in the Introduction to the book *The Pat Hobby Stories* (New York: Scribners, 1962). All references to the stories are from this volume. Arthur Mizener mentions them briefly in their biographical context in, *The Far Side of Paradise* (Boston: Houghton Mifflin, 1965). Sheilah Graham does also in *College of One* (New York: Viking, 1966), but neither gives any critical perspective on them.

[2] Fitzgerald, *The Pat Hobby Stories*, p. 103.
[3] *Ibid.*, p. 105.
[4] *Ibid.*, p. 8.

LEONARD A. PODIS

The Beautiful and Damned:
FITZGERALD'S
TEST OF YOUTH

During the early years of the republic, America's youth had little choice but to find a living as soon as they reached physical maturity. As the country prospered with the maturation of industrialism, allowing the middle class to encroach upon the leisure-ground traditionally reserved for the elite, youth gained education and freedom of movement as well. That women's emancipation was coming into its own in the early 1900's is common knowledge. What is not so often realized is that youth – both young men and women – were also gaining new feeedom. People had begun to enjoy themselves before seeking the sober responsibilities of family life.[1]

F. Scott Fitzgerald was perhaps the first, certainly the best-known, writer to monitor this trend in American culture, and capitalize on it in his fiction. It was, in fact, largely Fitzgerald's glamorous conception and treatment of the "new" American girl that popularized the notion of the "flapper," and brought him early success. So completely was Fitzgerald tied to the public's awareness of wild youth and "the jazz age," that many readers (including a few critics) could never accept him as the writer of serious literature he was during most of his career.[2]

Taken together, *This Side of Paradise* and Fitzgerald's early short stories demonstrate his penchant for dealing with people I prefer to think of as "moral orphans." Stories like "The Ice Palace," "The

141

Off-Shore Pirate," "The Jelly Bean," and "The Camel's Back," to name but a few, are filled with supremely youthful characters who drink and dance through an amusement-park world uninformed by parents, or any sense of parental morality. The fact that they seem to have no parents is somehow less important than the feeling one gets from their antics that they never had any to begin with. By totally separating youth from parents and elders, Fitzgerald created the atmosphere which enabled him to write the shocking, unprecedented, "now" tales of the post-World War period.

Yet while it is true that Fitzgerald peopled his early works with youthful heroes and heroines, it is equally true that much of his writing, most noticeably beginning with *The Beautiful and Damned*, expressed a tragic vision of the consequences of unfettered, misspent youth, failing to condone, while hesitating to glamorize the idea of young life divorced from parental stability. As he later noted in retrospect:

> All the stories that came into my head had a touch of disaster in them
> — the lovely young creatures in my novels went to ruin, the diamond
> mountains of my short stories blew up, my millionaires were as beautiful
> and damned as Thomas Hardy's peasants. In life these things hadn't
> happened yet, but I was pretty sure living wasn't the reckless, careless
> business these people thought — this generation just younger than me.[3]

In *The Beautiful and Damned* we can see Fitzgerald's first major attempt ("May Day" was his most notable minor attempt) to reconcile his romantic faith in the magic of youth with his morally ingrained suspicions that life wasn't "the reckless business" for which he and his young creatures had been taking it.

As Fitzgerald wrote his publisher, Charles Scribner, the novel would show the ruin of a young marriage "on the shoals of dissipation."[4] That it succeeded in this end critics agree. Most, however, feel that Fitzgerald failed to supply the groundwork necessary to explain the couple's decline. Thus the book delineates very well the pathetic landscape of mental and physical deterioration, but sheds no light on underlying causes.[5]

Fitzgerald originally intended to call his second novel "The Flight of the Rocket."[6] To me, this provisional title seems more appropriate than the more poetic one he finally chose. For the characters are not really beautiful, and they are certainly not damned — morally irresponsible, to be sure, but not damned in that lofty, tragic sense the phrase might suggest. "The Flight of the Rocket" is a more adequate description of the temporarily brilliant exhaustion of youth which occurs in the novel. Anthony Patch and his wife, Gloria, launch their lives with all the majesty and fury of a moon rocket. But, losing sight of moral wisdom and truths in the thrust of their consuming onward motion, they slip into total hedonism. They lack responsibility in any traditional sense of the word. Living without work or apparent purpose, thinking only of each moment as it comes in terms of their own enjoyment, Anthony and Gloria exploit their ephemeral youth imprudently, and, inevitably, fizzle out like spent rockets, disintegrating as they plummet earthward with the recognition that youth alone has not been enough.

Fitzgerald's abundant use of moral orphans notwithstanding, Anthony Patch is one of his few literal orphans. He lives with his parents as a very small boy, but his mother, an opera singer, dies when he is not more than six or seven. His memories of her are faint and "nebulous."[7]

Anthony's father is often drunk, and generally negligent in the care of his son. "He was continually promising Anthony hunting trips and fishing trips and excursions to Atlantic City, 'oh, some time soon now'; but none of them ever materialized" (6). On the one trip they do take, Anthony's father dies amid "much sweating and grunting and crying aloud for air," leaving the child an orphan at eleven.

Anthony soon finds himself under the guidance of the fatuous Adam Patch, his paternal grandfather, who, had Fitzgerald so desired, might have been as moral a force as the image of Nick Carraway's father would later be in *The Great Gatsby*. But in *The Beautiful and Damned*, it appears that Fitzgerald felt he must portray youth unhindered by any ubiquitous sense of morality. Just as Henry James wrote about people who did not work so he could examine their everyday lives in a purer context, so Fitzgerald used moral orphans to enable him to study youth in an isolated setting. Thus, far from providing Anthony with a moral heritage, "Cross" Patch, a fanatical social reformer of the day, is a simpering prig who:

> levelled a varied assortment of uppercuts and body-blows at liquor, literature, vice, art, patent medicines, and Sunday theatres. His mind, under the influence of . . . insidious mildew . . . gave itself up furiously to every indignation of the age. From an armchair in the office of his Tarrytown estate he directed against the enormous hypothetical enemy, unrighteousness, a campaign which went on through fifteen years, during which he displayed himself a rabid monomaniac, an unqualified nuisance, and an intolerable bore (4).

Fortunately for Anthony, his grandfather does not want much to do with him. Anthony goes abroad to study, and only occasionally pays a visit to his doddering benefactor – the closest thing to a father he has known since the age of eleven. During one conversation with Anthony, Cross Patch demonstrates his lack of cordiality and understanding. His mind appears to be as mired in its own narrow conception of life as his body is confined in his gloomy Tarrytown estate, surrounded by a "veritable maze of walls and wire fences" (13). When Anthony states that he feels himself most qualified to be a writer, the old man winces, "visualizing a family poet with long hair and three mistresses" (15). Anthony wants to write a history of the Middle Ages, however, not poetry. To this, his grandfather characteristically replies, "'Middle Ages? Why not your own country? Something you know about? . . . Why you should write about the Middle Ages, I don't know. Dark Ages, we used to call 'em. Nobody knows what happened, and nobody cares, except that they're over now'" (15).

Thus, although Adam Patch might easily have been a solid moral influence on Anthony, he emerges as a burlesque of the values and wisdom associated with the traditional image of fatherhood. His laughable sententiousness and over-zealous chauvinism tend to encourage Anthony's *carpe diem* life style, not temper it. Quite understandably, Anthony chooses to disregard totally his grandfather's presence, and live a youth of moral orphancy.

The Beautiful and Damned is unique among Fitzgerald's completed novels in that it has a heroine as well as a hero. Gloria Gilbert is the girl who matches Anthony in charm, vanity, and hedonistic tendencies, and is therefore the logical girl for him to marry. Although Anthony is probably the book's central character, much of the third-person narration is centered in Gloria's point of view.

Gloria has parents who fade out of the picture shortly after we meet them, but it is quite apparent that they have been powerless to control her for a long while. Fitzgerald shows them just long enough to establish their negative qualities as parents and as human beings in general. The mother, Mrs. Gilbert, is like an old figurine, capable of little more than sitting about decorously. Her manner is extremely affected, as we see on her first meeting Anthony. "'How do you do?' She spoke in the conventional American lady-lady language. 'Well, I'm *aw*fully glad to see you– . . . . This is really lovely – lovely'" (38).

Mr. Gilbert is bland and ineffectual in his own right. "His ideas were the popular delusions of twenty years before; his mind steered a wabbly and anaemic course in the wake of the daily newspaper editorials" (40).

Thus Gloria, like Anthony, has lived a youth unguided by stable, sensible parental values. Just as Anthony has responded to false morality by completely rejecting Adam Patch, so Gloria rejects the parents she has been unable to obey, and joins with one of her own kind. The marriage of Anthony and Gloria consecrates the understanding they have made with themselves, and which they now make together — the terms of which are later outlined by Gloria — " 'to use every minute of these years, when I'm young, in having the best time I possibly can' " (304).

Youth is central to Fitzgerald's depiction of Anthony and Gloria. When we first see Gloria, she is twenty-two — certainly young enough — yet she looks "so young, scarcely eighteen" (62). She seems the personification of youth. When one of Anthony's friends tells of his accidental meeting with her, he says, " 'She seemed — well, somehow the youngest person there' " (48). Symbolically as well as literally, she is constantly devouring gum-drops, no matter what the company around her. Anthony, too, is a "young soul." His friend Dick Caramel, the successful writer, calls him "young Anthony" (50), and notes that he is "very romantic and young" (51).

But soon after these auspicious beginnings, life for the Patches turns into wearying confusion. Wild party succeeds wild party, followed by petty, but enervating arguments, and more wild parties. Each day becomes "a jelly-like creature, a shapeless, spineless thing" (53). Borne along by a vague anticipation of more dissipation, and the excitement of the knowledge that they will someday inherit Adam Patch's seventy-five millions, Anthony and Gloria seem grossly immature. They have no work whatsoever, manual or intellectual. Anthony makes several abortive attempts at writing his "book on the Middle Ages," but as he never gets a word of it on paper, it becomes a mocking, standing joke. Parenthood might have rescued the couple from their morass of self-destructive indifference, but although Gloria becomes pregnant, no child is born, and it must be assumed that she has had an abortion.

Each dispute between Anthony and Gloria takes "relentlessly its modicum of youth" (195). As they begin to run out of money and their youthful beauty fades, both begin to sense the waste of their lives. Anthony feels "first of all, the sense of waste, always dormant in his heart" (284). Gloria wonders "whether after all she had not wasted her faintly tired beauty" (391). At the novel's end, despite the inheritance of thirty million dollars from Adam Patch, both Anthony and Gloria are aged and broken. Anthony, having reached his breaking point, is "a little crazy" (448), and sits swaddled in blankets on a deck chair, and Gloria is now ironically " – sort of dyed and *unclean*" (448) – both seem the diametric opposite of what they were scarcely ten years before.

In reality, neither character is "old" (Anthony is only a year or two past thirty, and Gloria is three years younger), yet Fitzgerald has ironically divested them of their precious youth. They are now condemned to an "old-age-in-youth," somewhat reminiscent of the Ancient Mariner's cursed "life-in-death." Gone is " . . . The fruit of youth or of the grape, the transitory magic of the brief passage from darkness to darkness – the old illusion that truth and beauty were in some way entwined" (417).

In *The Great Gatsby*, written almost four years after *The Beautiful and Damned*, one finds another significant attempt by Fitzgerald to reconcile his faith in youth's promise with his inbred sense of conventional morality. In that novel he introduces a tangible parental morality in the image of the narrator's father. Nick Carraway is fit to pass judgment on "the whole damn bunch put together," and to escape Jay Gatsby's (the moral orphan's) fate, primarily due to the strength he has drawn from his father: "In my younger and more vulnerable years my father gave me some advice that I've been turning over in my mind ever since."

Yet this evidence will not allow us to conclude that Fitzgerald had come to terms with moral orphancy and parental morality, for although Nick's parental heritage allows him to avoid what "preyed" on Gatsby, the novel does not finally condemn Gatsby's life style: "No – Gatsby turned out all right at the end."

Thus, whether or not Fitzgerald had adequately reconciled his romantic beliefs with his staid insticts by 1925 is doubtful. As the responsibilities of parenthood and family life pressed ever more heavily upon him, however, and his own youth receded before him, the author's sympathies turned increasingly toward more traditional moral values. In his later short stories and *Tender is the Night*, he was to forsake unguided youth almost entirely.

But of *The Beautiful and Damned*, we can be certain that Fitzgerald displayed his first significant literary doubt as to the "magical glory" of youth he had previously celebrated. While one may find other reasons – factors and deficiencies in character which contributed to the Patches' fall, such as vanity, lust for money and pleasure, idleness and lethargy – it is clear that all these are the accoutrements of moral orphancy, the obstacles and temptations to be overcome by the morally stable. In *The Beautiful and Damned*, youth has its first serious moral test. Uninformed by parental values, it fails. But it was only by isolating youth from a mature, conventional morality that Fitzgerald could administer the test.

Case Western Reserve University

---

[1] Henry Dan Piper, in *F. Scott Fitzgerald: A Critical Portrait* (New York: Holt, Rinehart, and Winston, 1965, pp. 59-60) draws on Alexis de Tocqueville and Van Wyck Brooks to support his somewhat fuller discussion of youth's emancipation.

[2] Piper, pp. 58-61, 72-6.

[3] F. Scott Fitzgerald, *The Crack-Up*, ed. Edmund Willson (New York: New Directions, 1945), p. 87.

[4] *The Letters of F. Scott Fitzgerald*, ed. Andrew Turnbull (New York: Scribners, 1963), p. 145.

[5] For examples, see Arthur Mizener, *The Far Side of Paradise* (Boston: Houghton Mifflin, 1951), p. 142; William Troy, "Scott Fitzgerald — The Authority of Failure," and Edmund Wilson, "Fitzgerald before *The Great Gatsby*," both in *F. Scott Fitzgerald: The Man and His Work*, ed. Alfred Kazin (New York: World, 1951); and Kenneth Eble, *F. Scott Fitzgerald* (New York: Twayne, 1963), pp. 71-4.

[6] *Letters*, p. 145.

[7] F. Scott Fitzgerald, *The Beautiful and Damned* (New York: Scribners, 1922), p. 6. Hereafter, page numbers are given in parentheses following the quote.

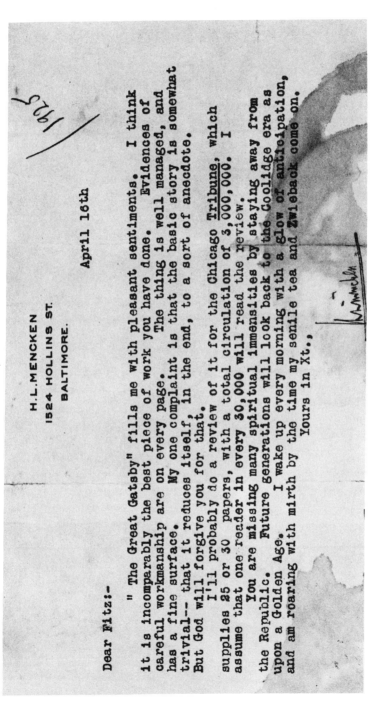

1925

H.L.MENCKEN
1524 HOLLINS ST.
BALTIMORE.

April 16th

Dear Fitz:-

" The Great Gatsby" fills me with pleasant sentiments. I think
it is incomparably the best piece of work you have done. Evidences of
careful workmanship are on every page. The thing is well managed, and
has a fine surface. My one complaint is that the basic story is somewhat
trivial-- that it reduces itself, in the end, to a sort of anecdote.
But God will forgive you for that.

I'll probably do a review of it for the Chicago Tribune, which
supplies 25 or 30 papers, with a total circulation of 3,000,000. I
assume that one reader in every 30,000 will read the review.

You are missing many spiritual immensities by staying away from
the Republic. Future generations will look back to the Coolidge era as
upon a Golden Age. I wake up every morning with a glow of anticipation,
and am roaring with mirth by the time my senile tea and Zwieback come on.
                              Yours in Xt.,

H. L. Mencken's letter about *The Great Gatsby* (Fitzgerald Scrapbook). Published by permission of the Mercantile Safe-Deposit and Trust Company, Baltimore.

CHARLES SCRIBNER'S SONS

PUBLISHERS, IMPORTERS AND BOOKSELLERS

597 Fifth Avenue
NEW YORK

No.

DATE October 13, 1934

CLAIMS FOR DAMAGES OR SHORT-
AGES MUST BE MADE IMMEDIATELY
ON RECEIPT OF GOODS.

TERMS: NET CASH
PAYABLE WITH EXCHANGE ON
NEW YORK

Sold To   Mr. F. Scott Fitzgerald

No.

Sent Per

QUANTITY	DESCRIPTION	EDUCATIONAL	TRADE	TOTAL
	To excess cost of corrections on:			
	TENDER IS THE NIGHT			
	Cost of composition and electrotyping	712.07		
	Cost of corrections		318.56	
	Allowance - 20% of $712.07, according to agreement		142.41	$176.15

The bill for F. Scott Fitzgerald's proof alterations in *Tender Is the Night* (Princeton University Library).

SCOTT FITZGERALD

IN

TRYON,

NORTH CAROLINA

My acquaintance with Scott Fitzgerald was only that. It never became warm friendship although we often saw each other. I am not sure when I first met him but I know it was Lefty and Nora Flynn who brought him to my house and introduced me to him. I felt it was an honor and a privilege for I regarded him then, as I do now, one of the greatest American writers.

Our meetings and contacts must have extended over a period of two or three years, because I have my first memories of him sitting on the edge of a pool table in a house I was renting in Tryon, and later memories of many visits and conversations in the house which I bought about a year later. The pool table was a bit fantastic. The house I was renting belonged to a gentleman who lived in Rye, New York, and used the Tryon house for recreation in the spring and fall months. He was a horseman so there were many silver trophies, riding whips, and bootjacks in it. He liked to play pool and he had installed this table in his long front hall where everyone who came in was surprised and temporarily blockaded. I wanted to take it out but the owner refused to let me do it — there was something about removal that would destroy its balance. So there it stayed and Scott thought it was an hilarious item. He used to plan stories featuring it, although so far as I know he never wrote one with the table as its chief character. Anyway, it served the purpose of giving us a constant joke and our acquaintance began around that table.

This was, as everyone knows, a period of anti-climax and defeat in Scott's life. Zelda was in a mountain sanitarium not far from Tryon. His daughter was in the Ethel Walker School and had applied for admission to Vassar when she would be graduated from the preparatory school. Scott needed money badly for both his wife and daughter and was trying to write stories that would sell.

He was not drinking a great deal. Nora Flynn was a good influence in keeping him sober, by stimulating him with her gay companionship. She was one of the Langhorne sisters of Virginia and her dislike — which was total — of alcohol derived from the fact that Lefty was a reformed alcoholic and she wanted to keep him from going back to the bottle. They did not serve drinks in their home which gave Scott a measure of safety there. We all heard that he did have drinking bouts now and then but I never saw one of them. For the most part he lived rather gloomily at the old Oak Hall Hotel, drank sodas at the drug store and wrote short stories almost furiously. I am fairly certain he was not working on a book at that time.

I never saw the glamor that had surrounded him a few years before. Of course, I had heard and read about it and he used to brag about it sometimes. "Margaret," he said once, "you wouldn't believe how Zelda and I were entertained by the truly great people of Europe." I did believe it. That was already on record, not only in the biographical pieces about him that were always popping out here and there, but also in his own novels. But what I saw in person was a pasty-faced man who didn't look healthy and wanted almost too desperately to sell what he wrote.

I was far more devoted to his work than I was to him personally. He was egotistical and certainly a literary snob. He would mock people who had been generous to him. At that time he seemed to me to be far more of a money-grubber author than I was, though I am certain that is what I was in his eyes. He resented the popularity I had with the magazine reading public at that time. He constantly talked about prices for stories — and wanted to know what I was getting for this or that one.

In one of his letters he refers with some disdain to a lady author whose fingers were covered with rings. This was supposed to be myself. At the time I was between marriages and didn't even wear a wedding ring. My only ring was an old-fashioned sapphire set with inconsequential diamonds so he made up that story out of the whole cloth.

I did not resent his feelings about myself. No one could possibly blame him. His stories were being rejected: his prices were going down; and he had to take it out on someone. A writer who he felt had a talent far inferior to his genius was fair game. But when I went to New York during that period I fought some battles for him. I would say to the editors and agents I knew, "He's a great writer — there's never been a better piece of American fiction than *The Great Gatsby* — why don't you editors do more for him?" And one or another would tell me, "Everyone has tried" or "You evidently haven't seen him rolling on the floor when he was dead drunk."

In one other letter he mentions judging a dog show in Tryon. I was one of the four judges on that occasion. Donald Peattie, the famous botanist, was another. Neither Donald nor Scott nor I knew a thing about the merits of dogs. So we left it all to the fourth member who was a local minister. We made wise-cracks. Everyone took our pictures and we took noble poses. There were days like that — not deeply gay for him but there was some laughter.

I was always rather tense with him, I think. I have no memories of really relaxed talks, nor of honest professional exchanges though we talked shop so often. But he knew I was there in the village and every now and then he found me useful.

One day he asked if he could bring Zelda to lunch and, of course, I was greatly pleased. I think I asked no one else, at his request. He brought her from the sanitarium and on the way she stopped at a pond and picked water-lilies to bring me. She seemed very vague and uncertain and Scott was magnificent with her that day, playing games, saying she was a princess in a castle. It was painful and it was beautiful to watch the effort he made to give her an hour of enjoyment.

On another day he telephoned and said he must see me about a very serious matter. He came to the house in a very troubled state of mind and told me that his daughter Scottie had been involved in some very slight escapade at school — I think she walked down the road and had a Coke out of hours — and he said that he was sure that now Vassar would not accept her. Since I was a Vassar graduate and had been a trustee would I get in touch immediately with Dean Thompson and intercede for Scottie? I told him that there was no need to worry, that Dean Mildred Thompson would not care in the least about some minor breaking of rules if his daughter's academic record was good enough to admit her to Vassar. I said I would telephone her if it would give him peace but I was sure of what I said. But he wouldn't believe me. Of course I was right.

He tried very hard to be a good husband and a wise parent. And when I think of Scott Fitzgerald — when I reread his work as I do so often — I am conscious, not of personal faults, but of his genius and his conscience, which never let him go but never could completely control his tragic life.

Duluth, Minnesota

DAVID TOOR

GUILT AND
RETRIBUTION
IN
"BABYLON REVISITED"

Roy R. Male's perceptive article on "Babylon Revisited" goes far in clearing up many of the unresolved problems that have recently been discussed in relation to the story.[1] Male has pointed out, as James Harrison had shown in an earlier note,[2] that Charlie Wales is in a sense responsible for the appearance of Duncan and Lorraine at the Peters' house at precisely the wrong moment. Male has further called into serious question the general interpretation of the story, most specifically Seymour Gross' contention that Charlie has been renovated and that the punishment he suffers is brought upon him from external sources. Gross says: "That moral renovation may not be enough is the injustice that lies at the center of the story."[3] Both Male and Harrison point out that had Charlie not given the bartender the Peters' address at the opening of the story, Duncan and Lorraine would not have shown up there and given Marion Peters a real reason to refuse to return Honoria to Charlie.

Gross' further statement, "Nor is there anything here of that troubled ambivalence which characterizes our response to that fantastic ambiguity, Jay Gatsby," seems quite wrong, because it is precisely in the troubled ambivalence of Charlie Wales that the meaning of the story is found. But Charlie's ambivalence is not the result of the fact that, as Male argues, "his is a story of suspension between two worlds," although to a great extent the story is structured on the contrasts between the past, as represented by Lorraine and Duncan, and the present, in the persons of Marion and Lincoln, but in a deeper awareness of Charlie's own guilt and his inability to work it out. It is in a kind of personal psychological morality that the meaning of the story is found.

It is convenient for Charlie to blame the errors of his past for the pains of his present — and future. But Fitzgerald's world is not a world of external retribution — you are not made to pay for what you've done — not at least by a God, or in Hemingway's words, "what we have instead of God," a code, or even by a deterministic fate. The payment is self-punishment, and the ironically disastrous result of such punishment is the intensification of the feelings of guilt. There is no expiation, only the further degeneration of the mind — neurotic reinforcement of behavior that leads eventually to total insanity or a form of suicide.

Charlie Wales is not torn between the poles of two opposing worlds so much as he is torn by his own inner sense of guilt and his inability to expiate it. He is not morally renovated, only sicker and less able to cope with the guilt. In one part of him he wants his Honoria (honor) back, but in the deeper man, the guilt-ridden one, he knows he doesn't deserve her. He has exiled himself to a dream world free of past responsibilities — Prague — where he creates the fresh image of himself as a successful businessman. Of course the image cannot hold, and his distorted view of the real world leads him into delusion and jealousy: "He wondered if he couldn't do something to get Lincoln out of his rut at the bank" (402). What kind of rut is Lincoln really in? A warm homelife that Charlie envies, children who love him, a neurotic wife, yes, but a reasonable contentment.

There are many hints through the story which point to these conclusions, and one of the most significant may be viewed as flaws in the technique of the tale. Fitzgerald chose a third-person limited point of view to tell the story, and the lapses, few as they are, are telling. All of the lapses — the shifts from limited to omniscient — are concerned with the Peters. The three most important ones directly involve Marion:

> She had built up all her fear of life into one wall and faced it toward him.

> Marion shuddered suddenly; part of her saw that Charlie's feet were planted on the earth now, and her own maternal feeling recognized the naturalness of his desire; but she had lived for a long time with a prejudice — a prejudice founded on a curious disbelief in her sister's happiness, and

which, in the shock of one terrible night, had turned to hatred for him. It had all happened at a point in her life where the discouragement of ill health and adverse circumstances made it necessary for her to believe in tangible villainy and a tangible villain.

Then, in the flatness that followed her outburst, she saw him plainly and she knew he had somehow arrived at control over the situation. Glancing at her husband, she found no help from him, and as abruptly as if it were a matter of no importance, she threw up the sponge.[4]

In a way these passages are indeed flaws. Certainly a craftsman like Henry James, whose meanings so much depend on careful control of point of view, would not have allowed them to pass. But Fitzgerald, as much a conscious artist as he was, as in the excellent handling of such matters in *The Great Gatsby*, for instance, did let them pass because, I think, perhaps he might have been too involved in the problems of this tale, as he was not in *Gatsby*. There is the possibility that these few passages can be read as consistent with a limited third-person point of view and that these were indeed Charlie's reactions to the situation.[5]

But what these flaws may represent is Charlie's attempt to somehow put himself in a position to account for the (subconscious) terrors that were plaguing him on this return to Babylon. All three of these cited passages are explanations of the sources of Marion's hostility and her resignation in the face of Charlie's apparent renovation. Charlie is convinced that Marion has seen that he is a changed man. But it becomes more and more clear as we examine the story that he himself was by no means convinced.

Aside from the early action of leaving the Peters' address for Duncan Schaeffer at the bar — and Charlie's subsequent denial of any knowledge of how Duncan could have found it out[6] — we need examine in some detail what Charlie does and says through the story to understand just how completely he is caught between the psychologically necessary self-delusion that he is somehow blameless and changed, and the deeper recognition of his own guilt.

Charlie's pose, once again, is that of the reformed alcoholic, allowing himself one drink a day to prove to himself he doesn't need it. " 'I'm going slow these days,' " he tells Alix at the beginning. " 'I've stuck to it for over a year and a half now.' " The reassurance seems to ring true — it has been a long time. But in the way that he tells himself he can face and beat alcohol, he hasn't allowed himself to try to face and beat the deeper problems. He lives in Prague, adding to Alix, " 'They don't know about me down there.' "[7] The dream world of escape, a foreign land where maybe Charlie too, doesn't know about himself. He is cooling it — going slow these days — even the taxi horns play the opening bars of *Le Plus que Lent.*[8]

The Peters' home reminds Charlie of what he has lost. It "was warm and comfortably American." He responds inwardly to the intimacy and comfort of the children in the house, but his outward reaction, while holding his daughter close to him, is to boast to the Peters about how well he himself is doing. He has more money than he'd ever had before. But he cuts it off when he sees "a faint restiveness in Lincoln's eye." His defensive opening had been wrong, he sees, but still he persists. He boasts also about the past: " 'We were a sort of royalty, almost infallible, with a sort of magic around us.' " And twice in three lines he repeats, " 'I take one drink every afternoon. . .' " (p. 386).

In one way Charlie is ready to admit to himself — and others — that he has a large burden of blame to carry, but too often this admission is qualified with either a denial, a shifting, or a sharing of the blame. As he looks at his daughter he silently hopes that she doesn't "combine the traits of both [Charlie and Helen] that had brought them to disaster." In his lyrical reminiscences of the past in Paris, especially about the money squandered, he tries to convince and justify himself: "But it hadn't been given for nothing." Hadn't it? The next passage is really quite confused, and although it sounds meaningful, in reality it is a pastiche of attempted self-justification and escape from responsibility:

> It had been given, even the most wildly squandered sum, as an offering to destiny that he might not remember the things most worth remembering, the things that now he would always remember — his child taken from his control, his wife escaped to a grave in Vermont (p. 388).

He thinks about Honoria being "taken from his control," not that "he had lost the right to her control." His wife has not "died," but has "escaped." The last part of the sentence essentially contradicts and yet reinforces the first part.

His encounters with Duncan and Lorraine demonstrate much the same kind of ineffectual self-justification: "As always, he felt Lorraine's passionate, provocative attraction, but his own rhythm was different now." After they leave the restaurant where he had been dining with Honoria, Charlie tries to separate himself from Duncan and Lorraine:

They liked him because he was functioning, because he was serious; they wanted to see him, because he was stronger than they were now, because they wanted to draw a certain sustenance from his strength (p. 391).

How do we understand this in terms of his later desire to get "Lincoln out of his rut at the bank?" We can't because of Charlie's inability to admit consciously the distorted state of his mind. Once again, it is not a conflict between the past and present, between Charlie Wales and Charles J. Wales of Prague, but between Charlie and his guilt. Charles J. Wales does not really exist, except in Charlie's limited perception.

Back at the Peters' on the evening of that first encounter with these spectres from the past, he proposes that he take Honoria back with him to Prague. He again boasts about his position and how well he is prepared to care for the girl, but he knows what he is in for — and in a way he is demanding to be punished, but he will put on an act for the Peters: "if he modulated his inevitable resentment to the chastened attitude of the reformed sinner, he might win his point in the end." But Charlie doesn't really know what his point is.

Marion, hurt and ill herself, pushes him to further self-justification: " 'You know I never did drink heavily until I gave up business and came over here with nothing to do. Then Helen and I began to run around with—' ". He is cut short, but he can't help but bring Helen into it. When Marion blames him for being in a sanitarium while Helen was dying, "He had no answer." Marion pushed him further. "Charlie gripped the sides of the chair. This was more difficult than he expected; he wanted to launch out into a long expostulation and explanation, but he only said: 'The night I locked her out—'" (p. 395).

When Marion asks him why he hadn't thought about what he had done before, and the damage he had caused to Honoria and himself, he again refuses to admit to the full blame:

"I suppose I did, from time to time, but Helen and I were getting along badly. When I consented to the guardianship, I was flat on my back in a sanitarium and the market had cleaned me out. I knew I'd acted badly, and I thought if it would bring any peace to Helen, I'd agree to anything. But now it's different. I'm functioning, I'm behaving damn well, so far as —" (p. 396).

His guilt at the damage he'd done to Helen is further reflected in the fear of what his daughter might learn about him: "sooner or later it would come out, in a word here, a shake of the head there, and some of that distrust would be irrevocably implanted in Honoria."

Marion hits Charlie hardest when she verbalizes the real and deepest source of Charlie's guilt: " 'How much you were responsible for Helen's death, I don't know. It's something you'll have to square with your own conscience.' " And this is just what Charlie can't do. "An electric current of agony surged through him. . . ." But his only outward response, after Lincoln's attempt to defend him, is, " 'Helen died of heart trouble' " (p. 397). There is no other answer Charlie can give, for to admit consciously, even for an instant that he might really have been to blame for Helen's death might permit him to face his guilt and thus enable him to start the cleansing process that might lead back towards balance.

In the reverie of Helen that follows the bitter scene ending with Marion's agreeing to return Honoria, we find evidence of his inability to admit to his blame. "The image of Helen haunted him. Helen whom he had loved so until they had senselessly begun to abuse each other's love, tear it into shreds." He excuses himself again for the events of the night he had locked her out. "When he arrived home alone he turned the key in the lock in wild anger. How could he know she would arrive an hour later alone, that there would be a snowstorm in which she wandered about in slippers, too confused to find a taxi?" The final scene of the vision of Helen that night is again part of his ambivalent attempt and refusal to find expiation. Helen seems to comfort him with tenderness and forgiveness, except that as she swings faster and faster the forgiveness is not complete: "at the end he could not hear clearly all that she said," leaving him to delude himself into half-believing the closing words of the story about Helen forgiving him.

The remaining two sections of the story, IV and V, reinforce what has gone before. Further self-delusions of himself as cured, even a garbled version of how best to raise a daughter:

> The present was the thing – work to do, and someone to love. But not to love too much, for he knew the injury that a father can do to a daughter or a mother to a son by attaching them too closely: afterward, out in the world, the child would seek in the marriage partner the same blind tenderness and, failing probably to find it, turn against love and life.[9]

This is just the kind of distortion that Charlie's mind would drive him to. Certainly there is a base in Freudian psychology for what he says, but only in his conscious rationalization of "not to love too much," can Charlie make sense out of his own inability to love fully and completely. He is too warped to see that the only love worth having or giving is one without reservations and limits.

Reference has been made in footnotes to some of the changes in the above passages between the 1931 and 1935 versions of the story. Two of the most significant changes between the two printed versions of the story occur in part IV. Both versions open with Charlie leaving the address of the Peters with the bartender to give to Duncan Schaeffer. Lorraine's later message reaches Charlie by different means in the two stories. In the 1931 version:

> Back at his hotel, Charlie took from his pocket a *pneumatique* that Lincoln had given him at luncheon. It had been redirected by Paul from the hotel bar.

In the final version:

> Back at his hotel, Charlie found a *pneumatique* that had been redirected from the Ritz bar where Charlie had left his address for the purpose of finding a certain man (p. 400).

It's likely that part of the confusion results from an oversight of Fitzgerald's in revising the manuscript.[10] But the confusion here may also be the result of Fitzgerald's intention to emphasize that Charlie was responsible for the appearance of Duncan and Lorraine at the Peters. The "certain man" in 1935 is still Duncan at the beginning of the story. And further, that if Lincoln had given him the message, as in the earlier version, Lincoln also would have known that Charlie had given out the address, and Charlie's denial would have been seen immediately as a lie. It was important that Charlie be able to continue his self-delusion without any real fear that Lincoln would know that Charlie was responsible.

Another important change is in Lorraine's invitation to Charlie after she and Duncan have barged in at the Peters: " 'Come on out to dinner. Be yourself, Charlie. Come on,' " reads the 1931 version. The final draft: " 'Come and dine. Sure your cousins won' mine. See you so sel'om. Or solemn.' " In the *TAR* version Lorraine is quite drunk, obviously intended to make Marion even angrier than in the magazine version. But Fitzgerald has cut the line, " 'Be yourself, Charlie.' " It is too obvious to Lorraine in that early version that Charlie is still Charlie, but more important, it is too obvious to Charlie that he is still what he was.

The ghastly scene at the Peters ends with Charlie getting what he was begging for subconsciously all along — Marion's rejection of his plea for Honoria. Before Charlie leaves he lies — consciously or not — to Lincoln: " 'I wish you'd explain to her [Marion] I never dreamed these people would come here. I'm just as sore as you are.' "

Charlie cannot make amends, cannot "conciliate something," as he puts it, and the story ends on a note of almost total despair. It is not by accident that his thoughts turn back to money and his imagination of the power of money. He reflects that "the snow of twenty-nine wasn't real snow. If you didn't want it to be snow, you just paid some money." Charlie hasn't been able to deal in love, but he has been able to handle money and the things money can produce. He still isn't convinced that the two are not equal, nor can he admit to himself the possibility that the main source of his troubles was his inability to love and that his present guilt feelings stem directly from that source. So he will turn back to the new old ways and instead of dealing with people, deal with things. "There wasn't much he could do now except send Honoria some things; he would send her a lot of things tomorrow. He thought rather angrily that this was just money — he had given so many people money. . . ." And that's all he had given.

In the tormented inner world of Charlie Wales, the world where God could not exist and therefore not punish, and where the individual retains, if not a sense of sin, at least a sense of guilt, we find the real conflict. "Babylon Revisited" is not a story about the inability of the world to forgive and forget, or even about a man drawn back to the past and therefore unable to come to terms with the present. It is a story about self destruction, about the human mind's ability to delude itself into thinking that what it does is based on logic and reason. The story ends with only the promise of emptiness to come in Charlie's life; it ends with the lie that may lead Charlie to destruction: "He was absolutely sure Helen wouldn't have wanted him to be so alone."

SUNY at Cortland

---

[1] Roy R. Male, " 'Babylon Revisited': The Story of the Exile's Return," *Studies in Short Fiction*, II (1965), 270-277.

[2] James Harrison, "Fitzgerald's 'Babylon Revisited,' " *Explicator*, 16 (January 1958), item 20.

[3] Seymour Gross, "Fitzgerald's 'Babylon Revisited,' " *College English*, XXV (November, 1963), 128-135.

[4] *Taps at Reveille* (New York: Scribners, 1935), pp. 396, 397, 398.

[5] Arthur Mizener, in his anthology *Modern Short Stories* (New York: Norton, 1962), contrasts the techniques of "Babylon Revisited" and Conrad's "Heart of Darkness," and, it seems to me, misses the point of these apparent lapses. He argues that a first-person narration is more effective for a presentation of "subjective reality" than one using third person (pp. 2-4). In many instances it may be true. But a strong case can certainly be made for an even more intense "subjective reality" through the use of the third person. See, for instance, the ways in which Henry James uses third-person limited narration in *Daisy Miller* or "The Liar."

[6] The denial is interesting. In the version of the story printed in 1931 in *The Saturday Evening Post*, CCIII (21 Feb. 1931), 3-5, 82-84, Charlie says, " 'They wormed this address out of Paul at the bar.' " The version printed in *Taps at Reveille* (1935), and most often anthologized, is " 'They wormed your name out of somebody.' " I discuss some further important changes between the two versions below, mainly in notes, but see William White, "The Text of 'Babylon Revisited,' " *Fitzgerald Newsletter*, No. 28 (1965), pp. 4-7, in which some of the minor variations between the different editions are discussed. White is concerned primarily with typographical errors and does not discuss the reasons for the changes between the two versions.

An interesting brief examination into some of the apparent inconsistencies and disparities in the different versions of the story is Kenneth McCollum's " 'Babylon Revisited' Revisited," in *The Fitzgerald/Hemingway Annual (1971)*, pp. 314-316. McCollum comments:

> Fitzgerald was obviously satisfied with "Babylon Revisited," as the number of revisions to the *Post* story was small . . . . Primarily, the revisions were directed toward shortening the story and sharpening the verbiage. Fitzgerald made no effort to improve the logic in the sequence of events and made only one small attempt to adjust the faulty time periods. Fitzgerald was interested in words and their effect. He chose his words carefully and well. "Babylon Revisited" can survive regardless of its faults in logic and chronology.

[7] In the magazine version the next line is "He smiled faintly," referring to Charlie. In *TAR*, this line is gone but there is a paragraph break and the next line − a paragraph by itself − is, "Alix smiled," possibly showing that Alix sensed more about Charlie than he himself knows. Alix has been in a position to have seen the changes in the Americans he had known so well when the money was flowing freely.

[8] The 1931 version does not contain the long paragraph describing the taxi trip around Paris. Fitzgerald inserted the part about the taxi horns and some further specific details and, most interestingly, the comment about never having eaten in a cheap restaurant in Paris. "Five-course dinner, four francs fifty, eighteen cents, wine included. For some odd reason he wished that he had" (384). Charlie's concern with money and its power and effect is discussed in some detail below. See also André LeVot in this number of the *Annual.*

[9] The changes from the magazine version show Fitzgerald trying to sharpen the prose and also some possibly revealing things. I italicize the words here in the earlier version that had either been cut or changed: "But not to love too much, for *Charlie had read in D. H. Lawrence,* . . ." and then, "the child would seek in the marriage partner the same blind, *unselfish,* tenderness and, failing *in all human probability* to find it, *develop a grudge* against love and life." *TAR*, p. 399.

[10]It may be the same kind of oversight we find in the *TAR* version with: "Lincoln was still swinging Honoria back and forth like a pendulum." The word "still" has no meaning here in the 1935 version, but in 1931 there is a section, later cut, about Duncan asking the Peters for a drink and we are told that Lincoln "had been somewhat uneasily occupying himself by swinging Honoria from side to side with her feet off the ground." This might relate, as some critics point out, to Charlie's vision of Helen swinging in his dream — the pendulum of passing time.

ELAINE P. MAIMON

F. Scott Fitzgerald's Book Sales: A Look at the Record

All legends do not fly at the mere touch of cold statistics. Most Fitzgerald buffs are familiar with the death and transfiguration of Fitzgerald's reputation. From the obscurity of his last years, Fitzgerald as artist first reemerged in 1951 with the posthumous publication of *The Last Tycoon*. After *The Crack-Up* in 1945 and *The Far Side of Paradise* in 1951, journalists legitimately spoke of a "Fitzgerald revival."

The purpose of the present article is to document the phenomenon of the Fitzgerald revival by studying the annual number of Fitzgerald's books that were sold in America from 1936 to 1968. Charts could proliferate, but a single one provides evidence for the major trends. The chart is derived from royalty records kindly made available by Charles Scribner's Sons, Fitzgerald's original publishers, who have always held the copyright to most of the author's work. Nevertheless, other publishers have frequently obtained licenses from Scribners to distribute books by Fitzgerald. Although these other companies have not always revealed precise annual sales, the best evidence available on these additional publications has been included here.

In 1936 nine of Fitzgerald's works — all of his novels to date, every short-story collection which he himself had compiled, and his one play — were still in print and available from Charles Scribner's

Sons. The Scribners royalty records show, nevertheless, that a total of only two hundred and ten books were sold during that year of general economic depression and particular decline of "the oracle of the Jazz Age." One must understand from this figure that the recently published *Tender Is the Night* and the later deified *The Great Gatsby* were at this time selling poorly. Although the Modern Library also had an edition of *The Great Gatsby* in print since 1934, the book was dropped in 1939 because it failed to sell.[1]

At Fitzgerald's death on 21 December 1940, his literary reputation was at its lowest point.[2] It is a commonplace of Fitzgerald criticism to repeat the inaccurate statement that all of his books were then out of print. Even Jackson Bryer falls into this trap.[3] The trap was set by Fitzgerald himself, who misunderstood certain correspondence from Scribners to imply that all of his books were going out of print in 1938 and 1939.[4] The misunderstanding was confirmed in his mind by his inability to find any of his works in Hollywood book-stores, when he wished to purchase copies for Sheilah Graham.[5] Fitzgerald's last letters to his editor, Maxwell Perkins, are thus impassioned pleas to publish an omnibus volume, revised versions of his novels, story collections – anything to reestablish his name with the reading public.[6]

In point of fact, all nine of Fitzgerald's books were in print in the year of his death, although the royalty record for *The Beautiful and Damned* was marked "out of print" as of 14 September 1940. Still this novel is included with the other eight of Fitzgerald's books in the Scribners catalogue for 1940. The real situation was actually worse than Fitzgerald himself had imagined: His books were available on order to Scribners, but no one was ordering them. On the last Scribners royalty record of which Fitzgerald himself may have been aware, that of 1940, only seventy-two copies of his books were recorded sold.

The sales charts do not tell the whole story, however. Characteristically, Fitzgerald did some informal research at the check-out desk of Los Angeles public libraries in the late thirties. On 24 December 1938, he wrote to Maxwell Perkins: "If you could see the cards for my books in the public libraries here in Los Angeles continually in demand even to this day, you would know I have never had wide distribution in some parts of the country."[7]

The thirties, we must recall, was not a decade for book-buying. In the spring of 1934, when *Tender Is the Night* first appeared, its sales were small, although it hovered between sixth and twelfth on the best-seller list.[8] Arthur Mizener maintains that during the thirties Fitzgerald had an "underground audience":

> " 'The Great Gatsby,' " says J. D. Salinger's Buddy Glass, "was my 'Tom Sawyer' when I was twelve." (Like Salinger himself, Buddy was twelve in 1931.) Writers like John O'Hara were showing its influence and younger men like Edward Newhouse and Budd Schulberg, who would presently be deeply affected by it, were discovering it.[9]

The young library-card-carrying Fitzgerald devotees in the early thirties did not limit their attention to *The Great Gatsby.* In fact, some had become Fitzgerald fans in prep school from their initial reading of *This Side of Paradise,* a book especially written to evoke a visceral response in early adolescents, who, later in life, would retain a vibration in the neurons at the name of F. Scott Fitzgerald. In a story written for *Esquire* in 1964 Vance Bourjaily speaks for many underground readers of Fitzgerald through his protagonist Professor Short. This English teacher, who was born during the twenties, as a youth devoured copies of *Tales at the Jazz Age* and *Flappers and Philosophers* in his prep school library. Later, he rediscovered Fitzgerald in Editions for the Armed Forces on "a troopship going to Africa."[10]

Although Fitzgerald devotees avidly read library copies of the master's works during the thirties, few could claim ownership of their favorite volumes. In 1941, as a reaction to Fitzgerald's death at the end of the previous year and to the widespread magazine and newspaper obituaries, Fitzgerald's sales reached a six-year high – but only of 237 books. On 27 October 1941, however, the incomplete *The Last Tycoon* (edited by Edmund Wilson) was published posthumously in a single volume with *The Great Gatsby,* "May Day," "The Diamond as Big as the Ritz," "Absolution," and "Crazy Sunday." This new publication brought the total sales figures for 1942 to 3669, although both *This Side of Paradise* and *The Vegetable* had gone out of print on 15 July 1941.

On 27 July 1942, both *Tender Is the Night* and *Flappers and Philosophers* went out of print. With the only five books in print, the sales of Fitzgerald's works for 1943 and 1944 were over five hundred volumes a year, better than the record during any of the last five years of his life.

In September 1945, the Viking Press published *The Portable F. Scott Fitzgerald,* selected by Dorothy Parker, with an introduction by John O'Hara. This volume included the complete texts of *The Great Gatsby* and *Tender Is the Night* along with selected short stories. According to Viking sales records, the Viking Portable sold over 18,000 copies in the four remaining months of 1945. In 1946, the composite volume sold over 11,000 copies and continued to sell well until it went out of print in October 1950, when Scribners withdrew from Viking its permission to publish the copyrighted material. Fitzgerald's books have frequently been popular choices for paperbound formats. In 1945 Bantam Books published a first printing of *The Great Gatsby*, which was in a fourth Bantam printing by 1951. It is important to note that during years when Scribners sales would indicate an almost forgotten Fitzgerald, his artistic creations were before the public through other sources. Not the least of these were excerpts from Fitzgerald's novels and entire short stories reprinted in various anthologies, especially between 1945 and 1950.[11]

New Directions also gave the Fitzgerald bandwagon a sturdy push in that key year, 1945, when in June it published Edmund Wilson's edition of Fitzgerald's *The Crack-Up.* Late in 1945 New Directions, obviously wanting to bring out something on the coat-tails of *The Crack-Up,* obtained a two-year license from Scribners for a New Classics ($1.00) edition of *The Great Gatsby,* which was published with a laudatory introduction by Lionel Trilling, who, in 1950, printed this introduction in an expanded form in his *The Liberal Imagination.*

The Scribners figures fail to indicate the groundswell of interest in Fitzgerald in 1945. *Publishers' Weekly* reported on this renewed popularity in September of that year:

> The first printing of "The Crack-Up" sold out three days after publication and a second printing, to be ready September 15, is all sold out in advance. The book has been widely reviewed and had the front page space in the *New York Herald Tribune Weekly Book Review* on August 12. Many of the critics, in reviewing the book, have also written at length of Fitzgerald's early novels.[12]

Whereas *The Crack-Up* stimulated widespread response in the press, the two Fitzgerald titles published by Editions for the Armed Services probably initiated interest in Fitzgerald among a great many young readers. *The Great Gatsby,* distributed in 1945, and a special anthology, *The Diamond as Big as the Ritz and Other Stories,* distributed in 1946, appeared among the 1324 titles sent free to American armed forces at home and overseas. Between the autumn of 1943 and the autumn of 1947, these paperbound volumes, especially designed to fit into a soldier's pocket, were the only books easily accessible to millions of Americans.[13]

The interest planted by the Two Fitzgerald titles in the Editions for the Armed Services took some time to germinate, although in 1946 Scribners published an inexpensive edition of *The Great Gatsby,* which sold two thousand copies in its single year of publication.[14] In 1947, However, the volume including *The Last Tycoon* and *The Great Gatsby* and selected stories was the only Fitzgerald publication produced by Scribners' presses. On 7 May 1947, *All the Sad Young Men, Tales of the Jazz Age,* and *Taps at Reveille* joined the growing number of books by Fitzgerald in the "out of print" column. So in 1947, 1948, 1949, and 1950, Fitzgerald's original publishers printed only one volume by a top author of the twenties.

Grosset and Dunlap partially filled the gap left by Scribners in the late forties. In 1947 they brought out *This Side of Paradise* in their "Books of Distinction" series, and, in 1949, they printed an inexpensive edition of *The Great Gatsby.* Although this publisher has not made the precise sales figures available, we must take note of these additional publications.

In 1950 Scribners took advantage of their copyrights by gradually withdrawing the licenses which they had granted to other publishers to produce the works of F. Scott Fitzgerald. In the same year Scribners' own sales for their only Fitzgerald publication, *The Last Tycoon* (together with *The Great Gatsby* and Selected Stories), tripled the sales of the previous year by jumping to 866. By the next year, 1951, *Tender Is the Night* and *This Side of Paradise* were back in print and matching or exceeding the sales of *The Last Tycoon,* which itself was selling over five thousand copies. In addition, scribners' new full-size publication, *The Stories of F. Scott Fitzgerald* (edited by Malcolm Cowley), sold over thirteen thousand copies in the first six months of publication. Among the few outside editions that Scribners did allow to appear in 1951 was a thirty-five cent Bantam edition of the original version of *Tender Is the Night,* which sold out a first printing of 240,000 copies within the first month of publication, with sixty-two per cent of the sale in the first ten days.[15] Permabooks, also in 1951, published their edition of *The Beautiful and Damned.* These sales figures provide objective evidence that the Fitzgerald revival was well underway.

Books written about Fitzgerald were also in great demand during the revival years of 1950 and 1951. Budd Schulberg's *The Disenchanted,* published by Random House late in 1950, sold five thousand copies in the single month of January 1951. Five days after publication in January 1951, Arthur Mizener's biography of Fitzgerald, *The Far Side of Paradise,* had already sold twenty thousand copies.[16] By the end of that year Houghton Mifflin had sold 42,287 copies of the biography, while the Book Find Club distributed an additional 30,032 copies.

After these large sales in the peak year of 1951, the revival entered a period of relative quiescence between 1952 and 1958. In 1953 Scribners' diminishing sales might have indicated that the Fitzgerald revival had been nothing more than a nostalgic fad of the season. But in 1954 the graphs began to climb again until the total sales of Fitzgerald's works in 1958 nearly doubled those of 1951.

One factor which helped Fitzgerald sales after 1958 was Holt, Rinehart and Winston's 1958 publication of Sheilah Graham's *Beloved Infidel.* The first edition of twenty thousand copies was sold out before publication.[17] The cover of the Bantam paperback announces that one million copies are now in print. On the tide of this renewed popular interest in the Fitzgerald legend, Scribners completed their trade list of Fitzgerald's novels in the late fifties. In 1958 Scribners reprinted *The Beautiful and Damned,* reissued the single volume trade edition of *The Great Gatsby,* and published *The Last Tycoon* alone in its own volume. Although Mizener's edition of *Afternoon of an Author* had been published in 1957 by the Princeton University Library, Scribners brought out a trade edition, also in 1958.

In 1959, *Flappers and Philosophers* was reissued, while *Taps at Reville* was reissued in 1960. Although *Tales of the Jazz Age* has never been reissued as such, Scribners have published *Six Tales of the Jazz Age and Other Stories* in a trade edition (1960) and in paper (1968). Besides Malcolm Cowley's edition of *The Stories of F. Scott Fitzgerald* in both a trade and Scribner Library format, other story volumes include *Babylon Revisited and Other Stories,* trade and paper (1960) and *The Pat Hobby Stories,* trade (1962) and paper (1970).

In the past decade Scribners has been the sole publisher of Fitzgerald's works, except for Dell Publishing Company which was granted a license in 1966 to print *The Letters of F. Scott Fitzgerald* in a paperbound edition. Scribners published the trade edition of the *Letters* (edited by Andrew Turnbull) in 1963 and a selection, *Letters to His Daughter,* in 1965. For an evaluation of Fitzgerald's popular reputation indicated by the sale of his books in the sixties, we need not look beyond Scribners' royalty records, which show that well over 100,000 of Fitzgerald's books have been sold annually.

The major upswing of Fitzgerald sales in the sixties must be accounted for, in part at least, by the soft-cover Scribner Library editions, which provide well-bound, easy-to-read volumes at reasonable prices. Not only has Fitzgerald always done well in paperbound volumes, but the Scribner Library editions have helped to disseminate the author's works to a student population. College English instructors tend to limit their selection of novels in a six or seven book literature course only to books available in soft-cover. As early as 1953 Scribners appealed directly to this large college market with a clothbound omnibus volume, *Three Novels of F. Scott Fitzgerald: The Great Gatsby, Tender Is the Night, The Last Tycoon.* This edition is still in print and doing well. In 1957, *The Great Gatsby* appeared alone in a student's edition, which was incorporated into the Scribner Library in 1960. Still in print, however, in addition to the trade and Scribner Library editions of *Gatsby,* are two editions, one hardbound (published in 1961), the other in paper (published in 1968), with a format and exercises designed specifically for high school students.

Most recently, in 1968, *The Great Gatsby* was published in a large-type edition, indicating, perhaps, that Fitzgerald's appeal extends to the old and myopic as well as to the youthful and clear-eyed. As the new decade develops, the sales figures indicate that Fitzgerald's artistic reputation is assured. The annual sale of Fitzgerald's books is now within range of the half-million mark.

Haverford College

AMERICAN SALES OF BOOKS
WRITTEN BY F. SCOTT FITZGERALD,
PUBLISHED BY CHARLES SCRIBNER'S SONS

Year	Number of Single Books (in Various Editions) in Print	Total Sales
1936	9	210
1937	9	173
1938	9	96
1939	9	114
1940	8	72
1941	8	233
1942	7	3,669
1943	6	519

1944	5		546
1945	5		433
1946	2		2,941
1947	1	*Last Tycoon*	173
1948	1	*& Great*	340
1949	1	*Gatsby* in	278
1950	1	single volume	866
1951	4		29,821
1952	4		3,851
1953	5		4,366
1954	5		4,915
1955	5		6,992
1956	5		11,178
1957	6		22,276
1958	9		57,351
1959	9		56,063
1960	12		177,849
1961	12		156,104
1962	13		205,831
1963	15		249,188
1964	15		274,325
1965	16		344,080
1966	16		454,973
1967	16		480,256
1968	16		448,420

[1] Arthur Mizener, "Gatsby, 35 Years Later," *New York Times Book Review* (24 April 1960), 46.

[2] For an early clarification of this problem, see "Did F Die OP?" *Fitzgerald Newsletter* (Washington, D. C., Microcard Editions, 1969), #16 (Winter 1962), p. 76.

[3] Jackson R. Bryer, "Introduction," *The Critical Reputation of F. Scott Fitzgerald: A Bibliographical Study* (New Haven: Archon, 1967), p. xiii.

[4] *The Letters of F. Scott Fitzgerald*, ed. Andrew Turnbull (New York: Scribners, 1963), pp. 277-282, 290.

[5] Sheilah Graham and Gerold Frank, *Beloved Infidel: The Education of a Woman* (New York: Bantam Books, 1959), p. 141.

[6] Fitzgerald, *Letters.* pp. 280-282.

[7] Fitzgerald, *Letters,* p. 282.

[8] Fitzgerald, *Letters,* p. 537.

[9] Mizener, "Gatsby, 35 Years Later," p. 46.

[10] Vance Bourjaily, "Fitzgerald Attends My Fitzgerald Seminar," *Esquire,* LXII (Sept. 1964), 195.

[11] Henry Dan Piper, "F. Scott Fitzgerald: A Check List," *Princeton University Library Chronicle,* XIII (Summer 1951), 196-208.

[12]"The F. Scott Fitzgerald Revival," *Publishers' Weekly*, CXLVIII (8 Sept. 1945), 965.

[13]John A. Jamieson, *Editions for the Armed Services, Inc.* (New York: Editions for the Armed Services, 1948), pp. 1-31.

[14]Although I have never seen a copy of this printing of *The Great Gatsby*, royalty records at Scribners indicate that in 1946 a "cheap" edition of *The Great Gatsby* sold 2,000 copies.

[15]"Tips for the Bookseller," *Publishers' Weekly*, CLIX (10 Feb. 1951), 879-80.

[16]"Tips for the Bookseller," pp. 879-80.

[17]Sheilah Graham, *The Rest of the Story* (New York: Bantam, 1965), p. 158.

JOAN M. ALLEN

THE MYTH

OF

FITZGERALD'S PROSCRIPTION

DISPROVED

Scott Fitzgerald was ever acutely aware of his mortality. A man who lived so frenetic a public life and who in his private times often fought not to succumb to the "dark night of the soul" had faced the awesome inevitability more often and truly than most. Before it came, he had made known his wishes about his funeral and burial both in conversation and legal document.

After his father died, Fitzgerald often said that he wanted to be buried with him and his family in the Catholic St. Mary's Cemetery at Rockville, Maryland, because it "was very friendly leaving him there with all his relations around him."[1] Optimistic about his financial future in Hollywood when he made his will in 1937, Fitzgerald stipulated that "Part of my estate is first to provide for a funeral in keeping with my station in life." Later when it became clear that the vagaries of his employers would not allow him to amass a fortune as he had hoped, he replaced "for a funeral" with "the cheapest funeral" and added "The same to be without undue ostentation or unnecessary expense."[2]

Even though he had made preparations, Fitzgerald was hardly ready to die. In his work on *The Last Tycoon* he knew that he had found his novelist's voice again and that he was creating a work with the economy and power of *The Great Gatsby*. He was excited about his new novel, and the work was going well when his second heart

175

attack killed him and ended his dream of personal and artistic vindication.

Fitzgerald had not been ready for his death in another respect. In order for a Catholic to be buried in consecrated ground with the rites of the Church he must have been in a "state of grace" at the time of his death. To achieve this he must have been a practicing Catholic, have received final absolution from a priest, confessed his guilt and asked for forgiveness on his own, or received absolution even after his death. The latter is made possible by the Church's concession that absolution can be given until that time when all life has left the body. Although this is a clinical medical matter, the Church has set a general limit of three hours after death. Not one of these conditions had been met in Fitzgerald's case. We know that he had ceased to practice his religion almost twenty years before, and a priest was not summoned either before or after his death. In her affective account in *Beloved Infidel,* Sheilah Graham tells us that she and Fitzgerald were alone when he abruptly lost consciousness and died within a few minutes, and in the confusion that ensued she lost control of the situation. That in any event it would not have occurred to her to call for a priest is evident in her letter to Fitzgerald's daughter written a few weeks later. One of his relatives had asked Miss Graham if a priest had been with Fitzgerald. She replied that it had been too sudden for such considerations, but she told Scottie, "I didn't tell her that Scott had abandoned the Catholic religion years ago and was definitely against all that sort of thing."[3]

Nevertheless, in accordance with his wishes, shortly after his death, Fitzgerald's body was sent from California to Baltimore and then on to the Pumphrey Funeral Home in Bethesda. There he waited in silent appeal like Gatsby while a few friends tried to arrange the burial he had requested.

Arthur Mizener in his account of the circumstances of Fitzgerald's burial in *The Far Side of Paradise* inadvertently created a bit of mythology that has endured for twenty years. Mizener said that Fitzgerald was refused burial in St. Mary's Cemetery because "his books were proscribed and he had not died a good Catholic."[4] The latter is certainly true, but, in fact, Fitzgerald's books have never been proscribed by the Catholic Church. Andrew Turnbull did not repeat the error in his biography where he states the case thus: "Fitzgerald had wanted to be buried with his family in the Catholic cemetery in Rockville, but since he had died a non-believer the Bishop raised objections, and he was buried in the Union Cemetery not far away."[5] However, Mizener's statement has been repeated without documentation in subsequent books by Kenneth Eble,[6] Nancy Milford,[7] and Sara Mayfield,[8] and in a recent newspaper feature article.[9]

Mizener has said that he based his assertion that Fitzgerald's books were proscribed on the narrative of one of the men who was involved in arranging the burial, John Biggs, who was Fitzgerald's Princeton roommate.[10] Judge Biggs with Eben Finney, who had also known Fitzgerald at school, and Fitzgerald's lawyer, Edgar Poe, made repeated requests to the office of Michael Joseph Curley, the Archbishop of Baltimore, for permission for a Catholic burial, and at this late date Judge Biggs can recall only that he was told by a monsignor in the Bishop's office that Fitzgerald would not be allowed a Catholic funeral because his writings were undesirable and he had not made his "Easter duty."[11] "Easter duty" refers to a Catholic's obligation each year to receive the sacraments of Confession and Communion within the six weeks before and the eight weeks after Easter Sunday and the fact that one is in a state of excommunication if he does not fulfill this requisite.

Although Mizener, Turnbull, and Mayfield attribute the refusal of a Catholic burial to the Bishop, there is no hard evidence to support this. Since there is no trace of anything to do with Scott Fitzgerald in the records of Archbishop Curley's administration, nothing concerning either censure of his books or the difficulties of his burial, it is not clear that Curley himself was involved in this matter.[12] The appeals of Biggs and the others could very well have been handled by a minor official. It is possible that Curley either privately felt that Fitzgerald's writings were undesirable or that he publicly denounced them from his pulpit, but he never took any official action against them, nor did he record his disapproval of Fitzgerald.

Further evidence is provided by a brief examination of the history and nature of the *Index Liborum Prohibitorum.* The first list of forbidden books was compiled by Pope Innocent I in 405, but it was not until the onset of the era of the printed word and the growth of literacy that Innocent VIII in 1476 decreed that all books must be submitted to local Church authorities for examination, and the use of the Imprimatur was thus begun. The Council of Trent which met in the years 1545-1563 elaborated and codified the regulations governing Church sanction of literature, and they remained in force for the next three hundred years. Leo XIII amended the general rules in 1897, and the revised *Index* was published in 1900 with the stipulation that "Henceforth, only those books pertaining to matters of faith and morals were to undergo the requirements for Church approval before publication."[13] Prior to this, not only books of an heretical nature but also those containing anything even mildly critical of the Church or a social or political theory not in accord with the Church's position were the objects of censure. Thus the works of Descartes, Hobbes, Mill, Rousseau, and Locke are listed in the *Index*. Although the *Code of Canon Law* governing the composition of the *Index* was set down by Benedict XIV in 1917, there is no general rule concerning novels. Thus it is only from inferences drawn from a survey of the novels which have been listed that one can conclude what sort of fiction the Church has found objectionable. Some of the novels mentioned in the *Index* are *Pamela, A Sentimental Journey Through France and Italy, The Red and the Black,* and *Madame Bovary.*[14]

The *Index,* which is a summation of all condemned books referred to the Vatican for official pronouncement, has never been a complete list of objectionable literature. It is conceivable that some American churchmen disapproved of Fitzgerald's writings, but none of them followed the prescribed procedure to condemn them officially, for Fitzgerald never appeared in the *Index*. Furthermore, none of the obituaries or retrospective assessments of Fitzgerald's career published at the time of his death mentioned proscription, a point which would have been of great interest and importance.

All appeals denied, Fitzgerald's friends arranged a service for him not without its ironies. They found a young, newly-ordained Episcopal minister, the Reverend Raymond P. Black, who was willing to officiate. When he was told who the deceased was, he said that "it made no particular difference to [him]" who it was.[15] Mr. Black conducted the brief service at the chapel, and Andrew Turnbull, who was present, observed that "It was as if nothing were being said *of* him or *to* him that the heart could hear."[16] Then as if in cruel parody of Gatsby's obsequies, the mourners drove in the rain at dusk to Rockville Cemetery where the simple Episcopal graveside rite was intoned. Dorothy Parker had earlier echoed the benediction of Owl-eyes for Gatsby which was painfully appropriate, "The poor son-of-a-bitch."

The decision of the representative of the Church has been difficult to accept for those who do not share his principles and commitment and, especially, the dogmatism of the Church he served. Although it may not allay one's resentment or anger, one should consider, however, that he acted as he felt he must in accord with his beliefs. Some small comfort may be drawn from the fact that this clergyman inadvertently set the stage for the reunion of Fitzgerald with his wife, Zelda Sayre, beneath a common headstone.

Toms River, New Jersey

---

[1] F. Scott Fitzgerald, *Tender Is the Night* (New York: Scribners, 1934), p. 267.

[2] Arthur Mizener, *The Far Side of Paradise: A Biography of F. Scott Fitzgerald*, 2nd ed. rev. (Boston: Houghton Mifflin Sentry, 1965), p. 336.

[3] Sheilah Graham to Frances Scott Fitzgerald, 14 January 1941, F. Scott Fitzgerald Papers, Princeton University Library, Princeton, New Jersey.

[4] Mizener, p. 336.

[5] Andrew Turnbull, *Scott Fitzgerald* (New York: Scribners, 1962), p. 321.

[6] In this and the following footnotes I quote the passage to show the writer's obvious indebtedness to Mizener. Kenneth E. Eble, *F. Scott Fitzgerald* (New Haven: College and University Press, 1963), p. 58. "At his death his books were proscribed by the Church, and he was not permitted burial in hallowed ground."

[7] Nancy Milford, *Zelda: A Biography* (New York: Harper and Row, 1970), p. 350: "Scott was denied the Catholic burial he had wanted because he had not died within the church. His books were proscribed. Therefore, he was not buried in the old tiny Catholic cemetery among the Scotts, the Keys, and the Fitzgeralds, but close by in the Rockville Union Cemetery."

[8] Sara Mayfield, *Exiles from Paradise* (New York: Delacorte Press, 1971), p. 279: "Because he had renounced Catholicism, died without supreme [extreme] unction, and his books had been proscribed, the bishop refused to allow him to be interred in hallowed ground."

[9] "Inconspicuous Tombstone Marks Fitzgeralds' Grave," Times-Post Service, *Asbury Park* [New Jersey] *Sunday Press* (April 2, 1972) sec. 3, p. C8: ". . . when Fitzgerald died . . . the Catholic Church denied his request. Church officials stated that Fitzgerald had not died a good Catholic because his books were proscribed by the Church . . ."

[10] Arthur Mizener to Joan M. Allen, 7 December 1971.

[11] John Biggs, Jr. to JMA, 10 March 1972.

[12] Rev. Michael J. Arrowsmith, Assistant Chancellor, Archdiocese of Washington, D.C. to JMA, 13 February 1972.

[13] Redmond A. Burke, *What Is the Index?* (Milwaukee: Bruce, 1952), p. 8.

[14] *Index Liborum Prohibitorum*, Iusso Editus (Roma: Typis Polyglottis Vaticanis, MDCCCCXLVIII).

[15] *Asbury Park Sunday Press*, p. C8.

[16] Turnbull, p. 322.

LAWRENCE D. STEWART

"ABSOLUTION"

AND

The Great Gatsby

It is no secret that Scott Fitzgerald's short story, "Absolution," began as a prologue to *The Great Gatsby* but was dropped because, as Fitzgerald himself wrote in 1934, "I preferred to preserve the sense of mystery."[1] The merit of this revision has been much debated: it is unlikely that Mrs. Wharton knew of "Absolution's" connection with the novel, but her letter of 8 June 1925 to Fitzgerald – which Fitzgerald called one of the few "intelligable" criticisms his book had received – would seem to argue for inclusion of the short story.[2] Other critics hold to judicative indecisiveness, observing either that "Actually the book gains as well as loses by the blurredness of Gatsby; it gains in mystery what it loses in defini- tion,"[3] or that "The blurring of Gatsby, if it is a defect, is also a virtue, in that it renders his fantastic illusion more believable."[4]

Such statements – including the one by Fitzgerald – sound as though the omission of "Absolution" had been a matter of taste. If the *Gatsby* prologue was much like the published short story, how- ever, I think that Fitzgerald was compelled to eliminate it; for "Absolution" and *The Great Gatsby*, though they share a few super- ficial similarities, are basically irreconcilable.[5]

I

The manuscripts and galley proofs of "Absolution" seem to have disappeared; Fitzgerald's records, however, indicate that the story was written in June 1923.[6] The only extant manuscript of *The Great Gatsby* makes no allusion to "Absolution"; therefore, the only evidence for what the story was is what the story is. First published in the June 1924 *American Mercury* — nearly a year before the novel came out — it was in 1926 included in *All the Sad Young Men,* Fitzgerald's third collection of short stories. For this volume, Fitzgerald made incidental verbal revisions in sixteen places, only one or two of them suggesting any change in his intention.[7]

The published story shows certain clear affinities to *The Great Gatsby:* both Mr. Gatz and Mr. Miller greatly admire James J. Hill; neither Rudolph Miller nor Jimmy Gatz believes himself the son of his parents, each having invented an alter ego; the imagery of rundown clocks and falling leaves is common to both accounts; and there is even occasionally heard the same voice as storyteller: "Perhaps in the houses of delinquency among the dull and hardeyed incorrigible girls can be found those for whom has burned the whitest fire" (115-116) must be Carraway speaking, the same man who once said of Tom and Daisy (in the manuscript, in lines not published), "they didn't seem quite so remotely rich if they enjoyed the supposition that I was possessed by the flowery lust. After all they too had once walked in all innocence through the charmed garden."

We might best try "Absolution" as an adjunct to *The Great Gatsby* if we view the novel's protagonist as an Alger hero and find "the deepness of the roots of Gatsby's dream in the deprivations of his past."[8] But the hypothesis will not stand the testing; for how do the deprivations in Rudolph's life account for the preposterous expression Gatsby gives his dreams? In Rudolph, Fitzgerald emphasizes the universality of all boyhood daydreams as release valves from unpleasant pressures. But Gatsby's dreams, like the man himself, are more than this: he has singularity ("an extraordinary gift for hope, a romantic readiness such as I have never found in any other person and which it is not likely I shall ever find again," says Carraway); and as he becomes the dream, there is no longer for him an out-of-dream existence.

Only once in "Absolution" did Fitzgerald even momentarily suggest that Rudolph's fancies could evolve into Gatsby's dreams. The passage comes after the boy's second lie in confession:

An invisible line had been crossed, and he had become aware of his isolation – aware that it applied not only to those moments when he was Blatchford Sarnemington but that it applied to all his inner life. Hitherto such phenomena as "crazy" ambitions and petty shames and fears had been but private reservations, unacknowledged before the throne of his official soul. Now he realized unconsciously that his private reservations were himself – and all the rest a garnished front and a conventional flag (124).

But Fitzgerald did not end his paragraph with notions of Rudolph's uniqueness. Instead, he concluded: "The pressure of his environment had driven him into the lonely secret road of adolescence" – and we pass from the individual to the universal. The eleven-year-old boy is already moving toward "the air cushions that lie on the asphalts of fourteen," Fitzgerald's *This Side of Paradise* survey of the road through adolescence.

In the worlds of "Absolution" and *The Great Gatsby* few characters worship the same god; certainly Rudolph Miller and Jay Gatsby do not stand before the same god. Orthodox religion threatens and terrifies Rudolph, and his consuming fear of God makes him shift defensively into feelings of superiority to the Divinity. The priest's madness confirms his suspicion that "There was something ineffably gorgeous somewhere that had nothing to do with God" (131) – this, the outcome of his earlier practice of reserving "a corner of his mind where he was safe from God, where he prepared the subterfuges with which he often tricked God" (117). Ultimately, "He no longer thought that God was angry at him about the original lie, because He must have understood that Rudolph had done it to make things finer in the confessional, brightening up the dinginess of his admissions by saying a thing radiant and proud" (131). He never felt identification with God, and the last remark suggests the shaky alliance he formed with the Divinity.

Jay Gatsby, however, "sprang from his Platonic conception of himself. He was a son of God—" and his dreams develop in Biblical imagery: Jacob's ladder, the confrontation in the Temple, the Platonism of the Gospel of John. With respect to this parallelism between Christ and Gatsby we can ironically appreciate Fitzgerald's use of "mystery" as an explanation for the story's cancellation, for we learn of Gatsby's life only at selected moments, in the same way that we know of Christ's at isolated intervals. Little in either account tells us of the protagnoists except when their actions are fulfillments of their inspired purposes. We cannot therefore legitimately want "more" about Gatsby's childhood when "more" would violate this aspect of Fitzgerald's intention. Even if that objection were met, "Absolution" itself never would have served: for in the use of religious imagery and ideas, Jay Gatsby has his predecessor not in the small boy, Rudolph, but in the priest, Father Schwartz.

II

With an account of the priest's plight we begin "Absolution"; with a final vision of his despair, we leave it. Assuredly, the story is much concerned with "the transition in Rudolph,"[9] but desire to connect the story to the novel has deflected attention from the equally important, dedicated man "who, in the still of the night, wept cold tears . . . because the afternoons were warm and long, and he was unable to attain a complete mystical union with our Lord" (109).

The priest is driven mad by contacts with this world, and he finds the shrill laughter of girls "a terrible dissonance," the scent of cheap toilet soap "desperately sweet," the Dakota wheat fields "terrible to look upon," and four o'clock of the afternoon a "hot madness." The only thing in the world lovely to him is an amusement park, because "it won't remind you of anything, you see. It will all just hang out there in the night like a colored balloon − like a big yellow lantern on a pole" (130). But even it must be regarded circumspectly − "a little way off from it in a park place − under dark trees . . . But don't get up close . . . because if you do you'll only feel the heat and the sweat and the life" (130). He never forgets his own repeated admonition: "my theory is that when a whole lot of people get together in the best places things go glimmering all the time" (129). It is a curiously inappropriate conversation to hold with a child; no wonder Rudolph thinks the priest is mad.

But nothing indicates that Fitzgerald himself regarded the priest's dilemma with amusement. One of the revisions he made in the story after its first publication was the alteration of the priest's concluding words with Rudolph: once "inarticulate and dim and terrible," they are now "inarticulate and heart-broken" (131); it is a small revision, but it suggests Fitzgerald's increasing sympathy for the priest as we see him − significantly, not through Rudolph's uncomprehending eyes.

The priest's disappointed desire for "a complete mystical union with our Lord" balances with his awareness of the physical unions which are presumably everywhere possible. Living in a world where all is ripeness, he finds denied him the one union he desires. Sexual frustration probably does contribute to the involutions in his behavior, but surely it is an oversimplification to dismiss Father Schwartz's problem as "the incoherent frustrations of the old Catholic priest, celibate by profession."[10] Certainly Fitzgerald's treatment of the man encourages another interpretation.

Was it not Fitzgerald's intention to use the language of physical fulfillment in a mystical sense, to suggest the priest's permanent three o'clock in the morning? The priest desperately needs an object to symbolize his yearning for God, and finds it, ironically, in a glittering amusement park because "it won't remind you of anything, you see." Only by comprehending his character can we understand how he has changed a "vast, vulgar, and meretricious beauty" into a mystical symbol. But this was to be the practice too of Jay Gatsby when he converted the tawdriness of the world into his secret symbols: a green light into a girl, a girl's voice into magical money, a girl herself into a manifestation of the Divine.

Until the creation of Jay Gatsby, Father Schwartz remained Fitzgerald's best example of the tragic, dream-haunted man. Because Father Schwartz is a Father, Fitzgerald can take these longings and, through the character of the man, transform them into a gaudy, glittering symbol without implying that the dreams themselves are worthless. With Gatsby, Fitzgerald worked conversely: cheap and obvious dreams were spoken of in religious language to point up Gatsby's devotion without implying that the objects ever became what the hero saw in them. We always keep a double vision with these committed men. We know the amusement park is sordid; but we also appreciate how to Father Schwartz it is pure. We know the worthlessness of Daisy and all of Gatsby's pursuits; but because we look through his eyes too, we see her and them as he would have us do.

"Absolution" stands as prologue to *The Great Gatsby* only as the harbinger of tragedy: the destruction of the priest foreshadows what must inevitably happen to Gatsby and his more intense dreams. But the short story's alleged Gatsby-as-boy is a child who has no awareness of Father Schwartz's dilemma and who uses the priest's behavior as justification for developing quite different notions. It takes uncommon faith to believe that Rudolph could have evolved into the man who gave his name to Fitzgerald's most polished novel.

San Fernando Valley State College

[1] *Letters of F. Scott Fitzgerald,* ed. Andrew Turnbull (New York: Scribners, 1963), p. 509. Ten years earlier, on 18 June 1924, Fitzgerald had told Max Perkins the story "was to have been the prologue of the novel but it interfered with the neatness of the plan" (p. 164). Recently Henry Dan Piper in his *Fitzgerald's "The Great Gatsby": The Novel, The Critics, The Background* (New York: Scribners, 1970) has said that "Absolution" "served at one stage as the first chapter of a discarded early version of the novel" (p. 1) and that Fitzgerald "intended 'Absolution' at one time to be the opening chapter of an early version of *The Great Gatsby"* (p. 83). Prof. Piper gives no evidence justifying the translation of Fitzgerald's term, "prologue," into either "first chapter" or "opening chapter."

[2] F. Scott Fitzgerald, *The Crack-Up,* ed. Edmund Wilson (New York: New Directions, 1945), p. 309; however, Mrs. Wharton appears to have been interested more in the first years of the newly-created Jay Gatsby than she was in the formative years of Jimmy Gatz. Fitzgerald's editor similarly complained about the vagueness of Gatsby's history when he first read the manuscript; cf. letter of Maxwell Perkins to Fitzgerald, 20 November 1924, asking for more details about Gatsby's present as well as past (*Editor to Author: The Letters of Maxwell E. Perkins,* ed. John Hall Wheelock [New York: Scribners, 1950], p. 39).

[3] Malcolm Cowley (ed.), *The Stories of F. Scott Fitzgerald* (New York: Scribners, 1951), p. xviii.

[4] James E. Miller, Jr., *F. Scott Fitzgerald: His Art and His Technique* (New York: New York University Press, 1964), p. 116. Also cf. Robert Sklar, *F. Scott Fitzgerald: The Last Laocoon* (New York: Oxford University Press, 1967), p. 174: "there was a plan, and its form required that the hero's origins remain mysterious to the end." Cf. also pp. 223-24.

[5] For an interpretation that sees *Gatsby* growing out of "Absolution," and not irreconcilable to it, cf. Henry Dan Piper, *F. Scott Fitzgerald: A Critical Portrait* (New York: Holt, Rinehart & Winston, 1965), pp. 13, 103-7. Also cf. Henry Dan Piper, "The Untrimmed Christmas Tree: The Religious Background of *The Great Gatsby,"* in *Fitzgerald's "The Great Gatsby",* pp. 93-100. Also cf. Sklar, pp. 159-60, 173-74, 186.

[6] Piper, *Fitzgerald: Critical Portrait,* p. 103.

[7] Rudolph's father originally was described as being "Somewhat gross and utterly deficient in curiosity . . ." Fitzgerald recast this to "Somewhat gross, he was, nevertheless, insufficiently hard-headed . . ." (118). (All parenthetical page references are to F. Scott Fitzgerald, *All the Sad Young Men* [New York: Scribners, 1926].) The punctuation of the two versions differs considerably. Fitzgerald revised primarily to smooth the flow of his rhetoric. One small change recalls his fascination for certain words: in 1925, after the first printing of *Gatsby* had come from the press in April, "echolalia" began reverberating in Fitzgerald's mind. Before the second printing in August 1925 he had the plates amended to replace "the chatter of the garden" (p. 60) with "the echolalia of the garden." Originally "Absolution" neared its conclusion with the priest collapsed upon the floor, "filling his room, filling it with voices and faces until it was crowded with shadowy movements, and rang loud with a steady, shrill note of laughter." For *All the Sad Young Men,* Fitzgerald converted "shadowy movements" to "echolalia."

[8] Miller, p. 115.

[9] Miller, p. 103. Arthur Mizener, *The Far Side of Paradise* (Boston: Houghton Mifflin, 1965; revised ed.), p. 214 sees the story as a contrast between "a romantic young man, who has a bad conscience and dreams of himself as a worldly hero named Blatchford Sarnemington, with a spoiled priest, who is filled with piety and a maddening dream of a life like an eternal amusement park."

[10] Miller p. 104. Piper, *Fitzgerald: Critical Portrait*, pp. 106-7, insists: "Rudolph is so much more attractive a character than Father Schwartz that it is hard to accept the foolish priest as an appropriate symbol of the faith he so unworthily serves. Fitzgerald's personal dislike obscures the priest's aesthetic function in the story. He was undoubtedly a portrait of someone Fitzgerald had known, and it is pretty clear that Schwartz's treatment of Rudolph is connected in some way with Schwartz's latent homosexuality." I know of no evidence that will support these assumptions.

OUTWARD FORMS
AND
THE INNER LIFE:
COLERIDGE AND GATSBY

That Fitzgerald associated many of the elements of *The Great Gatsby* with Keats and the "Ode to a Nightingale" is obvious enough and has been frequently noted. In the most thorough study of this question, Dan McCall has pointed out that "The distinguishing and complicated similarity [between Keats and the novel] is in a realization of the ambivalence of beauty."[1] This parallel is useful for our understanding of Gatsby himself, but it is of limited value in a study of the more central issues of the novel — the yearning, the dreams, and particularly Fitzgerald's elaborate and explicit comments (largely through Nick) on the inadequacy of specific ideals. In these terms, a more fruitful analogy is Coleridge's "Dejection: An Ode," a poem with which *The Great Gatsby* has some extensive affinities.[2] By examining them, we can acquire a precise understanding of the nature of Fitzgerald's comment on the American Dream.

The basic "situation" of the central figure in each work may first be noted. In both, the focus is on a downcast man, essentially isolated, unconscious even of the world about him; for both, the characteristic posture is one of motionlessness, while staring fixedly upon some far-distant object at night — in each case a green light.[3] Further, both have their hearts set upon an unattainable ideal — a woman who, for different reasons, is not to be theirs. In each work, the power of the mind to transcend physical realities is a basic facet of such reverie – although in the case of Fitzgerald, of course, Gatsby simply makes of Daisy something she is not.

The similarities between the situations, though striking, could be ascribed to mere coincidence were it not for the presence in *Gatsby* of most of the major symbols at work in Coleridge's poem – and each of these symbols is primarily associated with Gatsby himself. Most central in the novel are the moon and the light imagery, in particular the green light. Of secondary importance, but worth re-marking, are such other symbols as the clouds, eyes, water, and specific colors. Only the wind of Coleridge's poem does not appear in *Gatsby,* in part because the wind connotes a spiritual reality in Coleridge that is outside Gatsby's world; more immediately, Fitzgerald's purpose was not to dramatize natural tensions.

In Coleridge's poem, the moon is described as follows:

> For lo! the New-moon winter-bright!
> And overspread with phantom light,
> (With swimming phantom light o'erspread
> But rimmed and circled by a silver thread)
> I see the old Moon in her lap, foretelling
> The coming-on of rain and squally blast. (9-14)

And in stanza two Coleridge refers to "Yon crescent Moon, as fixed as if it grew/ In its own cloudless, starless lake of blue" (35-36).

Our first introduction to Gatsby shows him in the moonlight, gazing at Daisy's dock.[4] After repeated associations of the moon with Gatsby, we can see that the image functions in much the same way in each work – partly as symbolic in the traditional way of an unattainable ideal; but also as an image of a stasis, permanence, and peace that reflect the beholder but ultimately serve as a contrast to his inner turmoil. In every subsequent reference to the moon in the novel, Gatsby is present, usually alone, occasionally with Daisy. We may also make note of the fact that, in one instance, Fitzgerald refers to "A silver curve of the moon" (143) – thus directly echoing Coleridge.

In one significant scene, Daisy's first visit to Gatsby's mansion, the natural setting is again referred to:

> The rain was still falling, but the darkness had parted in the west, and there was a pink and golden billow of foamy clouds above the sea. (114)

Coleridge likewise describes the sky in terms of clouds and colors in lines 27-36. Here, as elsewhere, Coleridge's poem resembles *Gatsby* both in such details as the clouds, the westward looks, and the colors, and in the general emphasis on the blank gazing of the speaker. Eyes, in fact, are a central image in the poem, suggesting not only Fitzgerald's heavy stress on Gatsby's eyes, but also the sign of Doctor T. J. Eckleburg, whose eyes are "blue and gigantic" and "look out of no face, but, instead, from a pair of enormous yellow spectacles" (27). The yellow-on-blue image is repeated often in the novel, just as it is basic to "Dejection" (as in the above-quoted 11. 35-36).

But more essential than these parallels is the light imagery of the two works, and most important of all is that both center on green light:

> It were a vain endeavour,
> Though I should gaze for ever
> On that green light that lingers in the west. (42-44)

As with most romantic poets, light imagery is basic to Coleridge. What the persona in the poem comes to realize is that:

> I may not hope from outward forms to win
> The passion and the life, whose fountains are within.

Instead,

> . . . from the soul itself must issue forth
> A light, a glory, a fair luminous cloud
> Enveloping the Earth.   (45-46/53-55)

Light imagery is also common in *The Great Gatsby*. Interestingly, it first is associated with Daisy (an outward form?): "the last sunshine fell with romantic affection upon her glowing face" (17). The motif is then transferred to Gatsby, when he and Daisy meet again: "there was a change in Gatsby that was simply confounding. He literally glowed; . . . a new well-being radiated from him and filled the little room" (108). In the same episode, as elsewhere, his house (certainly an outward form!) is associated with light; for example, in the episode just referred to, Gatsby asks Nick to "See how the whole front of it catches the light." Yet another light image in the same scene refers to Daisy: when she comes out of the house "two rows of brass buttons on her dress gleamed in the sunlight" (109). What is most compelling about these various light images is that they are so precisely Coleridgean: light falls *upon* Daisy and the house, but it radiates *from* Gatsby ("from the soul itself must issue forth/ A light").

This distinction becomes more clear when the significance of the color green is examined. Primarily associated with Daisy, it is the symbolic object of Gatsby's extrinsic yearning. That Fitzgerald should so carefully stress its illusory quality indicates he is adopting the very distinction which informs Coleridge's poem: that between outward forms and an inner life. The first reference to the green light in *The Great Gatsby* occurs when we also see Gatsby for the first time. When he meets Daisy, Gatsby alludes to the green light — and identifies it as that which burns at the end of her dock (112). The image then is explicitly transferred to Daisy, as when she whispers at a subsequent party at Gatsby's that to kiss her, Nick should "Just mention my name. Or present a green card. I'm giving out green —" (126). At the end of the novel this motif is elaborated and extended in a description that brings together the other basic images of the "Dejection" ode:

> And as the moon rose higher the inessential houses began to melt away until gradually I became aware of the old island here that flowered once for Dutch sailors' eyes — a fresh, green breast of the new world. (217)

That Nick should have this insight is one of several indications that Gatsby, in his yearning for the outer forms of his world, had never perceived the inner light of his own existence.

The water imagery in the final passage of the novel points up what is another central parallel with "Dejection." In his concluding prayer for the "lady" of his poem, Coleridge states:

> To her may all things live, from pole to pole,
> Their life the eddying of her living soul! (135-136)

Similarly, Fitzgerald ends *Gatsby* by moving from the particular to the general, from past-present to the future, and with an image of the tide:

> Gatsby believed in the green light, the orgastic future that year by year recedes before us. It eluded us then, but that's no matter — to-morrow we will run faster, stretch out our arms farther. . . . And one fine morning —
> So we beat on, boats against the current, borne back ceaselessly into the past.

Scholars have often remarked on the presence in the novel of such themes as the yearning, the disparity between the apparent and the real, the worthiness of various ideals, even the joy-dejection tension.

But comparison with Coleridge's poem can make us appreciate how *related* these various themes are and how profoundly romantic was Fitzgerald's approach to them.

In one sense, *The Great Gatsby* is all about yearning – not just on Gatsby's part but that of everybody else in the novel. Even Nick reveals it, as when he admits that part of his summer routine was "to walk up Fifth Avenue and pick out romantic women from the crowd" (69). But it is also important to realize that not all yearning is the same (a point "Dejection" makes clear too): some dreams are illusory and unworthy, some are genuine.

Now this distinction and its respective consequences are not only romantic but explicitly Coleridgean. The idea may be illustrated elsewhere in Coleridge, but "Dejection" serves as well as any other text. The primary qualities that separate valid from false dreams are their immediate emotional effects (which may be summed up in one word – Coleridge's "joy"), their permanence, their internal origin, and their ultimate integrity (that is, wholeness). Gatsby does achieve a kind of joy (111) that, as we have seen, was innate. But in the long run he and the world he represents fail on all counts, as judged by their aspirations: they bring no joy (as Coleridge would have defined the word, that is, as distinct from transitory pleasure), they are of limited duration, and above all they are superficial, extrinsic, and fragmented.[5] Only Nick remains with his (symbolic) midwestern dreams to represent the genuine, the permanent, and the whole.

Thus, if "Dejection" is Coleridge's lament for the personal loss of "My shaping spirit of Imagination" (1. 86), *Gatsby* is Fitzgerald's expression of a similar but greater tragedy: man's loss of "something commensurate to his capacity for wonder" (218). The essential difference is that Coleridge's speaker is aware of the futility of continued striving, just as he is aware of the difference between valid and false ideals, whereas Gatsby and his world will continue to seek their false gods. If the conclusion to *Gatsby* has been the subject of some debate as to its specific import,[6] I would suggest that this comparison with "Dejection" and an awareness of Fitzgerald's romantic norms in the novel should settle the question: "boats against the current" is an exercise in illusory futility.

University of Cincinnati

---

[1] " 'The Self-Same Song that Found a Path': Keats and *The Great Gatsby*," *American Literature*, 42 (1970-71), 522.

[2] I can find no evidence that Fitzgerald read "Dejection," but his intimate

knowledge of English Romantic poets at large would seem to settle the matter. See, for example, Sheilah Graham, *College of One* (New York: Viking, 1967), passim and especially pp. 97, 207, where Fitzgerald mentions Coleridge's poetry. See also John Kuehl, "Scott Fitzgerald's Reading," *Princeton University Library Chronicle,* 22 (1961), 58-89, who shows that Fitzgerald had a full and intimate acquaintance with the poetry of Keats, Shelley, and Byron. We, of course, know that he took Romantic literature at Princeton, and years later he was writing to his daughter that "The only sensible course for you at this moment is the one on *English Poetry – Blake to Keats* (English 241)" – *The Crack-Up,* Edmund Wilson, ed. (New York: New Directions, 1945), p. 297.

[3] Further, both the persona of the poem and Gatsby are associated with "the western sky"; see, for example, 1. 28 of the poem and p. 143 of the novel, where this specific wording is used in both instances. This parallel, the green light in the west, has been noticed previously by Richmond Crinkley and Everett Fahy, *Fitzgerald Newsletter,* 15 (Fall, 1961), 67-68.

[4] *The Great Gatsby* (New York: Scribners, 1925), pp. 25-26. Subsequent references to the novel will be made parenthetically in the text.

[5] That Gatsby's own ideal was so thoroughly inadequate and unworthy of him leads me to believe that her name, Daisy Fay, is an ironic reversal of the Wordsworthian (and romantic) associations that both names contain. I refer in part to Wordsworth's fondness for the daisy as a subject (four poems on the subject, not to mention numerous allusions); "Fay," similarly, besides being the commonplace romantic term for "fairy," is reminiscent of the name Betty Foy in Wordsworth's "The Idiot Boy."

[6] For example, Arthur Mizener believes that "the dream is still the book's only positive good" – *The Far Side of Paradise* (Boston: Houghton Mifflin, 1951), p. 178. Even further removed from my interpretation of the novel is that presented by John Kuehl: "Jay Gatsby is a hero because he is a romantic, one who believes that illusion itself and not its materialization is important" – "Scott Fitzgerald: Romantic and Realist," *Texas Studies in Literature and Language,* I (1959-60), 424. As my analysis of "Dejection" should make clear, Kuehl's is a most unromantic use of the word "romantic"; and his description of Gatsby does not strike me as at all accurate.

ERNEST HEMINGWAY

WAYS
OF
SEEING
HEMINGWAY

The best-known article about Ernest Hemingway – and probably
the most widely discussed interview of its time – is Lillian Ross'
profile for *The New Yorker*. Many readers have persisted in regarding
it as an intentionally destructive job, despite the fact that neither
Hemingway nor Miss Ross regarded it as such. The summary of
Hemingway's career that accompanied the *New York Times* obituary
called the profile a "savage series" and noted, "But the most impressive riposte came from the novelist himself. When the profile was
published in hard covers, Mr. Hemingway in the *New York Herald
Tribune* listed it among the three books he had found most interesting that year." Miss Ross wrote to the *Times* pointing out that her
profile was "written out of affection and admiration and
knowledge"; that "Mr. Hemingway read and approved it" before
publication; and that she and the Hemingways were good friends
before and after publication of the profile – which was not a series.
She added that "there could not have been a 'riposte' when the
'profile was published in hard covers,' because it was never published
in hard covers [up to that time]." What the *Trib* published in
December 1951 was a list of three books Hemingway liked and six
made-up titles, including "He and Lillian: The Story of a Profile –
by Mary Hemingway".

Irving Howe, writing a re-appraisal of Hemingway in the 24 July

1961 *New Republic*, could find only negative qualities in the Profile. Howe admitted that Hemingway had approved the profile but judged that it shouldn't have been published because it shows Hemingway paroodying himself — that he should have been protected from himself.

After Hemingway's death Miss Ross prepared an account of the writing of the profile for the B.B.C. "Tribute to Ernest Hemingway" program, and this piece for the B.B.C. "Tribute to Ernest Hemingway" program, and this piece was published in revised form as the preface to *Portrait of Hemingway* (New York: Simon & Schuster, 1961). Miss Ross has made the text of her B.B.C. piece available to the *Annual*, which here prints the original version of her account of Hemingway's response to the profile.

An important chapter in our friendship involved a Profile I wrote about Hemingway in *The New Yorker* the following year — 1950. When it came out, it became — to my surprise and his — a controversial piece. At first, I didn't understand some of the reactions to it. Quite a number of people wrote in commenting enthusiastically about the Profile and about Hemingway, but others objected. Before the Profile was published, I sent it to Hemingway, in Cuba, and he read and approved it. The Profile was written out of affection and admiration and knowledge, and was intended to describe as precisely as possible how Hemingway looked and sounded when he was in action, talking, between books — to give a picture of the man as he was, in his uniqueness, and with his vitality and his enormous spirit of fun intact, rather than of the man as somebody sitting in judgment on him, however well-meaning, might wish him to be. But some people didn't like the way Hemingway talked. They didn't like his freedom. They didn't like his not taking himself seriously. They didn't like his wasting his time on going to boxing matches; going to the circus, talking to friends, going fishing, enjoying people, celebrating the finish of a book by splurging on caviar and champagne. They didn't like this and they didn't like that. In fact, they didn't like Hemingway to be Hemingway. They wanted him to be somebody else — probably themselves. So they came to the conclusion that Hemingway had not been portrayed as he was, and that he had, in fact, been "savagely criticized" and "devastated." Some people mistook an accurate description of Hemingway as criticism, and others, with dreary, small-minded preconceptions about how a great writer should behave, preferred their preconceptions to the facts. Hemingway, of course, didn't misunderstand the Profile for a minute, and neither did his wife, Mary. Over and over again, he wrote to reassure me and tell me not to be bothered by any criticism of the Profile. "I thought your piece was a good, straight, OK piece," he wrote on June 3, 1950. Another time, on June 16, 1950, he wrote: "Don't ever worry about losing me friends nor anything about the piece. It is just that people get

1ˢᵀ REVISE

G NYr A—395

APRIL 18, 1950—7-S—Q—MG
SOON—1ST REV. APR. 25
3336—ONE

ERNEST MILLER HEMINGWAY rarely comes to New York. He lives on a farm called the Finca Vigía, nine miles outside of Havana, with his wife, a household staff of nine, fifty-two cats, sixteen dogs, a couple of hundred pigeons, and three cows. When Hemingway does come to New York, it is only because he must pass through here on his way to or from somewhere else. On his way to France and Italy not long ago, he stopped in New York for three days. Shortly before, I wrote asking to see him when he came to town. He sent me a typewritten letter saying that would be fine, and went on to say, "I don't want to see anybody I don't like, nor have publicity, nor be tied up all the time. Want to go to the Bronx Zoo, Metropolitan Museum, Museum Modern Art, ditto of Natural History, and see a fight. Want to see the good Breughel at the Met, the one, no two, fine Goyas and Mr. El Greco's Toledo. Don't want to go to Toots Shor's. Am going to try to get into town and out without having to shoot my mouth off. I want to give the joint a miss. Not seeing news people is not a pose. It is only to have time to see your friends." In pencil, he added, "Time is the least thing we have of."

HEMINGWAY PROFILE

HOW DO YOU LIKE IT NOW, GENTLEMEN?

G NYr A—421

3336—THREE

"Elementary Italian Grammar," a book called "A Short History of Italy," and, for Hemingway, four woollen under-shirts, four cotton underpants, two woollen underpants, bedroom slippers, a belt, and a coat. "Papa has never had a coat," she said. "We've got to buy Papa a coat." Hemingway grunted and leaned against the bar. "A nice, warm coat," Mrs. Hemingway said. "And he's got to get his glasses fixed. He needs some good soft padding for the nose-piece. It cuts him up real bad. He's had that same piece of paper under the nosepiece for weeks. When he wants to get real cleaned up, he changes the paper. Hemingway gave another

3336—FIVE

I'd walk the prairies at low tide for snipe," he said. "It was a big fly route for ducks that came all the way down from the Pripet marshes. I shot good and thus became a respected local character. They have some sort of little bird that comes through after eating grapes in the north on his way to eat grapes in the south. The local characters ~~usually shoot them on the sit, and I would shoot them on the fly~~. Once, I shot two high doubles, rights and lefts, in a row, and the gardener cried with emotion. Coming home, I shot a high

[handwritten marginal note:] SOMETIMES SHOT THEM SITTING, AND I OCCASION-ALLY SHOT THEM FLYING,

G NYr A—429

3336—TEN

Hadley Richardson, ~~and Hemingway's third, Martha Gelhorn~~.   *?*

"Everything you do, you do for the sake of the children," Miss Dietrich said.

"Everything for the children," Hemingway said uncomfortably.

Hemingway refilled Miss Dietrich's glass.

I wanted to know what "true gen" meant, and Hemingway explained that it was a British term for information, taken from the word "intelligence."

"It's divided into three classes—gen; the true gen, which is as true as you can state it; and the really true gen, which you can operate on," he said. He looked at the green orchids and asked about Adeline and whether anybody had found out who she was.

"I forgot to tell you, Papa," said Mrs. Hemingway. "It was Mother. Adeline is *Mother*." She turned to me and said that her mother and father were now in their late seventies, that they lived in Chicago, and that they always remembered to do exactly the right thing at the right time.

"My mother never sent *me* any flowers," Hemingway said. "She never sent me nothin'." His mother was now eighty-nine, he said, and lived in Forest Park, Illinois, and he had not seen her for eighteen years. His father, who had been a physician, was dead. He had shot himself when Hemingway was a boy.

[handwritten marginal note: crowding eighty]

[handwritten marginal note: RIVER FOREST]

"Let's get going if we're going to see the pictures," he said. "I told Charlie to meet *me* here at one. Excuse me while I wash," he said. "In big city, I guess you wash your neck." He went into the bedroom. While he was out, Mrs. Hemingway told me that Ernest was the second of six children—Marcelline, the eldest, then Ernest, Ursula, Madelaine, Carol, and the youngest, his only brother, Leicester. All the sisters were named after saints, and all are married. Leicester, also married, is a businessman who lives in Bogotá, Colombia.

[handwritten marginal note: ATTACHED TO THE U.S. EMBASSY IN]

[handwritten marginal note: ?]

Hemingway came out in a little while wearing his new coat. Mrs. Hemingway and Patrick put on their coats, and we all went downstairs. It was raining as we came out of the hotel, and we got into a taxi. On the way to the Metro-

G NYr A—497

<u>3336—NINETEEN</u>

we all went downstairs. It was raining
as we came out of the hotel, and we got
into a taxi. On the way to the Metropolitan, Hemingway said very little; he
just hummed to himself and watched
the road. Mrs. Hemingway said that
he was usually unhappy riding in taxis
because he could never sit in the front
seat to watch the road. Once, he looked
out the window and pointed to what
looked like birds flying south. "In this
town, birds fly, but they're not serious
about it," he said. "New York birds
don't climb."

When we drew up to the Museum
entrance, a line of school children was
moving slowly inside. Hemingway im-
patiently led us past them. In the lobby,
he paused and took a silver flask from
his coat pocket. He unscrewed the top
and took a long drink. He put the flask
back in his pocket and asked Mrs. Hemingway whether she wanted to see the
Goyas first or the Breughels. She said
the Breughels, and so we started for the
room they were in, Hemingway leading
the way.

"I learned to write by looking at
paintings in the museums in Luxembourg and Paris," he said as the rest of
us hurried to keep up with him. "I never
went to high school. When you've got

G NYr A—498

3336—TWENTY

Mrs. Hemingway called to him. She was looking at "Portrait of the Artist," by Van Dyck. He looked at the painting, and nodded his approval and said, "In Spain, we had a fighter pilot named Whitey Doll, so Whitey came to me one time and said, 'Mr. Hemingway, is Van Dyck a good painter?' I said, 'Yes, he is.' He said, 'Well, I'm glad, because I have one in my room and I like it very much, and I'm glad he's a good painter because I like him.' The next day, Whitey was shot down and nobody ever found out what became of his painting."

G NYr A—582

3336—TWENTY TWO

"Huh!" Hemingway said. "Those painters always put the sacred scenes in the part of Italy they liked the best or where they came from or where their girls came from. They made their girls the Madonnas. This is supposed to be Palestine, and Palestine is a long way off, he figures, so he puts in a red parrot, and he puts in deer and a leopard. And then he thinks, this is the Far East. So he puts in the Moors, the traditional enemy of the Venetians." He paused and looked for something else the painter had painted in his picture. "Then he gets hungry, so he puts in rabbits," Hemingway said. "Goddam, Mouse, we saw a lot of good pictures. Mouse, don't you think two hours is a long time looking at pictures?"

G NYr A—597

3336—TWENTY-THREE

Scribner wanted to know where Hemingway could be reached by mail in Europe. Care of the Guaranty Trust Company of New York in Paris, Hemingway told him. "When we took Paris, I tried to take that bank and got smacked back," he said, with his bashful laugh. "I thought it would be awfully nice if I could take my own bank."

"Yuh, yuh," Scribner said. "What are you planning to do in Italy, Ernest?"

Hemingway said he would work in the mornings and see his Italian friends and go duck-hunting in the afternoons. "I shot three hundred and thirty-one ducks to six guns there one afternoon," he said. "Mary shot good, too."

"Any girl who marries Papa has to learn how to carry a gun," Mrs. Hemingway said and went back to her letter-writing.

things all mixed up." And the following December, he wrote: "About our old piece; the hell with them. Think one of the 'devastating' things was that I drink a little in it and that makes them think I am rummy. But of course if they (the devastate people) drank what we drink in that piece they would die or something. Then (I should not say it) there is a lot of jealousy around and because I have fun a lot of the time and am not really spooky and so far always get up when they count over me some people are jealous. They can't understand you being a serious writer and not be solemn." Death puts certain things in perspective. No doubt some of the people who misunderstood the Profile, were they to read it now, would see it for what it was – a loving portrait of a great and lovable man.*

The key evidence for determining Hemingway's response to the profile is the set of proofs that Lillian Ross sent to him for approval and correction before publication, and which he returned. There are 24 galleys, of which the first is slugged "1ST REV. APR. 25", and they have only 14 alterations. Ernest Hemingway's corrections are easily distinguished from the full-cap corrections made by Mary Hemingway.

galley 1   joint   [joints   *unidentified hand*

galley 3   real bad   [like mad   *Mary Hemingway*

galley 3   real   [truly   *Mary Hemingway*

galley 5   usually shoot them on the sit, and I would shoot them on the fly [sometimes shot them sitting, and I occasionally shot them flying   *Mary Hemingway*

galley 10   and Hemingway's third, Martha Gelhorn *[deleted with query by unidentified hand*

galley 19   "She never sent me nothin'." *[deleted with delete sign in unidentified hand*

galley 19   "eighty-nine   [crowding eighty   *Ernest Hemingway*

galley 19   Forest Park   [River Forest *Mary Hemingway*

galley 19   businessman   (Attached to the U.S. Embassy in *Mary Hemingway; query in margin*

---

*Copyright © 1973, Lillian Ross. This material cannot be reprinted without written permission from Miss Ross. The excerpts from Ernest Hemingway's letters are Copyright © 1973, Mary Hemingway and are printed with the special permission of Mary Hemingway to clarify the record: this permission is not to be interpreted as a relaxation of Ernest Hemingway's prohibition of the publication of his letters.

galley 19   in Luxembourg and Paris   [in the Luxembourg in
                Paris *Ernest Hemingway*

galley 19   went to high school   [went past high school *Ernest
                Hemingway*

galley 20   Whitey Doll   [Whitey Dahl   *Mary Hemingway*

galley 22   enecy   [enemy   *Mary Hemingway*

galley 23   I shot   [We shot   *Ernest Heminway*

These galley alterations are all simple corrections. If the Hemingways had objections to the substance of the profile, they kept them to themselves.

The latest attempt to reopen the Ross Case is Dennis Brian's "The Importance of Knowing Ernest" in the February 1972 *Esquire,* which uses the Profile as springboard for interviews with Miss Ross, A. E. Hotchner, Malcolm Cowley, Truman Capote, Carlos Baker, George Plimpton, William Seward, John Hemingway, and Mary Hemingway. Hotchner asserts that Hemingway said about the proofs of the Profile, "There's so much here that I don't know what to do with it − so I just said it was okay." But the final authority is Mary Hemingway, who told Brian: "I think that it's quite possible if someone is as clear as Lillian and as accurate as she is, everybody is a horse's ass . . . Hotchner came down after the thing was published, saying: 'YOU ARE RUINED!' Idiot things like that you know. And I remember saying: 'No single profile in any magazine, of Ernest, can ruin him, '. . . Ernest, if he did feel that, never game any impression of feeling it at all."

                                                                      M.J.B.

CHARLES E. ROBINSON

JAMES T. FARRELL'S
CRITICAL ESTIMATE
OF
HEMINGWAY

In the three years following Ernest Hemingway's death in 1961, James T. Farrell published three memorial articles: "Ernest Hemingway: The End of Something," *Thought* (30 September 1961), 13-15; "A Preface to Ernest" in the "Panorama" section of the *Chicago Daily News* (9 February 1963), p. 10; and "Notes on Ernest Hemingway" in the *Chicago Literary Times* (September, 1964), p. 5. In the last and briefest of these articles, Farrell acknowledged that his accounts of Hemingway had been "personal in character," but he also judged that it was "unfair to writers as a whole if one shifts interests from their work to aspects of their personal lives." Yet Farrell did continue emphasizing Hemingway's personal life, for in 1969 he published in the *Toronto Weekend Telegram* a series of his 1936 letters in which he described his first meeting with Hemingway. Wanting to be fair to Hemingway, Farrell in 1964 did begin a long critical essay on Hemingway's fiction, and this essay, though incomplete, is published here for the first time. Readers of both Hemingway and Farrell should welcome it for it complements Farrell's earlier analysis of and response to *The Sun Also Rises.*[1]

Farrell's interest in *The Sun Also Rises* and in Hemingway's volumes of short stories, especially *In Our Time* and *Men Without Women,* can be traced back to 1927, when he began to read Hemingway and decided to become a writer. For Farrell, Hemingway was more exciting to read than F. Scott Fitzgerald and the other younger writers of the 1920's, and he recalls that Hemingway's early fiction increased his awareness of the value of both ordinary life and the American vernacular which surrounded him in Chicago.[2] Within two years, Farrell began to incorporate this Chicago life and vernacular into his first novel, *Young Lonigan* (1932), which by 1935 was published with two other novels as *Studs Lonigan: A Trilogy*. When Farrell met Hemingway for the first time during the following year, on 29 November 1936, he was pleased to find that Hemingway had "read Studs Lonigan and liked it a great deal."[3] Farrell was on what he calls a half-vacation[4] to Key West, Florida, and he was pleased not only with Hemingway's response to *Studs Lonigan* but also with his cordiality. Hemingway the man was different from the myth, for "he didn't act up to any of the ham actor stories we had heard of him. To the contrary, he was modest about himself and his work and friendly."[5]

During the course of Farrell's short stay at Key West, Hemingway introduced him to his wife and to other friends, including J. B. Sullivan, and the two writers discussed such various subjects as Key West economics, bullfighting, prize fighting, *jai alai,* and contemporary fiction. Farrell, at ease with Hemingway, preferred baseball to bull fighting and made Hemingway laugh by parodying *Death in the Afternoon:*

> "Ernest, I'm going to write a book called *Death at 3 P.M. on The Diamond.* The first chapter will be called 'The Heroism of Ty Cobb's hook slide.' The second chapter will be 'The Tragic Stance of Paul Waner Batting at Home Plate'; and the third will be titled 'The Pathos of Lefty Grove's Fast Ball'; and I'll call the fourth chapter 'The Sadness in the Eyes of Silk McLaughlin when He Calls a Man out at Home.'"[6]

Apparently at ease with Farrell, Hemingway was quick to offer his opinions on other writers, for after but one day together, Farrell wrote the following account of Hemingway's literary judgments:

> He hates Cowley (Malcolm) in particular. He thinks Bunny (Edmund) Wilson is a bit dumb. It seems he didn't like what Bunny had written of him and claimed that Bunny hadn't read his books when he wrote of him. He doesn't know Bunny well. He likes Dos Passos very much.
> He says that he thinks the best part of Dos Passos are his portraits and that he also liked some of the early camera eye sketches, particularly those dealing with experiences he had known of. He thinks that Nathan (Asch) is utterly dumb. It seems once in Paris, Nathan pestered him and Hemingway

got sore and took a crack at Nathan and couldn't get rid of him any other way, so he had tried this way.

He thinks that Faulkner has more ability than any of us at writing, but that often, Faulkner is just faking. When he isn't faking, he is wonderful.

He thinks that Wolfe is a phoney. He thinks a lot of Dreiser. He said that this summer, or last, Dreiser went over to Europe and tried to get himself the Nobel Prize, and that by so doing, he damaged his chances. Dreiser, he said, had tried to impress the Europeans.

So he took along his mistress to show them that a man should go to Europe with a mistress, etc. and the Europeans didn't like that. Personally, he likes Dreiser as a man as well as a writer.[7]

Farrell has usually respected Hemingway's literary taste, and he was obviously intrigued in 1936 by the man who so quickly revealed his personal judgments about other writers. Farrell himself made a number of literary judgments at this time, including some about Hemingway who had loaned him copies of *Winner Take Nothing* and *The Green Hills of Africa.* After reading about one hundred pages of *Winner Take Nothing,* Farrell complained that the stories lacked the "surprise," the "same excitement and expectation" that characterized Heminway's earlier volumes, especially *The Sun Also Rises, In Our Time,* and *Men Without Women.* For Farrell, these three volumes contain a quality that Hemingway lost or could not equal after the 1920's, and while in Key West Farrell tried to explain the difference between Hemingway's earlier and more recent stories:

He has created his own style and his own manner. He has fashioned, as it were, a perfect instrument for saying what he wants to say. But he has not any great ambitiousness in his writing. His range is limited.

Consequently he does the following things: Descriptiveness, to "make" a scene, dialogue to reveal character, a slight bit of internal monologue and the emphasis is on feeling, sensation and on getting over a sense of pain, frustration, a nihilistic notion.

As a writer, he tends to be sensationalistic in the genuine sense of that word — to be largely concerned with shocks upon the senses, with the sensory feature of experience, and with the element of feeling. He has characters without ideation. Now Studs' does not really think, or order his world, but he has a lot of ideation going on.

Hemingway is less concerned with that. He wants to get a thing more through the feeling and sensory apparatus of his character, as it were. Also, his dialogue is good and clipped, but he has explored its range completely, and so there is, in the dialogue, no new element of surprise.[8]

I quote at length Farrell's 1936 remarks, for they introduce the substance of his later judgments on the strengths and weaknesses of

Hemingway's fiction. In 1943, while praising the freshness, originality, and suggestiveness of the technique in *The Sun Also Rises,* Farrell complained that Hemingway's main characters had no past or at least seldom reflected on it, and that without ideation they lived only for "new and fresh sensations." Hemingway's sensationalism was too simplistic: "He has tended to reduce life to the effect that sights, scenes, and experiences make upon the nervous system; and he has avoided complicated types of response. Herein we find one of the major factors revealing his limitations as a writer."[9] Farrell spoke more critically to this point three years later while participating in the Institute in American Studies at the University of Minnesota:

> Hemingway shows little development since early writing, no growth of perspective, no restatement of values. Retains juvenile masculinity, only shown in new settings (*For Whom the Bell Tolls* a compound of Hollywood and "Carmen"). Stronger and stronger shocks needed in sensationalist technique, if writer refuses to analyze complexities of problem. Hemingway notable for his biological hero, man with values and outlets reduced to those of boy of fifteen. Hemingway always exciting to new readers, but quickly exhausted.[10]

Without a past, without "ideation," living for non-complex, immediate, and sensational experiences, Hemingway's characters could not develop; and for Farrell, concerned with the past and man's changing and complex relationship to it, neither could Hemingway.

In his three memorial articles following Hemingway's death, Farrell chose not to emphasize Hemingway's lack of growth as an artist. But in the critical essay which he began in 1964 and which is published here, Farrell again questioned Hemingway's sensationalism with characters who have little past, who live for "immediate moments, and action and sensations of immediate moments," and consequently who lack intellectual depth. And when Hemingway in *For Whom the Bell Tolls* attempted "to cover a wider range of meanings and experiences" and "to implant ideas and abstract ideals in his chief protagonist, Robert Jordan," he failed. Notwithstanding Farrell's great liking for Hemingway the man and fond recollection of reading his early stories, he judged, albeit reluctantly, that Hemingway lacked the talent to intellectually universalize man's experiences. For Farrell, there was a sadness in this limitation and failure in a man he admired, a sadness in part anticipated by Farrell as early as 1936 when he isolated the danger in Hemingway's emphasis on ". . . sensation and feelings, with little ideation connected with it. . . . because you can run out of sensations quicker than you can run out of ideas — ".[1][1]

The basis for the text of the following essay is Farrell's 163-page holograph draft (c. 1964), entitled "Ernest Hemingway."[1][2] Written in various inks on lined paper (most of which was torn from spiral notebooks), considerably revised and repaged throughout, this MS (Text A) Farrell himself confessed to be in "rough" form. Accompanying this MS is a 6-page typescript of the first 39 pages of Text A. This typescript (Text B) differs but slightly from the holograph, and I conjoined Texts B and A into a reading text with Farrell's errors in punctuation, capitalization, and spelling silently corrected, with his short paragraphs frequently joined to make longer ones, with deletions marked by ellipses, and with alterations and statements about the MS marked by brackets. This "finished" MS (Text C) was submitted to Mr. Farrell for his approval on 2 August 1971; and on 19 August he returned a new typescript (Text D) which differed in style but not content from Text C: his revisions included further deletions, the rewriting of many sentences, and the omission of most of my editorial mechanics. Text D, with but a few minor changes on my part, is reproduced here and contains the substance of Farrell's judgments originally recorded in 1964. Finally, Text D was vetted by Mr. Farrell and approved for publication.

For their assistance in the preparation of this essay for publication, I wish to thank Mr. Nathaniel Puffer, Assistant Director of Libraries at the University of Delaware; the staff of the University of Pennsylvania Libraries, Rare Book Collection, for their help during my researches in the Farrell MSS deposited there; Professor Edgar M. Branch, Farrell's bibliographer, who kindly forwarded to me copies of Farrell's publications on Hemingway in the *Literary Times* and in the *Toronto Weekend Telegram;* Mr. Douglas Haneline, a graduate student at the University of Delaware, who helped me to read some of Farrell's occasionally indecipherable passages in the holograph; and, of course, Mr. Farrell himself.

---

[1]"Ernest Hemingway's *The Sun Also Rises,*" *The League of Frightened Philistines and Other Papers* (New York: Vanguard Press, 1945), pp. 20-24. Farrell first published this essay in the *New York Times Book Review* (1 August 1943).
    [2]Farrell has frequently made this point. See, for example, his essay in *The League of Frightened Philistines,* p. 22; and the notes from his talk on Hemingway as published in "The American Novelist and American Society — IV: Ernest Hemingway and Scott Fitzgerald," *Institute in American Studies, July 15 to*

July 20, 1946 (Minneapolis: Center for Continuation Study, University of Minnesota), p. 31.

[3]Quoted from Farrell's letter to Hortense Alden, 30 November 1936, as printed in "James T. Farrell's Unpublished Letters," *Toronto Weekend Telegram* (9 August 1969), Section 3, p. 5.

[4]The business half of Farrell's trip included requesting Hemingway to contribute to *The Nation.* Hemingway, according to Farrell, refused.

[5]Letter to Hortense Alden, 30 November 1936.

[6]Quoted in Farrell's "Ernest Hemingway: The End of Something," *Thought* (30 September 1961), 14.

[7]Letter to Hortense Alden, 30 November 1936. Compare "On another occasion, Ernest suddenly said to me: 'Jim, Faulkner is better than either of us,'" as quoted in "Hemingway: The End of Something," p. 14. Carlos Baker refers to this remark in the paragraph he gives to Hemingway's meeting with Farrell in *Ernest Hemingway: A Life Story* (New York: Scribners, 1969), p. 297.

[8]Letter to Hortense Alden, 2 December 1936.

[9]*The League of Frightened Philistines,* pp. 23-24.

[10]"The American Novelist and American Society: Hemingway and Fitzgerald," p. 31.

[11]Letter to Hortense Alden, 1 December 1936.

[12]This draft was among some unfinished critical essays which Farrell sold to Walter Goldwater of The University Place Bookshop in New York City. These essays were purchased by the University of Delaware Library in 1969.

.

JAMES T. FARRELL

ERNEST
HEMINGWAY

I

When Ernest Hemingway died, there were copious obituary notices; it was front page news. However, the obituaries were those of a public image, more than of a writer. Even his death was publicity. Anecdotes played more of a role in commemorating him than did accomplishments. How he fished and fought was more newsworthy than significant events in his career as a writer. He was praised for having "cooled" some night club characters who were left unnamed. The fracas with Max Eastman in which Ernest did not come out so well was revised so as to help make Ernest a slugging hero. The simple declarative sentences which he often used were treated by another obituary writer as a major innovation in literary style. It was all unseemly.

II

Not so long after his death, and in one of his last letters to me, Van Wyck Brooks wrote that fifteen years previously, Maxwell Perkins had told him, "Brooks, Hemingway is through." I would not put the sense of such a statement so harshly about a writer except for some exceptional reason. But editors and critics do make such statements and they are acceptable. Another writer cannot, or rather, should not speak in such a manner of a colleague.

If a writer reaches a point in his life when he is written out, this is something sad. More sad, however, is the writer who has disintegrated without having written himself out. This, let me observe, is the difference between Ernest Hemingway and F. Scott Fitzgerald.

The phenomenon of being written out is not understood. It is very difficult for anyone, seriously, in accordance with terms of truth and logic in interpretation, to defend any hypothesis which assumes that a writer has a certain quantity of things to say and that that is his limit. And once reached, he has nothing more to say. This interpretation does not provide for growth. And no one is an artist unless he or she grows. One of the great values of art (here, I am confining myself to literary art) is that it is an example of growth, on the part of an artist. I could hold it patent that an artist must grow. Growth is development of the spirit, of mind and emotion, of range, subtlety and delicacy of feeling, of flexibility in the use of the creative imagination.

In my opinion, Ernest Hemingway did not grow. His most important and most influential period was his first one. Then, gradually, he became a public personality.

Ernest Hemingway's early writings were exciting to read for the first time. This was back in the second half of the 1920's. There was a strong masculine appeal in these early stories. He caught the mood of the time, although some of the stories that had the strongest effect are the Nick Adams ones.[1] These were set in an earlier time. Nick Adams seemed an autobiographical image of Hemingway as a boy. The writing and dialogue were exciting aspects of these early stories. The sentences were simple but they handled experience adequately. They helped to convey experience and other background material. However, when quoted, they do not regain their original effect. "At the lake shore there was another rowboat drawn up. The two Indians stood waiting.

"Nick and his father got in the stern of the boat and the Indians shoved it off and one of them got in to row. Uncle George sat in the stern of the camp rowboat. The young Indian shoved the camp boat off and got in to row Uncle George."[2]

"Indian Camp" does not affect me now as much as the early Hemingway writings did back in the 1920's. I have given the quotation with the idea in mind that the reader can test, for himself or for herself, the impact of isolated Hemingway passages from an early story. Of course, it is not only unfair but downright idiotic to judge the story "Indian Camp" on the basis of these partial quotations. I hope that I need not elaborate on this comment. The story "Indian Camp" has held its interest for me notwithstanding all of the content in the time that has passed since I first read it almost 37 years ago. This is the Nick Adams story in which Nick's father, a doctor, performs a Caesarean operation with a jackknife and without any anesthesia. The locale is Michigan, where, ostensibly, the family of Dr. Adams spends time during the summer. In the area, there are Indians of the Ojibway tribe. An Indian comes to the doctor at nighttime because a pregnant squaw is in pain and difficult, frightening travail. The doctor takes his son, Nick, along. Uncle George also goes with them. A Caesarean operation is necessary. The doctor, Nick's father, goes boldly ahead in performing the operation. It is successful. A boy is born to the squaw. But when words are addressed to the Indian father of his newborn infant, there is no answer, no response. The Indian father is huddled under a blanket. When he does not respond the blanket is pulled down from his face and he is hideously dead. He has slit his throat while the squaw was in difficult labor. "Indian Camp," written close to the beginning of Ernest Hemingway's career, bears some comment. Just as in historic trends, the course of events in a literary career should be outlined. The early works of a writer frequently contain the elements and features of what is to come later in more expanded and clarified development. "Indian Camp" by Ernest Hemingway is a partial illustration of this pattern.

III

"Indian Camp" does not have evocative power in its opening lines. The characters are, at the beginning, merely names. They cross a body of water in canoes. The story is written from the standpoint of "the world of direct experience" to use a phrase I just happened to note in George Herbert Mead's *The Philosophy of the Act.* It is critically fair and proper to pose a question concerning the impact of experience within the story. In effect, I have already posed and answered this question. However, I shall phrase this again and briefly expand my comments.

When a story is told from the standpoint of immediate experience, the impact of words and of events acquires an obvious, if varying,

significance. A childbirth by a squaw forced by a Caesarean operation performed with a jackknife and then the discovery that the
Indian father has cut his throat – all of this concentrated physiology,
and concentrated drama, is too much for a five-page story and the
casual reaction of the boy, Nick Adams. "Nick did not watch. His
curiosity had been gone for a long time."[3]

On various occasions, I have stated or written that Ernest
Hemingway's writing can be described as sensationalist in the real,
the essential meaning of this word – that is, a shock upon the senses.
This is not a total description of Hemingway's fiction. But it does
constitute some important aspects of his fiction. And I think that it
was Hemingway's "sensationalism" that contributed to the original
impact of his work.

<The original impact and effect of Ernest Hemingway's writings is
an interesting matter, but that effect and impact has been registered.
The young Ernest Hemingway did become an influence, and very
quickly, too. His way of writing, his dialogue, and his attitudes.>[4]
These often might better be termed attitudinizations and sometimes,
even affectations. For instance, in "The Killers," there is an atti-
tudinized stoicism which seems to be, in my view, affected.

"The Killers" is, of course, one of Ernest Hemingway's most
admired and famous stories. It is one of the first stories that won him
critical acclaim. When I read it many years ago, I liked it, but with a
core of doubt. So it seems to me now.

It has been observed, more than once, that Ernest Hemingway's
characters have no past, or almost no past. The effects of his writing
depend on immediate moments, and action and sensations of immediate moments. Perhaps this is why Hemingway was sensationalistic as a writer. Again I mean sensationalism in the real sense
of the word – a shock upon the senses.

One of the effects of Ernest Hemingway's first stories was an
excitement of shock in this sense. But this is only one aspect of
Hemingway's fiction. In other words, it is not a total characterization
or account of Hemingway's writing. There was his indescribable
talent of creating a sense of reality, and of achieving this with
characters in a setting that seemed real. His use of dialogue, and the
use of repetition in dialogue were very effective means of creating
this sense of reality.

The killers come into "Henry's lunch room." They are going to
eat. Their manner is insulting. They assert their superiority by a
sneering humor. They are hired killers, and their manner and their
talk befit their occupations. Also, their talk is part of their taking

command of the situation. Their sarcasm is either related to the orders they give, or else an overtone to an actual command. In all of this, there is a fine consistency.

Since writing the foregoing, I have looked at "The Killers" again.[5] Technically, it is Hemingway at his best, in the sense of control over his material, and sharpened clarity of impression. But my impression remains. The lack of past of the characters and the situation are of utter immediacy without background; this robs them of depth. In the 1920's, a story about gangsters could assume that the public would recognize their roles. The story had a strong impact. The times, however, added to the story's impact.

What I have written about "The Killers" can be subjected [to] a counter interpretation. When situations are so exposed that merely to state them conveys a "shock of recognition" and the excitement of the time, then isn't that justification enough for what the artist has done?

As I go back into this story, I have developed two critical estimations of it, one favorable, the other unfavorable. In each of these judgments, I retain the same descriptive account and attribute the same significance to the events. It is not unusual, however, to hold a different view of the same work read at various times and ages of our life. The fact of the matter is that we change, and our likes and dislikes become different, perhaps not totally, but in degrees. This is a commonplace generalization, but it is worth stating.

IV

The work of Ernest Hemingway consists of more than his first writing, his early stories. His life work is finished. We can see him in perspective, which for us can be final. I wish I could be as enthusiastic about his later works as I was about his first ones. So presented, this is not a critical statement. There are, however, some points which I wish to make which are critical in character.

Had Ernest Hemingway confined himself to short story writing, it is likely that he would have left a more sizeable body of lasting work. Two of his novels, *The Sun Also Rises* and *A Farewell to Arms* are worthy of attention, and hold up somewhat in the careless passage of time. Of *The Sun Also Rises,* however, I have already written, and I do not want to repeat what I said in an essay that has been read fairly widely.[6]

A Farewell to Arms is a war novel. It is also a love story. The love story is of the war in the sense that the war made it possible. But it is not a war time tragedy of love. In fact, *A Farewell to Arms* is not a tragedy except in the sense of the biological tragedy of man, and, perhaps, the double tragedy of woman. One could say that it is a personal tragedy. But it is not the war that enforces the death of Catherine at the end of the book.

The above is defining and descriptive. *A Farewell to Arms, The Sun Also Rises,* and the volumes of stories, *In Our Time* and *Men Without Women,* were quite sufficient to support some conclusions about Hemingway's writing. These are ones that I have already embodied, however, in this essay. I have in mind the observation that Hemingway was sensationalistic in the true meaning of the word. The psychology informing his work also is sensationalism. Hemingway, I might remark, is tied to the 1890's. Whether or not Stephen Crane influenced him, there is a real line of connection between Hemingway and Crane. Crane, of course, was of the 1890's. There is much of the same sensationalistic psychology in both men. Neither Crane nor Hemingway probably ever read the Austrian Mach.[7] Mach's ideas of sensationalism lead toward either a revived Berkeleianism or toward Behaviourism. The climate of opinions, the climate of the *fin de siècle* of the nineteenth century, and of the earlier years of the twentieth century were affected by these ideas, and writers were indirectly affected, through "the climate of opinions," "the cultural climate." The sensationalism in Hemingway's writing has another character, however, and this should be noted. It was a kind of basis of a personal doctrine of the immediate.

There was reason, a kind of logic in this attitude, which Ernest Hemingway embodied in stories and his first two novels. What was he to believe in? What big words? What banners? What hopes? It was not cynicism. It was disillusionment to some extent, at least. But this is insufficient to convey the quality, the character, the tone of this attitude. To a degree, at least, it was a traumatic disillusionment. It was, also to a degree, disillusionment without there ever having been illusion.

We can relate Ernest Hemingway's stories of Nick Adams and of earlier times than the First World War in the context of illusion and disillusionment. If we do, we fail to find in these stories any illusions that serve as foils for, or any illusions that provide a dramatic contrast for disillusionment.

V

I shall skip over some of his later books to *For Whom the Bell Tolls.* This novel is his most serious effort and his longest book. It runs to 471 pages, and seems even longer. This novel is his most serious effort, in the sense that he tried to cover a wider range of meanings and experiences than in any of his other novels, and he strove to implant ideas and abstract ideals in his chief protagonist, Robert Jordan. He tried to be more significant than in his other books.

Many readers are more or less familiar with the content. *For Whom the Bell Tolls* is a novel about the Spanish Civil War of the 1930's. Something to take quick note of is the impression you gain from this novel (which you do not get, or at all events, you get in a much milder degree, in others of Ernest Hemingway's novels), is the degree to which this novel depends upon circumstances and events that, in turn, depend upon emotions and feelings outside of the novel itself. There is a parallel criticism to be made of the title which is universal, but Robert Jordan, the chief protagonist is, himself, not universal. And by method, by focus of mind, by life-long habit, up to the writing of *For Whom the Bell Tolls,* Ernest Hemingway was not equipped to achieve universality equal to the title in content.

PART TWO

I

When Ernest Hemingway died, I wrote a memorial article, in which I declared, that I was concerned about writing about the positive aspects of his work.[8] I believed it fair to consider the constructive features of his main work. Was I dodging making critical judgments that could run against the current of mourning? No.

The immediate reaction to the death of Ernest Hemingway was almost personal. The process of publicity and mythmaking went into quick operation. It was an indiscriminate performance, and the columnist, not the writer, was given the dominant role by [the] obituaries.[9] <Ernest Hemingway had influenced me. He had been a friend. I felt I had to write of him as an artist because he was an artist.>[10]

There was some criticism of Hemingway during the 1930's, especially in connection with his novel, *To Have and To Have Not.* It is not fair to dismiss this book without a reason. I have no intention of giving any detailed analysis of this novel, because it is not the best use of time or paper. *To Have and To Have Not* was criticized when it first appeared in 1936. Nevertheless, the book did enjoy a considerable sale.

I would describe *To Have and To Have Not* as sentimentalized toughness, and equally sentimental having not. The principal character of *To Have and To Have Not* is Harry Morgan, who runs rum between Key West, Florida, and Cuba. Morgan is poor, as was nearly everyone in Key West, during the 1930's. He is courageous and tough, and to earn his wherewithall of life, he encounters and meets danger. For Morgan "To have," he must face danger, and risk his life.

When *To Have and To Have Not* originally appeared, there were some comments pro and contra, in reference to the categorical notion of proletarian literature, and the insistence that a writer have what was termed "social consciousness." Such comment was, however, pretty banal and, at times, foolish. Actually, Harry Morgan is closer to *The Old Man and the Sea* than to a 1930's character with social consciousness. In *The Old Man and the Sea,* the old man is divorced of close to all social relationships, also. He is struggling to have what is only partially tangible, and clear. The Old Man is after an illusory fish. The illusory "having" is Morgan's "fish." (I am not extracting any symbol here, but drawing a limited parallel.)

II

For Whom the Bell Tolls is about the Spanish Civil War. Robert Jordan is an American who has joined up with the Loyalist government forces. Here Ernest Hemingway was able to get back to the subject of war. It was a new war, and it was linked up with the major world crisis after that of the First World War. It involved the politics of this country and politics was developing, with new types and credos. It touched on the concerns, interests, fears and angers of most people who read books.

The Spanish War was history. It remains history. Hemingway had been in history in the sense that he had been in war. And he had written of war. But *A Farewell to Arms* is far different from *For Whom the Bell Tolls. A Farewell to Arms* is not history. It is not history with historic meanings that are a part of the context of the story, and of its organization and direction. *A Farewell to Arms* and

For Whom the Bell Tolls are different as novels. The difference has to do with history.

For Whom the Bell Tolls is simply, not subtly, related to history. The Spanish Civil War and Revolution is the general subject matter of this novel, and it was written quite quickly after that war had ended in the victory of the forces led by Generalissimo Franco. Hitler and Mussolini were his allies. Spain became a great cause because of this alliance, and because of the prior successes of Mussolini and Hitler. The enemy was fascism, and fascism was the enemy of man's freedom.

Ideology, as it were, broke loose in America in the 1930's. When I state that ideology struck America, I am well aware that there had been ideologies and ideological clashes in America prior to the 1930's. But it was in the thirties when ideological issues connected with the modern relationships of nations, and within nations, and the co-relationships of power among nations, and the shifts of power within nations occupied so much of the attention of men — <including poets, writers, Vassar girls.>[1][1]

For Whom the Bell Tolls involved revolution and counter-revolution. The difficulties of the treatment of a war such as the Spanish Civil War and Revolution, must be recognized in any discussion of *For Whom the Bell Tolls.* Clausewitz, *On War,* emphasized that "War is a continuation of politics by another means." The Spanish War from 1936 to 1939 was rife, ridden, and riddled with politics. And the politics of this war was a number of diverse strains. The politics of other nations, international politics, and politics of Spain past.

Hemingway was not interested in ideology; and he was not prepared for any such event as the Spanish Civil War. I speak of Hemingway, the novelist and short story writer. This is not a criticism, in any necessary sense of the term; it is descriptive. I do not hold that a writer must be consciously ideological. Likewise, I do not hold that a writer must be consciously political. My comments are concerned with understanding or not understanding, knowing or not knowing, in reference to the ideological and political play which are relevant in attempting to reach any meaning concerning the Spanish Civil War.

The point to be raised here is not that a novel must be history or specifically that *For Whom the Bell Tolls* must be a history of the Spanish Civil War. I shall state my point first as generalization.

Some conception of responsibility in the writing of historical novels must be established. This is but part of the broader question of truth in the novel, and in fiction as a whole; more broadly still, we might say — all creative writing. However, too much is involved here for me to try to deal with the full subject, and the major and inescapable question and problems that are involved in this subject matter. At the same time, I need to make some statement no matter how tentative it may be. I assume that a writer is open to criticism if he tampers with events and relationships of a historic character and sequence. Furthermore, when there are involved and complicated inter-relationships of a historic order, it would seem to me that it is just to hold the writer responsible for learning the character and co-relationships of these involvements and inter-linked relationships. This much stands to reason.

III

The case of *For Whom the Bell Tolls* is clear cut. In the Spanish Civil War and Revolution, the war was not an issue of discipline versus lack of discipline on the Loyalist side. The Loyalist government was a Popular Front government at the time hostilities erupted. The Popular Front was a union of a loose order between parties designated as, or considered, bourgeois or *petit bourgeois,* and parties considered working class parties. Their principal aim was to defend democracy against fascism.

The Popular Front was decreed by Moscow in August, 1935, ending the so-called Third Period of the Communist International, the Third International which was very frequently called the Commintern. The so-called Third Period was one of leftism in a somewhat technical sense insofar as revolutionary theory is concerned. Spain had scarcely any Communist Party prior to the Civil War and revolution. The Spanish Popular Front government was not the same as that called for from Moscow by the Third International in August, 1935. The clash of politics and the growth of the Stalinist Communist influence in Loyalist Spain are essential features of the civil war and revolution.

However, the foregoing is but background in relationship to *For Whom the Bell Tolls.* This novel only touches on the war, in general, and for the main confines itself to an episode which, in its military sense and meaning, is tactical and concerns one locality. There are excursions away from this locality, and general comments, but the heart and the matter of the big novel, is a small corner of the war. But I hasten to add[12]

[1] I refer to the stories appearing in the books Scribner published, that is *In Our Time* and *Men Without Women* [Farrell's note].

[2] "Indian Camp," *The Fifth Column and The First Forty-Nine Stories* (New York: Scribners, 1938), p. 189.

[3] Ibid, p. 191 [Farrell's note].

[4] The sentences in these angle brackets are not found in the University of Delaware collection which lacks two pages of Farrell's holograph (Text A). The transcription is taken from carbon copies of these two pages found among the Farrell papers in the Rare Book Collection, University of Pennsylvania Libraries.

[5] This sentence is contained in Farrell's original holograph (Text A); thus Farrell is not introducing a new judgment in his revised version of this essay (Text D).

[6] Cf. "Ernest Hemingway's *The Sun Also Rises,*" *The League of Frightened Philistines and Other Papers* (New York: The Vanguard Press, 1945), pp. 20-24.

[7] See Ernst Mach, *Contributions to the Analysis of Sensations,* trans. C. M. Williams (Chicago: The Open Court Publishing Company, 1897).

[8] "Ernest Hemingway: The End of Something," *Thought* (30 September 1961), 13-15.

[9] Following this sentence in the holograph (Text A), Farrell repeated his preference for the early Hemingway in some passages which I deleted in Text C. At the conclusion of these deleted passages, Farrell had offered the following footnote: "I have also tapes of a long analysis of Hemingway and Fitzgerald, which I delivered a few years ago, but which I have been unable to get transcribed, let alone published."

[10] These comments in angle brackets are not contained in Farrell's original essay and were added in his revised version (Text D).

[11] This bracketed phrase is not contained in Farrell's original essay and was added in his revised version (Text D).

[12] Farrell's holograph (Text A) is unfinished at this point, and he did not choose to "add" any more in his revised version (Text D).

AN UNRECORDED
HEMINGWAY
PUBLIC LETTER

Although Abner Green's letter to Ernest Hemingway states that the American Committee for the Protection of Foreign Born was distributing Hemingway's letter as widely as possible, only one copy of this mimeographed public letter has been located (Collection of W. Jones). The *Fitzgerald/Hemingway Annual* invites information.

00 Fifth Avenue, New York City   ★   Tel. — ALgonquin 4-2334

February 1
1 9 3 9

Dear Hemingway:

I am enclosing a copy of your letter and what we did with it. We are now in the process of shipping it as widely as we can because it is one of the best means that we have right now of raising any funds to take care of the veterans' cases.

Your help is really very much appreciated. Right now there's only one thing standing in the way of taking care of all of these cases on hand – and that's funds. It's a matter, mainly, of paying for the necessary papers and transportation costs to some country other than their native countries.

It may look somewhat that I'm swapping a compliment for a favor, but I'd like the record to show, Hemingway, that I read the Fifth Column and thought it a fine piece of work. It's not meant just as a compliment.

I never liked reading plays too much, because they were much too sketchy for short-stories. Plays and short stories have a story to tell, the former lacking something in the telling when it's read. The Fifth Column suffered similarly somewhat, but at the same time it had a certain short-story technique one could say that made it a lot better reading than the average play.

Then of course the subject, treatment, characters, etc., being about Spain made me somewhat prejudiced in favor of you and the play, to say the least. But, all considered, handicaps and personal prejudices, I think it was a good play.

By the way, when are you going to write that long novel you used to speak about writing? Is there still a chance of your getting it done? Well, thanks again for your letter and I hope you like the job. Best regards.

Abner Green

American Committee for Protection of Foreign Born

100 Fifth Avenue, New York City ★ Tel. — ALgonquin 4-2334

Dear Friend:

Patrick O'Donnell Read was born in Ireland forty-two years ago. During the World War he served in the Canadian Army and after he was honorably discharged he came to the United States. Last year he went from this country to Spain to volunteer his services in the International Brigades.

There were hundreds like Read, men of all walks of American life, of different political and economic opinions, who offered their lives to fight Fascism in Spain. These men are heroes. I saw them fighting in Spain, bringing honor to the name of America as an exponent of freedom and democracy. Instead of a hero's welcome on their return, however, Read and sixteen other veterans were stopped at Ellis Island and ordered excluded from this country because they are not citizens and failed to take the necessary steps to insure their reentry before leaving.

These seventeen veterans — their heroism and their value to American society — are being disregarded and cast into disrepute by an avalanche of legal technicalities that block their efforts to rejoin their families and friends. At the same time, a cruel fate awaits each and every one of them should they be returned to Europe to face eventual deportation to totalitarian countries.

We must do everything we possibly can to save these men. The American Committee for Protection of Foreign Born, which is defending them, informs me that legal steps can be taken in their behalf. The Committee informs me also that the defense of these men is seriously handicapped by the lack of necessary funds.

Approximately two hundred and fifty dollars is needed to enable one veteran to escape imprisonment and possible death in Germany or Italy or Greece or Yugoslavia. I feel sure that you, too, will want to do your utmost to help save these men. I am asking you to send your contribution to the American Committee for Protection of Foreign Born, 100 Fifth Avenue, New York City, immediately. It is the least we can do to help these heroes.

Sincerely yours,

ERNEST HEMINGWAY

uopwa – no. 16

JILL RUBENSTEIN

A Degree of Alchemy:
A Moveable Feast
as
Literary Autobiography

> Things may not be immediately discernible in what a man writes, and in this sometimes he is fortunate; but eventually they are quite clear and by these and the degree of alchemy that he possesses he will endure or be forgotten. Writing, at its best, is a lonely life. Organizations for writers palliate the writer's loneliness but I doubt if they improve his writing. He grows in public stature as he sheds his loneliness and often his work deteriorates. For he does his work alone and if he is a good enough writer he must face eternity, or the lack of it, each day.[1]

In *A Moveable Feast* Hemingway transforms the materials of auto-biography into the materials of art through that "degree of alchemy" he says the writer must possess. The book is Hemingway's portrait of the artist as a young man, a retrospective account of the end of innocence and the confrontation of experience in the loneliness that is the only mode in which the artist may thrive. His subject is the search for validation of the values most basic to his vision, the faith that the good life is clean and simple and that the elemental pleasures are the most meaningful ones. To preserve the good life, however, the writer, especially, must be continually on the defensive. Hemingway believes that other people are naturally jealous of happiness and successful work and will destroy them, if possible. This belief becomes the basic orientation of *A Moveable Feast;* it molds most of the relationships in the book and Hemingway's attitude toward them.

In the Preface he gives the reader a choice: "If the reader prefers, this book may be regarded as fiction. But there is always the chance that such a book of fiction may throw some light on what has been written as fact." This deliberate confusion of factual material and fictional technique constitutes the "degree of alchemy" of *A Moveable Feast.* Hemingway sees a direct relationship between fiction and the life of the writer: "You invent fiction, but what you invent it out of is what counts. True fiction must come from everything you've ever known, ever seen, ever felt, ever learned."[2] In *A Moveable Feast* he employs the techniques of fiction to reinforce and emphasize his theme. Like the novelist, he selects and shapes reality into the quality of illusion. But *A Moveable Feast* is still autobiography, and the "I" remains unequivocally Hemingway. This interpenetration of autobiographical focus and fictional technique endows the book with a dimension that extends beyond either autobiography or fiction.

Throughout *A Moveable Feast* Hemingway uses figurative and allusive language and symbolism in much the same way that a novelist uses these devices and for the same general purposes. They extend the book's realm of significance; and they provide a unifying structure of images and references, creating reverberations of earlier chapters in the later ones. The title was imposed on the manuscript by a friend of Hemingway's when he and the author's widow were preparing to publish the Paris memoirs posthumously. The phrase comes from Hemingway's ruminations on the advisability of giving up a career in journalism to live in Paris to write seriously. He told A. E. Hotchner, "Yet, there's this to consider as a guide, since it's a thing I truly know: If you are lucky enough to have lived in Paris as a young man, then wherever you go for the rest of your life it stays with you, for Paris is a moveable feast."[3]

The phrase is derived from the Catholic calendar; a moveable feast day is one that is not fixed to a certain date, but is determined by the date of another, which also varies; for example, a moveable feast may occur a certain number of days before or after Easter. The title thus epitomizes Hemingway's conviction that happiness is dependent not on time or place, but on the individual, on his state of mind, and on the human relationships of a given moment. The attitudes that the book will develop toward happiness and art are applicable beyond Paris, beyond the decade of the twenties, even beyond youth.

The most pervasive symbolism of *A Moveable Feast* concerns the idea of escape. In a book devoted to an exploration of the good life, the threats to it, and the possibilities of preserving it, Hemingway sees escape as a better solution than resignation, which is self-destruction, or resistance, which is self-dissipation. To preserve the integrity of both self and work, the artist, especially, must be permitted to retire frequently into his own realm of imaginative concentration.

Hemingway describes his working quarters at "the hotel where Verlaine had died where I had a room on the top floor where I worked. It was either six or eight flights up to the top floor. . . ."[4] He links his own *atelier* to the French poet's and symbolically exaggerates its distance from the life of the world below. However, although he is conscious of the need to detach himself from this world in order to work effectively, he relishes both realms and does not forsake one for exclusive devotion to the other: "Going down the stairs when I had worked well, and that needed luck as well as discipline, was a wonderful feeling and I was free then to walk anywhere in Paris" (13). He repeats this pattern of ascent and descent several times, most notably in his accounts of trips to the mountains. Just as the return to the world from the upper story gives him "a wonderful feeling," a trip to the mountains refreshes his perspective, and he sees everything in Paris as "clear and cold and lovely." The first paragraph of chapter two presents, after an interval of escape, a total contrast to the initial description in chapter one. Instead of "The leaves lay sodden in the rain and the wind drove the rain against the big green autobus at the terminal . . ." (3), we have, "The trees were sculpture without their leaves when you were reconciled to them, and the winter winds blew across the surfaces of the ponds . . ." (11). The concluding chapter (to be discussed more fully below) picks up this symbol of escape to the mountains and presents it in a near-tragic light when it fails to provide the renewed vision so necessary to both happiness and writing. These same elemental symbols, mountain and rain, recur frequently in the fiction, most notably in *The Sun Also Rises* and *A Farewell to Arms*.

Although simplicity characterizes Hemingway's prose style, he constructs several equations which function as implicit, unstated metaphors to advance his theme. The most meaningful of these connects literature and love, both in their effect on him as an individual and in their effect on his relations with others. Writing leaves him with mixed emotions: "After writing a story I was always empty and both sad and happy, as though I had made love . . ." (6). What binds them together for Hemingway is the sacrosanct nature of both acts and the need for absolute concentration and privacy: "I said that I was working hard and it was murder to interrupt and that to interrupt a man while he was writing a book and going well was as bad as to interrupt a man when he was in bed making love."[5] In *A Moveable Feast* writing and love are the sources of Hemingway's greatest joys. The intense beauty and the terrifying vulnerability of each result in the ambivalent, bittersweet tone of the book and its preoccupation with protecting both literature and love from intrusion.

Hemingway uses horse-racing and its influence on him as a metaphor for an alluring but dangerous friend:

> Racing never came between us, only people could do that; but for a long time it stayed close to us like a demanding friend. That was a generous way to think of it. I, the one who was so righteous about people and their destructiveness, tolerated this friend that was the falsest, most beautiful, most exciting, vicious, and demanding because she could be profitable (61).

Racing required too much self-devotion for the rewards it paid. Picking up the symbol of escape to the mountains and the rewards it brings, Hemingway contrasts it, in implicit metaphorical terms, to the vitiating effect of racing: "But it was not the climbs in the high mountain meadows above the last forest, nor nights coming home to the chalet, nor was it climbing with Chink, our best friend, over a high pass into a new country. It was not really racing either. It was gambling on horses. But we called it racing" (61). He felt himself drawn to Enghien, "the small, pretty and larcenous track that was the home of the outsider" (50). Only when he realizes that he is no longer an outsider, that his obsession makes intolerable demands on his time and energy, can he give it up: "You knew many people finally, jockeys and trainers and owners and too many horses and too many things" (62). He repeats this pattern of withdrawal from intimacy in the case of several human relationships that threaten to become demanding and destructive.

This use of allusion, symbol, and figurative language is one of Hemingway's principal catalysts in the alchemical transformation of memory into literary autobiography. These devices unite various sections of *A Moveable Feast* which might otherwise seem disparate and unrelated to each other. Using to best advantage these verbal techniques of fiction, he recreates and shapes memory to "throw some light on what has been written as fact."

A. E. Hotchner, a close friend during the last decade of Hemingway's life, writes that "in Ernest's lexicon, Paris and happiness were synonomous."[6] The setting of *A Moveable Feast,* the great city itself, is the most all-pervasive aspect of the book. Like any accomplished novelist carefully manipulating spatial setting, Hemingway deliberately selects from Paris of the twenties, emphasizing some aspects of it and ignoring others. His feeling toward Paris is ambivalent; a striving for identification coexists with a simultaneous awareness of inevitable difference. He frequently traces his route in the closest detail, and the meticulousness of his walking itinerary indicates a self-consciousness in Hemingway's use of setting that recurs throughout the book. No matter how hard he tries, he cannot take Paris for granted.

The city itself is the most encompassing and well-developed symbol of escape in the book. During his Paris years, when he was working on *The Sun Also Rises,* Hemingway was acutely aware of the common stereotype of the decadent, escapist expatriate. Bill Gorton tells Jake Barnes:

> "You're an expatriate. You've lost touch with the soil. You get precious. Fake European standards have ruined you. You drink yourself to death. You become obsessed by sex. You spend all your time talking, not working. You are an expatriate, see? You hang around cafés."[7]

Although this passage is obviously ironic, Hemingway himself rejected the "strange-acting and strange-looking breed that crowd the tables of the Cafe Rotonde." He described their self-delusive way of life in a Paris dispatch to the *Toronto Star:*

> They are nearly all loafers expending the energy that an artist puts into his creative work in talking about what they are going to do and condemning the work of all artists who have gained any degree of recognition. By talking about art they obtain the same satisfaction that the real artist does in his work. That is very pleasant, of course, but they insist upon posing as artists.[8]

In the same article he referred to Baudelaire who, he suspected, "parked the lobster with the concierge down on the first floor, put the chloroform bottle corked on the washstand and sweated and carved at the Fleurs du Mal alone with his ideas and his paper as all artists have worked before and since." He expresses a similar contempt in *A Moveable Feast:* "People from the Dôme and the Rotonde never came to the Lilas. There was no one there they knew, and no one would have stared at them if they came" (81). Like the fire-eater he met in Lyon, Hemingway regards these fakes as "ruining the *métier*." In failing to acknowledge the sacred nature of art and in refusing to grant it the single-minded devotion that Hemingway knows it deserves, they violate one of his most devoutly-held credos.

To avoid the stifling crowd of American expatriates and poseurs, Hemingway chooses to frequent the smaller cafés filled with "much nicer-looking people that I did not know" (100). He prefers these to the three principal cafes, because they do not involve him in any relationships that linger beyond the moment. Sometimes he even chooses to write in the sanctuary of a café, a process that requires notebooks, pencils, a pencil-sharpener and luck. "Then you would hear someone say, 'Hi, Hem. What are you trying to do? Write in a café?' Your luck had run out and you shut the notebook" (91). Hemingway seems to take a savage pleasure in relating incidents like these in which he can be as rude as possible and still feel morally justified. The moments devoted to his work should be inviolable, and he will brook no interference.

In addition to the smaller cafés, the things Hemingway especially likes about Paris are significant. He consistently singles out for his attention people and things that make no demands upon him because they remain merely objects of observation, and he can maintain his detachment. He is struck by a beautiful girl in a café, and he feels comfortable in possessing his image of her because she remains anonymous and unapproachable, no threat either to his ego or his work. Watching the fishermen on the Île de la Cité, he finds: "It was easier to think if I was walking and doing something or seeing people doing something that they understood" (43). Because he need not interact with them and they leave him free to pursue his own meditations, he accepts them unquestioningly. He generally reserves his benevolence and compassion for people like waiters and garage mechanics. They are neither artists nor writers, and they have no aspirations in that direction, so they exist in another sphere, a completely different realm of endeavor that cannot threaten his.

His relationships with other writers are less straight-forward. He reserves the bitterness of *A Moveable Feast* primarily for rivals, real or imagined, and his praise is usually equivocal and grudgingly given.

Only when he can regard another writer as an object, something fixed, static, and therefore unthreatening, can he feel really comfortable. In Sylvia Beach's bookshop, "a warm, cheerful place," he notes "photographs on the wall of famous writers both dead and living. The photographs all looked like snapshots and even the dead writers looked as though they had really been alive" (35).

His insecurity becomes a rather offensive egotism in his treatment of Fitzgerald. At the end of the chapter called "A Matter of Measurements" in which he makes Fitzgerald look pathetically naive and ridiculous, he discusses him with a bartender who cannot recall "this Monsieur Fitzgerald that everyone asks me about." Hemingway promises Georges "to write something about him in a book that I will write about the early days in Paris. . . . I will put him in exactly as I remember him the first time that I met him" (193). The inference is clearly that Fitzgerald will be immortalized only through the medium of Hemingway's art, an exercise in egoism unsurpassed anywhere else in *A Moveable Feast.* The example is extreme, but the mode of thought has by this time become familiar. In order to preserve his integrity as a man and as a writer, Hemingway often feels compelled to negate human relationships with bitterness and sarcarsm or to reduce people to the status of objects which can be easily controlled.

His manipulation of the Parisian setting of *A Moveable Feast* is remarkably effective. He never attempts indiscriminately to recreate the atmosphere of post-World-War-I Paris. He selects details carefully to contribute to his theme, the possibilities for the preservation of individual fulfillment and artistic dedication. This process of selection creates a meaningful milieu which suggests the tenuousness of the good life that Hemingway seeks to preserve and the human shortcomings that render it so easily vulnerable.

A Moveable Feast is a sustained memory, and Hemingway uses the retrospective point of view to reinforce the theme of lost innocence. Like the photographs in Sylvia Beach's bookshop, memory places people and events at a distance where they can no longer threaten his sense of well-being. This distancing creates irony; the author views his own lost naiveté and reacts to it, and the reader watches the interactions of innocence and experience. Sometimes, however, the irony breaks down, and the tone changes from nostalgia to viciousness. This process occurs in the chapter on Ford Maddox

Ford. Hemingway initially resents Ford as an intruder upon his reverie, and he treats him with irony lightly hidden under a guise of politeness. The clever verbal manipulation, critical but not yet malicious, degenerates rapidly as Hemingway loses his retrospective, ironic point of view and begins mercilessly to play with Ford.

Even when he tries to be gentle and laudatory in his recollections of other writers, retrospective irony frequently becomes harsh criticism. He praises Pound but obviously disapproves of his subordination of aesthetic criteria to personal considerations: "He liked the works of his friends, which is beautiful as loyalty but can be disastrous as judgment" (107). Hemingway goes to the opposite extreme with Scott Fitzgerald. Although he obviously feels a rather strong distaste for his personal conduct, he allows Fitzgerald's genius to compensate for it:

> When I had finished the book I knew that no matter what Scott did, nor how he behaved, I must know it was like a sickness and be of any help I could to him and try to be a good friend. . . . If he could write a book as fine as *The Great Gatsby* I was sure that he could write an even better one (176).

Sometimes Hemingway unintentionally becomes the victim of his own retrospective irony. In the detachment of temporal perspective, he professes to feel sorry for Gertrude Stein and to perceive her literary frustrations and jealousies. But his own feuds with Ford and Wyndham Lewis and Ernest Walsh are equally petty and betray fears and insecurities analogous to Gertrude Stein's.

A sense of the fragility and ephemerality of apparent greatness is implicit in the temporal stance that Hemingway chooses. The retrospective point of view ironically emphasizes the discrepancy between the naiveté of youth and the sophistication of the mature writer. Naiveté, however, cannot be equated with gullibility. Hemingway's innate distrust of people was apparently deeply rooted even in the Paris days: "In those days we did not trust anyone who had not been in the war, but we did not completely trust anyone . . ." (82). The wariness often blends retrospective irony with more than a dash of bitters, and the combination is effective in reflecting Hemingway's sense of an innocence never to be recaptured.

In 1935 Hemingway wrote some important advice to a young writer who had asked for his counsel: " 'As a man,' he explained, 'things are as they should or shouldn't be. As a man you know who is right and who is wrong. You have to make decisions and enforce them. As a writer you should not judge. You should understand.' "[9] One of the problems implicit in the autobiographical mode is, of course, the unavoidable lack of detachment and objectivity. Writer and man are conterminous in the author, and moral distinctions and value judgments inevitably intrude. In *A Moveable Feast* Hemingway overcomes this handicap by enlisting it in his service. He deliberately creates a tone of moral superiority and, to a certain extent, self-righteousness that does not offend the reader because it so well serves the author's purpose. He uses this tone to advance his defense of the values that the entire book is designed to vindicate — the supremacy of art, the need for loneliness in its creation, and the beauty of the simple, uncluttered life.

His nearly religious veneration for the purity of literature is evident throughout *A Moveable Feast,* and the value-judgment never seems intrusive because "writer" and "man" are synthesized and subsumed in "artist." Hemingway derives great pleasure from the favors he does for other writers. He made Ford promise to publish in his *transatlantic review* the beginning of Gertrude Stein's *The Making of Americans,* and he edited the manuscripts for her because she felt this sort of work was degrading and odious. When Ernest Walsh had to return to the United States because of illness, Hemingway promised to attend to details of publication for his periodical. He apparently enjoyed these tasks and regarded them as services in the cause of literature. However, when these efforts began to encroach on his own work, he drew back. The first consideration was always to maintain his freedom from entanglements that might compromise his own writing.

> The way it ended with Gertrude Stein was strange enough. We had become very good friends and I had done a number of practical things for her such as getting her long book started as a serial with Ford and helping type the manuscript and reading her proof and *we were getting to be better friends than I could ever wish to be* (117, italics mine).

He and his wife learned "about the system of not visiting people" in order to preserve both their time with each other and his time to work. The self-righteous light in which Hemingway regards his assistance to others and the importance of his own privacy emphasizes his two inter-related themes of the supremacy of art and love and the vigilant care required to preserve them from intrusion and destruction.

Hemingway glorifies the simple life he led in Paris and endows himself with a certain moral superiority to those who cannot share it. He takes a rather perverse satisfaction in the realization that Gertrude Stein is jealous of his happiness, but he handles this satisfaction so well that it endows youth and love and writing with an aura of indefinable beauty. The same stance of moral superiority recurs in his attitude toward creature comforts. To the truly dedicated, literature, love and Paris ought to provide ample compensation for the lack of material wealth. The attitude is somewhat smug, and it could easily be offensive if treated less tactfully. But Hemingway makes it one of the highest values of *A Moveable Feast* and transforms autobiographical complacency into lyrical celebration.

His real or fancied empathy with Paris and the French people gives him another source of superiority. He dislikes foreigners who fail to understand the French, and he presents them as overly-sophisticated, decadent, and lacking the capacity for imaginative sympathy that is the first requisite for the writer. Although he is a snob of another sort, Hemingway cannot tolerate social snobs; and when Ford condescendingly talks about going slumming among the French, Hemingway demolishes him. He is only slightly less harsh with Fitzgerald:

> I thought of telling Scott about this whole problem of the Lilas, although I had probably mentioned it to him before, but I knew he did not care about waiters nor their problems nor their great kindnesses and affections. At that time Scott hated the French, and since almost the only French he met with regularly were waiters whom he did not understand, taxi-drivers, garage employees and landlords, he had many opportunities to insult and abuse them (168).

Hemingway makes Fitzgerald seem prejudiced and self-contained, while he, himself, values openness, flexibility and receptivity to new impressions and ideas. Again, the sense of moral superiority serves the larger conception of *A Moveable Feast.* Instead of trying futilely to eliminate the inevitable autobiographical bias, Hemingway molds it to his own purposes and employs it as part of the "degree of alchemy" that transforms memory into art.

The last chapter, "There is Never Any End to Paris," may serve well as a paradigm of how Hemingway applies the techniques of fiction and poetry to autobiography. This final chapter emphasizes the inter-relationships among Hemingway's three main themes — the high calling of literature, the happiness of simplicity and innocence, and the destruction wrought by intruders on both art and happiness.

The village of Schruns in the Austrian Alps is the ultimate physical symbol of escape and deliberately sought isolation. Hemingway seems happiest when he and his wife are skiing as high as they can go. Only when they descend do they rediscover the terrible fragility of their happiness:

> I loved her and I loved no one else and we had a lovely magic time while we were alone. I worked well and we made great trips, and I thought we were invulnerable again, and it wasn't until we were out of the mountains in late spring, and back in Paris that the other thing started again (210).

Related to the mountain symbolism is the symbol of the avalanche. He recalls digging a man's body out of the snow: "He had squatted down and made a box with his arms in front of his head, as we had been taught to do, so that there would be air to breathe as the snow rose up over you" (204). This account is a physical analogue of what Hemingway attempts to do throughout *A Moveable Feast;* he, too, wishes to make a box for himself, to preserve a small but vital area around himself that will remain inviolate from intrusion and prevent him from being stifled. Like the man buried by the avalanche, he, too, fails.

Hemingway uses metaphors of naturalistic destruction and animal imagery for the vulnerability of happiness and his own egocentric naiveté. A "pilot fish" comes, leading the rich who spoil the rural idyll. Two people who love each other are like a beacon that draws migrating birds, and the rich, "when they have passed and taken the nourishment they needed, leave everything deader then the roots of any grass Attila's horses' hooves have ever scoured" (208). He bitterly condemns his own gullibility in the same animal terms: "Under the charm of these rich I was as trusting and as stupid as a bird dog who wants to go out with any man with a gun, or a trained pig in a circus who has finally found someone who loves and appreciates him for himself alone" (209). The autobiographical narrative stance permits him effectively to combine anger at the intruders and profound disgust with himself.

In this last chapter Hemingway uses the retrospective point of view to illustrate the central paradox of *A Moveable Feast.* Although he can never return to the Paris of his innocence, "There is never any ending to Paris"; he returns despite his loss, and "Paris was always

worth it and you received return for whatever you brought to it"
(211). He sees his early days more clearly now in the perspective of
lapsed time, but he inevitably sees them with a vision that is partly
formed by the experiences that constitute it.

University of Cincinnati

---

[1] Nobel Prize acceptance speech, quoted in Carlos Baker, *Ernest Hemingway,
A Life Story* (New York: Scribners, 1969), pp. 528-529.

[2] A. E. Hotchner, *Papa Hemingway* (New York: Random House, 1966), p.
103.

[3] Hotchner, p. 57.

[4] *A Moveable Feast* (New York: Scribners, 1964), p. 4. Page references will be
placed in parentheses following subsequent quotations.

[5] Hotchner, p. 147.

[6] Hotchner, p. 58.

[7] Ernest Hemingway, *The Sun Also Rises* (New York: Scribners, 1926), p.
118.

[8] *By-Line: Ernest Hemingway,* ed. William White (New York: Scribners,
1967), p. 25.

[9] Quoted in Charles Fenton, *The Apprenticeship of Ernest Hemingway* (New
York: Farrar, Straus & Giroux, 1954), p. 155.

JOHN RAEBURN

Death in the Afternoon,

AND

THE LEGENDARY HEMINGWAY

John Peale Bishop remarked in 1936 that the author of *The Sun Also Rises* and *A Farewell to Arms* had been transformed into the "legendary Hemingway," a public figure whose personal fame equalled or even outstripped his literary renown.[1] From the very outset of his career Hemingway attracted more attention than young novelists usually do, but his fame in the 1920s was primarily literary in character and confined for the most part to the intellectual elite; by the mid-1930s, however, not only had his fame become as much personal as literary, but it also had spread beyond the intellectual elite to a much larger and more heterogeneous audience. More than any other novelist of his generation he fit the definition of a celebrity: a public figure who is more renowned for his personality than for his accomplishments, however substantial and meritorious those accomplishments might be.

The principal question, of course, is what was it that precipitated this remarkable transformation from private artist to public celebrity? Hemingway himself was still producing fiction in the 1930s with much of the same skill and energy he had demonstrated in the previous decade; between 1930 and 1936 he wrote nearly a score of short stories, among them such superior works as "A Clean Well-Lighted Place," "Fathers and Sons," "The Snows of Kilimanjaro," and "The Short Happy Life of Francis Macomber." But during these same years he had also begun to publish another kind of writing — vividly personal non-fiction — and it was this work which more than anything else elevated him to the status of a celebrity. Measured in terms of bulk this non-fiction of the early and mid-1930s outweighed his fiction: it included two books, *Death in the Afternoon* and *Green Hills of Africa;* twenty-five "letters" for the fledgling slick magazine, *Esquire;* and a scattering of essays and letters for other periodicals. The proportion itself of non-fiction to fiction suggested that he was reorienting his relationship with his audience; rather than remaining the anonymous presence behind the mask of his fictional narrators, he more often than not was discarding that mask in order to address his readers directly. The most striking feature of all this non-fiction, moreover, was the intimate, personal tone he characteristically adopted; whatever the nominal subject might be, the real subject was always Hemingway himself — his character, his tastes, and his attitutdes. By focusing his readers' attention upon himself in this way, he succeeded in bringing his personality, as distinct from his literary accomplishments, to the forefront of the popular consciousness. In all of his non-fiction he elaborated a public personality which, in turn, became the cornerstone of the legend which journalists helped to build around his life. The "legendary Hemingway," in short, was created by an ongoing dynamic relationship between his self-advertisment in his non-fiction and the mass media's exploitation of his public personality.

All of the non-fiction he published in the 1930s was important to the growth of his personal fame; but it was *Death in the Afternoon* (1932) which was most important, not only because it signalled the shift in his relationship to his audience, but also because it was, more than anything else he ever wrote, the most nearly comprehensive formulation of his public personality. He said that he wrote the book because there was no other work in either Spanish or English which provided an introduction to modern bullfighting, and as a beginner's guide it is still unsurpassed in English and, probably, in any language.[2] But it was much more than simply a technical manual of the mechanics and aesthetics of the bullfight; it was also a portrait of its author as he wished to appear to the public. It marked the beginning of Hemingway's vigorous self-advertisement of his personality, an activity which was to lead eventually to his enshrinement as a celebrity. It was, moreover, the first major work in a project that would occupy the novelist off and on for the remainder of his life: the creation of an adventure saga with himself as hero.

Hemingway is less obviously the hero of *Death in the Afternoon* than he is, for example, in his subsequent *Esquire* essays (1933-1936), *Green Hills of Africa* (1935), or *A Moveable Feast* (1964); unlike his role in these later works, he is in the earlier one only a spectator, and hence the possibilities for dramatizing his own activities are somewhat reduced. Nevertheless he is the hero of the book simply because no one or nothing else — neither bullfighter nor bullfighting as a subject — dominates the book with the same authority that the personality of the author does. As one reviewer of the book wrote, "the quality of its author's character is imprinted in the ink of the type on every page."[3] The portrait of himself that Hemingway limns in *Death in the Afternoon* reveals a man who is worldly, knowledgeable, hardened, and a bit cynical, but who is nevertheless charged with enormous gusto.

This self-portrait is a composite of a number of sketches interpolated throughout the book, each of them highlighting a distinctive aspect of the author's personality. These sketches cluster, to change the metaphor, around nine stances, or roles, that Hemingway assumes in the book. These nine roles are the basis of the novelist's public personality, and each of them recurs again and again in his subsequent advertisements of his personality. Journalists who later wrote about Hemingway discussed him in large measure in terms of these self-defined roles. *Death in the Afternoon* thus not only promoted his public personality, it also forecast the contours his personal reputation would assume in the media.

The first and most obvious of these roles is Hemingway the sportsman. Any reader of *The Sun Also Rises* would know of the novelist's interest in bullfighting, but *Death in the Afternoon* gave Hemingway wider scope than his fiction ever could to demonstrate his love for bullfighting and particularly his expertise in it. The quantity of information in the book is staggering. Every aspect of the sport, from where the best bulls are bred to what is done with the dead animal after the *corrida,* is fully covered in the text. The discussions of the strengths and weaknesses of various matadors, contemporary and past, are extensive and detailed. Hemingway was never a dabbler in any of his pursuits; rather, he always gave the impression that he was one of the leading authorities on whatever activity was currently engaging him. His characteristic tone in his nonfiction was a pedagogical one — the master speaking to his somewhat callow pupils. He always implied that his justification for this assumption of authority was experience; he repeatedly advertised himself as a man who had "been there" in the most immediate sense. He had on several occasions jousted with calves and cows in village *capeas,* amateur events which, if not really dangerous, simulated the conditions of the corrida; moreover he was an intimate of some of the great bullfighters, a fact that he clearly indicates in *Death in the Afternoon* (pp. 79, 87, 503-506). Not only had he seen them perform in the ring, but he had also talked with them in cafes, observed them in their dressing rooms, and watched them having their wounds treated in the infirmary. By underlining his position as an insider, Hemingway was lending credence to his self-anointed status as an expert. The stance of the expert was one he characteristically assumed in his nonfiction; it gave to his public pronouncements the impress of authority, and suggested that he was a man who could be relied upon to discover the truth in situations where other men might falter or be deluded.

After *Death in the Afternoon,* Hemingway turned his attention to sporting realms other than bullfighting, particularly to hunting, fishing, and boxing, only returning to bullfighting in "The Dangerous Summer," published less than one year before his death. The role of sportsman, while always significant in his public reputation, achieved particular importance between 1932 and 1936. During these four years he would vigorously and regularly advertise his expertise and competence as a sportsman, assuming the stance of an authoritative commentator and a champion competitor. After discussing the performance of others in *Death in the Afternoon,* he would in much of his subsequent non-fiction turn to descriptions of his own sporting triumphs. The discussion of his own sporting achievements created, in turn, a journalistic interest in them, with the result that newspapers and magazines began to make frequent reports of his prowess. This publicity inevitably created controversy about Hemingway himself. Many of his critics saw his preoccupation with sports as a manifestation of his lack of seriousness as a writer and as evidence that his career as a major literary figure was finished. Others, including the novelist himself, defended his activities on the grounds either that what he did with his own life was nobody else's business, or that his interests in sports connected in some usually undefined way with his skill and success as a novelist. This extensive airing of Hemingway's sporting interests and accomplishments and the concomitant discussions of what they signified about him thrust his self-assumed role as a sportsman to the forefront of his public reputation. Much of what was written about him and his work after *Death in the Afternoon,* and particularly between 1932 and 1936, treated directly or indirectly his concern with sports.

Closely related to his interest in sports was his self-advertised role as a paradigm of masculinity. Bullfighting, after all, to many non-Spaniards is a relic of barbarism, a cruel and brutal blood sport. For a widely-renowned American writer to make it the subject of a very long book inevitably raised questions about the writer himself. As one reviewer of *Death in the Afternoon* put it, the important thing was ". . . not only whether the book [was] good but whether Mr. Hemingway himself [was] good."[4] The very subject matter of the book inevitably suggested that its author prided himself on his hard-boiled, unflinching view of life and death, and that he was deeply, perhaps inordinately, interested in physical courage. Hemingway's treatment of various aspects of the sport did nothing to alleviate these impressions. He insisted that he was not writing an apologia for bullfighting, and indeed seemed to take special pains to demonstrate his imperviousness to some of the usual criticisms of it. He rails, for example, against a recent law which made protective quilts obligatory for the picadors' horses; this innovation, he says, destroys the comic aspect of the disemboweled horses trailing their entrails after they had been gored by the bull (pp. 7-8). He also argues for the "spiritual enjoyment" of killing, calling it "one of the greatest enjoyments of a part of the human race" (p. 232). He adds that because killing and death are so central to bullfighting, it is a manlier sport than Anglo-American games which look only to winning (p. 22).

His celebration of the physical courage of the bullfighters in *Death in the Afternoon* unequivocally suggested that this quality held a paramount position in his own system of values. Whether or not a man had physical courage was the test of his manliness, whether he was a bullfighter or not. While Hemingway does not explicitly discuss situations in which his own courage was tested (with the possible exception of an ironic allusion to his own exploits in the bullring), he implies in several references to his own experiences with violence and death that physical peril is no stranger to him. By extolling what he sees as the masculine virtues of courage, honor, and pride, and by implying the preeminence of these virtues in his own code of behavior, Hemingway was clearly advertising his own manliness.

He also advertises his masculinity in another, more direct way. *Death in the Afternoon* contains several contemptuous references to homosexuals which suggest that Hemingway's disdain for their abnormal sexuality is an unimpeachable demonstration of his own manliness. He singles out for particular contempt several homosexual writers: Jean Cocteau, Raymond Radiguet, Oscar Wilde, Walt Whitman, and Andre Gide; he categorizes them collectively as "the mincing gentry" (pp. 205, 71). He makes his own sexual proclivities clear in a discussion of Waldo Frank's *Virgin Spain,* which he dislikes primarily because of its ornate style. Frank, he says, is unable to make a clear statement about Spain because his style is inflated by a pseudo-scientific jargon and a distorted mystical vision. He calls this kind of style, which he thinks is generally fashionable in America, "erectile writing," and then proposes a remedy for it. "I wonder what such a book as *Virgin Spain* would have been like if written after a few good pieces of that sovereign specific for making a man see clearly. . . . it seems as though, had the brain been cleared sufficiently, by a few good pieces, there might have been no book at all" (p. 54). In other words, Hemingway, who had been hailed as a master of clear, stripped, un-mystical prose, is asserting that sexual intercourse is the necessary prelude to writing honestly and clearly. His suggestion in this discussion that his sexual life and his creative life were organically connected was another advertisement of his own masculinity. The implication was clear enough that the author of *The Sun Also Rises* and "Big Two-Hearted River" had a very active and satisfactory sex life.

One of the characteristics of a truly masculine man according to Hemingway is his ability to recognize and expose sham when he encounters it. He has this capacity for seeing clearly because his experiences with danger and death have taught him that any man's hold on life is tenuous; as a consequence of this knowledge he can perceive what is essential and true more accurately than other less experienced men. The badge of his masculinity, in short, is his ability to see through pretention. *Death in the Afternoon* is filled with assaults on various people and ideas which the author conceives of as phony, hypocritical, or witless. Often these expostulations have a jeering tone about them. The matador Nino de la Palma (the model for Pedro Romero in *The Sun Also Rises*), for example, demonstrated "cowardice in its least attractive form; its fat rumped, prematurely bald from using hair fixatives, prematurely senile form" (p. 88). The New Humanists, a school of critics whom the novelist disliked because they were antagonistic to his work, were ignorant and foolish, and, moreover, were the products of "decorous cohabitation" despite the fact that "the position prescribed for procreation is indecorous, highly indecorous" (p. 139). Waldo Frank's book on Spain was a fake not only, as Hemingway implies, because Frank's sex life was not active enough, but also because he did not have even a minimal understanding of the country about which he was writing, and relied instead on a flatulent and abstract mysticism to sustain it (pp. 53-54). Abstractness or "any over-metaphysical tendency" he said, was "horseshit" (p. 95). Years later he would formulate this idea into a general theorem. "The most essential gift for a good writer," he told an interviewer, "is a built-in, shock-proof, shit detector."[5] Hemingway's portrayal of himself as a man who could easily recognize cant and folly and expose them suggests the third role that he defined for himself in *Death in the Afternoon:* the destroyer of pretention.

The obverse of this trait of unmasking meritriciousness is the advancing of positive standards. Hemingway is not simply concerned with negative valuations in *Death in the Afternoon,* but energetically makes positive ones as well. These judgements embrace a variety of areas, not only bullfighting, but also drinks, paintings, books, cities, cafes, and so forth. The fourth role that he assumes, then, is of an arbiter of taste. *Death in the Afternoon* is filled with asides detailing the author's opinions on painting, wine, literature, foods, and other sundry matters. By interlarding these short essays on questions of taste with his discussions of bullfighting, he was able to demonstrate his expertise and knowledge in a host of realms. Near the beginning of the book, for example, he makes an extended comparison between enjoying bullfights and enjoying wine. This comparison allows him to introduce his own preferences in wine, which he sententiously calls "one of the most civilized things in the world," and to establish a standard by invidious comparison:

> In wine, most people at the start prefer sweet vintages, Sauternes, Graves, Barsac, and sparkling wines, such as not too dry champagne and sparkling Burgundy because of their picturesque quality while later they would trade all these for a light but full and fine example of the Grand crus of Medoc though it may be in a plain bottle without label, dust, or cobwebs, with nothing picturesque, but only its honesty and delicacy and the light body of it on your tongue, cool in your mouth and warm when you have drunk it (pp. 10-11).

Hemingway's promotion of himself as a man supremely capable of differentiating the genuine article from the spurious one is one of the dominating leitmotifs of the book and, indeed, of the public image he projects throughout his career. This pedagogical stance, with which the novelist establishes guidelines for proper discriminations of quality in a number of realms, literary and non-literary, was a characteristic feature of his public personality. By vigorously making public his preferences in questions of taste, he was in effect conferring on himself the status of an expert in matters often beyond the usual purview of a novelist.

Hemingway's fifth role in *Death in the Afternoon,* and one closely related to his stance as an arbiter of taste, is his promotion of himself as the knowledgable world traveller. *Death in the Afternoon* is as much a travel book about Spain as it is a treatise on bullfighting. Hemingway put into it much of the knowledge that he had acquired on his many trips to Spain since the early 1920s; one critic has suggested that the book is "a cross between Baedecker and Duncan Hines."[6] The discussions of various cities and regions are full and detailed; Hemingway even tells his readers what to order at various cafes: "On hot nights [in Madrid] you can go to the Bombilla to sit and drink cider and dance and it is always cool when you stop dancing there in the leafyness of the long plantings of trees where the mist rises from the small river. On cold nights you can drink sherry brandy and go to bed" (p. 48). He also informs his readers about proper comportment when visiting Spain. There is a long discussion, for example, of the proper way to ogle women at the bullring: it is bad taste to use field glasses from the actual ring (in those where spectators are permitted before the fight), but a compliment if they are focused from the *barrera,* the first row of seats (pp. 40-42).

Hemingway's novels and short stories had suggested the depth of his knowledge of France, Spain, and Italy, and contained a good deal of what might be called travel advice (e.g., from the ending of *The Sun Also Rises* one would surmise that the Casa de Botin was a good place to eat in Madrid), but *Death in the Afternoon* gave him more opportunity than his fiction afforded to demonstrate in detail how familiar he was with a foreign locale. His familiarity, the book carefully shows, is not that of the casual tourist, but of the insider who knows precisely what to see, where to eat and drink, and how to act. As a guidebook to the pleasures of visiting Spain, *Death in the After-noon* is highly prescriptive. It implies that to see Spain truly, the prospective visitor could do no better than to follow the explicit guidelines set out by its author. In subsequent non-fiction works he would treat Spain again, France, Africa, Cuba and Bimini, and, to a lesser degree, Italy, Switzerland, Austria, and Turkey. Some of his nonfiction also advised travelers in America, notably those going to Key West or the mountain states of the West. In every case Hemingway demonstrated his thorough and intimate knowledge of the area he was describing and suggested how visitors might enjoy it as much as he obviously had. This extensive advertisement of his role as a knowledgable world traveller was so successful that *Vanity Fair* in 1934 dubbed Hemingway and his wife "America's favorite gypsy couple."[7]

His advertisements of his preferences in wine and food, his descriptions of *ferias* and bullfights he had attended, and his discussions of what to do in Spain all suggest the sixth role which was a part of his public personality — the exemplar of the good life. The impression *Death in the Afternoon* gives of its author's life is that it was an extremely glamorous one, charged with excitement, filled with pleasure, and, as he once said of bullfighters, lived "all the way up." As a *cognescente* he was supremely prepared to marshall his experiences in such a discriminating way as to make them yield their full measure of enjoyment. The picture that he draws of himself travelling in Spain, drinking fine wines, eating *langostinos* in Madrid bistros, and watching bullfights suggested that his life had nothing of the mundane about it. It was full, rich, and completely satisfying. The implicit assumption that he was a master at the art of living was a perennial characteristic of Hemingway's non-fiction and of his public personality; he always conveyed the impression that he was absolutely in control of the course of his life and would not trade it for any other life that could be imagined.

The satisfactoriness of his life was in part due to his intimate knowledge of those things which interested him. His enjoyment of bullfighting was greatly enhanced, for example, by his personal acquaintance with several of the great *toreros*. He could write with authority about Spain because he saw it, not with the eyes of the superficial tourist, but as a native would. Madrid, he says, "has none of the look that you expect of Spain. It is modern rather than picturesque, no costumes, practically no Cordoban hats, except on the heads of phonies, no castanets, and no disgusting fakes like the gypsy caves at Granada. There is not one local-colored place for tourists in the town. Yet *when you get to know it,* it is the most Spanish of all cities, the best to live in, the finest people, month in and month out the finest climate . . ." (p. 51, italics added). The stance of the insider, the seventh role which Hemingway adopts in *Death in the Afternoon,* is a characteristic one in all of his non-fiction. Wherever he was or whatever he was discussing, he always assured his readers that the accuracy and genuineness of his perceptions were indisputable because he occupied a privileged position of familiarity. Most often this demonstration of his status as an insider would take the form of a dramatization of his friendship with other members of an in-group, whether they were bullfighters, soldiers, white hunters, or whatever. The line between the initiated inner-circle and the uninitiated outsiders was as firmly drawn in his non-fiction as it was in his fiction, and Hemingway never failed to make clear his membership in the former group. The impression his non-fiction invariably gave was that he was an enormously attractive and likeable man whom other men readily admitted to their counsels because of his *savoir-faire* and his engaging personality.

A commonplace of criticism of Hemingway's fiction is that his heroes are distinguished by their capacity for enjoying sensuous pleasure. They have earned the right, for example, to be insiders and to eat and drink well by virtue of their knowledge of the rigor and tenuousness of life. This knowledge has been dearly bought: the Hemingway hero has paid for it by enduring shattering and ofttimes violent experiences which leave both physical and psychic scars on him. His enjoyment of sensuousness is the manifest of his knowledge of essential reality. In *Death in the Afternoon* Hemingway suggests that what is true of his heroes is also true of himself. The eighth role, then, which he adopts is the battle-scarred stoic. The portions of the book devoted to his connoisseurship are balanced by sections in which he describes or implies his own intimate acquaintance with violence and tragedy; he has paid heavily, in other words, for the privilege of being an exemplar of the good life. While he rarely goes into detail, the implication that he has seen and suffered much is clear enough.

His preoccupation with violent death, which he calls the "most fundamental" of all human experiences (p. 2), is itself a warrant of his own intimacy with the harsh realities of existence. The book is filled with the killing of men as well as animals, deaths which the author has witnessed and often describes in detail. Death, he says, "is the unescapable reality, the one thing any man may be sure of; the only security . . . it transcends all modern comforts and . . . with it you do not need a bathtub in every American home, nor, when you have it, do you need the radio" (p. 266). Besides recounting the deaths of bullfighters, he describes in grisly detail some of the deaths he had witnessed in Italy during the war. He notes what putrefying bodies looked and smelled like, and recounts his experiences burying victims of a munitions-factory explosion near Milan (pp. 135-138). All these graphic accounts of death suggest that the author's life had been marked by encounters with violence and tragedy, and, like his fictional heroes who had been initiated into knowledge by their immediate awareness of the reality of death, he also spoke with the indisputable authority which is derived from experience. The notion that he was a man who had endured much hardship and seen much suffering and then emerged stronger because he had experienced so much was an important part of the Hemingway legend. One of the reasons why it was so important was that he advertised himself as such a man so frequently in his non-fiction.

The final role which Hemingway assumes in the book, and indubitably the most important one in his public reputation, was of the heroic artist. The artist, he says, pays a high price for the knowledge that he transmutes into art.

> There are some things which cannot be learned quickly and time, which is all we have, must be paid heavily for the acquiring. They are the very simplest things and because it takes a man's life to know them the little new that each man gets from life is very costly and the only heritage he has to leave. Every novel which is truly written contributes to the total of knowledge which is there at the disposal of the next writer who comes, but the next writer must pay, always, a certain nominal percentage in experience to be able to understand and assimilate what is available as his birthright and what he must, in turn, take his departure from (p. 192).

The artist is heroic because he suffers pain and loss for the sake of his art. He is also, in a sense, a sacrificial figure: he must experience and feel more intensely than most men (and for Hemingway consciousness is usually equated with pain) in order that his art add to the store of human knowledge. By professing this romantic view of the artist, Hemingway was inevitably focusing attention on his own personality. This formulation, stressing experience more than craft, suggested that an understanding of the artist's life was a suitable complement to reading his works and an aid in understanding them.

Hemingway discovers in bullfighting a paradigm for the role of the artist. He was first attracted to the bullfight because it was the only place in the post-war world where he could observe violent death, one of the "simplest things" and therefore one of the most important for a writer to study (p. 2). But the sport also provided him with a standard of heroism, derived from the code of the bullfighters, which emphasized the importance of physical courage, self-control, and stoicism. The great bullfighters, as Hemingway explained it, all had "cojones." They all shared the willingness to take chances with their lives, relying only upon their skill and dexterity to preserve them, in order that those observing the performance might vicariously experience the feeling of a triumph over death itself (p. 213). The bullfighter, rather than being an athlete in the Anglo-American sense, is an artist; similarly, the bullfight is not a sporting event but an artistic performance that parallels classical tragedy (pp. 20-21, 99).

In general terms, then, the bullfighter is an artist who confronts violence and possible death in the service of his art. He must risk his life repeatedly; and any reduction in the danger to himself is cheating which destroys the integrity of the artistic expression and negates the cathartic experience for the audience. Unlike spectators of any of the other arts, the viewers of a bullfight are privileged to witness the very act of creation itself; they can immediately judge the precise quantity of skill and danger involved.

The willingness to confront danger that Hemingway saw as a central feature of the successful bullfighter's psychology was a quality that he shared himself; stories of his derring-do and eagerness for various kinds of combat were already legion by 1932. By celebrating the bullfighter as an heroic artist, he was implicitly suggesting his own conception of how the artist should live and what his social function should be. The artist's obligation was to seek out danger and test himself against it; if he was not a bullfighter he ought to find other spheres of comparable risk. Out of the encounter between artist and violence would emerge, not only the material for art, but also the self-confidence of "knowing truly what you really felt, rather than what you were supposed to feel . . ." (p. 2). If this self-knowledge was translated into art, the audience for the work could partake in the truth that it held. The artist's life, therefore, was a perilous but noble one: he staked his very existence in order that others might share the knowledge that he found.

What Hemingway does in *Death in the Afternoon* is to frame criteria by which the success of an artist's life may be judged. These criteria implicitly take the form of a series of questions. Are the novelist's experiences legitimate ones, i.e., are they profound? Do they involve an element of risk? How did he comport himself? What did he learn? Hemingway's formulation in *Death in the Afternoon* of a standard of personal conduct for the artist links that book with the rest of the non-fiction he produced during his long career, works in which he focuses more completely on himself than he does in the bullfighting book. Many of his non-fictional works after 1932 answer the questions raised in *Death in the Afternoon* about the artist's behavior by documenting how successfully Hemingway lived up to the standards he fixed for the ideal artist's life. Regarded in this way, *Death in the Afternoon* is a prolegomenon to the adventure saga that featured the novelist himself in the leading role.

The question of why he should feel the necessity to make public these details of his private life is a complicated one, and no single answer is ultimately very satisfying. Presumably he could have met his own standards of behavior and never written a word of non-fiction about their achievement, simply using what he had learned as the basis of his fiction. Whatever in his psychic life stimulated his itch for publicity and self-aggrandizement may only be guessed at, but that the itch was there is undeniable.

The celebration of the artist as hero in *Death in the Afternoon* furnishes one clue which explains why he periodically advertised his own exploits. The artist, in Hemingway's view, occupies a position of paramount importance in his society; he operates on the frontiers of experience and consciousness and sends back reports of his findings. These reports, if they are stated truly and honestly enough, are to the audience surrogates for actual confrontation, allowing it to share in the artist's experience and the knowledge he has gained from it. Thus far Hemingway's theory of the artist's role differs little from other widely-held ones. Where it does differ, however, is in his admiration for the artist who actually performs his creative act directly before his audience – this artist is, of course, the bullfighter. In no other art is the impact of the artist's skill and daring so immediate to the audience.

In watching a bullfight the spectators could experience directly the danger in which the artist placed himself; they watched him pass the bull's horns close to his body. The writer had no such opportunity to enact his encounters with danger before his audience; his novels presumably contained the distillation of the knowledge he had gained, but they were obviously not the experiences themselves. Readers might make inferences about the author from the novels, but they would remain only guesses. But this gap between the writer's experiences and the audience's perceptions of them could be considerably narrowed by first-person accounts of events in the writer's life. If these accounts were not the actual events, they at least described real experiences without compelling the writer to don a fictional mask that confused imaginative reality with literal reality.

By writing in the first person about his experiences, Hemingway was able to simulate for his audience something of the immediacy of the bullfight. He could portray himself as an artist who, like the bullfighter, was experiencing danger and perhaps potential death in the service of his art. The precise measure of his courage in confronting experience could be weighed and judged, and thus his stature as an artist-hero could be assessed.

In his short stories and novels, moreover, Hemingway had taken physical courage, violence, and death to be his provinces as a writer. In his non-fiction, by dramatizing his own courage and describing his brushes with violence and death, he was giving to his fictional voice the stamp of authenticity. He was, in other words, suggesting that because he had experienced so much danger himself, his authority to write about it was unassailable. Norman Mailer proposes that Hemingway wrote so much about himself in order to "enrich his books." His work would have seemed silly, Mailer says, "if it had been written by a man who was five-four, had acne, wore glasses, spoke with a shrill voice, and was a physical coward. . . ."[8] By publicizing his personality and his activities so prodigiously, Hemingway was, in Mailer's sense, enriching his books by conveying to his audience his notions of what kind of man he was.

These nine roles that Hemingway assumes in *Death in the Afternoon* — sportsman, paradigm of masculinity, destroyer of pretention, arbiter of taste, world traveller, exemplar of the good life, insider, battle-scarred stoic, and heroic artist — all focused attention on his personality. Even the role of heroic artist emphasized his personal experience more than it did his mastery of craft. His assumption of all of these roles might be inferred from his previous fiction, but these inferences were inevitably complicated by the fictional mask the novelist wore. There was, of course, no such ambiguity about *Death in the Afternoon,* where he was clearly writing about himself and his own personality. The book suggested that Hemingway wanted to be known as more than a great writer; indeed, it seems clear that what he wanted was to be recognized as no less than a hero in his own right.

The decision to make public his personal life carried with it grave dangers for the artist, dangers Hemingway was acutely aware of. While he was writing *Death in the Afternoon* he was invited to contribute a foreword to a bibliography of his works then in preparation. He refused the offer on the grounds that anything of this nature that he wrote might deflect attention away from his works, where it properly belonged, to his own personality. He was adamant that he wanted his fiction to be evaluated solely on its merits without reference to anything he personally said or did.[9] Later, shortly after *Death in the Afternoon* had been published, he publicly replied to a reviewer who had taken exception to his disparaging comments in the book about Jean Cocteau. Cocteau, Hemingway said, was a "public character" and therefore not exempt from personal criticism.[10] Thus he recognized that the artist who became a "public character" was likely to have his work judged in terms of his personality, or, more drastically, to have his work completely disregarded and only his personality judged. Nevertheless, Hemingway's desire for personal celebrity and public recognition of his heroic stance overrode his misgivings. *Death in the Afternoon* signalled the fact that he would not shrink from making public revelations about himself, and that, indeed, he would lavish the same kind of attention on the creation of a public personality as he might on the creation of a character in a work of fiction. It was a successful and memorable creation, so memorable, in fact, that it often overwhelmed his substantial literary accomplishments. Hemingway's "rich and roaring life," as one mass-circulation magazine later characterized it, "was his own best story."[11]

The publication of *Death in the Afternoon* inaugurated, to borrow a term from economics, the take-off phase of Hemingway's personal reputation. It helped to create an apparently unquenchable thirst for details about his private life, a thirst which the mass media and the novelist himself quickly moved to assuage. It is safe to say that without *Death in the Afternoon* and his subsequent non-fiction, Hemingway might have had a limited celebrity, but it would never have reached the gigantic proportions that it did. The self-advertisement of his personality set in motion a process of response by journalists and critics that kept Hemingway's name before the general public for the rest of his life and transformed him into a celebrity.

University of Michigan

---

[1] John Peale Bishop, "Homage to Hemingway," *New Republic*, LXXXIX (11 November 1936), 40.

[2] Ernest Hemingway, *Death in the Afternoon* (New York: Scribners, 1932), p. 517. Subsequent references to this work will be placed in parentheses in the text.

[3] Lincoln Kirstein, "The Canon of Death," *Hound and Horn*, VI (January-March, 1933); reprinted in John K. M. McCaffery, ed., *Ernest Hemingway: The Man and His Work* (Cleveland and New York: World, 1950), 60.

[4] E. L. Duffus, "Hemingway Now Writes of Bullfighting as an Art," New York *Times Book Review* (25 September 1932), p. 5.

[5] George Plimpton, interview with Hemingway in *Writers at Work: The Paris Review Interviews, Second Series* (New York: Viking, 1963), p. 239.

[6] Phillip Young, *Ernest Hemingway: A Reconsideration*, rev. ed. (University Park, Pa.: Pennsylvania State University Press, 1966), p. 96.

[7] "The Hemingways on Land and Sea," *Vanity Fair*, XLII (July, 1934), 25.

[8] Norman Mailer, *Advertisements for Myself* (New York: Putnam, 1959), p. 20.

[9] Carlos Baker, *Ernest Hemingway: A Life Story* (New York: Scribners, 1969), p. 211.

[10] Ernest Hemingway, letter to Robert M. Coates, "Books," *New Yorker*, VIII (5 November 1932), 74.

[11] Cover, *Saturday Evening Post*, CCXXXIX (12 March 1966).

KENNETH E. BIDLE

Across the River

and

Into the Trees:

RITE DE PASSAGE À MORT

Ritual informs the writing of Ernest Hemingway. No other American author involves his characters in ritualistic action and thought as frequently as does Hemingway. His characters use ritual to intensify experience, to bring a semblance of order from a chaotic universe, to unify empathetic people through totemic affiliation, and – of significance for this article – to prepare for and signify changes in one's status in relationship to the cycle of life, i.e., the rite of passage.

Rites of passage are easily identified in modern religious ceremonies contingent upon baptism, confirmation, marriage, and burial. Likewise, secular activities such as graduation, initiation into Hellenic and fraternal organizations, and presentation of prizes or awards for meritorious performances are rites of passage. Such rites serve two major functions: to proclaim to the public that the individual has a new position or role in society and to impress upon the individual the importance of his new role and its concomitant responsibilities. In addition, the ritual assures the individual that he has the qualities necessary to meet his new obligations, giving him confidence in his ability to deal with the challenges and threats of his new status.

As with many of Hemingway's works, close examination of *Across the River and into the Trees* clearly reveals that the leading character, Colonel Richard Cantwell, repeatedly resorts to ritualistic actions.

Perhaps the critics who dealt harshly with this book would have presented more accurate appraisals if they had accepted Hemingway's *donnée:* an old warrior prepares for death in the same way that he lives – on the primitive, instinctive level – by performing rituals that are timeless and universal. True, Cantwell's rituals are partially self-created and self-imposed, but anthropologists and psychologists insist that such actions are in keeping with certain personality types; that is, certain humans lack satisfactory orientation within their own culture and can only achieve a form of integration by creating a self-world of ritualized behavior.

Psychologists, especially Carl Jung, repeatedly insist on the indispensable role of ritual in human activity. Jung specifically cites ritualistic actions practiced to invoke *numinosum,* an alteration of consciousness in the ritual participant. One achieves *numinosum* by invocation, incantation, sacrifice, meditation, self-inflicted torture, and confession. When *numinosum* is achieved, the ritual participant feels at ease with his world, for he has confidence that the malevolent powers have been placated and the benevolent powers have been invoked.

In keeping with his belief in a two-part unconscious (personal and archetypal), Jung avers that man practices two types of rituals: those common to the culture in which he exists and those which are the product of his unconscious inheritance, actual as well as mythical. It is necessary to keep Jung's dual sources of ritual in mind when examining *Across the River.*

On the literal level, the book is set in the post-World-War-II period and concerns a U.S. Army Colonel, Richard Cantwell, fatally ill with heart trouble. Knowing the seriousness of his affliction, the Colonel, now stationed at Trieste but having fought in Northern Italy during World War I, returns there for three days, ostensibly to hunt ducks but in actuality to die. He first visits Venice to renew acquaintances and to be with the nineteen-year-old Italian noblewoman who loves him. After two days in Venice, the Colonel goes duck hunting, overexerts himself, and dies on the return to Trieste. These bare bones of the plot reveal that the book does have a certain amount of dramatic possibility.

The book, however, was condemned because of the Colonel's vulgarity and his obsessive desire to conduct every conversation – even those with his sweetheart – as an interview. Critics complained that the Colonel even resorts to interviewing himself when he has no confessor around. (It will be shown later that this act of confessing is central to the book and was included deliberately and consciously by

Hemingway.) Most critics failed to perceive Hemingway's all-encompassing intent. They looked at the parts rather than the whole. They erred in failing to note the fidelity with which Hemingway integrated his subject and theme.

The subject of the book is the death of a professional soldier, a man who has lived keenly and on the margin of life and death. The theme of the book is that such a person (and by implication, all of us) comes to satisfactory terms with death only by performing an elaborate, precisely organized ritual. Hemingway superbly integrates and fuses subject and theme by focusing on the ultimate ritual of human existence, the *rite de passage à mort.*

As has been said, Colonel Cantwell, the protagonist of the book and identifiable with the warrior clan, is faced with the irrefutable knowledge that his death is imminent. Having seen death on an elemental level as a soldier and being a "primitive" in orientation to life, Cantwell prepares himself for his own passage to death by performing a series of elaborate, yet fundamental rites. These rites include, in a mythical but obvious fashion, baptism, confirmation, holy orders, sacred dining, matrimony, penance, extreme unction, and blood sacrifice. In fact, Cantwell participates in the various rituals in the order in which they are listed above, an order which gives the novel unity and structure.

The plot is constructed so that the book opens as Colonel Cantwell is being ferried out to the spot where he will perform the last ritual − that of blood sacrifice − as the final propitiatory act of his life. In Cantwell's instance, blood sacrifice involves the slaying of ducks in a precise, considered fashion − more of this later, however. As the colonel is waiting in the half-sunken wooden hogshed which serves as a duck blind, he relives the activities of the previous three days. Actually these are the last days of his life, for at the end of the book the action returns to the conclusion of the duck hunt which is followed immediately by the Colonel's death.

In the sunken hogshed awaiting the arrival of his sacrificial game, the Colonel recalls his interview with an Army physician three days previously. The physician, a friend of the Colonel, had implied the seriousness of the Colonel's illness by failing to offer him medicine. This scene is an excellent example of Hemingway's use of implication to achieve meaning beyond that of the dialog itself. When the physician calls the Colonel, "You poor son of a bitch,"[1] the reader is made aware of the gravity of the illness.

Hemingway also uses this scene to establish a mood appropriate for the primitive rituals to follow. The Colonel invites the physician to go on the hunt, but the physician declines, saying that he is a "city boy" who buys his "ducks at Longchamps on Madison Avenue" (p. 11). To which the Colonel retorts, "All right, City Boy. You'll never know." The last three words — "You'll never know" — imply the City Boy's inability to perceive the utter necessity of performing the primitive act of hunting as partial preparation for death. The City Boy is outside the pale: he is not among those initiated into the primitive but essential mysteries of life.

In his mind, the Colonel next relives the trip from Trieste to Venice. His driver, a corporal named Jackson, reveals he is also among the uninitiated by his lack of concern for the devastation wreaked by the medium bombers and his complete insensitiveness toward the religious paintings which he had seen in Florence. He calls them "sort of a manifest, say, of this whole bambini business" (p. 15). The Colonel, whose thoughts reveal that he does have a great understanding of Renaissance Italian painting, makes no attempt to enlighten Jackson.

Rather, he turns his thoughts to the surrounding terrain, for he had fought here and had been wounded here in World War I. He recalls that only a few weeks earlier he had located the exact spot where he had been wounded, the wound being a baptism by his own blood into the world of those who possess an intimate knowledge of their own personal death. He now detours to that sport, relieves himself:

> "A poor effort. . . . But my own."
> "Now I'll complete the monument," he said to no one but the dead, and he took an old Sollingen clasp knife such as German poachers carry, from his pocket. It locked on opening and, twirling it, he dug a neat hole in the moist earth. He cleaned the knife on his right combat boot and then inserted a brown ten thousand lira note in the hole and tamped it down and put the grass that he had cored out, over it.
> "That is twenty years at 500 lira a year for the Medaglia d'Argento al Valore Militare. The V.C. carries ten guineas, I believe. The D.S.C. is non-productive. The Silver Star is free. I'll keep the change," he said.
> It's fine now, he thought. It has merde, money, blood; look how that grass grows; and the iron's in the earth along with Gino's leg, both of Randolfo's legs, and my right kneecap. It's a wonderful monument. It has everything. Fertility, money, blood and iron . . . (pp. 18-19).

Here is the primitive ritual of sacrifice at its most intense. Cantwell's merde, money, blood, and iron are appropriate sacrifices to commemorate his passage from innocence to knowledge, his baptism under fire, and his confirmation into the warrior clan. Likewise, the Colonel's sacrificial act of excretion (a fertility rite commonly practiced by many cultures) invokes the beneficence of those powers which govern the regenerative processes of the world, a rite he must perform to be ready for the obligatory sexual ritual which occurs later. By returning the money which his medals have earned him, he liberates himself from obligation to them; in essence, he partially frees himself from the duties and restrictions of his profession.

It is significant to note that after performing this ceremony the Colonel is self-assured. He awakens his driver, who has characteristically slept through the Colonel's rite, and with confidence tells him: " 'Turn her around and take that road toward Treviso. We don't need a map on this part. I'll give you the turns' " (p. 19). Cantwell is now in control; he is experiencing the spiritual ecstasy resulting from having performed a ritual well and precisely.

On the remainder of the trip into Venice, Cantwell is "strictly controlled and unthinking *[sic.]* his great need to be there" (p. 20). He has performed the first of the requisite death rituals and now feels compulsion to complete the rest. Impatient for the proper turn in the road, the Colonel, as in all his actions, is not content to take the shortest, most convenient route to Venice: he must take the proper one, the one which leads through the area where he had fought in World War I. Along this route he recalls the actions of that war which provided his initiation into the mysteries of war and easy death. Further, the Colonel again reveals his primitive streak when he observes an oxen. "Why does it move my heart to see the great, slow, pale oxen? It must be the gait as well as the look of them and the size and color. But a good fine big mule, or a string of pack mules in good condition, moves me, too. So does a coyote every time I ever see one, and a wolf, gaited like no other animal, gray and sure of himself, carrying that heavy head and with the hostile eyes" (p. 24). Note the primitiveness and wildness of the scenes which stir him; they are something out of man's primeval past, not of the twentieth century. They are scenes from dim antiquity, but the Colonel, with his elemental orientation toward life, thrills to them.

Cantwell also thrills to the sight of Venice: ". . . he continued to look and it was all as wonderful to him and it moved him as it had when he was eighteen years old and had seen it first, understanding nothing of it and only knowing that it was beautiful" (p. 31). Here we learn why he had to approach Venice from one direction and why he had assumed control of the car's route: To achieve the full intensity necessary for completion of this phase of his *rite de passage,* he must reconstruct the circumstances and emotions surrounding his first view of the city. He must relive consciously his initiatory period.

As the auto moves closer to Venice, Cantwell recalls his World War I experiences. He remembers his first wounds, "small wounds in the flesh of the body without breaking bone, and he had become quite confident of his personal immortality" (p. 33). Then he was hit "properly and for good" and his feeling of grace is lost forever: "No one of his other wounds had ever done to him what the first big one did. I suppose it is just the loss of immortality, he thought. Well, in a way, that is quite a lot to lose" (p. 33).

Such thoughts remind him of his own imminent death: "For a long time he had been thinking about all the fine places he would like to be buried and what parts of the earth he would like to be a part of. The stinking, putrefying part doesn't last very long, really, he thought, and anyway you are just a sort of mulch, and even the bones will be some use finally" (pp. 34-35). He is moving closer to death, and he still has much to do by way of preparation.

They finally arrive at the *imbarcadero* for Venice. Waiting for the launch, Cantwell visits a special bar and is greeted with reverence by the bartender, with whom the Colonel has previously established a bond of comradeship. They shake hands; the bartender has already ordered the Colonel's regular drink, a Gordon's gin and Compari; and they take new delight in an old joke about Italian Minister of Defense Pacciardi. "The seriousness with which the Honorable Pacciardi took the post of Minister of Defense of an indefensible country was a bond between the Colonel and the bar-tender" (p. 40). With intense pleasure they extend and amplify the joke. It assumes gross proportion, but is interrupted by the appearance of an outsider, Corporal Jackson, the driver. He moves "in different circles" (p. 36) and is among those who can violate the sanctity of the Colonel's ritual. Thus, a new ritual has been brought in – that of holy orders or the initiated vs. the uninitiated.

This ritual is extended when Colonel Cantwell reaches the hotel where he is to stay. His first question is, "Where is the Grand Master?"; and the reader is introduced to *El Ordine Militar, Nobile y Espirituoson de los Caballeros de Brusadelli,* a purely fictitious organization which the Colonel and his Italian friends have organized in jest but which they treat with extreme seriousness. Evidence of the exclusiveness of the *Ordine Militar* occurs when Cantwell greets the hotel barman: " 'Good evening, Privy Counsellor,' he [Cantwell] said to the barman, who was not a full paid-up member of the order but whom he did not wish to offend" (p. 54).

Shortly thereafter the Grand Master of the Order makes his appearance:

> He advanced smiling, lovingly, and yet conspiratorially, since they both shared many secrets, and he extended his hand, which was a big, long, strong, spatular fingered hand; well kept as was becoming, as well as necessary, to his position, and the Colonel extended his own hand, which had been shot through twice, and was slightly misshapen. Thus contact was made between two old inhabitants of the Veneto, both men, and brothers in their membership in the human race, the only club that either one paid dues to, and brothers, too, in their love of an old country, much fought over, and always triumphant in defeat, which they had both defended in their youth.
>
> Their handshake was only long enough to feel, firmly, the contact and the pleasure of meeting and then the *Maitre d'Hotel* said, "My Colonel" (p. 55).

Note the intensity of their meeting, the emphasis on brotherhood and shared secrets, and the almost formal, ceremonial way in which they shake hands. After this obviously fraternal greeting, they conclude the reunion with a drink. Then in a mock-serious tone, the Colonel conducts the business of the Order, after which they commune with one another by recalling the World War I experiences that form the strong bond between them. They talk of the heroism and valor and relive old glories but, " 'There aren't any such times any more,' the Colonel said and the spell was broken" (p. 63). Nevertheless, the Colonel has participated in the third – holy orders – of the eight rituals which he must observe by way of preparation for death.

The substance of the fourth ritual is implied in the concluding exchange between the *Gran Maestro* and Cantwell when Cantwell inquires about reservations for dinner. The *Gran Maestro* desires to know how many to expect and the Colonel responds, " 'We'll be two' " (p. 64). Hemingway then introduces into the novel the Colonel's young sweetheart, Renata (rebirth), a lovely Italian girl of aristocratic background. Renata and the Colonel eventually meet, talk, drink and dine – in that order – with such precision and exactness that one is forced to notice the ritualism of their behavior. Their every word and every action are calculated for the effect. The words are said "with caution," and the drinks must satisfy a prescribed formula, "fifteen to one." Here also we learn that the Colonel's misshapen hand (the one with which he had greeted the Grand Master of the Order) has become a symbol between Renata and him.

She wishes to hold it and caress it; it represents all the wounds — physical, psychological, and otherwise — which he has ever suffered. Later it is vital in the by-play of their sexual union.

Their reunion at Harry's Bar establishes the infrangible relationship between Renata and Cantwell, but sanctitude is threatened by evil, alien forces. At a nearby table are four lesbians; at another is a man with "a strange face like an over-enlarged, disappointed weasel or ferret. . . . pock-marked and as blemished as the mountains of the moon. . . . Above this face . . . was black hair that seemed to have no connection with the human race. . . . A little spit ran out of the corner of his mouth . . ." (p. 87). Obviously these hostile forces riolate the sacred atmosphere required for Renata and the Colonel's meeting, so they return to the Hotel Gritti to eat their dinner, a meal infused by ritualistic implications.

On the way to the Gritti, the girl forces two emeralds upon the Colonel: " 'I would like you to have the emeralds and you could keep them in your pocket like a lucky piece, and feel them if you were lonely' " (p. 103). Such a gift of stones harks back to ancient fertility rites which preceded mating and sexual union. Primitive marriage ceremonies often include a ritual meal of cereals, seed-bearing fruit, flesh of animals, and drink. The meal usually follows an exchange of gifts (our modern rings). The bride often gives an amulet composed of magic stones which is to be worn near the genitals to ward off evil spirits and to impart fertility. Renata stipulates that Cantwell is to carry the stones in his pocket and to feel them if he is lonely.

Ultimately they reach the hotel and partake of the ceremonial dinner with the *Gran Maestro* supervising the rite. The *Gran Maestro*, in effect, is the ritual priest. He is assisted in the ritual by a waiter who "was a member of the Order" (p. 124), but it is the *Gran Maestro* who selects the food and the wine. He directs the service; he serves the food "adroitly and with respect both for the food, and those that were to eat it. 'Now eat,' he said. 'Uncork that Valpolicella' " (p. 124). There is no mistaking his priestly role, and he fulfills it well and fully. Thus, Renata and Cantwell complete the fourth ritual, sacred dining.

The conversation during the meal leaves little doubt about what is to follow. Renata and the Colonel leave the Hotel, taking with them a bottle of wine and a U.S. OD blanket given them by the *Gran Maestro,* and embark in a gondola. After suitable preliminary ritual, they consummate sexual congress under the blanket furnished by the *Gran Maestro,* who again has functioned as a priest. A brief excerpt from the conversation prior to the sexual union illustrates the ritualistic quality of their preparation. The Colonel says:

"You know just what you want?"

"I do indeed. Is it un-maidenly? I learned that word too from my governess."

"No," he said. "It's lovely. Pull up the blanket good and feel that wind."

"It's from the high mountains."

"Yes. And beyond there it's from somewhere else."

The Colonel heard the slap of the waves, and he felt the wind come sharply, and the rough familiarity of the blanket, and then he felt the girl cold-warm and lovely and with upraised breasts that his left hand coasted lightly over. Then he ran his bad hand through her hair once, twice, and three times and then he kissed her, and it was worse than desperation (p. 152).

The wind is from the high mountains but "beyond there it's from somewhere else," a mysterious unknown source which furnishes them with a timeless setting suitable for their love making. As part of the preliminary play, Cantwell strokes Renata's hair three (the traditional magical number) times.

During the first union, "The Colonel said nothing, because he was assisting, or had made an act of presence, at the only mystery that he believed in except the occasional bravery of man" (p. 153). The terms "act of presence" and "mystery" suggest the religious nature of the second act between Renata and the Colonel. The number three assumes further significance in that they unite sexually three times during the evening in the gondola. After the completion of their sexual congress, they conclude the sexual ritual by carefully and precisely phrased conversation accompanied by the drinking of the wine furnished by the *Gran Maestro*.

Thus, the fourth (sacred dining) and fifth (matrimony or sexual union) rituals are now complete, and the Colonel has three more rituals to perform to complete his *rite de passage à mort*. Left are confession and penace, extreme unction, and ritual blood-letting.

In actuality, the Colonel has been conducting a partial confession in all of his conversations with Renata, but such confessions have been peripheral to the rite at hand. He must achieve a purgation under the proper circumstances, circumstances which are arranged on the day after the sexual ritual was completed. The Colonel had returned to his hotel and slept alone. Renata had wanted to stay with him, but he had refused her: ' "It wouldn't be right. For them. Nor you. The hell with me' " (p. 159). The next morning they go for breakfast at the Hotel Gritti Palace, after first meeting at a restaurant where breakfast was available, but which was not the proper place to commence the confession ritual. " 'Breakfast is worthless here, and I don't like the square when it is flooded. It is said. . . . Should we go and have breakfast at the Gritti?' " (p. 200. The *Gran Maestro* again administers their meal, after which they go to the Colonel's hotel suite.

Once there, Renata prepares the Colonel for confession by asking him to leave his tunic on. It represents his worldly identity and he needs to be suitably garbed for the forthcoming ritual. As they lie quietly on the bed, she leads him into a discussion of the two great failures of his life: his third divorce and the loss of his general's stars. Holding his wounded, misshapen hand, Renata guides the discussion so that it becomes a confession. She demands that he tell her "Everything" (p. 220). She forces him to cleanse himself of all pent-up hostilities.

First, the agony of his marriage is relived. Renata forces Cantwell to think of that wife and the venom he has accumulated. Ultimately, they achieve success: " 'She is forgotten,' the Colonel said. And, strangely enough, she was." The purgation has been so effective that the ex-wife is "gone now, for good and forever; cauterized; exorcised and with the eleven copies of her reclassification papers, in which was included the formal, notarized act of divorcement, in triplicate" (p. 214).

Next, he talks of World War I "and now his head was turned to her head, and he was not lecturing; he was confessing" (p. 222). Note the word "confessing." He becomes vitrolic in his denunciation of those who had taken away his command, but she chastens, " 'Please don't be rough. Just tell me true and hold me tight and tell me true until you are purged of it; if that can be' " (p. 225). Ultimately he is purged, but only after she implores him to talk on and on. " 'Go on,' the girl said. 'Please let me fill your glass and you, please look at the light on the ceiling' " (p. 239). Thus she administers a ritual drink while, "The Colonel looked up at the play of the light on the ceiling. It was reflected, in part, from the Canal. It made strange but steady movements, changing, as the current of a trout stream changes, but remaining, still changing as the sun moved" (p. 235). The "strange," "steady movements, changing" yet "remaining," of the lights form the proper background for the purgation, and represent the Colonel's own mood. To him, they represent the mysterious patterns under-lying existence and give a clue to its meaning.

Inevitably the confession turns to the Colonel's death and burial. Renata vows he will be buried where he wishes and suggests the primitive rite of suttee as an appropriate complement of his burial.

". . . I will see that you go where you wish to go and I will go with you if you like" (p. 228). Cantwell vehemently refuses her suggestion; and the purgation, at her insistence, is resumed:

> "I bore myself, Daughter."
> "I don't think you do, Richard, you would not have done something all your life if you were bored by it. Don't lie to me please, darling, when we have so little time."
> "I won't."
> "Don't you see you need to tell me things to purge your bitterness?"
> "I know I tell them to you."
> "Don't you know I want you to die with the grace of a happy death? Oh I'm getting all mixed up. Don't let me get too mixed up."
> "I won't, Daughter."
> "Tell me some more please and be just as bitter as you want" (p. 240).

Thus, she administers extreme unction by helping him "to die with the grace of a happy death." Finally, the Colonel, in the state of exhaustion typically resulting from such a purgation, sleeps. Throughout this entire confessional scene, Hemingway repeatedly employs words with religious connotations, a random sampling of which includes "exorcised," "sacrifice," "purge," and "contrition." His use of such words intensifies the confessional aspect of the passage.

After purgation, the Colonel and Renata partake of a ritual meal during which the Colonel precisely and solemnly selects food and wine appropriate to the rite of confession. Everything is methodically and ceremoniously consumed. During this meal, Renata is initiated into the Order with due rites, and at the meal's conclusion the Colonel departs for duck hunting, the last of his pre-death rituals — sacrificial blood-letting.

The book, then, has moved full circle; it starts with the Colonel's duck hunting, moves back three (that number again) days to his confrontation with imminent, inevitable death, and then traces the Colonel's ritualistic behavior during the last three days of his life. During those three days he has lived carefully and properly. He has sacrificed merde, blood, iron, and money at the spot where he had first been baptized into war. He has confirmed his membership in an Order limited to those who were baptized in war. He has eaten ritualistically and received a fertility symbol, an amulet from his mate. After a satisfactory preliminary ritual, he has participated thrice in a sexual act. He has confessed himself in order "to die with the grace of a happy death" (p. 240), and now he has only to complete the last rite — to kill, not viciously or in anger, but carefully and consciously, with control and exactness. He completes the blood-letting and the *rite de passage* is concluded. He is ready for death; and he dies, quietly and with grace, in the backseat of his automobile as Jackson drives it into the night.

By utilizing Christian and primitive ritual, Hemingway has achieved organic fullness. His central character, with his totemic identification with war and its demands for fundamental living, is a man who would naturally have observed the rites recorded in the book. Perhaps his rituals are the product of a neurotic or perhaps they rise from the collective unconscious of man's primitive inheritance and his need to establish *numinosum;* whatever their source, they fit appropriately into the novel. The ritual acts, along with the mythological and literary allusions, give *Across the River* dimensions which the near-sighted critics failed to observe. They should not be forgiven their oversight and the wounds which they dealt Hemingway by faulting this rich book. The book is not self-parody: it is a richly sensitive book of an old warrior's preparation for death. Surely, the old warrior swears, but old warriors who have seen men suffer and die do swear. Therefore, the main character does not have a "behind-the-barn-door" mentality; rather, he is keenly aware of life and of death and reveals his awareness in his elaborate preparation for passage from life to death, his own personal *rite de passage à mort.*

Those who condemned the book failed to see that Hemingway achieved exactly what he had intended, the fifth dimension in prose — the fifth dimension which can only be achieved if "one is serious and had luck." Hemingway was serious; he had luck; and he produced a truly significant book.

Elmhurst College

---

[1] *Across the River and into the Trees* (New York: Scribners, 1950), p. 10. Subsequent references are to this edition and will be placed in the text.

JOHN STUBBS

LOVE

AND

ROLE PLAYING IN

A Farewell to Arms

A Farewell to Arms is Hemingway's novel about the discovery of the smallness and powerlessness of human beings in a world indifferent to their well being and about the defenses they construct to protect themselves from the crippling effects of such a discovery. Frederick J. Hoffman, in his discussion of war literature in *The Twenties,* has shown how the novel opens out from a study of war to a consideration of the hard, gratuitous quality of life in general.[1] Other critics have discussed at length the naturalism and existentialism inherent in Hemingway's picture of man in a harsh world.[2] What remains to be considered more fully is Hemingway's treatment of the defense Frederic Henry and Catherine Barkley put up by means of their "love" to guard themselves against the paralysis that awareness of human insignificance can produce.

Almost since the time of the novel's publication, the love of Henry and Catherine has been attacked by critics. Edmund Wilson has objected on aesthetic grounds that the love is an "idealized relationship" founded unrealistically on "the abstractions of a lyric emotion."[3] More psychologically inclined critics such as Isaac Rosenfeld, Leslie Fiedler, and Robert W. Lewis, Jr. have characterized it as "immature" and "adolescent."[4] These attacks are, I believe, mistakenly founded on the assumption that Hemingway wrote a double book: a war story and a love story. Nothing could be further from the truth. The love, if it is to be understood, must be seen as a direct consequence of the characters' war experience. Recently, critics Richard B. Hovey and Stanley Cooperman have suggested that the peculiar nature of the love reflects the "psychic need" of Henry and Catherine.[5] In this essay, I wish to extend their suggestion and to examine the way the love of Henry and Catherine serves their "need" for a psychological defense. Much attention in the past has been directed at the defense mechanisms in Hemingway's own personality. Yet the psychological defenses he depicts with great subtlety in his characters have not received as much scrutiny as they deserve.

The "love" between Frederic Henry and Catherine Barkley is built on role playing.[6] Both characters select parts for themselves in an ordered game of love which allows them to shut off, or at least minimize, the overwhelming aspects of the knowledge of human mortality that the war brings them. The defense of role playing, of course, is not unique to *A Farewell to Arms* in the Hemingway canon. In "Big Two-Hearted River," for instance, Nick Adams carefully builds a role of sportsman for himself to block out the trauma of his wound and to recapture belief in himself as an individual competent to function in the world around him. He contrives a series of tasks: setting up a good campsite, cooking and eating properly, catching his bait, and fishing the river well. Nick designs the tasks to be difficult enough to produce self-satisfaction when he performs them, but not so difficult that he risks failure in attempting them. The hard task of fishing the swamp, Nick postpones until he is stronger. He knows that fulfillment of any task chosen in advance — no matter how banal — brings a certain feeling of satisfaction. And Nick is a master at choosing the right tasks and the right role to restore his self-esteem. Similarly, Hemingway's "code heroes" create roles for themselves and derive pleasure from playing them well. Jake Barnes can maintain his self-esteem by imitating the bullfighter's "grace under pressure" in *The Sun Also Rises,* and the major in "In Another Country" can preserve his dignity by acting out the pose of military stoic. Role playing is their way of imposing order on chaotic life. Seen this way, role playing is a heroic gesture. But seen another way, it is an escape into an artificially constructed world. Hemingway is always clear on the first aspect, but only occasionally is he willing to treat the second with the fullness it deserves. In *A Farewell to Arms,* Hemingway deals carefully with both the heroic and the escapist qualities of role playing, and as a result, the novel is his richest and most successful handling of human beings trying to come to terms with their vulnerability.

At the beginning of the novel, Frederic Henry sees an order in the army and wishes to fit into it. Although he can't detail reasons for joining the army, he is convinced Italy must avoid the consequences of defeat, and he is prepared to act on his conviction. He works with great energy on the details of running the ambulances. He is irked to find out that his men can function smoothly when he is away on leave. And he takes his duty to bring back his vehicles during the retreat so seriously that he shoots one of the sergeants who deserts him. On a more mundane level, he is fastidious about his uniform, worries about the Italian salute, and wishes to have his Italian accepted as the speech of a native. Like many Hemingway heroes, he exists on the outskirts of an ordered world and tries to enter it. The important thing for us to realize, however, is that his life has, at the outset, the comfort of direction and purpose.

In contrast, Catherine Barkley is disoriented. She has no structure to give order to her life. The death of her fiancé – not by a sabre cut as she had imagined, but by a shell that blew him to bits – has destroyed her conception of a benign and romantic world. She is frightened by the world of gratuitous event which she has now come to recognize. She morbidly fears the rain because she sees death in it. Her guilt about denying sex to her fiancé has brought her to distrust, in particular, the conventional moral structure of her society. Her nursing offers the only structure she can use for a sense of order, but that is not very satisfactory since it only brings her near the gratuitousness and death she fears. She is close to an emotional breakdown when she meets Henry.

Gradually in the first half of the novel, Henry loses his sense of order. Moving toward Catherine's situation, he comes more and more to see himself as a participant in a series of events that proceed indifferent to his sense of what ought to be. First, he is wounded. The wound, as Frederick Hoffman has pointed out, is an "un- reasonable" one.[7] The shell lands, absurdly enough, in the dugout when Henry and the ambulance drivers are eating macaroni. They are not combatants, and the drivers even consider themselves pacifists. We get few details of Henry's internal, emotional reaction, since he tries to rivet his mind on the surface proceedures of his medical care in order to minimize his reaction. But the details we do get are sig- nificant. Henry awakens at night in the hospital, "sweating and scared." He can sleep only fitfully in the dark and needs the comfort of daylight before he can sleep soundly. His sense of being secure in an orderly world has been profoundly shaken. This kind of exper- ience is repeated during the retreat from Caporetto. This time, Henry sees Aymo shot down by the sniper fire of his own men, and then Henry encounters battle police who intend to execute him as a spy after he has struggled and even killed to do his duty in bringing back the vehicles. Now he has to recognize his relative powerlessness to control the events around him and find a personal order in them. It remains for the death of his son and the impending death of Catherine near the end of the novel to convince him of the utter gratuitousness of the world and bring him to his famous declaration of human vulnerability in his comparison of human beings to ants on a log in a fire. For the moment, though, we may content ourselves to note that when Henry deserts the army he completes the movement begun with his wounding. He breaks with the strong sense of order in the army which had supported him at the outset. As was the case with Catherine, he comes to need a new means to organize his life.

An ideal of order and harmony is given to Henry by the priest.[8] When Henry prepares for his leave, the priest describes to him the countryside in the Abruzzi mountains where the priest grew up. In the hospital, Henry recalls the priest's description:

> At Capracotta, he had told me, there were trout in the stream below the town. It was forbidden to play the flute at night. When the young men serenaded only the flute was forbidden. Why, I had asked. Because it was bad for the girls to hear the flute at night. The peasants all called you "Don" and when you met them they took off their hats. . . . For a foreigner to hunt he must present a certificate that he had never been arrested. There were bears on the Gran Sasso D'Italia but it was a long way. Aquila was a fine town. It was cool in the summer at night and the spring in Abruzzi was the most beautiful in Italy. But what was lovely was the fall to go hunting through the chestnut woods. The birds were all good because they fed on grapes and you never took a lunch because the peasants were always honored if you would eat with them at their houses.[9]

The scene is idyllic. In the midst of the doubts that come to Henry during the war, its appeal for him is strong. It is a world of beauty and innocence, but more than that it is a world of absolute harmony. Men are in perfect harmony with each other and with nature. The peasants receive visitors ceremoniously and politely. Courting goes on under careful rules. Nature is an attractive area for sport. Birds and trout are there, but the more dangerous bear is at a distance. The hunters must present their certificates before they are allowed to hunt. Nothing exists, or is permitted to exist, that might disrupt harmony. Such a world as this would offer Henry security. Here he would not need to worry about seeing himself powerless in an indifferent world. This world would be stable and benign. To duplicate the sensation of living in just such an ideal world as the priest describes, Henry and Catherine come to invent a private world and take on roles that define and perpetuate it.

The role playing begins during their third meeting. Catherine gives Frederic Henry lines to speak, and they fall into the parts of romantic lovers:

> "You did say you loved me, didn't you?"
> "Yes," I lied. "I love you." I had not said it before.
> "And you call me Catherine?"
> "Catherine." We walked on a way and were stopped under a tree.
> "Say, 'I've come back to Catherine in the night.'"
> "I've come back to Catherine in the night."
> "Oh, darling, you have come back, haven't you?"
> "Yes."
> "I love you so and it's been awful. You won't go away?"
> "No. I'll always come back" (p. 31).

The line "I've come back to Catherine in the night" is, of course, too melodramatic for their situation. It is a line for a hero in a dramatic monologue written by someone like Tennyson. Also Catherine's statement "I love you so and it's been awful" appears overly romantic when we remember that they kissed for the first time only at the end of their last meeting and that Henry has been away for just two days. Also perhaps excessive is her introduction of the word "love" at this point. But we know Catherine dislikes the "nurse's-evening-off aspect" of meeting Henry, and so we can consider her role playing an attempt to put a good face on the situation. In addition, Catherine is obviously trying to recapture some of the chivalric notions of love she had before her fiancé was killed. (She makes clear that she is using Henry as a substitute for her fiancé, when toward the end of the scene she compares their pronunciations of her name.) The scene she has Henry act with her is an attempt to blot out the death of her fiancé and return her to a more benign world than she now lives in.

Both Henry and Catherine are aware of what they are doing. Henry describes his reaction to the scene: "This was a game, like bridge, in which you said things instead of playing cards" (p. 32). He takes the role Catherine gives him because he knows it will lead to a sexual relationship. The game is more interesting than the one he has been playing with the prostitutes: "This was better than going every evening to the house for officers where the girls climbed all over you and put your cap on backward as a sign of affection between their trips upstairs with brother officers" (pp. 31-32). On her side, Catherine comes to label their scene "a rottęn game," to tell Henry he plays his part well, and to call the game off since it has served its purpose: " 'I had a very fine little show and I'm all right now' " (p. 32). Their awareness of what they are doing is a measure of their sophistication and complexity. Neither mistakes role playing for a truly intimate relationship, but both recognize that it can be a useful device for satisfying certain emotional needs.

In the first scene of role playing, Henry and Catherine pursue different, almost antagonistic goals. Henry wants an entertaining diversion, and Catherine wants to regain her conception of a benign, chivalric world. After Frederic Henry is wounded, the nature of their game shifts. They stop playing as adversaries and begin acting together for the mutual goal of shutting out the threatening sense of disorder which the war imposes on them. As we have seen, the wound initiates a change in Henry. After the wound, he starts to need the reassuring order of a romantic love as much as Catherine does. It is after Henry's fear in the night, immediately on Catherine's appearance at the hospital the next morning, that Henry discovers he is "in love" with her.

In the Milan hospital, Henry and Catherine pretend that they are married. At night, Henry unpins her blond hair, and it falls over him on the bed like a tent with both their heads inside. They call each other husband and wife in this secure, private world. In addition, they continue to use the highly romantic language of the earlier role playing. " 'You're my religion. You're all I've got' " (p. 123), Catherine tells Henry. When they are apart, they try to think the same thoughts. "It seemed to work sometimes," Henry comments, and then he adds realistically, "but that was probably because we were thinking the same thing anyway" (p. 121). The law that informs their game is the romantic ideal of two becoming one, an ideal inherent in the earlier lines of returning to Catherine in the night and always returning. This ideal offers the promise of mutual support. Obviously such support appeals to characters who are sensitive to their human vulnerability. At first, their use of the notion of "marriage" with its connotations involving practical problems might seem to us counter to the highly romantic notion of two becoming one, but on closer inspection we find this is not the case. They use the terms "marriage" and "husband" and "wife" primarily as a means to talk about things and places which belong to them collectively: *their* home in the hospital and *their* waiter at *their* restaurant. "Marriage" has no legalistic or practical connotations as they use it in their role playing; it is mainly a summary term for the ideal of two joining into one.

Despite the tenderness of the game they are now involved in, they are still conscious of the fact they are playing roles. Catherine asks for instructions in how to please in the role of lover or wife, and when the conversation turns toward the subject of separation after Henry convalesces, Catherine asks him to revert to their romantic game with her hair in order to block out the painful thought of separation. " 'We won't think about that until you go . . . ,' " she says. " 'Would you like me to take down my hair? Do you want to play?' " (pp. 123-124).

At one point, Catherine asks Henry about his evenings with prostitutes. When he gives her back a pleasing lie, she concedes that he is playing exactly the role she wants him to.

> "How many have you — how do you say it? — stayed with?"
> "None."
> "You're lying to me."
> "Yes."
> "It's all right. Keep right on lying to me. That's what I want you to do. Were they pretty?"
> "I never stayed with any one."
> "That's right. Were they very attractive?"
> "I don't know anything about it."
> "You're just mine. That's true and you've never belonged to any one else. But I don't care if you have. I'm not afraid of them. But don't tell me about them. When a man stays with a girl when does she say how much it costs?"
> "I don't know."
> "Of course not . . ." (pp. 111-112).

The scene is a good illustration of the nature of their relationship in Milan. Henry speaks lines from his role as the romantic lover who "belongs" to only one love. They both acknowledge the role playing, and both enjoy their smoothness at the game. Role playing has become a kind of bond between them. It provides a way for them to show how atuned to each other's emotional wants they are. In this scene, Henry recognizes Catherine is uneasy about the immorality of their relationship, despite the logical necessity she propounds for their not marrying. He turns her questions about prostitutes back into their pleasant game and cuts off the unpleasant direction the conversation threatens to take. He uses the game to stop her from equating herself with a prostitute and suffering the recriminations of conventional morality. He also uses the game to reaffirm their oneness after her questions threaten to emphasize their separateness.

In the scene in the railway station hotel before Henry's departure for the front, Catherine uses role playing in much the same way to reassure herself and to avoid moral recriminations. The garishness of the room's red plush disturbs her. " 'I never felt like a whore before,' " she tells Henry (p. 163). He explains that the garish hotel is the only place they can be alone, given the circumstances and the time. She accepts this and wills herself to be a "good girl." She calls the room their "home." " 'The red plush is really fine,' " she says. " 'And the mirrors are very attractive' " (p. 164). What Catherine does in this scene is convert a potentially unpleasant situation, by an act of will, into a pleasant one. She does here what Henry did for her in the previously mentioned scene. She incorporates the situation into their pretend world. Her act could be considered a triumph of her will over the situation.

They use role playing quite effectively as an emotional shield. But the fragility of their defense becomes obvious almost at once. Their defense can work only as long as the outside world does not intrude too forcibly on their make-believe. They can play their game effectively only when they are in private. At the race track in Milan, Catherine becomes annoyed by the people who cluster around them. It is necessary for Henry and her to go off by themselves to recapture their sense of closeness. This escapist quality of their role playing is an indication of its weakness. The outside world cannot always be avoided. This we see certainly enough when Miss Van Campen discovers Henry's drinking and gets his leave revoked. She, literally, breaks into their private world.

The breakdown of Rinaldi also provides a forewarning. He is a role player *par excellence.* As a surgeon, he tries to stay so busy he doesn't have time to think about the number of deaths around him. He puts it this way: " 'I never think. No, by God, I don't think; I operate' " (p. 177). He claims the role of cynic. He believes in no "sacred subjects," stuffs his holster with toilet paper, and tells Henry that the only difference between sex with a virgin and an experienced woman is the pain for the virgin. If he holds nothing sacred, then he can lose nothing. But on Henry's return to the front, we see that Rinaldi's defense of work and cynicism does not succeed in shutting out the war. During the lulls, when there isn't enough work for him, Rinaldi's mind begins to tabulate the deaths he has seen and, presumably, to form a world view similar to the one Henry gives us in his ants-on-the-log-in-the-fire analogy. " 'I don't operate now and I feel like hell,' " he tells Henry. " 'This is a terrible war, baby. You believe me when I say it' " (p. 178). Without enough work to keep him occupied, he begins to crack. The failure of his role playing is an ominous sign for Henry and Catherine.

After Henry's desertion from the army, his role playing with Catherine becomes the only source of order left in his life. He throws himself into it fully and desperately. Conversely, Catherine's sense of order has grown more secure. The game she started is now of utmost importance to Henry. He needs her help and her game in this period of crisis. She has a clear-cut role in ministering to his needs, just as at the beginning of the relationship he had been the main support of her.

They flee to the idyllic mountains of Switzerland. The world they find almost exactly resembles the ideal described by the priest.

> The snow was packed hard and smooth by the hay-sleds and woodsledges and the logs that were hauled down the mountain. . . .
> There was an inn in the trees at the Bains de l'Alliaz where the wood-cutters stopped to drink, and we sat inside warmed by the stove and drank hot red wine with spices and lemon in it. . . . The inn was dark and smoky inside and afterward when you went out the cold air came sharply into your lungs. . . . We looked back at the inn with the light coming from the windows and the woodcutters' horses stamping and jerking their heads. . . . There was frost on the hairs of their muzzles and their breathing made plumes of frost in the air. . . . Then the road was clean-packed snow and led through the woods, and twice coming home in the evening, we saw foxes.
> It was a fine country and every time that we went out it was fun (pp. 322-323).

The mountain area is clean and orderly in the snow. Catherine and Henry feel themselves in harmony with the woodcutters in the inn. They consider the scene with the animals in the snow-scape a picture that delights them. There may even be an equation between the humans' reaction to the cold air and the horses' reaction. In any case, Henry and Catherine are perfectly at ease in their surroundings. Here they can project their private game of romantic lovers and happily married family members on the outside world with little fear of disruption.

They continue to use the dialogue of their roles to hold off thoughts that might disturb them. The following conversation is in the pattern of their dialogues in Milan. A topic of conversation that could be emotionally dangerous opens up suddenly.

> "I'd like to see you with a beard."
> "All right. I'll grow one. I'll start now this minute. It's a good idea. It will give me something to do."
> "Are you worried because you haven't anything to do?" (pp. 318-319).

The conversation begins innocently enough, but the anxieties of both characters begin to manifest themselves. Henry has put behind him the extremely active role he had in the army. The role was important to him. He has replaced it with the relatively passive one of lover and husband. Both he and Catherine worry whether the new role will provide him with enough occupation to crowd out thoughts of human vulnerability inspired by the war and guilt feelings for having deserted. These worries come out in the conversation. The next phase of the dialogue indicates that Henry's mind has been dwelling on the war picture.

> "What are you thinking about now?"
> "... I was wondering whether Rinaldi had the syphilis."
> "Was that all?"
> "Yes."
> "... Did you ever have anything like that?"
> "I had gonorrhea."
> "I don't want to hear about it. Was it very painful, darling?" (p. 319).

This development opens up again the area painful to Catherine, Henry's life with other women. His nights with other women and his war experiences are aspects of his life that Catherine can't share. The conversation, then, has drifted in a direction which calls attention to their separateness. This is counter to their game of two lovers as one. The conversation has become a challenge to their defense. So Catherine, while she allows the conversation to continue, warns Henry to revert to their role playing when she tells him, "I don't want to hear about it. Was it very painful?" When he continues, he is to recognize that to tell her at length about the gonorrhea is to emphasize their separateness. The warning is picked up by Henry. He clips his answer to a minimum and allows Catherine then to steer the conversation back to the safety of their game.

> "Very."
> "I wish I'd had it."

"No you don't."

"I do. I wish I'd had it to be like you. . . ."

"That's a pretty picture."

"It's not a pretty picture you having gonorrhea."

"I know it. Look at it snow now."

"I'd rather look at you. Darling, why don't you let your hair grow? . . . Let it grow a little longer and I could cut mine and we'd be just alike only one of us blonde and one of us dark."

"I wouldn't let you cut yours."

"It would be fun. I'm tired of it. . . ."

"It might be nice short. Then we'd both be alike. Oh, darling, I want you so much I want to be you too."

"You are. We're the same one."

"I know it. At night we are" (pp. 319-320).

By the end of the conversation, they are back to their roles of lovers professing their oneness and even considering the possibility of looking alike. The dialogue seen as a whole is a masterpiece of defense. A rift opens between the two characters. They recognize it. And by mutual consent, they slip into roles which close it up before it can become serious.

There is, of course, a kind of desperateness behind their skill. They must constantly be on guard for the sudden gulfs that can open up in their game, exposing it as a pleasant myth. This is obvious at Stresa when Catherine leaves Henry for a few hours and thoughts of the war and of his desertion come rushing back on him. At all costs, they must keep in their roles if they are to shut out thoughts of vulnerability and powerlessness. They must make the game seem a continuous reality.

Their role playing can be criticized as a relationship inferior to true intimacy. If Henry and Catherine were utterly open with each other, they might well discuss together their fears that life is without design and is indifferent to the hopes of individual men. Facing this reality, they might then agree to patch together what order human beings can bring to their lives. Instead, they avoid moving toward such openness. At least at this point in their lives, they aren't strong enough for such candor. They try to leap over recognition of their fears into the direct construction of a new sense of order. As a result, they adopt a new myth of order that is no less an illusion than their earlier conceptions of order. We must admit that Henry and Catherine have their weaknesses, but we may also recognize their strengths. Together, with mutual support, they do struggle not to submit to circumstances. The roles they play, while they don't lead to real intimacy, do lead to a bond between them. The priest offers us a working definition of love: " 'When you love you wish to do things for. You wish to sacrifice for. You wish to serve" (p. 77). The definition comes close to describing the relationship of Catherine and Henry.[10] By entering the game, they enter a relationship where they support, or serve, the other. We could require more of them. But what they offer is significant.

Playing roles allows them to act with kindness and strength. Nowhere is this more obvious than in Catherine's performance during her death scene. She tells Henry she is going to die, and when he takes her hand to console her, she tells him, with the anger the dying bear the living, "Don't touch me" (p. 353). Then recognizing the pain Henry is undergoing, she slips smoothly back into her role of lover.

> "Poor darling. You touch me all you want."
> "You'll be all right, Cat. I know you'll be all right. . . ."
> "You won't do our things with another girl, or say the same things, will you?"
> "Never."
> "I want you to have girls, though."
> "I don't want them. . . ."
> "All right," Catherine said. "I'll come and stay with you nights" (pp. 353-354).

Catherine knows she is going to die. Death frightens her, and she resents it. But she sees Henry is not prepared to talk about it as openly as she is. When he tells her, "You'll be all right," he is, in effect, signalling her to keep the conversation on the level of comforting pretense. For a moment, she tries to talk realistically about their relationship as one where certain things were done and certain lines spoken according to pattern. However, his romantic responses, "Never," and, "I don't want them," indicate Henry wishes them to avoid such a candid view of their relationship and wants them instead to keep up their roles as lovers whom nothing can part. Catherine chooses to console Henry. This she does by responding to his wishes. When she tells him she will return in the night, she is deliberately taking up again her role in their game. She speaks to him the same romantic lines she required him to speak to her at the beginning of the novel. Her strength and kindness in carrying out her role playing to the end are clear. She is doing the one thing in her power to support Henry emotionally at the moment when he must take in the shattering prospect of her loss and the loss of their ordered world together.

The novel's conclusion, however, balances her kindness and courage against Henry's final realization of the inadequacy of their game to last. After Catherine has died, he returns to see her. "But after I had got them out and shut the door and turned off the light," he tells us, "it wasn't any good. It was like saying good-by to a statue" (p. 355). Nothing remains of their "love" after her death. Its support for him is over. The order it brought his life, like the order supplied by the army, has been destroyed. He must look directly at the indifference which the events of the outside world bear toward his private world and the ease with which they can crush it.

The balance at the end of the novel suggests the proper view for us to take toward Catherine and Henry. Ultimately their game of love and their role playing break down. The game and the roles are not strong enough to withstand the intrusion of life at its harshest. But while the game and the roles go on, they provide a means for two people to try to support each other emotionally and psychologically against the overwhelming challenge of reality that suddenly opens up before them. Through the defense of role playing, Hemingway explores both the strengths and weaknesses of his two characters. If we put aside preconceptions of what "mature love" ought to involve, we can appreciate Hemingway's psychological probing of characters looking desperately for order.

University of Illinois

---

[1] Frederick J. Hoffman, *The Twenties: American Writing in the Postwar Decade* (New York: Viking Press, 1955), pp. 67-72.

[2] Charles C. Walcutt, *American Literary Naturalism, A Divided Stream* (Minneapolis: University of Minnesota Press, 1956), pp. 258-289, and John Killinger, *Hemingway and the Dead Gods* (Lexington: University of Kentucky Press, 1960), pp. 46-49.

[3] Edmund Wilson, "Ernest Hemingway: Bourdon Gauge of Morale," *Atlantic Monthly,* CLXIV (July, 1939), 36-46.

[4] Isaac Rosenfeld, "A Farewell to Hemingway," *Kenyon Review,* XIII (1951), 147-155; Leslie Fiedler, *Love and Death in the American Novel* (New York: Dell Publishing Company, 1966), Revised Edition, pp. 317-318; and Robert W. Lewis, Jr., *Hemingway on Love* (Austin: University of Texas Press, 1965), pp. 39-54.

[5] Richard B. Hovey, *Hemingway: The Inward Terrain* (Seattle: University of Washington Press, 1968), pp. 73-91, and Stanley Cooperman, "Death and Cojones: Hemingway's *A Farewell to Arms,*" *South Atlantic Quarterly,* LXIII (Winter, 1964), 85-92.

[6] Role playing has recently become an important field for psychological investigation. Of special interest to psychologists are roles in social games which individuals play as replacements for true intimacy. See Eric Berne, *Transactional*

Analysis in Psychotherapy (New York: Grove Press, 1961) and *Games People Play* (New York: Grove Press, 1964). Hemingway's early interest in this aspect of behavior would seem to be a case where the artist anticipates the findings of the psychologist.

[7] Hoffman, *The Twenties*, pp. 67-72.

[8] *Cf.* Carlos Baker, *Hemingway: The Writer as Artist* (Princeton: Princeton University Press, 1963), pp. 94-116. Baker stresses the priest's world as one of the poles of the novel. It is a "home" world as opposed to the "not-home" world of the war.

[9] Ernest Hemingway, *A Farewell to Arms* (New York: Charles Scribner's Sons, 1929), p. 78. All subsequent page references to *A Farewell to Arms* will be to this edition. The page references will be given in parentheses in the text.

[10] The importance of the priest's definition of love has been well treated by Earl Rovit in *Ernest Hemingway* (New York: Twayne Publishers, 1963), pp. 98-106.

HAIL TO ARMS:
A VIEW
OF
For Whom the Bell Tolls

Robert Jordan continues to be considered one of the finest, if not *the* finest, of Hemingway's heroes. One recent discussion is Delbert Wylder's depiction of him as a mythic hero, the first of Hemingway's protagonists to bring together the "separated aspects of the human soul."[1] Wylder sees in Jordan's union with Maria a sacred marriage, which he considers to be the true center of the novel. The most important lesson Jordan learns is that man alone does not have a chance.[2] In his *Hemingway: The Writer's Art of Self Defense* (1969), Jackson Benson states that Robert Jordan is the hero who "interprets everything properly," who has a faith in himself, based on realistic grounds, that holds firm to the end. No other Hemingway protagonist is "so truly heroic" as Robert Jordan.[3] Benson considers *For Whom The Bell Tolls* a "morality play" in which man's ability to do his duty is not only the prime factor separating him from the animal but the sign of his Christian ethics. The rapid transition from lovemaking, for example, to the duty of fighting, is "more selfless than callous."[4]

A symbolic reading of *For Whom the Bell Tolls* is tempting, particularly regarding the relationship of Robert Jordan and Maria, with its air of unreality. Hemingway was undoubtedly placing new emphasis on both erotic and *agapé* love in an attempt to develop more complete, complex characters. But is it possible to ignore the events and the thoughts that actually occurred to Robert Jordan, despite what he or Hemingway might have felt were the properly humanitarian responses? Under the guise of Donne's brotherhood, Biblical thee's and thou's, a love affair, and talk of the evil of war, *For Whom the Bell Tolls* applauds a man for killing other men and for seeking his own death, all for a very remote cause. Although Robert Jordan fights in behalf of the Spanish Loyalists, we are never to forget that dying is an individual matter. The title from Donne becomes ironic. The test of a man is the same as elsewhere in Hemingway, that of individual courage, revealed through mortal combat, not through brotherly or romantic love.

With death at the heart of *For Whom the Bell Tolls,* the discussions of violence are the most vivid and effective sections. Seeing Maria's unbelievable sweetness and innocence, we might expect her to deter her lover from killing, or at least to shrink from war. But memories of the atrocities committed upon her and her family are a source of revenge for Jordan, whom she has made the center of her existence in the usual fashion of the Hemingway heroine. She reflects his appreciation of the kill in her most vivid and probably her longest speech, which relates why she carries a razor blade near her breast:

> "Pilar gave me this and showed me how to use it," she . . . took out a Gem type, single-edged razor blade. "I keep this always," she explained. "Pilar says you must make the cut here just below the ear and draw it toward here." She showed him with her finger. "She says there is a big artery there and that drawing the blade from there you cannot miss it. Also, she says there is no pain and you must simply press firmly below the ear and draw it downward. She says it is nothing and that they cannot stop it if it is done."[5]

Little Rabbit knows which skills are important to her lover. She knows a good deal more about killing than she knows about making love, never even having learned to kiss. Animal-like in all her functions, she brings food, sleeps with Jordan, and learns how to kill. Being little more than an extension of him, she shares his feelings as he is about to make his last important killing: " 'But will we kill Falangists? It was they who did it. . . . But can we not kill them in some way? I would like to kill some very much' " (p. 353).

Rabbit's protector, Pilar, a sort of lusty earth mother, has the instinct to preserve the race, not to kill. But she has long been in a world of soldiers and bullfighters and thrives on their kind of excitement. Many of her splendid stories tell of the violence she has seen, particularly in the life of her husband. Jordan seeks out Pilar for the story of Pablo's massacre of the fascists. Maria (who has not yet attached herself to Jordan) does not want to hear it, but at Jordan's insistence Pilar relates the vivid details. Her most dramatic affirmation of murder comes when Pilar votes yes to have her own husband killed. He is a foul-mouthed rascal, believed to be a traitor, but is death the obvious penalty? The reason for wanting to kill Pablo, it turns out, is actually not his treachery, but his crude remarks and sloppy drinking.

> "I liked you better when you were barbarous," the woman said. "Of all men the drunkard is the foulest. The thief when he is not stealing is like another. The extortioner does not practice in the home. The murderer when he is at home can wash his hands. But the drunkard stinks and vomits in his own bed and dissolves his organs in alcohol" (p. 208).

Maria says nothing in Pablo's defense, although he once saved her life. These are strange women who do little to preserve life, who have no children, and who hold no families together. They have taken on the savage values of the world around them. Life is cheap in the intimate circle of these guerrilla fighters where a woman can say of her husband, " 'Kill him,' . . . Her big face was dark and tired looking. 'I am for it now' " (p. 217).

Pablo's decline in popularity corresponds with his decline in courage, that is, his failure to kill. His murderous skill is only a memory as he bows over the table deep in drink; now he would restore to life every one he has killed. This kind of talk is brushed off as drunken foolishness, and the group votes to kill him. Only as he used to be is he admired. " 'Pablo was brave in the beginning. . . . Pablo was something serious in the beginning,' " Anselmo tells us. " 'He killed more people than the cholera' " (p. 26). Courage is equated with ability to kill, even by Anselmo, who does not like the killing of men. Pablo's main source of fame was his slaughter of the fascists and the dramatic disposal of their bodies over a cliff. While Jordan cannot openly sanction such violence, it is with a touch of envy that he calls Pablo a murderous bastard when he returns to help blow up the bridge. The fact that he was once a courageous warrior cannot be dismissed.

While Pablo was Jordan's last teacher, his first was also a capable warrior, General Golz. Although he plays a minor part in the novel, his military superiority sets a lasting standard for Jordan. After telling Golz that there is no time and place for women in war, he meets Maria and is later embarrassed to imagine what Golz's reaction to their romance would be. If love were as important to Jordan as he believes it is, he would hardly have shrunk so from thoughts of the military Golz. But since his first desire is to be a good soldier, it is important to please him. Like Jordan, he is no thinker: " 'I never think at all,' " he admits. " 'Why should I? . . . I never think. Do not try to trap me into thinking' " (p. 8). For both men, too much thinking might reveal, among other things, some distasteful truths about their motives as fighters.

As the leader of a nearby guerrilla band, El Sordo is another whose strength emerges during battle. So much are death and killing his particular forte that he is ecstatic at a time when his own death is imminent. Looking down on Lieutenant Berrendo, El Sordo shouts from the hilltop, " '*Bandidos!* Shoot me! Kill me!' " laughing as though his head would burst (p. 319). Is this giddiness merely the demeanor for horror? Or is it a cry of truth escaping during stress, a wild sort of death wish? El Sordo's opponent, Lieutenant Berrendo, is a cool killer. He tosses four grenades into a pile of dead horses (and possibly men) before he advances to take a last look. Joaquin, the only survivor, is disposed of quickly and "gently, . . . as Sordo had shot the wounded horse" (p. 322). Before killing him Berrendo makes the sign of the cross – then goes back to the bodies, tied across the saddles so they can be packed like equipment. As Berrendo sees the corpse that was El Sordo, he thinks it a good thing to "Cut the head off and wrap it in a poncho," and as an afterthought he orders, " 'You might as well take all the heads' " (p. 322) as one might instruct his chef to top a bunch of carrots. More Hail Marys. When the battle is finished, Berrendo feels, as Hemingway often did, "only the hollowness that comes after action" (p. 326).

In contrast to these men who love the kill is the pacifist, Anselmo. He fights sorrowfully, weeping when he kills a man, even though he sees a kind of cruel necessity in doing so. Each man's struggle is a private one in this world of war, but Anselmo's suffering is double, for what he must do goes against what he believes. No amount of experience in war has made him value killing, as Jordan says the true soldier must learn to do. Anselmo is the one man who might have shown, through preserving life, that "no man is an island," and yet he is lonelier than the others because no one shares his beliefs. His influence is slight. As Jordan's guide and teacher, he leads him from Golz to Pablo, but does little to change his ideas. Jordan admits that he is the most trustworthy Spaniard he has met, and yet "Jordan trusted the man, Anselmo, so far, in everything except judgment" (p. 4); and he never adopts his simple faith as he took up the views of

General Golz. The old man is followed by no one: his wife is dead, and he has no children. Anselmo alone understands the wrong of killing, even when there is a cause; and for him there is more cause than there is for Jordan – it is his Spain and his Republic. When he dies Jordan strides by his body almost as if it were not there:

> Anselmo lay face down behind the white marking stone. His left arm was doubled under his head and his right arm was stretched straight out. The loop of wire was still around his right fist. Robert Jordan got to his feet, crossed the road, knelt by him and made sure that he was dead. He did not turn him over to see what the piece of steel had done. He was dead and that was all.
>
> He looked very small, dead, Robert Jordan thought (p. 446).

Perhaps this account of Anselmo's death is merely a Hemingway understatement with the omission of what is most significant. But details of Jordan's thoughts are usually given us – his questions to himself about war, love, his past. His approach to Anselmo's death, while it may show a weariness of all death, appears to be more indifferent than controlled. Only later does he indicate anything significant about the old man's death, by considering it in relation to "The anger and the emptiness and the hate that had come with the let-down after the bridge, when he had looked up from where he had lain and crouching, seen Anselmo dead, were still all through him" (p. 447). First for him is the emptiness coming after action. Then the hate. Then the connection with Anselmo, whose death seems rather a further irritation than the source of the stronger feelings. Jordan *is* the central person in the novel, portrayed sympathetically, and if Anselmo's death means little to him, what he stands for seems not to mean much either. What manner of man is this strange hero?

Robert Jordan, the professor from Montana who desires action without thought, is a complex person. Fluctuating between an idealistic notion of heroism associated with a cause and the practical knowledge that he might be wrong, he stifles thought and concerns himself with killing and dying. His usual way of opening a conversation is by asking, "How many people have you killed?" Knowing of Pablo's reputation for massacre, he inquires, " 'Have you killed many civil guards?' " (p. 14). Then he wants the details. As a child he begged his grandfather to tell of the men he had killed when he was a soldier. Jordan's questions to Anselmo lead to a discussion of the difference between killing an animal and killing a man. He rebukes the old man for loving his hunting: " 'I do not like to kill animals.' " Anselmo's reply points up the great difference between them:

" 'With me it is the opposite, . . . I do not like to kill men.' " Jordan reasons that " 'Nobody does except those who are disturbed in the head, . . . But I feel nothing against it when it is necessary. When it is for the cause' " (p. 39). After finding a reason for killing, Jordan can appreciate it; Anselmo never can. The rise of fascism in Spain offered a cause that filled both Jordan's moral need and his need for a violent way of proving his courage. Yet he is uneasy and asks others how they have managed their consciences. He reminds Anselmo: " 'You have killed?' . . . 'Yes,' replies the old man, 'But not with pleasure. To me it is a sin to kill a man.' " Jordan continues — — " 'Yet you have killed.' " His resolution is that " 'To win a war we must kill our enemies. That has always been true' " (p. 41).

Even as a young boy Jordan was intrigued by death. The memory of a lynching has stayed with him, the terrifying night a group of drunks hung a Negro to a lamp post and burned him. The grotesque scene fascinated the boy peering over the edge of the window. In telling his Spanish friends about it, Jordan stresses the drunkenness of the killers, not their murder. " 'I have had experiences which demonstrate that drunkenness is the same in my country. It is ugly and brutal' " (p. 117), he tells them. Pilar agrees with him about the vice of drink but says nothing about the lynching. It is difficult for Jordan ever to say, unequivocally, that killing is wrong; when he does mention its evil, he gives conditions under which it is permissible to kill in order to prevent a worse wrong. Not only does Jordan relish the killing on the battlefield: in the closeness of the guerrilla band, he and the others thrive on the plan to kill Pablo. True, Pablo has been insulting and hostile to the plan of blowing up the bridge – but there is no proof that he has been a traitor. Yet they agree to kill him and nominate Jordan to do the job. He is pleased. "I'd like to kill him and have it over with" (p. 212), he thinks. With this in mind, he goes on to say, a few moments later as he toasts Pablo with a cup of wine, " 'We are good friends already' " (p. 213).

Jordan's conversations with Maria, though not as obviously de-ceptive, often seem as superficial as his statement of friendship to Pablo. Speaking of their love, he tells her that " 'No other thing has importance' " (p. 262), but as soon as she is asleep he checks the pistol by his side. As some readers have pointed out, Jordan's affair with Maria is not his central experience (as perhaps he would like to make it) but a way of filling the lulls between combat. Night time is the waiting period before the morning's battle. He shares little more than his body with Maria, and he can safely speak of marriage, for he fully expects to die in this war in Spain. It is difficult to imagine his marrying Maria and taking her back to his American life. In considering it he thinks of her as a kind of war trophy, the survivor of multiple rape who could deliver her story of atrocities to his colleagues, complete with details of how the Falangists sat on her head.

In the tradition of other Hemingway heroes, Jordan does not consider his woman as mother or himself as father. There is no place for birth in their world of death — he tells Maria he would not want to have children. Humanitarian as this view may be, it shows no concern for her wishes. When she tells him she may not be able to have children, he answers that it really does not matter at all — not to him, anyway. He is so insensitive to her feelings that when they are together on their last night and she tells him nervously, " 'I do not wish to disappoint thee but there is a great soreness and much pain,' " his reaction is: " 'There is always a great soreness and much pain. . . . That is nothing' " (p. 341). An act of love can quickly be exchanged for an act of war — for Jordan there is little incongruity. He can best describe their lovemaking by comparing it to dying, not a new comparison, but certainly an apt one for Jordan: " 'I feel as though I wanted to die when I am loving thee' " (p. 160). "For him it was a dark passage which led to nowhere, then to nowhere, then again to nowhere, once again to nowhere . . ." (p. 159).

In the name of love and brotherhood, Jordan is a kind of antichrist. Bronzed, fair-haired American god, in peasant clothing, he comes as a savior to the Spanish peasants. Maria immediately gives herself to him, and like a Mary Magdalene to Christ, she washes his feet, brings his food, and worships. Worldly Pilar, who appears to know a good deal about people, also considers him something of a god. Although she has had no experience with him which would lead to trust, she immediately and intuitively puts Maria in his care. The thee's and thou's add a Christ-like touch as do such pious statements as " 'I do not like to kill animals' " (p. 39). And Jordan's life is sealed with martyrdom as he dies fighting for the Loyalist cause. But to be Christ-like one must have Christian motives, and Jordan's thoughts are far from Christian. His words to Anselmo, " 'we must kill our enemies' " (p. 41), are a harsh parody of the Biblical "Love your enemies." The truth about his motives is made clear in a discussion with Augustin and Anselmo. At the thought of killing, Augustin feels the necessity on him " 'as it is on a mare in heat' " (p. 286). His fear is great, but there is no stronger thing than the other, the desire to kill.

Yes, Robert Jordan thought. We do it coldly but they [other national groups who have killed] do not, nor ever have. It is their extra sacrament. . . . only suppressed and hidden to bring it out again in wars and inquisitions. They are the people of the Auto de Fé; the act of faith. Killing is something one must do, but ours are different from theirs. And you, he thought, you have never been corrupted by it? . . . Nor at any time? *Qué va,* he told himself. At every train (pp. 286-87).

Jordan sees his resemblance to the inquisitors, those super antichrists, who in the name of good brought death. "Stop making dubious literature about the Berbers . . . and admit that you have liked to kill as all who are soldiers by choice have enjoyed it at some time whether they lie about it or not" (p. 287).

With Jordan's relish of killing, guerrilla warfare is appropriate; the air warfare being introduced into Spain would be too impersonal. His is the art of aiming at an enemy's heart: before dying he skillfully puts "the oblong of the foresight, settled now in the notch of the rear, onto the center of the man's chest" and squeezes the trigger gently (p. 434). He can see the expression of surprise and hurt on the man's face as he falls. When he meets Anselmo, weeping because he has killed, Jordan does not understand, much less share his sorrow; coolly continuing the duties of war, he is irritated to find Pablo still alive. He tells himself not to make moral judgments on him, but cannot resist an attack on the crime so close to his own: " 'What do you expect from a murderer? You're working with a murderer' " (p. 455). As Jordan prepares to die, he sends Maria away. To spare her? Surely not because he is embarrassed to be seen dying. But it is necessary for a man to die alone — his long awaited moment will be relished in privacy, which also allows him one last shot at the enemy.

Hemingway may well make much of Jordan's courage. And yet it is not the courage of the code heroes Francis Macomber or Manuel Garcia of "The Undefeated" — men who face a physical contest when they are frightened and beaten. Both of these men have social as well as physical courage. Macomber must perform in view of a wife who has belittled and cuckolded him with her lover, the experienced and courageous guide; Manuel must beg for a job and perform before a hostile crowd that knows he is beyond his prime. And although these heroes must kill to prove their manhood, there *is* a difference between killing animals and killing men. Jordan has no such social trials. Maria is a temporary pleasure he can dismiss when he wishes to be alone — she will be his in any event. In his last struggle he has no peers to judge him. Jordan, who has always resisted any identification with his suicidal father, whom he considers a coward, is perhaps closer to him than he imagines, as he goes off to fight in Spain expecting and possibly wishing to die. He is to be as pitied as any obsessively suicidal man.

The unnerving thing about the test of courage in Hemingway's novels is that it follows an increasingly murderous path. In *The Sun Also Rises* war has been a debilitating event. Jake Barnes and his friends are empty and wounded after war, showing no indication that they were ever fulfilled by it. Barnes's courage is in a stoic acceptance of his incapacity. Romero's manhood is proven in mortal combat, but not by killing men. In *A Farewell to Arms* Frederic Henry turns his back on war, valuing only his love for Catherine; but their love is not a healing force. Seeming a coward for leaving the responsibility of war, Henry is left in the bleakest of Hemingway's worlds. *Death in the Afternoon* states that the moment of killing the bull is an esthetic and even a spiritual climax. The joy of killing continues to be limited to animals in *Green Hills of Africa,* but we now hear of the "stench of comrades." Ironically, *To Have and Have Not,* which makes a departure for Hemingway into a new social consciousness, gives us a super killer in Harry Morgan. But at least we know Morgan for a killer. The disturbing thing about *For Whom the Bell Tolls* is not that it shows the art of killing men, in brilliant detail, but that it sanctions the killing by making it necessary to a cause and essential in proving the courage of individual men. All under the guise of romance and the trappings of Christianity.

West Hyattsville, Maryland

---

[1] *Hemingway's Heroes* (Albuquerque: University of New Mexico Press, 1969), p. 128.

[2] *Ibid.,* pp. 135, 155.

[3] Minneapolis: University of Minnesota Press, 1969, pp. 154-56.

[4] *Ibid.,* pp. 159, 163.

[5] Ernest Hemingway, *For Whom the Bell Tolls* (New York: Scribners, 1940), pp. 170-71. Further quotations from the novel are taken from this edition and are cited in the text.

C. E. FRAZER CLARK, JR.

RECENT
HEMINGWAY
AT
AUCTION[1]

Three unusually important groups of Hemingway letters recently appeared at auction with record prices paid at each sale. What made these letters special was the richness of Hemingway's critical and biographical comment; in each case, Hemingway was corresponding with a writer in whose work he had a stake.

The first group comprised ten letters to Charles Poore, book critic for forty years on *The New York Times,* who had met Hemingway in the late 1930s and remained a lifelong supporter. Poore, in the process of assembling *The Hemingway Reader* for Scribners,[2] had initiated a correspondence regarding the selection of material for the anthology. These letters were offered piecemeal in a much-heralded auction[3] by Charles Hamilton at The Waldorf-Astoria on the evening of 9 March 1972. The 10 lots brought a total of $5,875. The prize letter in the collection was a 7½ page A.L.S. in which Hemingway discusses many of his works, the locations where they were written, and alterations for *A Farewell to Arms* suggested by F. Scott Fitzgerald. This letter established a new record for a single Hemingway letter at auction, bringing $1,900. This and other letters were purchased for the Clark Collection.

Arthur Mizener's correspondence with Ernest Hemingway during the time Mizener was preparing his biography of F. Scott Fitzgerald was sold en bloc by Sotheby Parke-Bernet, 31 October 1972, for

$12,000. The core of the collection was a series of eight T.L.S. in which Hemingway describes at length his relationship with Fitzgerald and his views of Fitzgerald's work. Also widely publicized, the sale was highly competitive and the pre-sale gallery estimate of $4,000 to $6,000 for the lot was quickly surpassed with the record price of $12,000 paid by William Young, a Massachusetts dealer, who bought the letters for stock. Young later resold the letters to the University of Maryland.

The most recent Hemingway letter collection to reach auction was the early (1923-1927) correspondence with Edward O'Brien, editor and anthologist, who first published Hemingway in book form.[4] Eight Hemingway letters to O'Brien (4 A.L.S. and 4 T.L.S.) were auctioned by Sotheby Parke-Bernet, 20 February 1973. The letters discuss in detail Hemingway's early struggles to get published and portray his feelings about the first stories he had written. House of Books, Ltd., representing the University of Maryland, purchased the eight letters for $12,000.

The top prices paid for Hemingway letters at these three sales confirm the continued bullishness of the Hemingway market. Considering the great amount of Hemingway autograph that still remains in private hands, it seems certain that recent prices will soon lure more material into the sale rooms. This will be a good thing for scholars. How prepared or willing the Hemingway market is to continue to back its faith with hard cash is a matter of speculation.

Appendix

Charles Hamilton — 9 March 1972

Lot 144	$ 500.00	Parke-Bernet — 31 October 1972	
Lot 145	$ 500.00		
Lot 146	$1,900.00	Lot 203	$12,000.00
Lot 147	$ 400.00	Lot 204	$ 600.00
Lot 148	$ 475.00	Lot 299	$ 2,250.00
Lot 149	$ 575.00		
Lot 150	$ 475.00		
Lot 151	$ 325.00	Parke-Bernet — 20 February 1973	
Lot 152	$ 450.00		
Lot 153	$ 275.00	Lot 211	$12,000.00

[1] For a complete history of sales and prices realized, see *Hemingway At Auction,* ed. Matthew J. Bruccoli and C. E. Frazer Clark, Jr. (Detroit: Bruccoli Clark/Gale Research, 1973).

[2] *The Hemingway Reader, Selected with a Forward and Twelve Brief Prefaces,* by Charles Poore (New York: Scribners, 1953).

[3] "Revelations About And by Hemingway," by Alden Whitman appeared in the *New York Times* on the day of the sale, 9 March 1972.

[4] *The Best Short Stories of 1923,* ed. Edward J. O'Brien (Boston: Small, Maynard, 1924), printed "My Old Man," the first appearance of Hemingway's work in book form in the United States. The volume was dedicated to Hemingway.

GEORGE MONTEIRO

HEMINGWAY'S
PLÉIADE
BALLPLAYERS

Twenty years ago Ray B. West warned that baseball was not yet a mythology available to serious writers. His case in point was the recently published *Old Man and the Sea*. Baseball references in novels would inevitably perplex generations of readers, predicted West, and, consequently, future editions of Hemingway's titles would perforce carry a rather generous supply of explanatory rotes.[1]

So far West's prediction has not come about, not for English-language editions at least. But what *do* readers of the 1970's make of those references to Gonzalez, Luque, and Dick Sisler? There is probably little need as yet to gloss Santiago's references to "the great DiMaggio," but references to John McGraw already call for explanation.

In foreign-language editions Hemingway's baseball references have always called for explanatory notation, though that need has seldom been acknowledged. Happily, the recent two-volume Pléiade edition of Hemingway's work, edited and annotated by Roger Asselineau, recognizes that need.[2] Unfortunately, however, some of the baseball annotations are misleading, while at least two of them are just plain wrong.

The references Asselineau takes on first are those to the "Cards" and "Giants" in the early story "The Three-Day Blow." He identifies them as "names of well-known baseball teams" (I, 1368). Further references in the same story to "MacGraw" and "Heinie Zim," however, evoke no explanation. The editor does not tell us that John Joseph McGraw (1873-1934) was best known as the manager of the New York Giants for three decades beginning in 1902 and that Henry (Heinie) Zimmerman was an infielder who, having played for the Chicago Cubs from 1907 to 1916, had his contract sold in mid-season to McGraw's Giants. The reference to the trade which brought "Zim" to the Giants establishes 1916 as the date of the incidents of "The Three-Day Blow."

When Asselineau takes on *A Farewell to Arms,* his annotations verge on distortion. Breathes there anyone who does not know that George Herman Ruth, that graduate of a Baltimore orphanage, became "one of the greatest" players "baseball has ever known?" But it is misleading to imply, as Asselineau does, that Babe Ruth's reputation is based on his pitching, his success as a "lanceur" (I, 1392). Writing about events which took place during the Great War, Hemingway, it should be noted, invents true enough to history when he has Frederic Henry ruminate on Ruth's pitching exploits for the Boston Red Sox. It was not, of course, until Ruth's contract was transferred to the New York Yankees that he achieved his greatest fame, and that fame was based on his super-hitting. When Hemingway was at work on *A Farewell to Arms,* it was rather a cute historical touch to refer to Ruth's pitching, for by the mid-1920's Ruth's great reputation was that of a hitter who would in twenty-two seasons record 714 home-runs. Later on, glossing Hemingway's reference to Ruth in *Green Hills of Africa* (1935), Asselineau notes cautiously that Ruth was "a celebrated baseball player, a long-standing idol of sports fans" (II, 1635).

With *The Old Man and the Sea* Asselineau's record is only so-so. Joseph Paul DiMaggio, the "Yankee Clipper" of the sports-page, he gets without mishap, noting correctly that twice he was voted his league's most valuable player, and that after retirement he was voted into the Baseball Hall of Fame at Cooperstown, New York. Like DiMaggio, John McGraw is correctly identified as a Hall of Famer. But Asselineau comes a-cropper on Dick Sisler, erroneously installing him in the Hall of Fame, along with McGraw and DiMaggio. Asselineau has confused Richard Sisler with George Sisler, his father. As a first-baseman, primarily with the St. Louis Browns, the elder Sisler had a sixteen-year batting average of .341, amply qualifying him for the Hall of Fame. The younger Sisler, despite Santiago's fond memory of the long home runs he hit out of the Havana ballpark, had a rather lacklustre major league career, one hardly conducive to his being admitted to Cooperstown. As for "Luque" (Adolphe Luque, born 1890) and "Mike Gonzalez" (Miguel Angel Gonzalez, born 1892), Asselineau settles for the somewhat barren fact that they are "names of managers of well-known baseball teams" (II, 1735). That they were *local* luminaries as well, both because they were natives of Havana who became well-known players in the "Gran Ligas" and because, at one time or other, they managed teams in the Cuban Winter League, slips by without explanation.

Asselineau's howler, though, comes when he deals with *The Sun Also Rises.* Unaware that the reference he would annotate deals with baseball, he ventures an educated guess which catapaults him well beyond his limits. Trying to identify the "Frankie Fritsch" with Fordham University connections, Asselineau decides, rather plausibly given the context, that Fritsch must be some kind of "religious" personage. The dialogue surrounding the reference to "Fritsch" centers, after all, on the likes of Bishop Manning, Holy Cross College, Loyola University, and Notre Dame University. Since Fordham is still another Catholic institution, Asselineau follows through smartly. Frank Francis Frisch, an infielder whose nineteen-year Major League career was spent with the New York Giants and the St. Louis Cardinals, and who in 1946 was elected to the Hall of Fame, is boldly identified as "Frankie Fritsch, a celebrated agnostic" (I, 1424).

Brown University

---

[1] "The Sham Battle Over Ernest Hemingway," *Western Review,* XVII (Spring, 1953), 240. West's complaint re-surfaces in "Six Authors in Search of a Hero," *Sewanee Review,* LXV [Summer, 1957], 503. At the same time Charles Poore was arguing: "Somewhere, right now, I hope, a student inspired by the wonderful references to Mr. DiMaggio in *The Old Man and the Sea,* is tracing other ballplayers in other stories, such as Frankie Fritsch in *The Sun Also Rises* and Heinie Zimmerman in 'The Three-Day Blow' " (Introduction to *The Hemingway Reader* [New York: Charles Scribner's Sons, 1953], p. xx).

[2] *Oeuvres Romanesques d'Ernest Hemingway,* ed. Roger Asselineau (Paris: Gallimard, 1969). All references to this work — volume and page numbers — will be given within parentheses in the text itself.

JOHN O'BRIEN

I AM SURE
I SAW
ERNEST HEMINGWAY ...

I am sure I saw Ernest Hemingway in Harry's New York Bar in Paris on Thursday, 2 June 1927, at approximately 4:30 p.m., but if I were cross-examined under oath some doubts might arise.

I was eighteen years old and so overwhelmed that I did not have the guts to ask him his name nor to introduce myself. I had read *The Sun Also Rises* when it was published in 1926, and in a two-months stay in Paris the next year I think I visited every cafe mentioned in the book.

It is difficult to explain now the impact of that book on me and my generation. It swept the clutter from literature and demonstrated that we could be writers without sprinkling classical allusions around and resorting to deep analysis. The simple declarative sentence became respectable and my generation had been waiting for a Hemingway to spring us free.

This explains the failure to engage him in conversation. To an 18-year-old he was a mountain, larger than life and not to be bothered by the ignorant and callow.

I kept a faithful diary of the tour, which was made with an ancient brother aged 23. Here is the entry for 2 June 1927 exactly as written:

"I got up at 9 and had petit dejeuner in bed. Petite dejeuner is commonly known as breakfast. It consists of a roll and a cup of coffee. It was raining a lot so we didn't go to Longchamps as we expected. Especially since the Herald says the field is poor.

"I got a telegram from Bob saying that A. was married so I crossed her name out of my address book, cried a little, and then we walked along the Des Italiens.

"We didn't know what to do, so finally dove into a French movie. They had pictures showing Lindbergh arriving at Le Bourget. Everybody clapped. Good movie except for a lot of rot with Racquel Meller in it.

"Got out about 4:30 and went over to Harry's and listened to some guy talk about bull-fighting in Spain. We knew he was Hemingway because:

1. He knew all about Spain.
2. He had a moustache.
3. He was a newspaperman.

"After Clem won a package of Luckies playing with Chips the bartender we walked around in the rain looking for a cab but couldn't. Got a metro and back to the hotel.

"Forgot to say that during the day we signed up with Kelley Tours to go to Fontaineblau tomorrow.

"Had dinner and after I went up to Bowman's room and we discussed England and U.S.A. from several angles. He didn't give me the fr. 300 tho.

"Went for a walk up the hill [Montmartre], had some drinks, and came home to bed. God, I'm getting fat."

All I can add to this is that I stood next to Hemingway at the bar and eavesdropped on his conversation with the barman. He was asked how things were in Spain and he said that the bull-fighters had to play closer to the critics than to the bulls.

This remark was not recorded in the diary, which was a sort of went-here, went-there work, but I have treasured it some forty-five years.

Perhaps another diary entry might interest students of *The Sun Also Rises*. Here is Monday evening, 30 May:

"Had dinner at the hotel and after it as Clem and Bowman were feeling vulgar we went to the Gaity Theatre which was vulgar enough for anybody. I'll never think of that rear end scene without laughing. And singing about it! And Jesus wept, as Bowman would say. [Explanation not contained in diary: Backdrop had a round hole in it with sun rays radiating from it. Man played a guitar to the sun, whereupon a lady behind the drop stuck her *derrière* into the hole and was serenaded. This wowed a boy from Detroit.]

"After the show jumped in a horse cab and drove to Zellis famous dive. Everybodies been there or wants to. We stood at the bar and Bowman introduced us to the mgr. Bushby. Vermouth is 10 fr. a shot here. That's about 40¢ but its damn robbery anyway. The crowd pulled in about 1:30 so we took a table and got a bottle of champagne (180 fr.) Charlie Heidsicks, y'know.

"Bowman's friends Mimi and Gaby came along after while so we got another bottle of champagne. They have a Negro orchestra that's damn good especially Buddy the drummer who put on an act on the dance floor.

"I lent Bowman 300 francs. I hope he's good for it."

Buddy is Hemingway's "nigger drummer . . . waved at Brett" and of whom she said: "He's a great friend of mine. Damn good drummer." This may have been what started a rumor about Buddy and Brett.

Bowman was an Englishman working in Paris selling real estate and renting apartments and houses. He was not good for the 300 fr. but we parted friends when I left Paris.

Those were the days.

The Detroit News

ROBERT MURRAY DAVIS

IRONY

AND

PITY

ONCE MORE

Matthew J. Bruccoli traces the Bill Gorton-Jake Barnes conversation about "irony and pity" in *The Sun Also Rises* to Gilbert Seldes' review of *The Great Gatsby (F/H Annual 1970)*. Without disputing his case, one can find a source still closer to the final stages of the novel's composition: Paul Eldridge's *Irony and Pity: A Book of Tales* (New York: Joseph Lawren, 1926).

Mr. Eldridge, now in his eighties and the author of many other books (see *Who's Who in America*, 1970-71) writes that he and his editors at Liveright's assumed that Hemingway was referring to his book, but that he has no proof. However, it is almost certain that Hemingway knew his name, since Mr. Eldridge published a poem, "Potiphar's Wife," in the same issue of *The Double Dealer* that included Hemingway's "A Divine Gesture." The stories in the collection were first published in such literary magazines of the period as *The Double Dealer, The Reviewer, This Quarter,* and *The Smart Set;* their publication in book form, would probably have excited some comment.

Though external evidence for Hemingway's knowledge of the book is not presently available, it seems probable that he had at least heard of it. The earliest review, March 28, 1926, in *New York Herald Tribune Books,* indicates that *Irony and Pity* was available at least several weeks earlier, and according to Carlos Baker's biography,

Hemingway was in New York during February in very literary company and was revising *The Sun Also Rises* until August.

Perhaps the strongest support for this case is internal to Hemingway's novel. Because Bill is giving Jake the very latest literary gossip from New York, it seems far more likely that he would refer to a current book title than to a phrase in a year-old review. However, it is certainly arguable that he expected a few friends to recognize and smile at the covert allusion to Seldes.

University of Oklahoma

CHARLES A. NORTON

THE ALCOHOLIC CONTENT

OF

A Farewell to Arms

Three things, war, sex, and alcohol, dominated much of the social, political, and literary thought of Americans during the years between 1914 and 1929. It has been well recognized that Ernest Hemingway in his novel *A Farewell to Arms* had much to say about the first two, but the third, alcohol, also plays an important part, yet very little has been written about its significance in the work.[1]

The alcoholic content of the book becomes apparent during even a casual reading. It becomes more apparent after a careful reading. This can be confirmed easily as a matter of quantity by counting the pages upon which some reference is made to alcoholic beverages. Such shows that 104 pages out of a total of 342 printed pages bear some reference to alcohol. Since the themes of war, sex, and alcohol nearly always merge, it is improper to make a flat declaration that at least one-third of the book concerns the matter of the use and effects of alcoholic drinks, thus leaving the remaining two-thirds to the themes of war and sex. Nevertheless, considering that Hemingway used the names of no fewer than 30 types and kinds of alcoholic beverages, not counting duplications, and has used alcoholic beverages in at least 72 instances of varying critical significance in the work, the importance of alcoholic content from the point of quantity alone rates some attention.

This degree of quantity is justified to some extent due to the setting of the story in Italy. "Italians love the vine and the vine loves Italy, flourishing in every region and festooning the trees in those where other crops have the field."[2] There, as elsewhere on the European Continent, alcoholic beverages are a common part of most meals and a regular substitute for unreliable water. One study has noted that ". . . it could be said that for Italians drinking is a part of eating, even a form of eating, for wine is food."[3] Yet, the fact that impresses is that the alcoholic content, while being less than that of *The Sun Also Rises* where over one-half of the pages carry such references, is of more importance in this later work than that of mere background. Therefore, other factors than that of quantity need to be considered for a more thorough understanding.

Unlike quantity, the aspect of quality must often be interpreted from that which is left unsaid as well as from that which is said. Assuming that it is Hemingway who speaks through the first person narrator of this work, we can believe that what we read are his personal judgments regarding those wines and other beverages which he mentions. Some are mentioned with direct comment, some without, but an opinion of quality is more or less always present. We should recall that in *The Sun Also Rises* the narrator, Jack Barnes says to Count Mippipopolous, " 'You ought to write a book on wines, Count.' "[4] Perhaps Hemingway acting upon the thought decided to incorporate the idea in Lt. Frederic Henry. Hemingway created his young hero and narrator as almost a connoisseur. As if he had kept careful notes, Lt. Henry recalls what he drank, where and when and for what reason.

The list of beverages named, either with only brief or implied comment, is an extensive and an impressive one, including such wines as Asti (Asti Spumante, a famous bubbly wine); Strega (an Italian liqueur); Grappa (an Italian brandy); Capri Bianca (a white wine); Cognac (a French brandy, but loosely any brandy from France); Cinzano (a well-known vermouth, also mentioned in *The Sun Also Rises* somewhat commercially in all capital letters); Chianti (a red Italian wine, noted for the fiasco, or flask in which it is sold, usually protected from breakage with a wicker covering); Barbera (a red Italian table wine); Margaux (a red French wine); Marsala (a brown, dessert wine from Sicily); Fresa (a liqueur made from strawberries, or supposed to have the flavor of that fruit); and St. Estèphe (a red wine of the Medoc district in France). As to the types of alcoholic beverages mentioned, these are as many as they are various, running from red wine and white wine to rum, brandy, vermouth, egg-nog, sherry, whiskey, kümmel, zabainone, champagne, the martini, champagne cocktails, Munich beer, glühwein, kirsch, and marc. In nearly all cases, these are named with hints or outright suggestions in respect to their usage, such as with meals, for medical purposes, for companionship, for toasting, for a love tryst, for drinking alone, and so on. "Let them bring the ice separately. That way you could tell how much whiskey there was and it would not suddenly be too thin from the soda"[5] is offered as directly as if being stated in a handbook for imbibers, and "a bottle of capri bianca in a silver bucket full of ice"[6] is suggested for the love tryst. Only in the case of fresa is a wine accorded a negative opinion, this when the narrator comments with a typical Hemingway understatement, "It was not much of a wine."[7] The most naive reader would hardly finish this work without feeling some effect of the judgments made in respect to quality.

The thorough manner in which Hemingway covers the alcoholic drinking habits and observances of Lt. Henry, beyond the aspects of quality, also reveals upon deeper analysis of the work some important aspects of the author's questioning. As noted, Hemingway comments heavily on the factors of war and sex, but prohibition of alcoholic beverages, which became a legal fact in the United States from 1919 until 1933, also drew Hemingway's attention. His attitude, throughout the book, can be sensed, time after time, as accepting the use of alcoholic beverages as a fact equal to accepting war and sex. He seems to hold that alcoholic beverages were made for man and that man was made for them. At one point he even falls back upon the Bible when he has Rinaldi comment, " 'Take a little wine for your stomach's sake. That's Saint Paul, you know.' "[8]

Although Hemingway was not above a biblical quotation, he drew mostly on his own experience and was keenly aware that prohibition was both a sad fact and a heated issue in the United States. While he had begun and later completed revision of *A Farewell to Arms* in Europe, during most of its creation he had lived in the United States. Consequently he was able to observe at firsthand how his fellow Americans living at home had to satisfy their common urge with home-brew, bootlegged concoctions often watered down or improperly labled if not outright poisonous, and the occassional, very expensive sip of the "real thing" at a speakeasy bar. Another expatriate, Malcolm Cowley expressed an opinion similar in feeling when writing in *Exile's Return:* "Our own nation had passed the Prohibition Amendment as if to publish a bill of separation between itself and ourselves; it wasn't our country any longer." The total situation was as Horton and Edwards describe it: "Unquestionably the major cause of violence and lawbreaking in the Twenties was the experimentation with the prohibition of alcoholic beverages."[9] With direct suddeness there developed in the 1920's the unwritten folk-laws of bootlegging, numerous speakeasies, and gangsterism—all making the federal law quickly seem a foolish and regrettable act.

It seems inevitable that along with the other factors influencing the direction of his thoughts and consequently his writing, Hemingway's distaste for prohibition would seek a way to be expressed. Thus it may be argued that he made some very pointed comments on the type of individuals who would have promoted the prohibition laws when he wrote of Miss Van Campen, the superintendent of the American hospital (a symbolic America) to which the injuried Lt. Henry is sent in Milan to recuperate.[10] When Lt. Henry asks permission to have wine with his meals, as freely practised in Italy, the superintendent replys to the request, firmly, " 'Absolutely not.' " Later, Lt. Henry comments to Miss Gage, the friendly nurse, that Miss Van Campen was " 'snooty.' " When Miss Van Campen relents slightly and sends up Miss Gage with a glass of egg-nog containing a dash of sherry for the patient, an act comparable to the serving of a glass of near beer,[11] Hemingway has Lt. Henry speak with a tone of subtle sarcasm and false remorse, " 'She's a splendid woman . . . Thank her very much.' " Lt. Henry's answer, and therefore Hemingway's, to this act of prohibition in the hospital (and in America) was to smuggle in, or bootleg under the snooty nose of Miss Van Campen, a supply of real stuff.

That this provides only a temporary solution, and not a good one at that, is shown later when Miss Van Campen discovers that Lt. Henry has a case of jaundice and an armoire filled with empty bottles. She says, " 'I suppose you can't be blamed for not wanting to go back to the front. But I should think you would try something more intelligent than producing jaundice with alcoholism.' " The scene comes to its conclusion as Miss Van Campen commands the porter to remove a rucksack filled with forbidden bottles. Of the porter carrying the rucksack, the narrator comments, "He knew what was in it."[12]

Although at the time of its writing Hemingway made claims to being a "Catholic," throughout this book and others he made numerous criticisms regarding the performance of organized religion. Usually he showed a preference for a more natural and less confining religion. But he does not so finally reject Saint Paul as Rinaldi does. In fact, in this work, he places heavy emphasis on the idea of the sharing of wine as an act of communion, the sharing of the symbolic blood as a ritual of brotherhood among believers. We may note how Hemingway sharply divides between those Lt. Henry considers to be friendly and those he would distrust by allowing the former to be willing to share a drink and by having the latter refuse to drink. This can be seen profoundly in the scene where the wounded man needs an operation on his leg. He asks of the house doctor, whom he does not trust, " 'Will you have a drink?' " The answer is a very definite, " 'No thank you. I never drink alcohol.' " Then to the surgeon who is allowed to perform the operation, he says, " 'Will you have a drink, Dr. Valentini?' " And the answer is again very definite, but in the affirmative: " 'A drink? Certainly. I will have ten drinks.' "[13] While this is done on the personal, man-to-man basis, earlier in the book Lt. Henry comments: "They talked too much at the mess and I drank wine because to-night we were not all brothers unless I drank a little . . . ,"[14] thus suggesting the universal application of the same principle.

That the book touches on themes more serious than those of sex and war is apparent several ways. Also, because the author has the narrator avoid any frankly realistic or detailed physical description of himself, the work facilitates the projection of the narrator as a type of *Everyman*. This attitude is fostered through such statements by the narrator as, "I explained [to the priest], winefully, how we did not do the things we wanted to do; we never did such things."[15] Thus, it is also with added significance that the one who *saves* Lt. Henry from arrest, the only one who stands between his escape to peace and return to certain death is the barman, the symbolic provider of the wine, who wakes the deserter from an innocent sleep during a storm-swept night and provides the warning of the impending disaster, and then the means of escape — the barman waving deprecatingly as the escaping soldier slips into darkness, then to the safety and peace of another country.[16] It was every bit as the barman had promised (speaking of the padlock restraining the boat), " 'Any time you want it . . . I'll give you the key.' "[17]

What Hemingway has attempted to say in this novel is not always easy to determine. Perhaps it is as Lt. Henry said to Catherine in one of their first conversations, " 'There isn't always an explanation for everything.' "[18] Nevertheless, what is certain is that attention to the alcoholic content of this work is important to a proper interpretation of its meaning in many of its finer points.

Cincinnati, Ohio

[1] Ernest Hemingway, *A Farewell to Arms.* (New York: Scribners, 1929).

[2] Article on WINE, *The Encyclopedia Americana,* 1954 ed., V. 29, p. 391.

[3] Mark Keller, "Introduction," p. xiv., *Alcohol in Italian Culture* by Giorgio Lolli, et al. (Glencoe, Ill.: The Free Press, 1958).

[4] Ernest Hemingway, *The Sun Also Rises.* (New York: Scribers, 1926), p. 62.

[5] *A Farewell to Arms,* p. 330.

[6] Ibid., p. 40.

[7] Ibid., p. 120.

[8] Ibid., p. 184. Also: *Holy Bible,* I Timothy 5:23.

[9] Rod W. Horton and Herbert W. Edwards, *Backgrounds of American Literary Thought.* (New York: Appleton-Century-Crofts, 1952), p. 310.

[10] *A Farewell to Arms,* pp. 93-94.

[11] The only beer allowed under the Prohibition Act. It contained no more than ½ of 1 per cent alcohol.

[12] *A Farewell to Arms,* pp. 153-155.

[13] Ibid., pp. 106-107.

[14] Ibid., p. 40.

[15] Ibid., p. 13.

[16] Ibid., Chap. XXXVI. Hemingway's use of "deprecatingly" in this chapter can be understood by considering the Latin root for "deprecate." (dēprecāri: to ward off evil by prayer.) This interpretation strengthens the possibility of the symbolism outlined here.

[17] Ibid., p. 273.

[18] Ibid., p. 18.

MICHAEL PEICH

HEMINGWAY

AND

Kiki's Memoirs

Kiki's memoirs, including Hemingway's introductory essay, became mildly famous in 1930 when the United States Customs barred it from entry on a charge of alleged obscenity. Audre Hanneman's *Ernest Hemingway: a Comprehensive Bibliography* (Princeton: Princeton University Press, 1967), p. 94, lists eight editions under B7 in which Hemingway's *Introduction to Kiki of Montparnasse* appeared. Louis Henry Cohn, in his 1931 Hemingway bibliography, says that the introduction was published separately in 1929 by Edward W. Titus in an edition of twenty-five copies in order to protect Hemingway's copyright.

Boar's Head Books, New York, reissued the volume in 1950 under the title *The Education of a French Model: The Loves, Cares, Cartoons and Caricatures of Alice Prin.* Lee Samuels, in *A Hemingway Check List* (New York: Scribner's, 1951), notes that Hemingway probably did not approve the publication of the Boar's Head edition.

I recently discovered a copy of Prin's memoirs entitled simply *The Education of a French Model.* Although Hanneman does not list this edition, it is similar to the Boar's Head printing, yet distinct from it. The book has black boards, with the title printed in yellow on the spine; it measures five inches by eight and a quarter inches and contains 160 pages of text. Hemingway's introduction appears on pp.

7-10; a publisher's note faces the copyright page, and notes by Samuel Putnam (the original translator) and Edward Titus appear on pp. 154-156 and pp. 157-160 respectively. The title page lists Bridgehead Books, New York, 1954, as the publisher; yet the copyright page establishes the copyright date as 1955 by Seven Sirens Press, Inc. The text of Kiki's life is illustrated by semi-erotic sketches highlighting her "career." One eye-catching feature of this edition is a sixteen-page section entitled "A Few of Kiki's Beautiful Friends"; it photographically displays fifteen nude women (most likely *not* friends of Kiki's) in a variety of suggestive poses.

It is most unlikely that Hemingway authorized the publication of his introduction in the Bridgehead edition. *Books in Print* and *Publisher's Weekly* for 1954 and 1955 make no mention of the publication of *The Education of a French Model*. Furthermore, neither the 1954 or 1955 Directory of Publishers in *Books in Print* nor *The American Book Trade Directory* for 1952 or 1956 lists Bridgehead Books as a known publisher. If the book was authorized and not pirated, why is there no record of its publication or publisher? The answer appears to be all too obvious: like *The Collected Poems of Ernest Hemingway,* it is a pirated book.

West Chester State College

STEPHEN LONGSTREET

Hemingway and the SUN Set.
Bertram D. Sarason.
Washington: Bruccoli Clark/
NCR Microcard Editions, 1972. $15.00.

Hemingway and Jake.
Vernon (Jake) Klimo and Will Oursler.
New York: Doubleday, 1972. $7.95.

The Hemingway industry — both feet solidly planted in the air — is as active in the United States as IBM or Kentucky Fried Chicken franchises. The boom in F. Scott Fitzgerald stock has passed its peak, but a burst of activity is expected in William Faulkner in the very near future. I am, however, happy to report that Professor Sarason's splendidly researched book is far ahead of anything yet produced on the actual personalities behind the 1926 novel, *The Sun Also Rises,* and does it with an appetite for responsibility. On the other hand, *Hemingway and Jake* is a curb issue, with almost no assets behind it. It is one of those "told-to" items. Contains almost no ore worth assaying, and presents the curious stealth of some vague speculation.

Everyone who ever met Hemingway — and he was on the surface an exhilerating phenomenon — seems to be moving towards print. When I was a teen-age art student, on the fringe of the School of Paris in the middle 1920's, there were several thousand Americans in Paris, as a colony, in the main of sloth and insufficiency, isolated in the City of Light. So knowing "Hem" was as casual as greeting the passing *flic* or going to the American Express office in hope of a check from home. Professor Sarason is very good in his tight texts in pointing out this isolation. Few of us met any of the French except waiters, profit-seekers, and whores. Most Americans spoke hardly any French except for some basic questions as to food, drink, pliant

319

love, and directions outside the stockades of the Left or Right Banks. (Gertrude Stein's French was miserable, and I recall Gide remarking on the horror of her accent.)

While alcohol, paranoia, suicide, *and* nostalgia gone to senility have cut down the number of people who claimed to have boxed with Hemingway (like *Mayflower* descendants a mighty army), the game goes on. I had had some training as a ring fighter, so observing Hemingway boxing, it was clear to me he was a lousy boxer. But noting his powerful chest and muscled arms, and his cruelty — power as an end in itself — and his desire to win, I sidestepped that simple road to fame. No, I never put on the gloves, so did not collect an anecdote for someone's text.

What Professor Sarason set out to do was to track down the surviving originals of the characters in *The Sun Also Rises,* for it was no secret that the author of this *roman à clef* had used the circle of Americans of the first half of the 1920's in the literary set in Paris and their hangers-on. Charted their amorous, drinking, and sport-hunting activities, and used them pretty much directly from life. With mellifluous and quivering imaginings of his own.

Harold Loeb, we told each other, is clearly Robert Cohen; Ford Maddox Ford is Braddock; Lady Duff Twysden, that wrinkled, genteel babe, is Lady Brett Ashley. (What a blow to discover she was born Mary Smurthwaite, and her father was actually in trade, as a wine merchant). Pat Guthrie was Mike Campbell, Bill Smith and Donald Ogden Steward made up Bill Gorton. A few other bar-flies, horrendous cafe sitters, fringe characters of the arts are also identifiable. And Jake Barnes with his cock shot off, very much Ernest Hemingway himself, the tough observer with a new angle of vision, speaking with a new exactitude of language.

I remember Harold Loeb as a much more decent person than Hemingway's picture of Robert Cohen in the novel. Loeb never played the part of a drifting rich boy moving in a kind of experience-seeking euphoria. Rather I sensed this was a properly brought up Jew, now free of his background of Temple Emmanuel and *tantes,* all the *mispoche* — and loose among women for the first time. Escaped into an atmosphere where Mamma and the relatives couldn't point a finger of shame at him — a *shanda* to the Harmony Club, Princeton, Kuhn Loeb & Co., Loeb was a mild victim of Hemingway's Jew-baiting. Professor Sarason tries and fails to absolve Hemingway of deep seated anti-Semitism. Hemingway was a Jew-hater, I remember. And calling himself "Hemingstein" was a sort of humorless, ironic tease of playing at being what he called in conversation "a Hebe."

However, in fairness I must point out that Hemingway was *not* a revolting, dangerous, anti-Semite, as was his friend, Ezra Pound, nor like T. S. Eliot a perfect fascist in his talk. Eliot frankly said he'd like to keep a few Jews around "as flavor," but the rest — well . . . He'd give us a flick of the wrist and a silence. This was all *before* the rise of Hitler, and none of the *Sun* set advocated concentration camps or furnaces. There was a naive inexactitude in Hemingway's crudeness towards Jews — unlike his rigid rage about homosexuals.

Professor Sarason's book clearly shows Loeb brought out the anti-Jewish feeling in Hemingway by Loeb's affair with Lady Duff. The Professor feels there was no actual fornication between Duff and Hemingway; many of the people he interviewed, nearly fifty years after the events, agree with him.

The book sets itself the hard task of correcting the untrue images of people as distilled into good Hemingway fiction. The actual personalities as they drank and talked and sexed (a great deal of all three often) and acted out their aspirations and despairs, became literature. They existed, of course, in a different world from the one we now historically live in.

As a young painter I had little interest in the American literary set in Paris. My main objectives were the studios and table-talk of the artists' painterly sensibilities, and drawing sustenance from the museums, the galleries. Being very young in the wonderful sense of being out of sight of home, and rather callow, I had no profound feeling for mere prose writers. I was delighted with the café life, the bike races, the racetracks, the *vin ordinaire* and the horse-meat eating places, and the various parties given on check-arriving days. I was selling drawings to an English-language magazine *The Paris Boulevardier,* run by Erskine Gwynne — which gave me contact with folk who were later to be famous or notorious in Hemingway's fiction. He was already by 1925 the receiver of some small fame. I read and thought his early short stories were the work of a genius.

When *The Sun Also Rises* was published — "how well he caught the transience of our fleeing moment" (from my journal) — it was like an explosion of some fully defined, great truth. It is difficult today in 1972, nearly half a century later, to explain what a newness, directness, wonder – the maximum of feeling done with the minimum of detail – *Sun* was to us. The language was still so new-stripped down, bleached Baroque. Hemingway had not yet parodied himself into the strained efforts of Papa. The settings of *Sun* were as close to us as our skins. We wallowed in the delicate nuances that bring physical actions, sensations over into prose. The book was a revelation. I knew most of the people in the novel on sight – not as close friends. I was never part of the La Stein-*transition*-Scotty-Black Sun Press-Flanner-Sylvia Beach inner circle; I considered only painters worthy of cultivation. But at bars, cafés, and parties we overlapped with writers and we talked, drank wine, sat together at the six-day bike races, wondered on what horse to bet ten francs. So *Sun* hit us hard; it was a novel that transcended the reality of any book most of us had read before. Professor Sarason wisely does not overdo the "how fine it was then" stuff.

Only years later was it apparent that we all lived then not a reality but rather in a kind of romantic Paris haze, a Post-War (the Great War) chic, fake toughness, loving the tag "the lost generation." *The Sun Also Rises* actually left out more than it told. Missing was that seamy, clapped-up, sleazy side. The lonely despair, the mean, greedy French, the dirt and filth of bug-infested, cold studios. All the stink and reek of the Paris of the 20's so many Americans lived in. Not that we minded too much – but it *was* there. All of this Hemingway waxed and polished into the fêtes, the gay cafés, the names of drinks: Fundador Brandy, Dubonnet, Grand Marnier. All the bitter-sweet candy of sad love and the naming of all the cafés: Dome, Select, Lipps, the Flora. And the color of Paris, a pointillism of its silver-grey-blue tones. The *Sun's* pictures in many cases were as untrue to actuality as the Western legend in American films starring Gary Cooper (a Hemingway hero in films and in private a greatly admired friend). I tried to avoid this gloss in my own genre history book, *We All Went to Paris*.

Professor Sarason takes no sides on the book's merits. I have reread *The Sun Also Rises* about five times since 1926. I went through it again before attempting this review. Today it is a bore; the *mystique* has fled. The color has run from it; the language I once found so wonderful, the dialogue glowing like bubbly wine has seeped away to corny stuff (by its over-use by Hemingway's imitators accepting the great service he did for them; clarifying, cleaning up English prose). The newness is all gone like paint off an over-fondled old toy. The dialogue seems merely chi-chi, in part caustic, bitchy. And the wonderful people once accepted as so exciting, often come through in the pose of window dummies in the better shops, the male sports as pictures from a catalogue by Abercrombie and Fitch.

When Hemingway said, "We all had a girl and her name is nostalgia," he said a hell of a lot better than he knew. In our Orwell-Bernstein *Mass* age, with the planet hearing the Doomsday Bomb ticking (and in Yeats' words an awareness by many that "the center will not hold"), there is a reason why so little of the magic is left in *Sun*. A book that was so true for us, so valid and marvelous, is now perhaps just shadows of neurotic narcissism.

Professor Sarason has dug deeply and come up with many new facets. He has talked long with Loeb, and Kathleen Cannell (Loeb's mistress in the novel). He has brought out statements from Bill Smith and Donald Ogden Stewart, who went to Pamplona for the bulls. The book hunts down a great deal there was left to know of Lady Duff Twysden.

The text is for students and specialists. There is just too much detail, cross-filing, collection of names, for the average reader to follow, or even care about. Reading the many names today is like trying to find the ghosts of the old Bolsheviks that Stalin executed.

In the middle 1920's the café gossip was that Hemingway and Lady Duff had actually been lovers. Elliot Paul, one of the editors of *transition* told me so, and he was a fairly reliable witness as to the doings of the American colony. But of actual documentary proof there is none. ("Is there proof for Christ's miracles or Jonah's whale?" — Balzac). *Hemingway and The SUN Set* goes a long way to reestablish the reputation of Lady Duff, and in this the author appears to be right. I knew her casually as a drunk, but not as an alcoholic. Almost everyone drank heavily, and there were some hopelessly hooch-addicted people. But she seemed to be able, as she proclaimed once in public in Harry's Bar, "to take the sauce or leave it alone." Was she a sex maniac? *The SUN Set* says no, and that Hemingway made her out to be worse than she was. Except for Pat Guthrie and Loeb, the book names none of her other lovers but for a mysterious Negro, never actually proven or identified. Yet in the middle 1920's in Paris the listing of her bed partners was common gossip, though there was no suggestion of a mad nymphomaniac drive. The casual, often inchoate love-making of the Americans and English in Paris was part of most lives. There were wives and husbands who didn't play around; however, it was for most what today would be called a swingers' society of mistress and wife-swapping, and there were folk who did make out with casual strangers.

The book claims that Lady Duff was most likely sexually frigid, and not really a great lay. Elliot Paul in conversation with me claimed she was much better in bed than the model Kiki, or Mistinguett — and two other people he knew who had fabulous sexual reputations in Paris at that time. Elliot Paul was an inquisitive bastard, often positively telepathic.

Professor Sarason does not go into Hemingway's sexual abilities in any great detail. Yet the true key to *Sun is* sexual — *not* money, as he suggests. Perhaps an error to an understanding of Hemingway. Virgil Thomson has written that Gertrude Stein was in love with Hemingway and offered to go to bed with him. He rejected her. He himself has admitted his periods of impotence at the beginning of his second marriage. There is other evidence that he had sexual problems. One is noted in the estate of a friend of e. e. cummings, the late painter, Elise Cavannah; a letter to her from a woman who tried sex with Hemingway and had a frustrating experience. One line I read in that letter notes: "It went on hour after hour, and it was like sawing a woman in half."

Perhaps this is a key to Jake Barnes, whom Hemingway identified with himself later in writing about *Sun.* Jake is sexually out of it. Was it more than just a literary gambit? Did it reflect a great deal of the author's sexual hangups? I leave the answer to the professors. But I do know that like Fitzgerald he retained a sexual puritanism. And as to the claims he was a latent homosexual? If so, he fought it by being over-manly, and going out of his way to cut down faggots in his prose.

Actually most of the people I knew in Paris felt he was immature all his life; he had the code of an earnest boy camping-out, playing Huck Finn. Robert McAlmon when boozed up, I remember, claimed Hemingway knew little about women and that he actually feared them. That they were all to Hemingway, he said, "a high-school football player's idea of a dream lay." This can be borne out in a way by the unreal sex toys the women are in Hemingway novels. The too *too* willing rubber doll nurse in *Farewell;* the cropped-haired boy-girl in the sleeping bag in *Bell;* the Sevres china contessa in the gondola in *Across the River.* He never created real, sweating women, except for what may be a half-portrait — the distorted image of Lady Duff.

Duff did not die romantically, a Lady of the Camellias. She actually made a happy marriage with a Texan ten years younger than herself. Hemingway — gone to Poe — invented a funeral for her with her coffin being carried by her drunken lovers, who dropped the casket and it split open. This is as true as his claim to have banged Mata Hari. (She was shot in 1917 by the French, and Hemingway didn't get to Europe until 1918.)

Professor Sarason does an excellent job of separating the early Hemingway genius (and I think he was a genius then) from the mean and cruel human problem he actually was. Whatever the reason for his ungracious side, as an artist he flickered golden as a little Pentecostal flame. In Paris before *Sun* was published, he was respected as a great, promising talent who would do important work. Re-reading those early stories they stand up, in the main, as major contributions to American literature. The novels do not. They have brilliant spots, but, like Kipling, Hemingway was not a good novelist. Flawed, with inner scar-tissue, he could not sustain a long emotional odyssey.

We doubt if anyone will again produce so detailed, so hunted-down a text as *Hemingway and The SUN Set.* It is a labor of love and admiration for a very original artist, but one who lived a pilgrimage of misdemeanors. In the end the book seems to fill out the image of Ernest Hemingway as a baffled man, and for me, keyed to a remark a girl from Arizona made to me at the Select one chilly morning when Paris was turning the proper autumnal gray-and-gold, and you could see your breath vaporize before you: "As a human being E. H. wasn't really the shit he made himself out to be . . ."

Of the book *Hemingway and Jake* (jacket blurb, "An Extraordinary Friendship") there isn't much to say. There is almost no Hemingway in the strident, unpleasant book. Jake may have had a few drinks with "Stein" (as he calls Hemingway) and been on his boat. But it's much too casual, and third-rate, with the heavy hand of Mr. Oursler. Most of the jumbled text is not about "Stein" but about Jake, who claims to have been a smuggler, pirate, jailbird, *and* drifter in Key West in the 1930's. He wouldn't mind if you thought of him as the original of Harry Morgan in *To*

Have and Have Not. Not that he does; just kind of acts coy about it in the exuberant assumption of being a character. The book is mostly about his drifting, his jail terms. There is some quoted dialogue with Hemingway, hardly the nut-hard stuff (maybe it wasn't so good that day, not running good at all). Samples: "Jake, what are you getting into?" Another line hints with a knowing wink of the final shot-gun blast: "I don't believe you have the guts to shoot yourself."

The book reminds me of what the artist Hilaire Hiler once said in Paris: "Kant is to Hegel as a hole is to a bagel."

It is this side of the "I-knew-him" Hemingway industry that is growing. I have made a promise: never to write *Steve and Hemingstein.*

Beverly Hills, California

SHELDON NORMAN GREBSTEIN

A Reader's Guide to Ernest Hemingway.
Arthur Waldhorn.
New York: Farrar, Straus and Giroux,
1972. $8.95.

Toward the close of this estimable book, these sentences appear. Although they specifically refer to the hero of *Islands in the Stream,* they might also serve as paradigm for Arthur Waldhorn's general critical method: "Despite these shortcomings as a fictional character, Hudson does — in his resemblance to Hemingway — contribute to the compelling force the novel somehow musters. What one knows about Hemingway inevitably inspills over into any reading of his work." That is, *A Reader's Guide to Ernest Hemingway* is fundamentally biographical criticism, and its major concerns are, typically, character and theme rather than technique. Fortunately, Waldhorn's treatment of these matters takes its authority not only from a deep knowledge of the writer's work but also from a compassionate understanding of Hemingway as a man.

Considering that we now possess much intimate information about Hemingway's life and personality, and that most of our recent knowledge is for the worst, it is truly admirable for someone to write biographical criticism which is neither thesis-ridden nor clinical. In Hemingway's case we can no longer delude ourselves — as we could during much of his lifetime — that the writer perfectly enacted in his own conduct those virtues exemplified by his heroes. (Note, by contrast, that a mantle of dignified mystery still surrounds Faulkner.) Thus, as biographical critic, Waldhorn has achieved a rare condition: to confront unblinkingly the salient weaknesses in Hemingway's sensibility as these manifested themselves in his books, and yet to treat them with persistent intellectual fairness and sympathy. In consequence, the reader comes voluntarily to share the critic's own attitude: to love the writer and his work, despite the occasions when one doesn't like or respect them. What better guide than the critic at once loving and scrupulous?

In addition to its subtle ambience of human warmth and good sense, *A Reader's Guide to Ernest Hemingway* is commendable in other ways. Waldhorn writes with consistent grace and clarity, even in his discussion of complex issues. At moments, indeed, the critic's style is inspired to an eloquence excelling that of its subject, particularly in the concluding chapters dealing with *The Old Man and the Sea, Islands in the Stream,* and *A Moveable Feast.* These are suffused with an elegaic tone almost as instructive as the overt formulation of the critic's ideas.

Another of Waldhorn's praiseworthy qualities is his taste. He likes the right books and usually for the right reasons. Accordingly, in the Hemingway cannon Waldhorn rates *The Sun Also Rises* and *A Farewell to Arms* at the pinnacle, *The Old Man and the Sea* just below them, and *For Whom the Bell Tolls* next. He admits that *To Have and Have Not* and *Across the River and into the Trees* are grossly flawed, but takes them seriously nevertheless. His judgment of the stories is likewise cogent. My quarrels with him on this score are minor. I rank *For Whom the Bell Tolls* with the two masterpieces of the twenties because its magnitude, its richness of texture, and its intricacy of structure far surpass its weaknesses. I think *To Have and Have Not* is a bad but interesting book, far more consequential than *Across the River and into the Trees,* which is intolerably pontifical in attitude and inexcusably decadent in manner. Waldhorn also discusses another poor book, *Green Hills of Africa,* with more ardor than it deserves.

If Waldhorn errs, then, it is toward generosity. He is notably too harsh only in his treatments of *Death in the Afternoon* and *A Moveable Feast. A Moveable Feast,* especially, for all its shameful vindictiveness, has some marvelous writing, a quality which the critic recognizes but tends to minimize in his preoccupation with the work as dark mirror of the man. Here a sharper focus on the volume as a figurative narrative, not merely a memoir, might have saved him from the all too tempting mistake of biographical criticism: to slight craft in favor of content. Whatever its value as a record of Hemingway's mind and heart, to me the most remarkable and enduring aspect of *A Moveable Feast* is its imaginative achievement. Many of its episodes employ the style and structure characteristic of some of the writer's best short stories, and are far superior to such earlier satirical sketches as "Mr. and Mrs. Elliott." Nevertheless, in Waldhorn's book I found myself in the cordial company of an agreeable person, an uncommon situation in too much Hemingway criticism.

Nor is there sharp provocation to dispute Waldhorn's interpretations. I think he misreads the protagonist's motives in "Fifty Grand"; and in another text, "Macomber," he mistakenly insists on an interpretation of character which derives from a bio-graphically-influenced argument, whereas the real issue is technical. Furthermore, Waldhorn is a little too kind to Jake Barnes at Robert Cohn's expense, for the same reasons as already suggested: because the critic argues what he perceives to be Hemingway's worldview while slighting the problems posed by narrative perspective. Other than these examples, and they are notoriously controversial, there is little in Waldhorn that needs rebuttal. He inclines to a less systematic and less emphatic account of Hemingway's symbolism and symbolic structure than I do, and, accordingly, he undervalues Carlos Baker's work. But this is a matter of judgment, like his concentration on character and theme – critical decisions beyond reproach or indictment.

Now, after all this praise freely bestowed upcn an intelligent and sensitive book, here is a paradox although by no means a recantation. I can say in one breath that I am glad we have Waldhorn's study and glad that I read it, and in the next that it is not a "contribution" in the fullest sense. I mean, to put it bluntly, that it did not teach me a great deal. There are some keen new insights, but in the main its strength is synthesis, not discovery. Moreover, I suspect that others familiar with Hemingway criticism will respond similarly. Only in his illuminating discussion of *Islands in the Stream,* wherein Waldhorn did not have a mass of previous commentary to surmount, did I find him profoundly instructive. Waldhorn's treatment of that mediocre novel shows him at his best, skillfully interweaving the diverse strands of life and art into a unified tapestry of meaning.

This vital point, the status of *A Reader's Guide to Ernest Hemingway* as a contribution, can perhaps be clarified by comparison. Before Waldhorn's book the most recent Hemingway study I had read was Emily Stipes Watts' *Ernest Hemingway and the Arts.* In comparison, Waldhorn's book is wiser, more sophisticated in its literary scholarship and taste, a finer model of expository prose, and far greater fun to read. In these respects Waldhorn is a seasoned, skilled professional, whereas Watts' work is a bit clumsy and dense, hinting of an apprenticeship only recently served. But, withal, Watts makes a *contribution* and thereby attains an importance to Hemingway scholars that Waldhorn may not achieve. She takes a new slant on Hemingway, brings to bear the formidable resources of another body of knowledge, assembles impressive data about a special area of Hemingway's experience, and, above all, opens up hitherto unexplored dimensions of Hemingway's craft.

I had thought I was utterly weary of hearing about Hemingway's themes and Code and heroes-as-personae. Waldhorn surprised me and refreshed me by proving he could do it all again, and do it so well it seemed fresh. His work demonstrates not only the power of sympathy but also the power of synthesis. As is eminently suitable to a reader's guide, his book contains most of Hemingway and many of Hemingway's best critics, all ably compacted and distilled. I will praise the book to students and recommend it immediately after Young and Baker and Rovit. I will speak of it favorably to colleagues in other specialities and press it urgently upon those who, for whatever reason, read Hemingway eccentrically. But for the veteran Hemingway scholar-critic it mainly performs only the pleasant service of evoking and confirming what he has already learned for himself.

State University of New York at Binghamton

JACKSON R. BRYER

F. Scott Fitzgerald: A Descriptive Bibliography.
Matthew J. Bruccoli.
Pittsburgh: University of Pittsburgh Press, 1972.

Simply stated, this is the most important book in Fitzgerald studies since Andrew Turnbull's 1963 volume of letters; and it far exceeds Turnbull's book in the meticulousness of Bruccoli's scholarship. To find a work on Fitzgerald which approaches this one in the quality of its research, one has to go back to Arthur Mizener's 1951 biography. And I daresay that, while Mizener's book is certainly more readable, Bruccoli's bibliography will prove the more durable and indispensable. Even to anticipate the innumerable ways in which it is likely to be useful is unfairly to suggest its limitations. It is not only a volume which every student of Fitzgerald must have, it is also a model for anyone planning to undertake a scholarly author bibliography. But Bruccoli's standards are so high that those who use his book as a model may well find themselves unable to match its thoroughness and completeness. It is the product of fifteen years as a collector, compiler, scholar, and bibliographer; and the results are a tribute to Bruccoli's expertise in all four areas.

It is divided into nine major sections, followed by ten appendices and an index. Section A is a chronological listing of "all books, pamphlets, and broadsides wholly or substantially by Fitzgerald — including all printings of all editions in English." For the first printing of the first American and English editions of each book, Bruccoli provides facsimiles of the title page, of the copyright statement on the verso of the title page, and often of the dust jacket. For each of these first editions he then gives a full collation, a listing of the contents, descriptions of the typography and paper, the binding, and the dusk jacket, the number of copies in the first printing, the date of publication, the price, the names of the printer and binder, and the locations of specimen copies. In addition, where warranted, he notes any special publishing circumstances, such as a complete collation of the differences between the first, fourth, and seventh printings of *This Side of Paradise,* or mention that *The Great Gatsby* was serialized after book publication in *Famous Story Magazine* (1926) and later in England in *Argosy* (1937), or the fact that, in the first edition of *The Crack-up* (1945), the titles of "Handle With Care" and "Pasting It Together" were transposed, with the essay entitled "Handle With Care" actually being "Pasting It Together" and vice versa (this error was perpetuated in the first English edition). Tucked away amidst the familiar Fitzgerald titles in this section are such exotic separate publications as the broadside mock issue of "The Saint Paul Daily Dirge" (1922), the 1928 printing of *John Jackson's Arcady,* the parody newspaper story of Grant's surrender to Lee at Appomattox which Fitzgerald had printed for distribution to his friends, and the special Canadian edition of *Turkey Remains* (1956). Subsequent printings and editions for each book are described more briefly but, in each case, number of copies, date, and locations are listed, and, for new editions, a description of the title page.

Section B presents a chronological list of all titles in which Fitzgerald material appears for the first time in a book or pamphlet. Previously unpublished pieces are noted; only the first printings of these books are described, although English editions are listed; and locations are provided for scarce items. Entries in this section range from the predictable first reprintings of Fitzgerald stories in anthologies and selections of the year's best short fiction to the more obscure *Ten Years of Princeton '17* (1929) and *Colonial and Historic Homes of Maryland* (1939), to which Fitzgerald contributed a Foreword. This section also lists the hard-to-find brief fragments of Fitzgerald letters and manuscripts which have appeared in books like Sheilah Graham's *College of One* or in the numerous autobiographies of such Fitzgerald contemporaries as Morley Callaghan, Helen Hayes, and Lillian Gish.

Section C lists all first appearances of Fitzgerald pieces in magazines and newspapers. Complete bibliographical citations are given for all American publications; while English printings are more briefly noted. Cross-references to reprintings in collections listed in sections A and B are provided; and, occasionally, reprintings in periodicals are mentioned when Bruccoli feels they are "especially important," as when an article or story was widely syndicated. One of the most striking facts which even a rapid survey of this section makes clear is that a surprisingly large percentage of Fitzgerald's work remains uncollected. This is particularly true of his later short stories.

Section D enumerates manuscript and typescript material by Fitzgerald quoted in auction, bookdealer, and library-exhibition catalogues. This section, of course, presents much previously unavailable information; and, because Bruccoli prints partial or full transcriptions of many of the letters and book inscriptions in the catalogues, it serves as the source of new Fitzgerald material. Section E lists published interviews with Fitzgerald, noting when these have been reprinted in collections. Section F consists of articles which contain material by Fitzgerald, such as quotes attributed to him. Section G arranges in chronological order the dust jacket blurbs which Fitzgerald wrote for books by other authors. Section H lists keepsakes (here defined as "a separately printed small item with a limited number of copies not offered for sale"), such as the four-page facsimile of "The Author's Apology" which was printed in conjunction with the first issue of the *Fitzgerald/Hemingway Annual*. Finally, Section I is a bibliography of Zelda Fitzgerald's publications, with full descriptions of the first American and English editions of *Save Me the Waltz* and listings of Zelda's stories and essays, some of which were by-lined either as by Scott or by Scott and Zelda (Bruccoli uses notes in Fitzgerald's *Ledger* to determine which were largely Zelda's work).

The ten appendices, successively, list: English-language editions of story collections published in Japan; unlocated clippings found in Fitzgerald's scrapbooks; published plays based on Fitzgerald stories; unpublished plays by Fitzgerald produced in St. Paul during his boyhood there; mimeographed film scripts by Fitzgerald (with the locations of these noted); Fitzgerald's movie-writing assignments; movies made from Fitzgerald's work; Fitzgerald publications available in Braille; facsimiles of Fitzgerald's book contracts; and a highly selective checklist of principal works (almost all full-length books) about Fitzgerald.

This rapid description of the book's contents, however

insufficiently it may suggest the wealth of material available, does indicate the wide range of Bruccoli's scholarly net and the incredible diligence with which he has pursued his task. It is thus with considerable hesitancy and a full understanding of their relative insignificance that I mention the very few errors and omissions which I found. There are minor proof-reading errors in entries C 75 and C 145. Entry C 209, "A Snobbish Story," is one of the Josephine Perry stories and should be identified as such, as are the others in that series. B. F. Wilson's "Notes on Personalities" (E 17) should be noted as reprinted in A 32, *F. Scott Fitzgerald in His Own Time: A Miscellany*. In Appendix 2, item 2.10, listed as an unlocated clipping, is located and has been included as item B 109 in my *The Critical Reputation of F. Scott Fitzgerald*.

No one who has waited for this bibliography to appear for the past several years will be disappointed in the final product. Bruccoli demonstrates that a bibliography can be far more than a dreary catalogue; it can clearly be creative scholarship, settling many critical issues and stimulating work on numerous others. This book sets a standard for the future which will be extremely difficult to match; it also provides a tool for scholars, critics, bibliographers, and collectors. Its value and its excellences can no more be summarized adequately here than they can be overestimated. This is one of those very few works which can legitimately be described as a monumental achievement.

University of Maryland

JAMES B. MERIWETHER

F. Scott Fitzgerald and Ernest M. Hemingway in Paris: An Exhibition at the Bibliothèque Benjamin Franklin in Conjunction with a Conference at the Institut d'Études Américaines 23-24 June 1972 Bloomfield Hills, Michigan, and Columbia, South Carolina: Bruccoli Clark, 1972. $5.00.

This attractively produced little pamphlet is, despite its modest scope, a significant contribution to our knowledge of an important literary relationship. In a prefatory note, Matthew Bruccoli and Frazer Clark explain that the occasion of the exhibition was a conference sponsored by the *Fitzgerald/Hemingway Annual* "to explore the significance of the Paris experience in the careers of the two writers." The illustrations and annotations in the catalogue make available, in whole or in part, a number of highly interesting letters and book inscriptions by Fitzgerald and Hemingway. Related materials include letters and inscriptions by other writers, proof sheets, and rare books and pamphlets. Fitzgerald's daughter contributes a delightful reminiscence of life with her parents in Paris in the 1920's.

The Hemingway material probably comprises the most interesting and useful part of the catalogue. The compilers of the catalogue have obeyed Hemingway's stipulation, in his will, that his letters not be published, but passages from several highly significant letters are made more widely available here by reprinting them from dealers' catalogues. Other materials that call for special mention include a copy of the first English edition of *In Our Time* annotated by Hemingway; a copy of the Crosby Continental

Editions *The Torrents of Spring* in a previously unrecorded printed glassine wrapper; and galley proofs of *A Farewell to Arms.*

University of South Carolina

BIBLIOGRAPHICAL MATERIAL

BRUCCOLI
ADDENDA

The following items were either omitted from Matthew J. Bruccoli's *F. Scott Fitzgerald: A Descriptive Bibliography* (Pittsburgh: University of Pittsburgh Press, 1972) or appeared after the bibliography was published.

M.J.B.

SECTION A

A5.8   *Note:* This 4-volume set was in its 17th printing in March 1973.

A6.3   *Flappers and Philosophers.* New York: Scribners, 1972. Scribner Library #371. A.8.72(C).

A11?   *The Great Gatsby.* 1969 Taiwan piracy reported, but not seen.

A14.1.a *Note: TITN* was serialized in *Scribner's Magazine,* XCV (January-April 1934). The serial text was slightly bowdlerized.

A20.2   *The Stories of F. Scott Fitzgerald,* ed. Malcolm Cowley. New York: Scribners, [1972]. Added to the 4-volume Fitzgerald set distributed by The Literary Guild of America and its associated book clubs. See AA5 correction and A5.8.

A33   *Note:* The Scribners first printing of *Dear Scott/Dear Max* was distributed in Canada by John Wylie & Sons Canada.

A33.1b   *Dear Scott/Dear Max.* London: Cassell, [1973].

A34   *Note:* The Lippincott first printing of *As Ever, Scott Fitz—* was distributed in Canada by McClelland & Stewart.

A34.1b   *As Ever, Scott Fiz—.* London: Woburn Press, 1973.

A35   *F. Scott Fitzgerald's Ledger A Facsimile.* Introduction by Matthew J. Bruccoli. Washington: Bruccoli Clark/NCR Editions, [1973].

A36   *The Great Gatsby A Facsimile of the Manuscript.* Edited with introduction by Matthew J. Bruccoli. Washington: Bruccoli Clark/Microcard Editions Books, 1973.

A37   *The Basil and Josephine Stories.* Edited with introduction by Jackson R. Bryer and John Kuehl. New York: Scribners, [1973].

A38   *Bits of Paradise.* Edited with introduction by Scottie Fitzgerald Smith and Matthew J. Bruccoli. London: Bodley Head, [1973].

SECTION AA

AA5   *Correction:* The Bodley Head 2-volume *Short Stories* edition adds 12 stories to the contents of the Scribners edition: "The Jelly Bean," "A Short Trip Home," "The Bowl," "Outside the Cabinet-Maker's," "Majesty," "A Night at the Fair," "He Thinks he's Wonderful," "First Blood," "One Trip Abroad," "Design in Plaster," "Boil Some Water — Lots of It," "Teamed with Genius." *No first book material.*

AA12   *Absolution May Day Babylon Revisited*, ed. A. Le Vot; trans. M.-P. Castlenau and B. Willerval. Paris: Aubier-Flammarion, [1972]. Bilingual edition.

SECTION B

America Awakes, by Jan Farrington. Richmond: Westover, [1971]. Facsimiles full 2-page inscription to Sylvia Beach in *GG.* See B51.

The American Credo, by George Jean Nathan and H. L. Mencken. New York: Knopf, 1920. Fitzgerald claimed items 22, 51, 193, 199, 248, 262, 429, 433, 442, 449, 450, 455. New edition in 1927.

Under the Red, White, and Blue ['The *Great Gatsby'*] *By F. Scott Fitzgerald: Apparatus for a Definitive Edition,* by Matthew J. Bruccoli. Columbia, S.C.: University of South Carolina Press, [1974].

Crazy Sundays, by Aaron Latham. London: Secker & Warburg, [1972].

The Left Bank Revisited Selections from the Paris Tribune, ed. Hugh Ford. University Park: Pennsylvania State University Press, [1972]. First book appearance of interview, p. 115. See Section E.

O'Hara, by Finis Farr. Boston: Little, Brown, [1973]. Previously unpublished inscription to John O'Hara in *TITN,* p. 14. See front end paper in this volume of the *Annual.*

Scott Fitzgerald and his World, by Arthur Mizener. London: Thames & Hudson, [1972]; New York: Putnam, [1972]. Facsimiles *GG* galleys, p. 67; facsimiles inscription in *GG* to Carmel Myers, p. 69; also signed photos, pp. 21, 39.

Spellbound in Darkness, by George C. Pratt. Rochester: University of Rochester School of Liberal & Applied

Studies, [1966]. First book appearance of interview by Margaret Reid, "Has the Flapper Changed?" vol. 2, pp. 385-386. See E21.

Section C

Blurb for *Appointment in Samarra, New York Herald Tribune Books* (7 October 1934), VII-17. This ad reprinted as keepsake to mark publication of Matthew J. Bruccoli's *John O'Hara: A Checklist* (New York: Random House, 1972).

Section D

Charles Hamilton Auction Number 55 (3 February 1972). #158: Quotes 17 July 1926 Fitzgerald ALS to Jimmy: "... I sobered up in Paris and spent three days trying to get Brigham into shape. Then down here I worked on it some more and made a tentative working outline ... I don't believe that I can make the grade and the more I struggle with it the more I'm convinced that I'll ruin your idea by making a sort of half-assed compromise between my amateur idea of 'good theme' and Werner's book. I think your instinct has led you to a great idea but that my unsolicited offer was based more on enthusiasm than on common sense. So I bequeath you the notion of the girl which I think in other hands could be made quite solid, and rather ungracefully retire hoping that Connelly or Craig will make the sort of vehicle of it that's in your imagination. It was great seeing you. You're a man after my own heart and I feel that we have by no means seen the last of each other even in a theatrical way ... It was so nice of you to come and see Zelda ..."

Charles Hamilton Auction Number 60 (3 August 1972). #66A: Quotes 24 April 1935 TLS to C.A. Wright: "I was on the *Tiger* staff at Princeton for three years and got out many issues ... though I was not chairman. It was never as big a thing at Princeton as was the *Record* at Yale ... because most of the local wit was concentrated on producing the hullabaloo of the Triangle show, and lately the 'Intime' reviews. My time was chiefly notable for the first acknowledgment in print that girls would be girls and the first use in the east of such words as 'necking' and 'petting' exemplified by a series which I started . . . called *International Petting Cues . . .*"

Charles Hamilton Auction Number 61 (14 September 1972). #160: Quotes 7 January 1934 TLS to E.S. Oliver: "The first help I ever had in writing in my life was from my father who read an utterly imitative Sherlock Holmes story of mine and pretended to like it. But after that I received the most invaluable aid from . . . headmaster of the St. Paul Academy . . . from Courtland Van Winkle in freshman year at Princeton . . . he gave us the book of *Job* to read and I don't think any of our preceptorial group ever quite recovered from it . . . Most of the professors seemed to me old and uninspired, or perhaps it was just that I was getting under way in my own field. I think this answers your question. This is also my permission to make full use of it with or without my name . . ." #161: Quotes 1 February 1935 TLS to E.S. Oliver: ". . . I don't want to be quoted . . . anything you may want to use from my letter is to be summarized . . ."

Fifty For The Fair Heritage Bookshop (September 1972). #11: Quotes inscription in *GG:* "For . . . , from an unknown admirer, F. Scott Fitzgerald. Autumn 1940". #12: Quotes inscription in *ASYM:* "For . . . , from F. Scott Fitzgerald, one sad young man to another. Hollywood, 1940". #13: Quotes inscription in *TITN:* "To . . . , from his friend F. Scott Fitzgerald, This story of a Europe that is no more. September 1940". #14: Quotes inscription in *TAR:* "For . . . , with gratitude from F. Scott Fitzgerald. Armageddon, Annus I (1940 Old Style)". All inscribed to Fitzgerald's Hollywood attorney in 1940.

Cyril Connolly's One Hundred Modern Books, catalogue by Mary Hirth. Austin: University of Texas, [1972]. #48B: Facsimiles ALS to Joseph Hergesheimer: "14 Rue de Tilsitt/Paris France/Dear Hergeshiemer: Scribners forwarded me a copy of the letter you were kind enough to write about *The Great Gatsby.* Thank you for what you said about it as well as for the permission you so courteously gave to use your opinion. I'm afraid its a financial failure and I enclose you one of comments which may interest you. I don't do Rascoe's intelligence to think he really believes I am like Chambers — *La Cousine Bette* or *Linda Condon* could be "criticized" on the same grounds, if one wanted to make out such a preposterous case — the trouble is that we snubbed his wife. None the less I find the enclosure rather saddening review. Looking forward to *From an Old House* of which I've read with delight the three parts I came across in Italy. Again thank you, and most cordial good wishes Scott Fitzg–/Excuse the blots! I'm awfully anxious to see the Dower House. You promised to invite us but never did."

First Editions . . . Catalogue Four (Joseph the Provider, 1972). #256: Quotes inscription in *B&D:* "From F. Scott Fitzgerald/Great-Neck, Long Island/October 15, 1922".

F. Scott Fitzgerald and Ernest M. Hemingway in Paris. Bloomfield Hills & Columbia: Bruccoli Clark, 1972. Facsimiles Fitzgerald's inscription to Van Wyck Brooks in *GG* and June 1925 ALS to Brooks. See F19. 650 copies in orange-brown wrappers, plus 5 copies in white wrappers.

GRM Catalog 16 . . . George Robert Minkoff (1972). #470: Quotes *GG* inscription: "For . . . /From us sincerely/F. Scott Fitzgerald/Feb. 1927". #471: Quotes *ASYM* inscription: ". . . /with best wishes/F. Scott Fitzgerald/(There is an original drawing by Fitzgerald of a long line of sad young men)/TYPICAL SAD YOUNG MEN".

Modern Literature . . . Black Sun Books (Catalogue 10, 1972). #110: Quotes inscription in *B&D:* "For —— /with best wishes/from/F. Scott Fitzgerald/This was a book about/things I knew nothing/about, a drawing upon/experiences that I had/not had. Much more than/my first book this/was a piece of insolence." Also offers TLS.

Thomas M. Fassell, Inc. autographs . . . (Catalogue 2, 1972). #23: Describes 27 March 1924 ALS to Miss Cornelia C. Abbot of Lynn, Mass. This letter later quoted in *Conway Barker List* 724-2: "The Post has sent me your accusation. I use to defend myself. (1) Baby had nurse mentioned in fourth or fifth paragraph of story. (2) Nurse found door locked, concluded Gretchen was in city & carried on. Q.E.D. Sincerely, F. Scott Fitzgerald."

SALE NUMBER 68 . . . THE FINE LIBRARY OF THE LATE INGLE BARR . . . FEBRUARY 18 . . . FEBRUARY 19 . . . SOTHEBY PARKE BERNET, LOS ANGELES . . . (1973). #214: Describes *ASYM* inscribed to Horace McCoy, "Paramount, 1939".

SECTION E

"Fitzgerald Back from Riveria; Is Working on Novel," *Paris Tribune* (9 April 1929). See Section B.

SECTION F

Kent, Beth. "Fitzgerald A Ghostly Figure of Another Time," *Twin Citian*, X (October 1967), 15-19. Quotes from letter and reports conversation.

Latham, Aaron. "The Making of 'Crazy Sundays.' " *Princeton Alumni Weekly*, LXXI (1 June 1971), 8-10. Facsimiles page of revised TS for *LT.*

Margolies, Alan. "F. Scott Fitzgerald's Prison Play." *Papers of the Bibliographical Society of America,* LXI (1st Quarter 1972), 61-64. Includes material from *Play* notebook.

West, James L. W. III. "The Corrections Lists for F. Scott Fitzgerald's *This Side of Paradise,"* *Studies in Bibliography,* XXVI (1973). 254-264. Includes letters.

SECTION H

F. Scott Fitzgerald's Projected Collected Works. Columbia: Matthew J. Bruccoli, 1972. 300 copies. Facsimile of holograph plan for the "Works of F. Scott Fitzgerald".

This Side of Paradise, The Grammarian, and the "Author's Final Intentions." [Blacksburg: James L. W. West III, 1972]. 100 copies. Facsmiles 2 pages of *TSOP* MS and 1 page of TS.

Telegram keepsake. Facsimile of 15 March 1934 Western Union wire to Perkins about *TITN*. Columbia: Matthew J. Bruccoli, 1972. 100 copies.

SECTION I

I3? A new printing of the Southern Illinois University Press edition of *Save Me the Waltz* was distributed by the Book-of-the-Month Club in 1972. Not seen.

CHECKLISTS

MARGARET M. DUGGAN

FITZGERALD
CHECKLIST

Except for items of special interest, this list does not repeat entries listed in "Bruccoli Addenda" in the present *Annual.*

Anon. "A Positive Postscript," *Johns Hopkins Magazine,* XXI (October 1970), 9. Notes public response to February article on the neglect of Fitzgerald's gravestone.

_____. "The First and only Novel Ever Written by Zelda Fitzgerald," *Book-of-the-Month Club News* (August 1972), 26. Advertisement.

_____. "F. Scott Fitzgerald . . . 'Nobody Ever Wrote Better Prose,' " *Pittsburgh Press Roto* (19 November 1972), 36. Interview with Matthew J. Bruccoli.

_____. "Scott," *Edinburgh Festival 1972 Play Program* (21 August– 9 September). Musical presented by Bristol University Players.

_____. "Zelda's Play by Vagabond Players," *Baltimore Sunday Sun* (10 September 1972). *Scandalbra* revival.

Bahnks, Jean. "Letters to the Editor," *Galena (Illinois) Gazette* (4 March 1971). Discusses Fitzgerald's maternal grandfather's life in Galena with reference to *Tender is the Night.*

Baritz, Loren, ed. *The Culture of the Twenties.* New York: Bobbs-Merrill, 1970, pp. 300-310, 413-424. Reprints seven letters and "Echoes of the Jazz Age."

Behrman, S.N. "People in a Diary – Part II," *The New Yorker,* XLVIII (20 May 1972), 39-95.

Birmingham, Frederic A. *The Writer's Craft.* London: Arthur Barker, 1959. Quotes from "Red-Headed Woman" and "The Night Before Chancellorsville" in his discussion of Fitzgerald.

Bruccoli, Matthew J. " 'A Might Collation': Animadversions on the Text of F. Scott Fitzgerald," *Editing Twentieth Century Texts,* ed. Francess G. Halpenny. Toronto: University of Toronto Press, 1972, pp. 28-50.

_____. *Under the Red, White, and Blue ['The Great Gatsby'] By F. Scott Fitzgerald: Apparatus for a Definitive Edition.* Columbia: University of South Carolina Press, 1974.

Bulhof, Francis. *"Le Grand Meaulnes* and *The Great Gatsby," Dichter und Leser/Studien zur Literature.* Groningen: Wolters-Noordhoff, 1972, pp. 276-286.

Cahill, Thomas and Susan. *A Literary Calendar 1973.* Jamaica, N.Y.: Cahill, 1972. Quotes Fitzgerald.

Caruthers, Clifford M., ed. *Ring Around Max/The Correspondence of Ring Lardner & Max Perkins.* DeKalb, Illinois: Northern Illinois University Press, 1973.

Chesler, Phyllis. "Women & Madness," *Ms.,* I (July 1972), 109-113.

Dekle, Bernard. "F. Scott Fitzgerald 'The Roaring Twenties,' " *Profiles of Modern American Authors.* Rutland, Vermont: Tuttle, 1969, pp. 102-107.

Ellis, James. "The 'Stoddard Lectures' in *The Great Gatsby," American Literature,* XLIV (November 1972), 470-471.

Eyre, Richard. "Scott," *Edinburgh Scotsman* (25 August 1972), 8.

Fitzgerald, F. Scott. "Babylon Revisited," *Great Short Stories of the World,* selected by editors of *The Reader's Digest.* Pleasantville, N.Y.: Reader's Digest, 1972, pp. 393-411.

_____. *F. Scott Fitzgerald's Ledger,* Introduction by Matthew J. Bruccoli. Washington: Bruccoli Clark/NCR Editions, [1973]. Facsimile.

_____. *The Great Gatsby: A Facsimile of the Manuscript*, ed. Matthew J. Bruccoli. Washington: Bruccoli Clark/NCR Editions, 1973.

_____. "The Last of the Belles," *Images of Women in Literature*, ed. Mary Anne Ferguson. Boston: Houghton Mifflin, 1973, pp. 206-218.

_____. "Letter to His Daughter," *Authors on Film*, ed. Harry M. Geduld. Bloomington: Indiana University Press, 1972, pp. 223-224.

_____. "The Passionate Eskimo," *Showpiece*, I (July, August, September 1972), 12-16, 46-48. Unauthorized publication.

_____. "Ring," *The Critic as Artist*, ed. Gilbert A. Harrison. New York: Liveright, 1972, pp. 131-137. Also Malcolm Cowley's review of *Tender is the Night*, pp. 86-90.

_____. #30, *The Scriptorium*, unnumbered catalogue, 1972. Facsimiles inscription to Harry W. Winston that has been previously facsimiled in other catalogues.

_____. Louis Zukofsky's copy of *Tender is the Night*, with his critical notes. #79C, *Cyril Connolly's One Hundred Modern Books*, catalogue by Mary Hirth. Austin: University of Texas, [1972].

Fitzgerald, Zelda. "A Love Story" ["A Couple of Nuts"], *Pageant*, XXVII (March 1972), 60-73.

Graham, Sheilah. *A State of Heat.* New York: Grosset & Dunlap, 1972.

Hemingway, Ernest. Letters to Arthur Mizener and Charles Poore. See "Hemingway Checklist" in the present *Annual* and *Hemingway at Auction.*

Hoffman, Nancy Y. "The Doctor as Scapegoat," *Journal of the American Medical Association*, CCXX (3 April 1972), 58-61.

Hunter, Paul. "An Interview with F. Scott Fitzgerald," *The Best Short Plays 1972*, ed. Stanley Richards. New York: Chilton, 1972, pp. 325-354.

Latham, Aaron. *Crazy Sundays: F. Scott Fitzgerald in Hollywood.* New York: Pocket Books, 1972.

Longstreet, Stephen and J. J. Godoff. *Remember William Kite?* New York: Simon and Schuster, 1966, pp. 155-156. Novel in which Fitzgerald is discussed.

Longstreet, Stephen. "Scott," *We All Went to Paris.* New York: Macmillan, 1972, pp. 369-372.

_____. "Sinclair Lewis: An Overdue Memory of a Friendship," *Midway Magazine,* VII (1972), 105-118. Discusses Fitzgerald and *The Great Gatsby.*

Lowes, Bob. "My Side of F. Scott Fitzgerald," *Washington University Student Life,* XCIII (10 December 1971), 13-16.

MacPhee, Laurence E. *"The Great Gatsby's* 'Romance of Motoring': Nick Carraway and Jordan Baker," *Modern Fiction Studies,* XVIII (Summer 1972), 207-212.

Madden, Charles F., ed. "Arthur Mizener on F. Scott Fitzgerald," *Talks With Authors.* Carbondale: Southern Illinois University Press, 1968, pp. 23-38.

Mathieson, Theodore. "The F. Scott Fitzgerald Murder Case," *Ellery Queen's Mystery Magazine,* LX (November 1972), 85-97. Nonsense.

Mayfield, Sara. "Exiles from Paradise," *McCall's,* XCVIII (July 1971), 64-65, 127-129, 131-132, 140.

Merchant, Larry. "Bow Wow," *New York Post* (10 November 1971), 92. W.S. Wojtkiewicz, former husband of Sheilah Graham, has Fitzgerald papers.

Milford, Nancy. "Gatsby, Where Are You?" *Lifestyle,* I (November 1972), 22-29.

Nelson, Gerald B. "Dick Diver," *Ten Versions of America.* New York: Knopf, 1972, pp. 43-60.

O'Donoghue, Michael. "The Zircon as Big as the Taft — Random Incidents in the Lives of the Jazz Babies," *The National Lampoon,* I (May 1972), 46-47. Parody.

Raymont, Henry. "Reprint Houses Vex Publishers," *New York Times* (21 March 1972), M-42. Mentions the piracy of Fitzgerald.

Sagan, Françoise. "Ils Comprennent les Femmes — Delahaye-Fitzgerald," *Vogue* (French edition), (October 1972), 177.

Schulberg, Budd. *The Four Seasons of Success.* Garden City, N.Y.: Doubleday, 1972. Cites Fitzgerald as example of destructive power of the success ethic of the American market place.

Sheed, Wilfrid. "Fitzgerald: Once Again in Fashion," *Harper's Bazaar,* No. 3134 (January 1973), 80-81.

Stevenson, Laura Lee. "New York Magazine Competition," *New York,* V (16 October 1972), 95. Parody of Fitzgerald.

Sullivan, Scott. "Remembering Ernest, Scott and Zelda," *Baltimore Sun* (16 July 1972), K-5.

Tate, Allen. "Miss Toklas' American Cake," *Prose,* III (1971), 137-161.

Tomkins, Calvin. *Living Well Is the Best Revenge.* New York: Signet, 1972.

Turnbull, Andrew. *Scott Fitzgerald.* Harmondsworth, Middlesex, England: Penguin Books, 1970.

_____. "A strange set of spiral bound galley proofs, with the Scribner imprint, of a biography of Fitzgerald. No author name imprinted, and as far as we can find out, this was never published. No date. From the library of W. H. Auden." #294, *Phoenix Book Shop,* Catalogue CVII, n.d. The mysterious biography described is Turnbull's biography.

Tuttleton, James W. "F. Scott Fitzgerald: The Romantic Tragedian as Moral Fabulist," *The Novel of Manners in America.* Chapel Hill: University of North Carolina Press, 1972, pp. 162-183.

West, James L. W., III. "The Corrections Lists for F. Scott Fitzgerald's *This Side of Paradise,*" *Studies in Bibliography,* XXVI (1973), 254-264.

_____. "F. Scott Fitzgerald's Contributions to *The American Credo,*" *The Princeton University Library Chronicle,* XXXIV (Autumn 1972), 53-58. Facsimiles pages from Fitzgerald's copy of *The American Credo.*

Willis, Martee. "A Writer Who Sought Peace in Florida's Backwoods," *Jacksonville Times-Union Floridian* (24 September 1972), 28-30. Marjorie Kinnan Rawlings recalls Fitzgerald.

Reviews of *As Ever, Scott Fitz–*: Dennis Brown, "Fitzgerald and Friends," *St. Louis Post-Dispatch* (4 June 1972), D-4; Jackson R. Bryer, "Fitz/Ober Letters," *Connecticut Review,* VI (October 1972), 100-103; Alice Digilio, "Scott Fitzgerald? He Wrote for Loans," Alexandria, Virginia *Journal Newspapers* (14 September 1972), A-4; Maurice Duke, "Fitzgerald's Letters to, From His

Agent Give Keen Insight Into Literary World," *Richmond Times-Dispatch* (13 August 1972), F-5; Maggie Irving, "Important Biographies," *Worcester, Mass. Telegram* (6 August 1972), E-8; Robert Kirsch, "More Bits of the Fitzgerald Mosaic," *Los Angeles Times* (18 May 1972), IV-19; Betty Leighton, "Letters Record Waste of Talent," Winston-Salem, N.C. *Journal* (3 September 1972), 18; David Lenson, "Old Times, Good Times With the Writer," *San Francisco Book Review*, No. 26 (December 1972), 8; Robert F. Lucid, "A Not-So-Great Gatsby in the Business World," *Los Angeles Times Book Review* (25 June 1972), 1, 9; Thomas S. Reigstad, "Fitzgerald's Letters to Ober," *Buffalo Courier-Express* (10 September 1972), 16; William White, "The letters of despair by F. Scott Fitzgerald," *Detroit Sunday News* (11 June 1972), E-5; Alden Whitman, "SR Reviews Books," *Saturday Review*, LV (8 July 1972), 60, 64.

Reviews of *Dear Scott/Dear Max:* Matthew J. Bruccoli, "Max, the man who took care of Scott," *Chicago Daily News-Panorama* (25-26 December 1971), 7; Joan Bunke, "Scott and Max — A Literary History Told in Letters," *Des Moines Sunday Register* (23 January 1972), C-9; Rod Cockshutt, "Scott, Max and 'Ecclesiastes,' " *Raleigh News and Observer* (19 December 1971), IV-6; Jeffrey Hart, "Fitzgerald and Perkins," *National Review,* XXIV (3 March 1972), 228-229; Robert Kirsch, "The Book Report — Fitzgerald, Editor Become Friends," *Los Angeles Times* (5 January 1972), IV-4; Theodore M. O'Leary, "How Close the Writer and Editor," *Kansas City Star* (12 December 1971), E-3; W. G. Rogers, "The Literary Scene," *New York Post* (29 November 1971), 22; Tom Saunders, "Editor and Author," *Winnipeg Free Press* (8 January 1972), 20.

FITZGERALD

IN

TRANSLATION

This list supplements "Fitzgerald in Translation" in the *1972 Annual* – M.M.D.

THIS SIDE OF PARADISE

Na Prahu Rāje, trans. Josef Hochman. Praha, Czechoslovakia: Libuše Vrbová, 1971. Czech.

Deze Kant Van Het Paradijs, trans. Clara Eggink and Omslagontwerp van Uniepers. Amsterdam: Contact, 1971. Dutch.

THE GREAT GATSBY

Veliki Gastby, trans. Gitica Jakopin. Ljubljani, Yugoslavia: Cankarjeva Založba, 1970. Slovene.

TENDER IS THE NIGHT

Natten er blid, trans. Helga Vang Lauridsen and Elsa Gress Wright. Denmark: Gyldendal, 1972. (Original version). Danish.

Az éj szelíd trónján, trans. Osztovits Levente. Budapest: Európa Könyvkiadó, 1972. (Revised version). Hungarian.

Sauve es la noche, trans. Marcelo Cervelló. Barcelona: Plaza & Janes, 1972. (Revised version). Spanish.

COLLECTION OF SHORT STORIES

F.S. Fitzgerald Short Stories/Nouvelles, ed. Andre Le Vot, trans. Marie-Pierre Castlenau and Bernard Willerval. Paris: Aubier-Flammarion, 1972. af 49. "Absolution," "May Day," "Babylon Revisited." Bilingual text – French and English.

ZELDA FITZGERALD — SAVE ME THE WALTZ

Darf ich um den Walzer bitten?, trans. Elizabeth Schnack. Olten: Walter-Verlag, 1972. German.

MARGARET M. DUGGAN

HEMINGWAY
CHECKLIST

Anon. "Author's Ailments Likened to Dad's," *Los Angeles Mirror* (5 July 1961). Interview with Carlos Baker.

_____. *Checklist 29 Ernest Hemingway.* Hyderabad: American Studies Research Centre, 1971. Revision of 1967 publication.

_____. "Figure in Stories by Hemingway Recalls Author," *The New York Times* (2 April 1972), 45. Interview with Joe Bacon.

_____. "Hemingway's Son Lives Father's Story in Tanzanian Bush," *Columbia* (S.C.) *Record* (20 March 1972), A-3.

_____. "Traveling Through Hemingway's Lower Michigan," *The Bloomfield Hills Eccentric* (4 January 1973), C-17.

Asselineau, Roger. *Ernest Hemingway.* Paris: Editions Pierre Seghers, 1972.

_____. "Un Romantique Américain du XXᵉ Siècle: Ernest Hemingway," *Le Romantisme Anglo-Américain Mélanges offerts à Louis Bonnerot.* Paris: Études Anglaises, #39, pp. 404-412.

Baker, Carlos. *Hemingway The Writer as Artist.* Princeton, N.J.: Princeton University Press, 1972. 4th edition, *revised.*

Botsford, Keith. *Dominguin.* Chicago: Quadrangle Books, 1972.

Bruccoli, Matthew J. and C. E. Frazer Clark, Jr. (Compilers). *Hemingway at Auction.* Detroit:Bruccoli Clark/Gale, 1973. Facsimiles major auction and dealer catalogues.

Butcher, Fanny. *Many Lives—One Love.* New York: Harper & Row, 1972.

Davidson, Arnold E. "The Ambivalent End of Francis Macomber's Short, Happy Life," *Hemingway Notes,* II (Spring 1972), 14-16.

Dekle, Bernard. "Ernest Hemingway A Life of Adventure," *Profiles of Modern American Authors.* Rutland, Vermont: Charles E. Tuttle, 1969, pp. 113-119.

Dowdy, Andrew. "Hemingway and Surrealism: A Note on the Twenties," *Hemingway Notes,* II (Spring 1972), 3-6.

Fisher, Edward. "Lost Generations, Then and Now," *Connecticut Review,* VI (October 1972), 13-25.

Gent, George. "Hemingway's Letters Tell of Fitzgerald," *New York Times* (25 October 1972), L-38.

Gingrich, Arnold. "That Slovenly Servant, Memory," *Esquire,* LXXVIII (September 1972), 6. On "Snows."

Groseclose, Barbara S. "Hemingway's 'The Revolutionist': An Aid to Interpretation," *Modern Fiction Studies,* XVII (Winter 1971-72), 565-570.

Hemingway, Ernest. "American Bohemians in Paris," and "Soldier's Home," *The Culture of the Twenties,* ed. Loren Baritz. Indianapolis: Bobbs-Merrill, 1970, pp. 297-300, 19-28.

———. "A Tribute to Mamma from Papa Hemingway," *Authors on Film,* ed. Harry M. Geduld. Bloomington: Indiana University Press, 1972, pp. 283-284. On Dietrich.

———. Blurb for John W. Thomason, Jr's *Texas Rebel.* New York: Berkley, 1961. Quoted from *Men at War:* ". . . it is a fine story as are all of his other stories . . .".

———. *E. H., apprenti reporter,* ed. Matthew J. Bruccoli, trans. Yves Malartic. Paris: Gallimard, 1972. Translation of *Ernest Hemingway, Cub Reporter.*

———. *For Whom the Bell Tolls.* Bombay, India: Thacker, 1944.

———. "Hemingway on Safari," *The Look Years 1937-1971.* New York: Cowles Communications, 1972, pp. 48-49.

_____. *Islands in the Stream.* Harmondsworth, Middlesex, England: Penguin Books, 1971.

_____. "The Short Happy Life of Francis Macomber," *Images of Women in Literature,* ed. Mary Anne Ferguson. Boston: Houghton Mifflin, 1973, pp. 141-163.

_____. "The Snows of Kilimanjaro," *Great Short Stories of the World,* selected by editors of *The Reader's Digest.* Pleasantville, N.Y.: Reader's Digest, 1972, pp. 165-188.

_____. *The Torrents of Spring.* New York: Scribners, 1972. Clothbound and Scribner Library #373. A-7.72[C].

_____. TLS to "Dear Erl," Key West, Florida, 20 November 1935. #235, *Seventy Two ABC Of Collecting, House of El Dieff,* n.d. See *Hemingway at Auction.*

_____. ALS and TLS to Paul Drus, Key West, Florida, 1 February and 28 July 1938. #204, *Sotheby Parke-Bernet Galleries,* Sale 3428, 13 October 1972. See *Hemingway at Auction.*

_____. TLS to Patrick and Gregory Hemingway, Havana, Cuba, 14 July 1939. #102, *Kenneth W. Rendell,* Catalogue 80, n.d. See *Hemingway at Auction.*

_____. 8 TLS to Arthur Mizener, Finca Vigia, 6 July 1949 through 4 January 1951. #203, *Sotheby Parke-Bernet Galleries,* Sale 3428, 31 October 1972. See *Hemingway at Auction.*

_____. 4 ALS, 5 TLS, and 1 memorandum to Charles Poore, Finca Vigia, 4 August 1949 through 21 May 1953. #144-#153, *Charles Hamilton,* Auction Number 56 . . . 9 March 1972. See *Hemingway at Auction.*

_____. TLS to W. G. Rogers, Finca Vigia, 29 July 1948. *We are pleased to offer an Ernest Hemingway Letter . . . Gotham Book Mart . . .* (1972). 4-page prospectus facsimiles letter in full; 100 numbered copies.

_____. TLS to Mrs. E. S. Russell, Cooke, Montana, 27 October 1936. #236, *Seventy Two ABC Of Collecting, House of El Dieff,* n.d. See *Hemingway at Auction.*

_____. *A Farewell to Arms,* inscribed: "To Mrs. Marchall Russell with very best wishes, always, Ernest Hemingway." #293, *M.A.C. Co-Operative,* Catalogue XIV, April 1972.

_____. *Death in the Afternoon,* inscribed: "To Tommy Shevlin's mother from his friend, who hopes he will be her friend Ernest Hemingway." #292, *M.A.C. Co-Operative,* Catalogue XIV, April 1972.

_____. *For Whom the Bell Tolls,* inscribed: "To Elizabeth Russell from Tommy's friend and her admirer Ernest Hemingway." #294, *M.A.C. Co-Operative,* Catalogue XIV, April 1972.

_____. *The Fifth Column and the First Forty Nine Short Stories,* inscribed: "To Gweneth Beam, in admiration always – Ernest Hemingway." #157, *William Young and Co.,* Catalogue 609, n.d.

_____. *Three Stories & Ten Poems,* inscribed: "To Philip Jordan Hommages Respecteies or x from Ernest Hemingway Paris October 1925." Facsimiles inscription. #299, *Sotheby, Parke-Bernet Galleries,* Sale 3428, 31 October 1972.

_____. Revised TS, 5 pp. Adaptation of "The Sea Change" into reading version. #33, *The Scriptorium,* unnumbered catalogue, 1972.

Hemingway, Mary. "Ernest's Idaho and Mine," *World,* I (7 November 1972), 34-37.

Higgins, George V. "Rooting in Papa's Closet to Discover . . . 14 Pages?!," *The National Observer* (29 April 1972).

Hillinger, Charles. "Hemingway Name Used for Selling Cats in U.S.," *Indianapolis Star* (17 September 1972).

Howell, John M. and Charles A. Lawler. "From Abercrombie & Fitch to *The First Forty-Nine Stories,*" *Proof,* II (1972), 213-281.

Hurwitz, Harold M. "Hemingway's Tutor, Ezra Pound," *Modern Fiction Studies,* XVII (Winter 1971-72), 469-482.

Kilmo, Vernon (Jake) and Will Oursler. *Hemingway and Jake.* Garden City, N.Y.: Doubleday, 1972.

Lacy, Mary. " 'New' City Library Gets Two Hemingway Letters," *Richmond News-Leader* (15 September 1972), 19.

Longstreet, Stephen. "Hem," *We All Went to Paris.* New York: Macmillan, 1972, pp. 307-314.

Lucia, Ellis. "A Good Place to Come Home to/Hemingway in Idaho," *Westways* (Part One), LXII (February 1970), 15-17, 42.

McHaney, Thomas L. "Anderson, Hemingway, and Faulkner's *The Wild Palms*," *PMLA*, LXXXVII (May 1972), 465-474.

McLendon, James. *Papa: Hemingway in Key West*. Miami, Florida: Seemann, 1972.

Moats, Alice-Leone. "A Day with Hemingway," *The Paris Observer*, No. 1 (July 1972), 3-11.

Monteiro, George. "Hemingway: Contribution Toward a Definitive Bibliography," *The Papers of the Bibliographical Society of America*, LXVI (Fourth Quarter 1971), 411-414.

Nahal, Chaman. *The Narrative Pattern in Ernest Hemingway's Fiction*. Cranbury, N.J.: Associated University Presses, 1971.

Nolan, William F. "Papa as Nick," *Newsletter* (Writers Guild of America, West) (June 1972), 21-22. First publication of narration for *Adventures of a Young Man* by Hemingway.

Nelson, Gerald B. "Jake Barnes," *Ten Versions of America*. New York: Knopf, 1972, pp. 23-42.

Pelfrey, William. "The Next Nick Adams," *The New York Times* (6 July 1972), C-37.

Pennington, Phil. "Hemingway Letters," *Los Angeles Mirror* (5 July 1961).

Plimpton, George. "Editor's Notes," *Esquire*, LXXVII (May 1972), 13, 32.

Prizel, Yuri. "Hemingway in Soviet Literary Criticism," *American Literature*, XLIV (November 1972), 445-456.

Root, Waverly. "Telegrams, Cablese and Newspapers," *International Herald Tribune* (4 August 1971).

Rubin, Louis D., Jr. "Writers View Other Writers as Spiteful Rivals," *Richmond News-Leader* (13 November 1972), 12.

Saroyan, William. *Places Where I've Done Time*. New York: Praeger, 1972, p. 60.

Sissman, L. E. "Raymond Chandler Thirteen Years After," *The New Yorker*, XLVIII (11 March 1972), 123-125. Discusses Hemingway as hard-boiled writer.

Stock, Ellen, ed. "The Papa Papers," *New York*, V (30 October 1972), 64.

Sullivan, Scott. "Remembering Ernest, Scott and Zelda," *The Baltimore Sun* (16 July 1972), K-5.

Sutherland, Fraser. "The First Time Hemingway Told of His Fight," *Toronto Globe and Mail* (3 November 1972).

Tate, Allen. "Miss Toklas' American Cake," *Prose,* III (1971), 137-161.

Waldhorn, Arthur. *A Reader's Guide to Ernest Hemingway.* New York: Farrar, Straus and Giroux, 1972.

Whitman, Alden. "Hemingway Letters Reproach Critics," *New York Times* (9 March 1972), C-36. On letters to Charles Poore.

Wills, Martee. "A Writer Who Sought Peace in Florida's Backwoods," *Jacksonville Times-Union Floridian* (24 September 1972), 28-30. Marjorie Kinnan Rawlings recalls Hemingway.

Woodward, Robert H. "Robert Jordan's Wedding/Funeral Sermon," *Hemingway Notes,* II (Spring 1972), 7-8.

Articles on Paris Conference and *Hemingway and THE SUN Set:* C.E. Frazer Clark, Jr., "Having a Wonderful Time in Paris, Wish Scott and Papa Were Here," *Detroit Free Press Magazine* (27 August 1972), 10, 12-15; Michael Harrawood, "Two Professors Stir Up 'Dust' of Noted Writers," *The State* (Columbia, S.C.) (20 August 1972), E-3; Gretchen Hitch, "At Parisian 'Roundtable' – Memories of Literary Greats Revived," *Bloomfield Hills* (Michigan) *Eccentric* (20 July 1972), C-1, C-11; Kathryn Kolkhorst, "SCSC Professor Gives New Voice to Hemingway Players," *New Haven Journal-Courier* (27 July 1972), 4; Irving Marder, "Beating the Drum About a Book Written 46 Years Ago," *International Herald Tribune* (26 June 1972), 14; Jonathan C. Randal, "Literary Lost Generation," *Washington Post* (26 June 1972), B-1, B-3; Ted Stanger, "Hemingway's Old Pals Retaliate," *Hartford Times* (23 July 1972), A-9. Anon., "Books," *Family Digest* (December 1972), 61; John O'Brien, "The Last Word on *The Sun Also Rises,*" *Detroit News* (4 August 1972), A-14; Quentin Vanistartt, "Hemingway and THE SUN Set," *Connecticut Review,* V (April 1972), 16-17.

GENERAL CHECKLIST

Baritz, Loren, ed. *The Culture of the Twenties.* New York: Bobbs-Merrill, 1970.

Beach, Sylvia. *Shakespeare and Company.* London: Faber and Faber, 1959.

Bridgman, Richard. *Gertrude Stein in Pieces.* New York: Oxford University Press, 1970.

Flanner, Janet. *Paris Was Yesterday 1925-1939,* ed. Irving Drutman. New York: Viking, 1972.

_____. "That Was Paris," *The New Yorker,* XLVIII (11 March 1972), 32-36.

Geismar, Maxwell. *Ring Lardner and the Portrait of Folly.* New York: Crowell, 1972.

Hubbell, Jay B. *Who Are the Major American Writers?* Durham: Duke University Press, 1972.

McCormick, John. *The Middle Distance A Comparative History of American Imaginative Literature: 1919-1932.* New York: The Free Press, 1971.

The Most of John Held, Jr., Foreword by Marc Connelly; Introduction by Carl J. Weinhardt. Brattleboro, Vermont: Stephen Greene Press, 1972.

Payne, Ronald. "Late Mr. Leverty 'Ideal Newspaperman,' " *Richmond Times Dispatch* (6 November 1972), A-14. MMentions the Fitzgeralds, Hemingway's style and their contemporaries.

Spiller, Robert E. and Willard Thorp, Thomas H. Johnson, Henry Seidel Canby, Richard M. Ludwig, eds. *Literary History of the United States: Bibliography Supplement II.* New York: Macmillan, 1972. Updated entries for Fitzgerald and Hemingway.

Szladits, Lola L. *1922 A Vintage Year.* New York: New York Public Library, 1972. Exhibition catalogue.

White, Ray Lewis, ed. *Sherwood Anderson/Gertrude Stein: Correspondence and Personal Essays.* Chapel Hill: University of North Carolina Press, 1972.

ANNOUNCEMENTS

Presentation Ceremony

On 17 November 1972, Scottie Fitzgerald Smith presented the first copy of Matthew J. Bruccoli's *F. Scott Fitzgerald: A Descriptive Bibliography* (Pittsburgh: University of Pittsburgh Press, 1972) to the Library of Congress. In a ceremony at the Library, Mrs. Smith gave the book to Dr. L. Quincy Mumford, Librarian of Congress. The occasion was attended by two of Mrs. Smith's children, Jack and Cecilia Lanahan; Frederick A. Hetzel, Director of University of Pittsburgh Press; officials of the Library; Dr. Ronald S. Berman and Dr. William Emerson of the National Endowment for the Humanities; J. M. Edelstein, Librarian of the National Gallery; Dr. O. B. Hardison, Director of the Folger Shakespeare Library; and Philip W. Bonsal, former U.S. Ambassador to Cuba.

Following the presentation ceremony there was a viewing at the National Portrait Gallery of the recently acquired, only surviving, life oil portrait of Fitzgerald, painted by David Silvette in 1936. The day was marked by publication of a keepsake which facsimiles a holograph list made by Fitzgerald of his projected collected works.

Francis Scott Fitzgerald Smith presenting the first copy of *F. Scott Fitzgerald: A Descriptive Bibliography* to the Library of Congress, 17 November 1972. Left to right: Frederick A. Hetzel (Director of the University of Pittsburgh Press), L. Quincy Mumford (librarian of Congress), Mrs. Smith, Matthew J. Bruccoli.

The only known oil portrait of F. Scott Fitzgerald from life, by David Silvette, now at the National Portrait Gallery, Washington, D.C. Marvin Sadik, Director of the Gallery previewing the portrait with Francis Scott Fitzgerald Smith — 17 November 1972.

REVISED BAKER

The fourth edition of Carlos Baker's *Hemingway The Writer as Artist* (Princeton University Press 1972 — $2.95) deserves more space than we can give it, for the revision and updating of this book are a model for the maintenance of scholarly books. After adding chapters to the second and third editions, Prof. Baker has now rewritten the first two chapters of the book and added new chapters on *A Moveable Feast* and *Islands in the Stream.* The author and his publisher merit compliments and thanks.

FITZGERALD'S *Ledger*

A facsimile of F. Scott Fitzgerald's *Ledger* was published in the spring of 1973. The key bio-bibliographical document for Fitzgerald, it consists of five sections:
"Record of Published Fiction — Novels, Plays, Stories"
"Money Earned by Writing since Leaving Army"
"Published Miscelani (including movies) for which I was Paid"
"Zelda's Earnings"
"Outline Chart of my Life"
The *Ledger* facsimile is limited to 1,000 copies priced at $35.00 (Washington: Bruccoli Clark/Microcard Editions, 1973). It is a bound book; it is not a microcard.

SCADE Gatsby

The first volume in the South Carolina Apparatus for a Definitive Edition series (SCADE) is an editorial kit for *The Great Gatsby* consisting of 1) emendations list, 2) textual notes, 3) alterations in the galley proofs, 4) list of Fitzgerald's revisions in his own copy, 5) explanatory notes. This volume does not print the text of the novel; it provides material for a definitive edition of *The Great Gatsby* prepared by Matthew J. Bruccoli. The emendations are keyed to both the 1925 first printing and the Scribner Library edition, thereby making it possible for readers to emend their own copies of the novel. This volume has been awarded the Center for Editions of American Authors seal for "An Approved Apparatus." To be published late in 1974 by The University of South Carolina Press.

Gatsby Manuscript Facsimile

A facsimile of Fitzgerald's manuscript for *The Great Gatsby* was published in fall 1973. The volume includes an introduction by Matthew J. Bruccoli reconstructing the composition of the novel and textual apparatus, as well as the offset lithography facsmile. This volume has been awarded the Center for Editions of American Authors seal for "An Approved Facsimile." The *Gatsby* facsimilie is limited to 2,000 copies priced at $45.00 (Washington: Bruccoli Clark/Microcard Editions, 1973). It is a bound book; it is not a microcard.

A Point of Considerable Interest in Key West

A little-publicized but highly interesting small Hemingway display is featured at the Martello Gallery and Museum. Among the items donated by Mary Hemingway are young Hemingway's arithmetic and spelling lessons, his nature and baseball scrapbooks, as well as the corrected galleys for the play version of *The Fifth Column* and the *Death in the Afternoon* dummy. And there is more: Hemingway memorabilia ranging from his boxing gloves to his "torn-and-bloody" World War I uniform. The Martello Gallery and Museum is located on South Roosevelt Boulevard, Key West, Florida.

Le Légume

A French production of *The Vegetable* opened at the Théâtre Hérbetut in Paris in 1972. *Le Légume* is reported to have been well-received and enjoyed a successful run.

Recent Princeton Library Acquisitions

A typescript with Fitzgerald's corrections entitled, " 'Mr. Consumer. Do you ever figure Cost Plus?' a recent snooze by F. Scott Fitzgerald."

Several Fitzgerald letters to Thomas Boyd, to Chester B. Sikking (7 April 1922) with a military pass signed for him by Fitzgerald, and to George A. Kuyper (13 March 1922).

A watercolor profile portrait of Fitzgerald.

An additional collection of Zelda Sayre Fitzgerald's papers, among which are letters written by her husband, typescripts of her own work, and related material.

Also, fourteen Hemingway letters and telegrams to Mr. and Mrs. Milford J. Baker, complete with photographs and collateral papers coveting the period 1930 to 1969.

EDITORIAL: THE DIFFERENT RICH

In 1967 Andrew Turnbull's *Thomas Wolfe* presented Maxwell Perkins' account of the famous put-down about the rich having more money, in which Hemingway — not Fitzgerald — was the straight man. But articles are still being published which give the "Snows of Kilimanjaro" version.

Here is the way it was, according to Perkins:

> Wasn't that reference to Scott in [Hemingway's] splendid story otherwise, contemptible, and more so because [Hemingway] said, "I am getting to know the rich," and Molly Colum said — we were at lunch together — "The only difference between the rich and other people is that the rich have money" (p. 243).

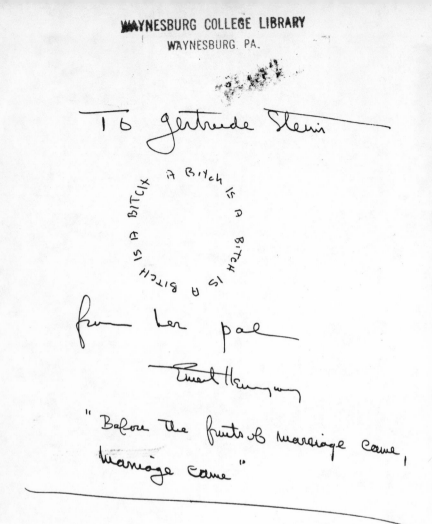

Inscribed copy of *Death in the Afternoon* (Lilly Library, Indiana University).